CLINICAL ANTHROPOLOGY

CLINICAL ANTHROPOLOGY

An Application of Anthropological Concepts Within Clinical Settings

JOHN A. RUSH

Westport, Connecticut
London

Library of Congress Cataloging-in-Publication Data

Rush, John A.
    Clinical anthropology : an application of anthropological concepts
within clinical settings / John A. Rush.
        p.   cm.
    Includes bibliographical references and index.
    ISBN 0–275–95571–0 (alk. paper).—ISBN 0–275–95572–9 (pbk. : alk.
paper)
    1. Anthropology—Methodology.   2. Anthropology—Philosophy.
3. Physical anthropology—Methodology.   4. Physical anthropology—
Philosophy.   I. Title.
GN33.R87   1996
301′.01—dc20   96–2203

British Library Cataloguing in Publication Data is available.

Library of Congress Catalog Card Number: 96–2203
ISBN: 0–275–95571–0
        0–275–95572–9 (pbk.)

First published in 1996

Praeger Publishers, 88 Post Road West, Westport, CT 06881
An imprint of Greenwood Publishing Group, Inc.

Printed in the United States of America

The paper used in this book complies with the
Permanent Paper Standard issued by the National
Information Standards Organization (Z39.48–1984).

10 9 8 7 6 5 4 3 2 1

Contents

Figures

Preface

The impetus for this work stems from a personal need to understand common threads that knit together both the biological and the social sciences. In other words, what factors do they all share in common, can these be useful in collecting and interpreting data, and can these common threads be used in clinical settings? In my opinion, the social sciences represent mainly a description of cultural content. Theories or models that have evolved are what I term "second level," in that they are constructed to look at small segments of the content and attempt to assign some sort of generalized meaning. This work represents an attempt to develop a first-level model that is not only useful in data collection, but also necessary when clinically applying the data to any system, social or biological.

All medical, psychiatric, and clinical psychological procedures are designed to, first, diagnose (a type of "word magic")--that is, define or name a condition of physical/emotional distress--and, second, apply concepts or procedures with one goal directed at individual and system stress reduction. The procedure should be no different for clinically applied anthropology. However, the anthropologist is in a unique position, in that he or she has the benefit of a cross-cultural perspective, which should reveal common factors of "curing" found in all cultures. In order to do this, the anthropologist need not refer to Western biomedical and/or psychiatric diagnostic categories or naming as these are, for the most part, culture bound.

One of the basic threads that ties all curing systems together is human information processing, or how the individual or system acts and reacts to specific as well as combined information input. Some information (or combination) is stress evoking, while other information is stress reducing; what enhances or decreases stress is determined by both the individual (biological/emotional) and the culture. Diagnosis, then, is a matter of defining which information (or combination) is stress enhancing and which is stress reducing; this information is then applied within the specific clinical and/or cultural setting.

This work is reductionist, in that I am attempting to boil down the content, models, and theories from many fields, again to uncover basic threads. In doing so, the reader might be inclined to say, "All this is self-evident," or, "It is too general or too simplistic." My answer to these observations is, first, when you have your nose pressed against a mirror, it is difficult to see your face. Although certain concepts presented in this work may seem familiar, they are less than appreciated, let alone self-evident, *until* they are pointed out. This is more than apparent, for example, when one takes the time to observe and listen to the communication styles around us. Most people, regardless of their educational or professional standing, are not aware of what is happening as they talk and listen. And, in the process of communicating and not under-standing, a great deal of social stress is generated. In a general sense, this is not necessarily a negative situation because unique combinations of in-formation, problem solving, and systems emerge from the resulting stress and conflict. On the down side, however, a great deal of personal and system stress can lead to many behavioral and/or medical conditions, as defined by a cultural belief system. Stress is generated as a result of a cultural/biological reaction to information intrusion, information alteration, information loss, insufficient information, inherited information, disguised information, and information imbalance. These informational categories cover all the curing/medical systems, in terms of a diagnosis and curing procedures, I have researched to date; this leads to a first-level concept or model of the stressors impinging on the group-oriented individual and the group. Second-level diagnosis, using these informational categories, looks at the specific cultural content of the stressors (the negative bits), out of which a "curing" procedure for rebalancing the system emerges. A balanced system swings within geometrical space; the cultures that refer to or use the concept of balance that have been researched by the author to date have a geometrical representation of this space-balance as expressed through oral or visual means. A Western way of rendering this is illustrated on page xiii.

A balanced system, or "health," could be seen as one that rotates within some information-processing, three-dimensional space; health would be defined as lying within specific parameters, and ill health prevails outside of these. The yin and yang are symbolic of balance in many Asian and Southeast Asian belief systems, and are analogous to this illustration.

This work also represents an attempt to define clinical anthropology and to show how it differs from the approaches found in Western medical, psychological, and psychiatric practice. I have defined the field from my perspective, which will certainly differ from the views of others. Hopefully, a dialogue can commence, clarifying, in a general sense, what it means to be a clinical anthropologist. If the public in general is to recognize the field of

Health, Illness, and the Concept of Balance

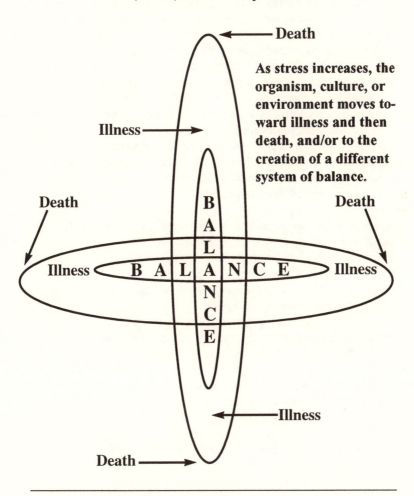

As stress increases, the organism, culture, or environment moves toward illness and then death, and/or to the creation of a different system of balance.

clinical anthropology, then what we do has to be more clearly defined *and* promoted. Even if my model is not acceptable to other anthropologists, at least it is a description of how I, in my clinical practice, approach stress in systems, and, if unacceptable, the challenge is for the reader to come up with other models distinct from those of Western biomedicine.

The term clinical anthropologist assumes that the individual with that title is actually applying anthropological concepts in clinical settings. Writing about clinical anthropology or discussing the concept in a classroom although certainly useful, is not clinical anthropology. For one thing, within clinical settings clients expect results, and, unless a model or theory can be directly tied to application, it remains a theory only. Having a theory--for example, Marxist (see Morsy 1990)--may describe stress factors in the system, but, in and of itself cannot be applied to a clinical setting without blaming, offending, and adding more stress to the system. The same is true of the concepts of power in relationships, utilized in marriage and family counseling by psychologists, MFCCs, and LCSWs, and put forth as an explanation of family violence and competition in male-female relationships in general. Again, suggesting that family violence, for example, stems from the individual's need to control is a statement of blame wherein the emphasis is placed on the individual to change his or her behavior. In fact, much of the violence that goes on in families and much of the observable hostility between males and females (as evidenced in part by sexual harassment lawsuits in the courts) has little to do with power in relationships. It has much more to do with unclear or implied rules--especially in our age of liberality--regarding male-female interaction patterns, a lack of appreciation and/or an ignorance of what happens when we send and receive messages, and our failure to be responsible communicators. We are responsible for the messages we send and we are responsible for our interpretations, regardless of our constitutional right to free speech, which is not the right to be irresponsible. Few people, in my experience, are willing to take responsibility for how they send and receive, regardless of their education or profession.

The approach to diagnosis presented in this volume differs in large measure from what one would encounter in either medicine/psychiatry or psychology. With reference to psychiatry, the current *Diagnostic and Statistical Manual of Mental Disorders (DSM-IV)* does not, in itself, lead to any therapeutic procedure for dealing with emotions and behaviors that, for the most part, have evolved out of social issues. In fact, the *DSM-IV* seems to stand as a weak analogy to medical textbooks on disease pathology. When the psychiatric and psychological communities began to see emotional and behavioral problems/ symptoms *as the problem* (and as codified in some word magic), they lost sight of cause, effect, and probable prevention. What this leads to, instead, is the psychiatrist--with many psychologists following close behind--attempting to emulate the wider medical system (and its preoccupation with the suppression of symptoms) with the prescription of numerous and dangerous mind-altering drugs to "cure" the problem. This has led to massive drug addiction (more than the Colombian drug cartels could ever wish for) and untold iatrogenic or prescription-drug-induced physical damage. This type of chemical psychiatry has also led to what some have referred to as a pseudoscience (see Ross and Pam 1995). Moreover, this obsession with chemical control of emotional/ behavioral issues successfully eliminates any genuine interest in the social/ environmental stressors (causal factors) relating to emotional problems, let alone cross-cultural concerns.

With respect to what would be considered medical issues by Western bio-medicine (i.e., arthritis, migraine headaches, Alzheimer's disease, etc.), the symptoms are considered the disease, and, again, codified by word magic, without really approaching cause. The model presented in this work is designed to consider the underlying causes with the ultimate goals of balance and prevention. One purpose of the clinician, then, is to teach systems, such as family (and individuals within), hospital, and government, how to send and receive information so that it is stress reducing *and* balancing at both the biological and social levels. As information intrudes on the individual from a multitude of sources, that is, the sun, the wind, temperature changes, bacteria, viruses, the mass media, diet, and general lifestyle, these likewise need to be factored into the equation, with some being more important than others in individual cases.

All psychotherapy, all curing, as it is approached from the perspectives of very diverse cultures, relies on information-sending and -receiving techniques designed, first, to interpret the condition/situation; second, to alter the client/patient or culture's meaning of the illness; and, third, to take steps, through some sort of information input, to alleviate or cure the problem, which, in much of non-Western curing, includes a *termination* of the curing process and a *reintegration* of the individual into the social level. In much of Western therapy, both medical and psychological/psychiatric, there is no termination out side of death. Because the psychiatric and psychological community stigmatizes individuals with diagnostic labels, such as schizophrenic, manic-depressive, and so on, and then pass down moral judgments to the public, reintegration is next to impossible. What results is a never ending supply of sick people to treat, sick people who are never cured. One of the reasons for this is that the diagnosis has nothing to do with treatment; the diagnosis does not tell you how to proceed toward cure and is, outside of trauma injuries, a stepping off point for suppressing symptoms. The diagnosis is likewise a process of depersonal-ization mirroring a cultural standard of depersonalization. In short, this type of diagnosis removes the individual and his or her symptoms from the social matrix and, when this happens, we lose perspective of not only cause and effect but who we are as social beings.

One of the keys to providing successful therapy as well as preventing many emotional and behavioral problems, can be found in the way we send and receive information. Diagnosing the individual and group's high risk messages offers a more practical approach because you also know how to proceed with treatment. Treating emotional issues, for example, is essentially a reframing of the individual and group's meaning of events, a procedure used in all cultures.

In order to develop a clinical perspective, we need to define who we are, determine where we have come from, and, in the process, uncover specific threads that knit us together as a species, threads that are also important and useful within clinical settings. Chapters 1 through 3 consider human universals from an information-processing perspective. This is a difficult undertaking because of space limitations, and I encourage the reader to contend with the bits and pieces until the synthesis at the end of each chapter. This information will then be used to reveal a general, first-level process for diagnosing illness and disease (Chapter 4). Directly evolving from this is an overview of procedures for applying the process to clinical settings (Chapters 5 through 7).

I wish to thank all the authors mentioned in the work and many others not included, as well as all my academic mentors and tormentors throughout my long academic career. I also wish to thank all my clients and students, who have provided me with important content and associated insights into human biological and social stress; such a perspective can only be gained within the clinical setting. And, finally, I wish to thank my wife, Katie, and my children--Erik, Jason, Damon, and Greg--for allowing me time and space to complete this work, and, more important, being patient with my anthropological study of our family unit.

CHAPTER 1

Becoming Who We Are

Clinical anthropology is the application of concepts from the field of anthropology to clinical settings. By clinical, I am referring to the use of such information/concepts in a holistic, helping, and therapeutic manner. Clinical settings could include hospitals, police and probation situations, individual and marriage and family counseling, and cross-cultural issues, as well as governmental policy. By therapeutic, I mean the educational delivery of concepts or behaviors that allow individuals or groups to reduce stress and move toward personal and group health. By holistic, I am referring to both physical and emotional health, taking into consideration the diverse factors or stressors that reduce health potential.

In order to understand our subject matter, reference points need to be established. As our subject matter is *Homo sapiens*, general ideas found within the anthropological literature would be useful in defining who we are, what we do, and why. Many of these concepts differ greatly from the perspectives of other disciplines, and, thus, to have a field of clinical anthropology, the subject matter of anthropologists, rather than Western psychologists, medical doctors, or psychiatrists, must be the primary reference, with Western concepts viewed as a cultural manifestation, and worthy of study, rather than as universal and truth.

The goal in reviewing anthropological and related literature is to find, as mentioned, who we are, what we do, and why. This will lead to universal statements about human behavior. Out of these universals will flow a model or theory useful in building a reasonable and general content description of the field, as well as a model and a philosophy for therapeutic intervention. Such a model must be observable and verifiable. Without such a definition and model, clinical anthropology has no form or function.

All the fields associated with the realm of anthropology are a vast resource of specific concepts and tools applicable to clinical settings. The problem is to isolate them and understand their significance; this demands that the researcher spend considerable time within both the intellectual community and clinical settings. Some of these tools and concepts evolve directly from the universals and will be discussed in more detail in the following chapters.

INTRODUCTION: SETTING THE SCENE

When we look at humanity prehistorically, historically, and currently, we notice the differences in skin colors, hair textures and colors, languages, mannerisms, attitudes, religious beliefs, art forms, culinary habits, and the "us" vs. "them" phenomenon, which seems to be universal. We see our group, our culture as holding a special place in the scheme of things, while others are regarded as more primitive, not God's chosen people, or perhaps less than human. The Japanese, for example, have a term for "inside" (*miuchi*) which translates as "within one's body" and "is a term that refers to the group of individuals most closely related to a person, with the parent-child relationship forming the nucleus of the group. . . . The term *tanin* (*ta* = the other; *nin* = person) refers to those outside the *miuchi*. The distinction often extends to the public domain, where the Japanese distinguish between people within one's own organization and outsiders. . . . The inside:outside classificatory principle also operates at the broadest sphere of social interaction, distinguishing between acquaintances and strangers" (Ohnuki-Tierney 1984:40). This "us" vs. "them" is a way of organizing the world and creating boundaries between things, a way of generalizing and making things less complicated, at least in the individual or group mind.

The boundaries that we create between people and things are artificial and only serve to order our thinking and to limit the confusion and the stress generated when we overload the nervous system with too much data. Generalizing, or "chunking" of information into all-inclusive units, serves to keep information within manageable limits. On the other hand, the observable differences between people and groups serve another, perhaps equally useful function, in that perceived diversity between interacting human groups and among individuals *breeds* stress and conflict (as individuals feel more comfortable with others similar in attitude, appearance, etc.).

On the biological, psychological, and social levels, individuals and groups move toward stress reduction or personal and/or group solutions designed primarily to reduce stress. Such solutions can be psychological rationalizations, diplomatic endeavors, and physical solutions, for example, warfare, political exclusion, murder, or even prison/psychiatric isolation from others. One generalization that we can make is that stress and conflict seem to be natural factors in group living and, at the same time, antithetical to individual psychological organization; they can either push us toward greatness as individuals or as a species or place us in the most hellish of situations.

Homo sapiens are statistically more similar to than different from one another at the genotypic or unobservable level. All peoples, in all areas of the globe, have the same cellular characteristics, and organs, and all fit into one of the four general blood groupings. There are typical differences in metabolism and quantitative differences in enzymes, electrolytes, and neurochemistry among individuals within any cultural or ethnic group. Such differences are not qualitative, but are, instead, "more or less" (quantity) factors that make up our individualism at the biological level. Skin color, hair texture, stature, nose size, and so on, are physical adaptations to environmental factors (i.e., cold, heat, humidity, dryness, etc.) that have occurred through group isolation and genetic drift involving long spans of time. Melanin in skin tissue, for example, differs in quantity, not quality, from individual to individual. This is not to say that qualitative differences cannot arise given long periods of time and circumstances. There may indeed be a few individuals existent on the face of the earth with qualitative differences in melanin, with a super-melanin that could possibly protect the individual from extreme forms of ultraviolet and other generally harmful radiation, just waiting for a Darwinian-type expression if or when the ozone layer is more seriously depleted. These physical differences are fortunate, as they have, for the most part, enriched the human gene pool and will hopefully include adaptive characteristics useful thousands of years from now (or even sooner).

Cultural beliefs and behaviors also play a part with respect to physical adaptation. It is theorized, for example, that Neanderthal robusticity is an adaptation to a rather inefficient hunting strategy (Trinkaus 1986), although there are other social factors perhaps equally important, and that human upright posture, loss of body hair, subcutaneous fat, loss of appocrine glands, and so on, are adaptations to an environment requiring a great deal of contact with water for acquiring food (Morgan 1990, Knight 1991). Make no mistake, however; cultural attitudes and consequent behaviors will have an effect on genetic changes and physical development over time. The fact remains, though, that irrespective of cultural background and phenotypic differences, all human groups are capable of interbreeding and producing viable offspring, hence the definition of a species or race.

What are the behavioral and psychological similarities between our ancestors and protoancestors? In order to answer this question, I will address the following three areas. First, I will explore and make generalizations about human behavior and adaptation from anthropological and psychological perspectives, in order to uncover and understand how problems in social living occur and how they are resolved. Within this frame, I will examine the paleontological and archeological data, as well as the historical data. Second, I will examine the models or belief systems different cultures use to explain certain types of behavior considered unusual or abnormal and requiring social intervention. Along with this, I will explore current cross-cultural psychiatric and psychological models explaining these problems. Third, I will consider a model that explains what all these different beliefs and practices have in common. Questions to be answered include these: Do current North American psychiatric models serve as useful frameworks of interpretation of unusual or abnormal behavior cross-culturally? Are the associated tools designed for resolving these issues adequate to the task, or do urbanized, North American concepts and tools miss the therapeutic point, so to speak, because they cultural bound? Do they attempt to make "scientific" certain phenomena that are best approached from an interpersonal and group communication perspective, a perspective that is ever changing? My goal is to offer another model for understanding stress and psychological problems, and their impact upon group functioning, and then discuss the part clinical anthropologists can play in applying this understanding to clinical and social issues. It must be understood that I am dealing with systems and not just individuals. Yes, individuals are important, but the existence of individuals and any psychological problems encountered is related to the bigger picture, the groups and the information, beliefs, and attitudes within which the syndromes occur. How a culture reacts to or deals with problem behaviors is as important as the behaviors themselves. This, then, is a second generalization when considering anthropology from a clinical standpoint: humans are a group animal, and human behavior can only be understood within the context of group interaction.

The psychoanalytic literature, some of which incorporates research in anthropology and spans nearly a century, has reported "psychological universals," which, unfortunately, are not universal, but which still color psychiatric and psychological thinking, theory, and, to a large extent, procedure when dealing with such emotional and behavioral manifestations in clinical practice. Psychiatry and psychology, as practiced in the West, tend to view themselves as scientific, with clinicians attempting to apply these models cross-culturally (see Berry et al. 1992:8-14). Westernized psychiatry/psychology is no more or less scientific than models presented by other cultures and should more properly be referred to as "ethnopsychological" (Lutz 1985:63). This is less of a criticism and more of a starting point in our understanding. If Westernized psychiatry/psychology is culture bound, and thus views other cultures through an ethnocentric lens (the "us" vs. "them"), then what generalizations does it find, and do these reliably represent a template upon which to describe and diagnose behaviors and emotional states in other cultures or even in our own? It is only through examining these generalizations within the social and ecological context of specific societies that we can refine our thinking and develop new models that are and perhaps more useful, from academic (knowledge for its own sake) and clinical (intervention) standpoints. The world is shrinking, in a metaphorical sense, and Western biomedical and mental health communities are being confronted with diverse and unusual symptoms and beliefs about cause and effect (see Tobin and Friedman 1983). Moreover, as we move toward a world with less and less cultural diversity, our models of physical, behavioral, and emotional cause and effect become more and more biased, although stated more and more dogmatically and offered as scientific. For example, Juillet Cheng, while living in China, had sought help for her arthritic daughter, utilizing acupuncture and herbal remedies with good results ("Today Show," October 8, 1990). After moving to the United States and consulting Western biomedical practitioners, their advice involved surgical procedures. Mrs. Cheng decided to continue with the traditional approach (i.e., acupuncture and herbal remedies) as prescribed by her culture of origin. The Western biomedical practitioners, because of Mrs. Cheng's refusal to take their advice, pressed for charges of child neglect. Alan Fleischman, M.D., a medical ethicest, agrees that Mrs. Cheng should be charged with child neglect, while Mrs. Cheng's attorney states that our Western medical community suffers from "cultural arrogance."[1] Such legal cases offer an interesting dilemma in the "us" vs. "them" phenomenon. These cases also present another dilemma: Who ultimately is in charge regarding decisions about our personal health? The individual, the medical community, the Food and Drug Administration, or the federal government? Are these humanitarian issues, economic issues, or both? Perhaps the old Chinese formula would be useful; that is, you pay the physician when you are healthy, but not when you are sick. This course of action would solve some of the economic issues. If the medical community desires to take responsibility for a person's health, let's place that responsibility within a preventative matrix.

Many anthropologists, especially adherents of the American School of Cultural Anthropology, have traditionally been involved in what I term "clinical anthropology"; that is, they have practiced as psychotherapists, (e.g., Alfred Kroeber and Margaret Mead) or consultants for understanding personality and psychological problems (e.g., Ruth Benedict and Gregory Bateson). Some anthropologists, on the other hand, cringe at the idea of action, or applied anthropology, desiring, instead, to maintain the prime directive or non-interference in the lives of others, including the culture in which they live. Human systems are complicated, to say the least, and it is difficult, if not impossible, to predict the outcome of new ideas, help in the form of food or agricultural technology, or even the introduction of seemingly less sophisticated technology (see Sharp 1966). I take the following position in this work:

1. Individuals or families moving into urban areas often experience a great deal of stress, which creates problems in individual, dyadic, and group functioning. Any information, techniques, or insights that can be used to alleviate or decrease that stress should be utilized.
2. Anthropologists have traditionally studied the family, small groups, and networks of kin and significant others. Another term for this is "social organization." Most

problems in social living evolve out of these relationships and are not simply individual psychopathologies. Anthropologists, therefore, have an advantage in understanding the interactive and communicative processes involved. All psychotherapy involves a process of retranslating dyadic and group communicative events in history and reassessing rules and roles within the family or group. As I will demonstrate, this process is universal, with different cultures utilizing different procedures and/or content for essentially comparable contexts in order to achieve similar results.

3. The potential for conflict exists on the dyadic and group levels (family, work, etc.) and spills out to the international level. Conflict is not a matter of simple individual psychology, but a combination of ingredients, including numbers of people involved, implied rules that no longer serve the common good, attitudes toward outsiders, economics, beliefs in power (what it is and how it is to be used), mythical charters, beliefs in supernatural agencies, technology, and world views, to name a few. From a psychological perspective, most studies in conflict have been geared to management of individuals and problems generated in institutional settings, such as, psychiatric wards, and jails and/or detention settings, and work environments. In this work, I will not only consider conflict at the individual level, but also include conflict in the family as well as factors at the national and international levels that stem from the interrelations of groups and ideas.

The world appears to be evolving into an increasingly dangerous place in which to live, although this may be an illusion created and fostered by the sensational objectives of the "news" media, and it is difficult to know if we are at a crossroads leading to a gentler and kinder world or on a continued downward spiral into worldwide ideological/economic conflict--the beginning of the end, so to speak. We need to reassess who we are and how we, as individuals and groups, get to be the way we are. Let's begin our journey, then, by exploring prehistory and what we know and can suggest about protohuman and small-group behavior.

Prehistoric Man: Information Processing and Culture

Anthropology as a formal discipline is approximately 100 years old. But anthropology, in the sense of humanity studying itself and its physical developments, social systems, customs, technology, beliefs, psychology, and relationships with the surrounding ecosystem has a historical depth of many thousands of years and a prehistory of speculative millennia perhaps spanning as much as four million years. And, certainly, the ability to study one's self and the surrounding environment has greater survival value if the knowledge acquired can be stored and passed on from generation to generation in an accumulative fashion through the use of symbols, initially prelanguage symbolizing systems, then language, and then, by analogy, other external chunking devices or systems such as cave painting (see Pfeiffer 1982), hieroglyphic writing, books, and electronic media. It would seem, as discussed by Donald (1991:18), that "[t]he most recent cognitive transition acknowledges the importance of external storage media on individual cognitive structure." After examinations of hominoid endocranial casts and other physical evidence, "it appears that hominids were fully bipedal, right-handed, and language bearing by 2Myr BP" (Falk 1987:26). Speculating then, the ability to symbolize through the use of language may have been part of human social evolution for approximately two million years (see also Klein 1989:201). The feature of the endocranial casts referred to by Falk is Broca's area, which lies on the back portion of the left cerebral cortex, and which research (see Kosslyn and Koenig 1992:211-285) has shown is a necessary component (but not the only component--see Lieberman 1991) in terms of formulating information, chunking it, and transmitting it by symbolic representations.

Although the brain had perhaps been "wired" for the possibility of spoken language for two million years (or earlier), the anatomy of the vocal tract may have had to await certain changes before fully articulate speech was possible (see Lieberman 1991). This would place the development of fully articulate speech in a time frame of 100,000 to 250,000 years ago. As Lieberman states, "The presence of a functionally modern human vocal tract 125,000 years ago and its subsequent retention and elaboration are consistent with the presence in this period of brain mechanisms allowing automatized speech motor activity, vocal tract normalization, and the decoding of encoded speech" (1991:77). Not everyone, however, is in agreement with Lieberman's position (see Trinkaus and Shipman 1993:353-355, 391; Bower 1992a:230).

Species survival depends on many factors, for example, brute strength, agility, fecundity or sheer numbers, abrupt changes in the surrounding environment, cunning, reasoning ability, intelligence, and genetic predispositions (i. e., tendency toward grouping, consciousness, and language), to name some of the more obvious. But one of the main factors is our ancestors' ability to study, observe, and come to conclusions about the surrounding environment in reference to the individual and the group. This ongoing attempt to understand motivation, desire, passion, and behavior and place these within a symbolic context (i.e., roles, rules, and rituals) and to understand the advantages of cooperation through the serial aligning of human brain power to solve problems, is our prehistoric and current tool of survival. The push factor leading to such curiosity and attempts at understanding can only be genetic in origin. According to Dawkins (1976:25), "The evolutionary importance of the fact that genes control embryonic development is this: it means that genes are at least partly responsible for their own survival in the future, because their survival depends on the efficiency of the bodies in which they live and which they helped to build."

Dawkins goes on to say, "Genes have no foresight. They do not plan ahead. Genes just are, some genes more so than others, and that is all there is to it" (1976:25). Dawkins' deterministic premise is that it is the genetic material, the information at the physical level, that is trying to survive, with all the man-

ifestations of the phenotype (physical, emotional, and intellectual) representing a test of the genotype. Crisis situations (e.g., extreme environmental
changes) offer a traumatic testing of the phenotype, and consequently the
genotype, allowing more and more possibilities. However, stability of
genotype may be more the rule than the exception, as Eldredge (1985) has
pointed out in his position on "punctuated equilibria." Human survival, then,
represents an interplay between genetic and extragenetic processes, that is, the
environment, the culture, and the related ability of humans to think or reason,
get curious, observe the world around them, and wonder about cause and
effect. There are, certainly, some important exceptions or additions to this
idea of punctuations in human evolution, to be discussed below, which are
quite relevant to one of the themes in this book. Chaos, uncertainty, confusion,
and conflict, for example, can be useful properties of human social
organization and individual psyche and are necessary considerations when
attempting to understand human physical and social development, clinical
analysis and evaluation of social stress, and the individual's adaptation to
specific stressors.

At this point, two more generalizations, to be expanded upon, come to the
surface, and they are the protohuman and human abilities to (1) observe or
perceive occurrences in the environment and (2) to store and retrieve that
information when needed. These imply a type of ancient consciousness,
contrary to Jaynes's extremely interesting thesis that consciousness is a
relatively recent phenomenon, perhaps only 3,000 or 4,000 years old (Jaynes
1990).

Information storage can exist on a number of levels, with the first being
ideas, generalizations, or specific symbols stored in the individual's brain
(Edelman 1989:186-192). A second level would be information communally
stored by the group, with certain members storing specialized knowledge
not necessarily known to others. Moreover, adults certainly have stores of
information, both qualitative and quantitative, that is not possessed by their
children, and that is only acquired with age and experience. A third level
involves information stored in the environment, that is, signs and signals that
trigger complicated responses. The environment, the information surrounding
and including the individual or group, is analogous to a cave painting or even a
book (the more tangible outside-the-individual storage systems) or to a story or
oral tradition rendering the group's origin and relationship to the world; this
is represented in the fourth level of information, which is purposely stored
outside of the individual and thus transcends the individual, the group, and the
surrounding environment. At this level not only is "reality" being created or
invented, but also this reality it is now in a more stable position to be
transmitted from generation to generation. At this point you have culture.

It is my position that there is no evidence of protohuman or human culture
until information is stored outside the individual and group in the form of tools
and other artifacts that are purposely manufactured *and* transported from place

to place for future use without the continual necessity of manufacture each time a tool or other artifact is needed.

The storage of knowledge (see Figure 1.1) likewise exists on a number of levels (and meta-levels); it is not just stored at the surface level of cave paintings, books, or on clay tablets or computer chips (see Wynn 1989; Renfrew and Zubrow 1994).

Figure 1.1
Storage of Knowledge

Level 1	Level 2	Level 3	Level 4
			Externally Stored
Environment <------->	**Individual**<------->	**Individual** <------->	**"Reality "***
	(cannot exist outside	**and**	|
	the context of the group)	**Group**	**Culture**

*The term "reality" here is not synonymous with fact or truth in the large sense of the word. Reality is a construction of the individual and group aided by group and environmental input, which is mediated by genetically derived "representations" (see Bickerton 1990:18-19, 198-199) necessary for survival within an environment.

For example, while computer software represents a program or task for the hardware to perform, the computer software and hardware are a vast storage area of ideas, facts, beliefs, and ideologies about us and what we know. Technology tells us about itself and the people who manufacture and use it. But the knowledge imbedded in practical application is not always self-evident, as with cave paintings or the so-called Venus figurines found at numerous Upper Paleolithic and Neolithic sites throughout Europe (Gimbutas 1989:163-65; Gadon 1989:3-20; Neumann 1972:94-119).

Our sensory equipment (visual, auditory, kinesthetic, olfactory/gustatory, etc. (see Rivlin and Gravelle 1984 for a discussion of other important sensory modalities) and our ability to store information, then, are of paramount importance. But preserving or storing these perceptions and interpretations outside the individual seems to be the overall purpose of culture and, as mentioned above, defines culture and its variations. Culture is essentially a set of rules and roles that instruct people in what to do in order to survive under existing conditions. Change in those conditions force adaptation culturally and/or physically. Our social systems are an environment in themselves; rapid changes in our social environments can be seen as analogous to rapid changes in the physical environment. And if examining diverse cultures tells us nothing else, it tells us that we can have different rules for doing very similar things, and that rapid changes in our social environments can be devas-tating, devastating for bands and tribes in terms of extinction because information and experience with alternatives are limited and devastating for nation states in that the altering of the systems within (economic, political) breeds tremendous individual and group stress. Nation-states, however, have momentum due primarily to the information available to the individual, and extinction, to the degree experienced by bands and tribes in North, Central, and South America during the past 500 years since European contact, is unlikely. The reader might ask, "Well, didn't the ancient cultures of Rome, Egypt, and Sumer become extinct?" The answer is, "No. We are the evolving, cultural products of those ancient peoples."

Prehistoric Man's Behavior

Most of the current thinking regarding the dynamics of prehistoric human behavior at the interpersonal and group levels is speculative, comparative, or educated guesswork generated from three general areas of theorization. The first area developed out of the speculations of the anthropologists of the mid and late nineteenth century. Through the works of Morgan (1870), Frazer (1890), and Tyler (1871), who were influenced by Darwin (1859, 1871), a picture emerges of humanity/culture slowly changing over time from one stage to another as information accumulated. Freud (1946), working from these studies and his interpretation of classical myths, the works of other anthropologists, and his own observations, added the psychic dimension (the id, ego, libido, superego), which pushed these systems along. A problem with all these views of early humanity is that they developed from information that was second- or thirdhand and speculative or inaccurate in the first place, as Franz Boas pointed out at the turn of this century (Kuper 1988:125-151; Harris 1968:250-289). It was also male centered. Moreover, Freud's use of myth as expressions of universal psychic conflict is questionable. As Eisner (1987:18) states, "[T]oo many modern interpreters, by removing the myths from their original poetic and cultural contexts, have transmogrified the deeds of the ancient characters into pale foreshadowings of modern behavior." This is likewise the case with Levi-Strauss (1967, 1969, 1970) and his rendering or interpretation of myth, although Levi-Strauss is attempting to uncover ex-planations for cultural or group development, while Freud and his followers are looking for universals in the human psyche per se.

Further, "[m]any of the Freudians suffer from a hermeneutic variety of paranoia, even as Freud described it. Typically, they attach the greatest significance to minor details of other people's behavior and draw far-reaching conclusions from the interpretations of these details" (Eisner 1987:40). I will have more to say about these problems of interpretation, and especially the Oedipus complex, in Chapter 5.

The second area of theorization of human social development comes from the observations by primatologists and the belief that, by observing monkeys and apes we could then, through analogy, develop a reasonable model of social evolution. However, by looking at the same data, one is able to propose numerous scenarios, male centered and/or female centered, as to the prime mover in our current social development (see Fedigan 1986 for an interesting discussion of these issues).

The third area of theorization comes from a regeneration of the social evolutionary position. That is, through observations of existing preliterate societies and extractions from more reliable ethnographic work during this century, an analogy can be made that, if this is how these individuals succeeded in surviving, then this is possibly how our distant ancestors and protoancestors might have organized their social groupings.

All three areas have something to offer. Information does accumulate; therefore, human culture evolves or takes on new dimensions. We develop more complex aligning of people, starting with family units and kinship in general (particularism) and then bridging to political units that can be more universalistically based (Parsons and Shils 1962:82). Explanations for the accidental or the unforeseen do change in complexity, thus mirroring the intricacy of the social structure within which they occur (Rush 1974:128-135). And, certainly, our technology changes or evolves with newer ideas or applications being built upon. Data collected by primatologists offer possibilities of group arrangements, just as an understanding of the !Kung, the Shoshoni, the Yahgan, the Athabascan Hunters, the BaMbuit, and other band-type societies gives us a feel for the possibilities for survival at that level of organization. What these studies cannot show or tell us are the other possibilities, the trials and errors of social organization that did not survive the test of time. Just as one would be hard pressed to find an unadulterated band-type organization on this shrinking planet today, there probably were short-lived experiments, perhaps resembling contemporary baboon- or chimpanzee- type organizations. The Neanderthals may be an example of such a short-lived experiment, just as *Homo sapiens* may turn out to be short lived as well.

Cultural Origins

Knight's recent synthesis incorporates all of the above areas of theorization (Knight 1991).[2] Using a Marxian and ecological perspective, he basically suggests that the origins of culture involved the synchronization of menstruation, with females banding together to limit sexual access by males. This allowed males more equal access to sex, thus cutting down conflict. Knight further suggests that economics emerged from this female "sex strike" through the process of males giving away large game kills to others, especially to females, who then can establish a "home base" from which to forage and within which they can protect offspring (Knight 1991:190-194). Knight goes on to amass credibility for his hypothesis by considering mythological statements from diverse cultures relating to menstruation, the moon, blood, snakes, and so on (Knight 1991:480-513). The mythology, however, is more recent in origin than any behaviors or attitudes it supposedly represents. Mythology represents or explains the chunking of experience, the whole and not the parts that led to it. Mythology is not fact. As Joseph Campbell states, once myth is believed *as* fact, it loses something and takes on a totally different significance (1989a). Knight's *Blood Relations*, however, is, in my opinion, a useful work, in that it helps to restore legitimacy to discussions of cultural origins, discussions that have not been popular for many years.

However, I have certain questions about Knight's synthesis. First, using a Marxist position, he draws a parallel between oppression of the masses by the ruling class and female oppression by males. He determines that initially there was a class society, that is, one of males and females in which the males ruled in such a tyrannical manner that the females synchronized their menstrual cycles, went on a sex strike, and thus created a starting point for building culture. By making such a statement, Knight is assuming that culture (with political underpinnings and sexual restrictions) already existed prior to and at the moment of the strike. Second, oppression is a relative thing. Can one feel oppressed without reference to some other non-oppressed group in the same category? Moreover, and according to Knight, these tyrannical males cannot move into culture because they are too busy "taking care of business," that is, making sure that interlopers do not get near members of their harem, essentially fighting with other males (doesn't such behavior represent sexual restrictions?). If, on the one hand, this is a true picture of our precultural selves, these males are operating on a genetic calling. And if, on the other hand, we can truly use the terms "oppression" (which equals politics) and "sex strike" (which implies unfair restriction), a terminology that implies the existence of culture, then who is the most "oppressed"? Is it the males, who put their position in the hierarchy and/or life and limb on the line every day, only to look forward to an injury or a violent death at the tooth and claw of a rival; or is it the females, who have to look forward to "wham, bam, thank you ma'am"? Both are oppressed (or neither is), but what is really oppressed is the ability of culture to evolve into a more plastic thing, a thing that will allow or accommodate a wide range of behaviors, political and sexual, necessary when various crises present themselves, rather than remaining mired in a genetic calling of raw emotional and habitual reactions.

Third, to state that it was females who invented culture is analogous to saying that males invented culture; neither one can be passive in the process. Knight's position as to the origin of culture is, in my opinion very interesting, and, at the same time, overly complicated. Instead, what is needed is a simpler scenario, one that could be reinvented and built upon, as culture often takes two steps forward and one step back. The key to unlocking the door to culture is (1) a brain (qualitative) that was environmentally selected for a consciousness that allowed for (2) an almost compulsive (quantitative) need to process information in an analogous fashion that (3) could then lead to a reassessment of relationships that already existed within the precultural hominid group--more specifically, the relationship between mother and child. Even the concept of "home base" (defined and considered in more detail in Chapter 2) has its basic antecedents in the brain's "internalized maps," representing the environment within which we have had to operate (Bickerton 1990:94-96), waiting for analogous thinking to push them into the home base arrangement described by Knight. A model combining the basic behaviors and relationships that led to culture will come to light as I continue and will then be detailed in Chapter 2.

Implied Rules and the Evolution of Cooperation

One factor that I think would be useful to Knight's hypothesis is the concept of implied rules. If we assume that behaviors that offer survival potential and act to decrease stress will survive in the long term, the first of our ancestors to willingly and with intent give away his kill to another, for whatever reason, initiated an implied rule. If the receiver reciprocated and, in turn, gave away his kill, even to the person who initially gave to him, you begin an asymmetrical cycle of give and take, of rights and obligations, which resembles Anatol Rapoport's Tit for Tat computer model (see Axelrod 1980a, 1980b, 1984). This is a simple, but ideal procedure, which could be reinvented over and over again for enhancing the individual's gain, but not at the expense of others. The rules of Tit for Tat are simple. First, there is an assumption of time depth in the relationship, that the players will be interacting for some time and are not just ships passing in the night, so to speak. Second, one player gives something to or does something for the other. Third, if the receiver reciprocates, then the first player continues to give, ideally a little more than was received; this asymmetry keeps the ball rolling because the books are not even. If the second player defects, then the first player discontinues giving, but does not retaliate in the extreme. If the second player resumes giving, the first player immediately resumes giving (see Axelrod 1984 and Poundstone 1992 for more detail and the history and implications of this model).

All the elements for this type of give and take, which could lead to extensive cooperation (i.e., economics and politics), can be found within the mother/child dyad. The dynamics of this relationship will be addressed in Chapter 2. Knight's economic model, on the other hand, was created when our ancestors had (1) difficulty determining when females would ovulate, and understanding that menstruation is a female's method of saying, "No, not tonight honey, I have a headache;" (2) a sex drive, but lacked the cues for knowing when to satisfy that sexual need; (3) established a rule with females, through the gift of food, that would help to secure a vagina to satisfy sexual needs. This, I maintain, is too complicated. However, the spontaneous giving of meat to females (or anyone), an implied rule, could begin a process of rights and obligations. But the giving of food, the give and take or implied rule for this important step toward culture, is more likely to be found in the already established biological process of a mother giving food to her child. While the reader is considering this relationship, the concept of implied rules needs to be defined. Implied rules are those behaviors or actions that "just happen." That is to say, a member of the group begins a behavior and the other members allow it to continue (or not to continue). Such rules are not explicitly stated or negotiated and can be seen as primary mechanisms of organization and power, a "glue," if you will, that gives stability to relationships and the cultures that evolved out of them. Implied rules are likewise the engine behind delayed gratification. Implied rules can be postulated as existing in early prehuman and human behavior and groupings and can be seen, for example, in contemporary North American family units; they likewise extend into international politics. Further, implied rules can be seen as a major mechanism in the self-assembling of cultures. The development of implied rules and roles among group members can be added to our list of generalizations. I will have more to say about implied rules in contemporary settings, their development and rather conservative nature in Chapter 3. For now, implied rules can be seen as stabilizing mechanisms for groups because they create expectations. However, because implied rules are stabilizing mechanisms for groups, their conservative nature can inhibit change, which might explain why tool types and most probably associated human interaction patterns changed very little for thousands and thousands of years once a cluster of rules was in place and met the survival needs of the group. Any crisis or conflict, though, can serve as a mechanism for possibly altering implied rules.[3]

What my model has to prove is the existence of a brain and a consciousness with the ability to think into the future, delay gratification, or display some type of extraordinary wisdom (which might even have been drug induced) and compulsive analogous thinking (a brain equipped to consider what is in the environment and compare and contrast this to its own existence within that environment).

A Hint of Language: Implied Rules, Processing Abilities, and the Chunking of Information

Linguists and anthropologists would generally agree that language development was an evolving process. As Bickerton points out (1990:7):

There are two ways in which evolution can produce novel elements: by the recombination of existing genes in the course of normal breeding, or by mutations that affect genes directly. Even in the second case, absolute novelties are impossible.

What happens in mutation is that the instructions for producing a new part cannot simply be added to the old recipe. There must already exist specific instructions that are capable of being altered, to a greater or lesser extent. What this means is that language cannot be wholly without antecedents of some kind.

He goes on to point out that there is such a qualitative difference between human language and the communication efforts of other animals that human language stands on its own as a departure from former systems. Moreover, the ancestral connection between "us" and "them" must reside within neural information processing common to both (1990:21).

Organisms, as they relate to their environment, and through a feedback process, develop varying sophistications regarding *representations* of that environment. A representation is what an organism processes and/or experiences visually, auditorially, kinesthetically, and so on, according to its neural sensing system. Different species, out of necessity, will sense and represent internally those aspects of the environment most directly related to meeting basic survival needs. The more complicated making a living becomes, the more sophisticated the representational capacity becomes. "As long as there are creatures whose motor capacities and environmental conditions allow them to benefit from it, evolution will always favor an increment in representational power" (Bickerton 1990:104). Bickerton goes on to discuss "Primary" and "Secondary Representational Systems," and how these coalesce with other neural/physical mechanisms for the expression of these representations, and to suggest that these were piecing together perhaps five million years ago. From here, Bickerton discusses the development of "protolanguage," which evolved out of neural representation systems, and the eventual development of language as we understand it today (1990:131). He further suggests that protolanguage and language coexisted by using a brief analysis of pidgin languages. His analysis shows that two speakers, both competent in dissimilar languages, can still communicate through a pidgin expression of the two which precisely represents protolanguage--a base line so to speak--so that needs and ideas can be expressed. As to when protolanguage came into being, Bickerton gives that honor to *Homo erectus* about 1.6 million years ago (1990:134). It is at this time in prehistory that we encounter a quantum jump in tool manufacture over that of *Homo habilis*, a tool type represented by Acheulean hand axes, which lasted for over a million years. The emergence of language as we know it can probably be dated to a time period of from 100,000 to 40,000 before present, when we notice a change to tool types (Mousterian) that are more sophisticated for engaging in specialized functions. Bickerton goes on to say that Creole languages, which evolve out of the pidgin languages by the next generation of speakers (the children of the pidgin speakers), "form an unusually direct expression of a species specific biological characteristic, a capacity to recreate language in the absence of any specific model from which the properties of the language could be 'learned' in the ways we normally learn things" (1990:171).

It is difficult to imagine culture without protolanguage or, more certainly, without language. Implied rules also can be seen as a possible mechanism in language development. Imitative gestures and calls, for example, modeled by infants from adults, would spontaneously occur when implied rules were adhered to or broken (see Roonwal and Mohnot 1977 for a discussion of facial gestures and calls among different primate groups in South Asia). Such spontaneity, although leading to meanings attached to sounds, has its down side as it can attract predators as well as scare away potential game. And, in terms of spontaneous calls being *the* push factor for developing language as such, as Bickerton suggests, we must look toward "referential units" (1990:155).

The first referential units of protolanguage were, more than probably, arbitrary units utilized during periods of low individual and group stress. Through time, and applying the idea of implied rules, these units were accepted for a particular group of hominids, as symbolizing another thing or idea. It is not unreasonable to assume that the far more ancient alarm calls would issue forth in situations creating high stress, as when people involuntarily scream at the instant of perceived danger or sigh when frustrated. Over time, however, the ability to conceal sounds or utilize sounds for functions that increased individual and group survival would be (and obviously were) maintained, and perhaps even lost and rediscovered (Bickerton 1990:155), although when and when not to speak is, in large measure, a learned behavior, as any parent or teacher will quickly attest. These sounds, once again, were more arbitrary and disconnected from the alarm calls, hoots, and hollers associated with the call-continuity hypothesis.

Once the neural mechanisms and protolanguage were in place that (1) allowed for self and group consciousness to be seen as part of, *but separate from* the environment; (2) were wrapped around some compulsive, innate need to organize the environment and self within it; and (3) provided an adequate physiology for articulating sounds, then the implied rules of doing and responding became the engine that pushed sounds and gestures into the recognizable content we today call languages. With the event of language, that is, a system composed of phonemes, morphemes, and syntax (all three of which combine the innate capacity for language process with the socially evolving content), then rules and roles/statuses (any idea, concept, or procedure) can be transmitted more explicitly and are therefore more open to negotiation or change. Language, therefore, can be seen as a bridge between conservative, implied rules and roles, and new ideas and attitudes, by placing a mirror of the group processes constantly in front of the speakers. Because language can (but certainly not always does) represent more exactness, detailedness, or explicitness in human interaction, it can communicate rules and rules about rules (meta-systems) regarding relationships, attitudes and/or emotions about people, behavior, and things or objects in the environment. In short, because language is an organized system for establishing rules and attitudes, it can add a great deal of stability or discussed "agreed-upon-ness" about procedure, and thus security to a system because the individual members know who they are and how they are supposed to behave. On the other hand, the content of language, the words and gestures, not only serves to organize, but also is subject to interpretation. It is a continual feedback process with a great deal of "instant" flexibility. It is like traveling down a highway with many on and off ramps in an automobile with many passengers, each taking his or her turn at the wheel (input) and being subjected to the proverbial back-seat driver (feedback). Interpretation as to where the auto is going and what its progress is in that direction is both an individual and a group process. Conflict and cooperation are bound to occur as the auto (culture, a gene pool carrier) continues on its way. Like our group participating in driving down life's highway, language is not always a simple "yes" or "no." It is often "maybe," which, when combined with other rules, opens the door to other considerations or possibilities (other off-ramps, traffic jams, and accidents).

Humans and Chimpanzees

As we are genetically very close to the chimpanzee, we can speculate (and only speculate) that, prior to culture and/or the idea or ability to transmit symbols about self and the group beyond direct observation (see Chalmers 1980), our preculture, like the chimpanzee, could be described as follows: "Three features stand out as especially characteristic of chimpanzees and worthy of further thought. These are the loose unstable groupings and apparent lack of group social organization, the lack of dominance hierarchies as regulators of behavior, and the impressive choruses of hoots, screams, and drumming" (Reynolds and Reynolds 1965:422-423). More recent observation (see Goodall 1986) suggests restrictions of sexual access, in-group and out-group aggression, tool use, food sharing, cannibalism, and a tendency toward sexual division of labor in food gathering (although McGrew 1979, through an analysis of ingested foods, suggests this might not be the case). This type of arrangement obviously lacks a number of elements conducive to the development of culture, that is, specific and consistent sexual restrictions, economics involving consistent cooperation, and a home base (see Knight 1991 for an extended discussion of these factors). There is obviously a large gulf between chimpanzees and humans, and any theory addressing the development of culture must take into consideration how and under what circumstances these three features evolved. Implied rules offer a mechanism for both social evolution and stability. But, once again, in order for humanity to develop, a type of mental apparatus, capable of separating itself from the environment and generating analogous ideas from observations of the environment and group interaction, must be in place for these behaviors to commence in the first place (i.e., a female giving away her milk equals giving away one's kill), thus leading to the rule.   Moreover, all this must be linked to a concept of time or cycles and of space, in which and within which events take place. Where did these mental processes come from?   Did they or do they simply become manifest once the brain reaches a certain size?   What factors might be responsible for forcing these behaviors into place?   Can we rely on a strict Darwinian model to solve these problems, or do we have to look elsewhere?

Topobiology

Edelman's (1987, 1988, 1989) discussion of "topobiology" is of interest. He states (1989:240-242):

Thus, a central problem that must be solved to allow an understanding of brain function is the problem of morphologic evolution. . . . I argue that to solve this problem, evolutionary theory requires an appropriate developmental theory. . . . As a basis for such a developmental theory, the morphoregulator hypothesis was formulated. According to this hypothesis, genetically regulated development of form rests on topobiological events--molecular events at cell surfaces occurring as a function of place and regulating or altering the primary processes of development. These processes include cell division, movement, death, adhesion, and differentiation. The hypothesis proposes that morphoregulatory molecules are key elements in topobiologically controlled events because they are under strict genetic regulation and because they are essential both for the formation of cell collectives and for cell migration and communication in development. Alteration of signals to the control loops affecting morphoregulatory genes (which control the structural genes for such molecules) leads dynamically to developmental changes in shape. This leads in turn to new boundaries between cells and their collectives and alters various other gene-signaling events. A heritable change in morphoregulatory genes followed by natural selection for fitness based on the changed morphology may lead to molecular heterochrony. This term refers to alterations in the timing of action of morphoregulatory genes governing key developmental events that are the basis of a given form. Obviously and a fortiori, all of these remarks apply to the evolution and development of brains.
    The morphoregulator hypothesis is important for our present concerns because it provides an obligate basis for the generation of neuronal diversity and individual variation in neural connections that underlie the TNGS (neuronal group selection).

The juxtaposition of cells, then, can lead to different signaling between cells, new boundaries and the time frames relative to morphology. This can lead to different information organization potentials--in short, a different *type* of information-processing unit, not only quantitatively, but qualitatively as well.

Crisis, Classical Darwinism, and Cultural Evolution

From a Darwinian perspective, mental processes would be altered by some sort of crisis. There seems to be agreement among most anthropologists (see Eldredge 1985:70-79, 1991:180-200; Calvin 1990:10-13) that an extreme environmental crisis can create rapid changes in the physiology of organisms within that environment, including everything from extinction to adaptive modification. With respect to our ancestors, that crisis had to be something that would tax mental functioning or processing itself, not something that would select the amount of melanin in the skin, the thickness of the skull cap, and so on. A likely candidate for such a crisis is population pressures occurring approximately 40,000 years ago in response to improved nutrition and availability of food, especially meat. This would have allowed more people to exist per square mile. With game plentiful and nutrition exceptional, infant mortality would have declined.

Behavioral Crisis

With more people in face-to-face contact, and with no competition for scarce resources, you create a crisis, an information-processing crisis that would put different, novel demands on mental processing and/or cause reassessment of behavioral choices. Behavioral choices in such a crisis are two (1) fissioning the group through conflict or (2) incorporating and organizing larger numbers of people into the group. The size of the group or the number of people with whom one has face-to-face contact is also an important psychological consideration. The human ability to process incoming information has its limits, and these limits have been with us from the beginning; we do not pay attention to everything, and there are even limits as to what we want to pay attention to.

One of the first researchers to consider how much information the human brain is capable of handling during a single time period is Miller (1956). Briefly stated, we are able to handle 7 +/- 2 chunks of information at any one time. A chunk of information is perhaps best defined as an "overlearned set" of behaviors or ideas that are generalized to be one unit in the mind. When stress is low, we are able to pay attention to seven to nine chunks; when stress is high, that number drops to five or less.

It is like starting a new job. As a new employee, your stress is probably high to begin with, as you do not know exactly what to expect. The supervisor, who takes you around and acquaints you with your duties, has, over time, overlearned many of the procedures and does them automatically. He has to break down procedures to their smallest unit, communicate this information to you, and then go on the next "learning station." As each thing is new to a new employee, by the time you have been presented with five or six new things or processes, your stress begins to increase, and it is difficult to remember the procedures, so maybe you begin asking the supervisor to repeat the procedure or you nervously start to jot things down. By the time the supervisor runs you through all your responsibilities, you are discouraged, and the supervisor thinks you are stupid. After being on the job for a few weeks, you superchunk certain procedures, which become a chunk, and you settles in.

Computer programs present the same problem. An individual purchases a word processor and starts to read the manual. By the end of the second page, his head is just swimming in procedures, and he wonders if, perhaps, going back to the pad and pencil would be a better idea. It becomes obvious that, although modern-day humans have to live within the limits of our own information-processing abilities, we loses sight of this when it comes to considering the problems presented to our ancestors. What seems common-place to us was novel and complex to them.

Getting back to our ancestors in groups, there are limits to the number of people with whom an individual can interact and cooperate. That is to say, when group size reaches a particular magnitude, there are diminishing returns on cooperation and survival; it becomes more and more difficult to keep track of and fulfill duties and responsibilities. People feel slighted, rejected, and resentful. Stress gets so high that the system either fissions or reorganizes (perhaps "superchunks" categories) on different principles. For example, the words "male" and "female" are categories in all languages. By lumping all people into one or the other,[4] two general behavioral categories allow the development of general expectations and interaction routines. The same would be true of the categories "brother," "sister," "wife," "husband," and so on. Language as a means of chunking or creating categories and rules of relationships simplifies interaction and reduces stress and conflict. With categories, one can always deal with the individual deviation, through, for example, exclusion or ritual.

Extending this to a larger level of organization, the superchunking of information can allow one type of organization to incorporate similar units (members of a set), that is, family units within a clan, clans within a tribe, and so on. With the development of these categories, one creates a mental set that extends from ego to group and is made legitimate because there is a terminology that encompasses each specific group and one's relationship to it. If the individual perceives himself/herself as part of something (i.e., family, clan, the tribe, nature, etc.), with group or nature's survival representing individual survival, he or she sets the stage for all types of cooperative strategies, from sharing meat to revering and/or appeasing or apologizing to the animals from which it comes.

Group identity is extremely important, and there are some very basic processes that push the individual into dependence upon others for survival.

But let's back up a bit and consider some of the mathematics of conflict, devised by Robert Carneiro, that could act as a push factor for creating categories and different types of social organization.

There is a mathematics of conflict. According to Robert Carneiro of the American Museum of Natural History in New York, tensions rise rapidly with the rise in the number of two-person relationships or dyads as group size increases. The formula is $(N^2 - N)/2=D$, where N is the number of individuals and D is the number o f dyads. Thus, ten dyads exist in a five-person family, while the addition of one more offspring increases the number of dyads by five. When the Yanomamo Indians of southern Venezuela and northern Brazil reach the 100 to 125 level, 4,950 to 7,750 dyads, the atmosphere becomes so charged with hostility that the group must split in two. (Pfeiffer 1982:191)

Adding to this, we have Wobst's (1974) research on optimum group size and survival, with the half-life of a five-member band being about a genera-tion and the half-life of a twenty-five member band being between 250 to 500 years. So, although there is the probability of limited stress with fewer numbers of people, there is also a minimum number required in order to ensure future survival. We are left, then, with a group of twenty-five on the lower limits of genetic survival and an upper limit of approximately 125 for social survival that maintains a particular type of organization. In terms of personnel, these groups are inherently unstable (genetically and socially), with the loss of a member in the group of twenty-five often tipping the survival balance. At the other end, adding any more personnel creates information overload and accompanying stress. Thus, any implied rule (and certainly any explicit rule) that enhances cooperation and reduces stress, especially in larger groupings, is extremely important if groups are to enlarge beyond this upper limit.

According to Hurtado (1990:18-21), "The average village community in central California probably numbered about one hundred souls. These autonomous units gave to aboriginal Californian life a separatist character quite foreign to our modern California organization into towns, counties, and state." But these villages were knitted together through kinship and ceremonial/economic relationships presided over by chiefs, with the larger units being called "tribelets." Such villages, one could theorize, using Carneiro's and Wobst's formulas, were existing near the limits of their information-processing abilities and optimal level of social survival. At the same time, mechanisms (e.g., ceremonial chief) appear to have been available (see Levy 1978a:410, 1978b:487; Smith 1978:439-440) to push these units into a higher level of organization (i.e., a tribe) given enough time and noninterference from the Europeans.

What we *might* have been witnessing with respect to the California tribelet type of organization at the time of European contact was (1) the gradual superchunking of the concept of power, power brought together from face-to-face control mechanisms, kinship identification, and supernatural agencies; and (2) the granting of decision-making power to certain individuals who either have some mythical charter for acquiring and dispensing power, settling disputes, or organizing for war or representatives of the "big man" phenomenon, which establishes power over social compliance through gift giving (essentially helping people ceremonially or economically and creating an implied rule of dependence).

So at the band and tribelet/tribal levels of organization, we need to explain the individual's innate information-processing abilities in conjunction with cooperation and stress and with the optimum group size necessary for survival over time. The mathematics outlined above help us with an explanation. Essentially what this tells us is that humans are indeed a small group animal; we are not designed for working in large systems. Even with special microsystems in place (e.g., police, courts), most, if not all, problem solving and simple day-to-day living occur in small groups. A nation-state, as an abstract entity, does not solve problems. The heads of the nation-state, in mass assembly, ritually shuffle information giving the appearance of solving national problems. Problem solving, even at this level of social organization, occurs in small groups by people who are and have been separated from the everyday realities or problems that they endeavor to solve. Many of the problem solvers, in fact, have developed amnesia for these everyday realities, as is common of most managers in large businesses. Moreover, because nation-states contain so much information and are composed of so many small interrelated systems, it is difficult to know what the problems are that need to be solved. At the national level, for example with the United States, all solutions lead to more problems and unexpected results of a magnitude quite unlike solutions generated at the family level of organization.

Negative Bits and High Risk Messages:
Physical and Emotional Stress

Homo sapiens are information processors at the genetic/biological as well as at the cultural/social levels. Information is processed on a priority basis; that is, information that is perceived as either uncomfortable or threatening will be given highest priority. This could involve personal physical discomfort (being wounded, eating a poisonous plant) or a more emotional level (being pursued by a predator or experiencing harsh words from a band member). This could also involve a threat to the group that is also a threat to the individual.

Any message/information that represents a physical and/or emotional threat I term a *negative bit*. Again, these negative bits can come from a predator, a witch, the enemy in the form of arrows or spears, an unkind word or gesture, or a pathogen. Negative bits imply rejection and imbalance; fear of rejection is innate because without the group, we cannot survive.[5] The fear of rejection is ever present in our minds and represents an endless loop as we are always on the lookout for any message that implies rejection. At the biological level, negative bits (bacteria, viruses, helminths) can cause an imbalance of metabolic processes and physical death.

Referring to social information, what implies rejection to one person may not exactly correspond to that of another. Thus, I have coined the terms, Individual High Risk Message (HRM), meaning that which is symbolically specific to the individual, and Cultural High Risk Message, meaning that which is common to a culture. Again, fear of rejection is innate, and HRMs are the social symbols, learned over time by the individual, that represent this fear. Negative bits that tap into a person's HRMs lead to an action or a reaction which could be a physiological response (vomiting, disease, death) or a physiological/emotional action or reaction (flight, fight, freeze, emotional conversion, sexual behavior), as well as an attempt to explain or put meaning to a situation that is perceived as high risk. Consciousness and analogous thinking are essential in terms of the development of the personal-emotional or social-emotional interpretation of negative bits that lead to the conception of HRMs. HRMs, then, are expressible and can be stored outside the individual.

As we will see in Chapter 3, personalized HRMs represent loops in the brain (because they are attached to the innate fear of rejection), or information that is gone over and over in an attempt to organize and explain. Looping leads to high personal stress, which can be converted to physical illness (internal reaction) or socially aberrant behavior. It is this looping behavior that leads to the explanations represented in myth and ritual and to the belief in superordinate agencies. Schizophrenia and manic-depressive reactions, discussed in Chapter 3, are the result of (1) information input (of a social or physical nature) and perpetual looping (2) combined with or exacerbating neurochemical predispositions (Gershon and Rieder 1992:126-133).

Emotional and social stress, then, has to do with, first, a genetic/biological substructure and, second, the interpretation placed on events or situations, essentially information in general, as sensed or experienced by the individual in a group-feedback setting. All social systems, from politics to religion, are designed to keep individual and group stress and reactions to that stress within manageable limits. If the stress is not contained, anarchy and chaos ensue. We can state, then, that the development of restrictions on sexual access, of economic cooperation, and of a home base is the product of information feedback in an attempt to minimize the destructive aspect of stress reactions, both physically and socially.

THE PHYSICAL EVIDENCE: HUMAN DEVELOPMENT, INFORMATION STORAGE, AND LANGUAGE

As Tuttle (1988) makes very clear, the physical remains, although increasing in number, do not permit us, at this time, to absolutely determine which of the fossil remnants represent our earliest protohuman ancestors, nor do they allow us to identify with certainty the lines of descent. There is indeed useful speculation, even when it is emotional and "adulterated with show biz" (Tuttle 1988:391), but the same evidence is often subject to many inter-pretations (see Lewin 1987 and Johanson and Shreeve 1989). What can the paleoanthropologists, archaeologists, and cultural anthropologists agree on?

As Tuttle (1988:408) states, "The most securely dated early remains of anatomically modern humans in Africa come from Middle Stone Age deposits at Klasies River Mouth, South Africa. The cranial remains are probably about 100 k.y. (thousand years), and no younger than 60 k.y. old. They have the closest morphological affinities with modern southern African peoples. Anatomically modern *Homo sapiens* appeared in Europe a mere 35-30 k.y. ago."

According to Rachel Caspari and Milford Wolpoff (see Bower 1990), it may be necessary to redefine the physical characteristics of modern humans because of the enormous variation in fossil evidence. This could possibly push the date of the appearance of modern humans back in time, but it could also place modern humans within a more recent time frame. The problem, however, involves assuming modern behavioral characteristics on the basis of anatomy. It is my position that modern humans, or those with a culture/ language-carrying capacity similar to our own, probably do not date much past 40,000 or 50,000 years, although Lieberman (1991) uses a 100 thousand year time frame based on anatomical characteristics.

With our current knowledge, this date of 40,000 to 50,000 years for spoken language as we perceive it, with adequate markers for metaphor and analogous thinking, is speculative at best. A much earlier date of two million years was previously mentioned. It would seem, however, and keeping Lieberman's anatomical consideration in mind, that for some reason(s) the social nature or purpose/function of language was altered during the late Paleolithic period (40,000 to 50,000 years ago). Speculating, prior to this above date, if fully articulate speech existed, it probably served mainly to communicate primary-order rules of relationships and division of labor. Secondary, more complex and analogous/metaphorical rules, that establish a connection to nature and the group through the expression of detailed myths and rituals, would have taken time to build and pass on from generation to generation, with a slow elaboration of content taking place. Complexity and richness of myth and ritual is likewise connected to a need for information storage and numbers of people in the group. I also believe that the knowledge of the existence of other social groupings (e.g., other bands somewhere in the known geographical space) likewise enhances the need for understanding and explanation through metaphor and myth. Once there is an oral tradition, a necessary element for building elaborate myths, such myths can then be created almost overnight, so to speak (Hurtado 1990:18-19). As technology increases, along with conscious participation with the environment, language takes on a more elaborate metaphorical and analogous function. Why? Because it aides biological survival by allowing the storage and transmission of knowledge about possible experiences, which the individual might or might not encounter. In some measure this would represent a strategy of preparing for future occurrences. Language, then, superchunks experience or potential experience. The modeling of behavior (e.g., flint knapping) would not necessitate an elaborate symbolizing system other than the behavior itself. Communicating ideas about game (i.e., behavior, geography, seasonal hunting grounds), concepts about life and death, and relationships with others, however, would have immense survival value. It builds a framework within which to act, react, and alter. Faced with some sort of cultural or ecological crisis, like the possibilities mentioned earlier, our ancestors would have been forced to adopt a more elaborate symbolizing system. Morphemes reflecting past, present, and future action, for example, would become quite useful. If Trinkaus (1986; see below) is correct in assuming that Neanderthals were opportunistic hunters and gathers, built for endurance and not efficiency, then their limited art and other symbols could suggest a language deficient in detailed structures for communicating on an elaborate metaphorical or analogous scale. This is quite possibly the way it was with most of our distant ancestors. Referring again to Lieberman (1991:63-77), Neanderthals may have lacked the ability to articulate certain sounds because of the position of the larynx relative to the nasal cavity, thus limiting phonetic ability. (On the plus side, Neanderthals would not have been able to aspirate food.) But, again, not everyone is in agreement with this position.

There is no such thing as a primitive language in today's world; all known languages contain phonemes, morphemes, and syntax. But certainly language did not just come into being in the intricate forms currently known. Moreover, a language could meet the criteria of phonemes, morphemes, and syntax without being particularly elaborate in metaphorical/analogous references. Keep in mind that language, in any form of development, is metaphorical. It transcends the individual by making things out of ideas, which then makes them "real." Again, language superchunks or compresses experience. Need or cultural necessity determines the elaborateness of metaphorical reference. Further, some ancient languages might have been more contextual than others, which is to say, much of the meaning is derived from the situations or experiences rather than the words used to relive the experience. Within such languages or cultural groups, language represents the immediacy within which things happen. As information accumulated, along with increasing cultural contact, the language and its function as a transmitter of ideas or knowledge would have faced a crisis necessitating more elaborate metaphors, analogies, or storytelling for the expressing of past, present, or future experiences (see Schank 1990 for a discussion of how storytelling enhances memory and recall and how this can lead to accumulated knowledge and group survival). In essence, the content would change, compressing, thereby allowing more meaning per unit and decreasing energy expended, and thus increasing efficiency of effort, while maintaining the underlying structure and processes. This elaboration of the content most certainly would have been recent in origin (e.g., 40,000 to 50,000 years ago) at precisely the time referred to by Pfeiffer (1982) as the "creative explosion." Why? Because rapid change evolves out of necessity, a crisis of some sort.

If basically contextual languages existed in the distant past,[6] it would have been more difficult to utilize the linguistic symbols and markers to transmit experience unless the experience is communal; the realities of the experience are bound to the context and are not well represented by the spoken language. Acting out or nonverbal representation would have been extremely important, but, at the same time, could limit efficiency of information transmission and lead to numerous interpretations of events and perhaps a lack of agreed-upon group reality. This would be similar in English and our cultural experience, for example, to relating an experience that was humorous for the participants, but that a non-participant in the experience fails to grasp, the "you had to be there" experience.

In more contextual languages/cultural groups, such as possibly the Neanderthals (perhaps limited to contextual elements because of anatomy), it would have been difficult to plan and thus adapt to new situations that rapidly befell them. Granted, some individuals are better at storytelling, at constructing metaphors and analogies that match the reality of the receiver. In a contextual language, the issue is not the intelligence of the receiver so much as the inadequacy of the descriptive content and amplified processes for describing events outside of their context.

Language is the key to modern humans and expanded cultural development, to our social and emotional successes and failures. It is the ability to symbolize, to store, to retrieve and pass on detailed instructions regarding social rules, roles, environmental information, and technology that explain our very existence within cultural groups. Obviously, one does not need a language in order to survive in nature, that is, to find food, procreate, and simply exist. Culture, and more specifically, language, is a long-term survival mechanism that transcends environment: It goes beyond time and space. However, there is little evidence of language as we know it, and of the types of cultures that would rapidly evolve, until 40,000 to 50,000 years ago. Yes, stone tools represent a symbolizing and transmitting of ideas over time. But as Klein (1989:216) states:

Overall, the European artifactual data, like those from Africa and southwest Asia, suggest remarkable behavioral conservatism over long periods. This in turn may reflect limited cognitive and communicational abilities in *Homo erectus* and early *H. sapiens* compared with modern *H. sapiens*. More specifically, the lack of innovation and the limited evidence for differentiation of tool types during the long Acheulean time span may mean that the stone tools were "the product of complex forms of imitative behavior in a pattern no longer to be found among the

Hominidae" [Jelinek 1977:15].

Speculating on primitive language or origins has been out of vogue for many years. I personally believe that we need to redefine language and its elements beyond phonemes, morphemes, and syntax in order to expand our thinking about our protoancestors. Although protolanguage will be considered in more detail later in this chapter, we must keep in mind Bickerton's statement that there exists a qualitative difference between animal communication and human language (1990:21).

Mitochondrial DNA

Considering our protoancestry once again, according to Allan Wilson, by making comparisons between mitochondrial DNA, which is only inherited from one's mother, the modern "mother" from whom *Homo sapiens* descended existed between 140,000 and 280,000 years ago, with the !Kung of southern Africa being "her" closest living relatives (see Vigilant et al. 1989; Vigilant et al. 1991; Brown 1990). This position has created a controversy, to say the least. The controversy was popularized in the August 1990 issue of *Discover*, with some anthropologists holding their ground of one million years plus or minus, using comparative anatomy and questioning if natural selection and random genetic loss skew the molecular clock model used by the biochemists, which then makes "Eve" look younger than she is. Some biochemists, however, are holding fast to their position as well.

On the other hand, Greenberg et al. (1986) state that, by studying prehistoric and modern teeth, modern humans may have originated in Southeast Asia and not Africa, as the biochemists contend.

But like language, "Eve" did not just show up without precedents (see Frayer et al. 1993 and Templeton 1993, for a detailed discussion of the problems with the Eve hypothesis). Indeed, modern humans may be only approximately 100,000 years old, but the fossils unearthed in Africa, Asia, and Southeast Asia do point back to an ancestry existing perhaps four to five million years ago. Moving back in time, some prime candidates for our protoancestors are *Homo erectus*, dated to approximately 500,000 years ago (see Rightmire 1992 and Bower 1992b:408-411 for an overview of the controversy regarding where *Homo erectus* fits into human evolution), *Homo habilis* (dated to approximately 1.8 million years ago), and the plethora of interpretations regarding *Australopithecus* (2-4 million years ago). As Buettner-Janusch (1966:167) pointed out in reference to the *Australopithecine* materials, "Although variability is apparent, the same kind of variation is evident in chimpanzee skills. No one would use the three chimpanzee in the figures as the basis for erecting three taxa. Yet three genera were proposed on the basis of the fossil australopithecine skulls."

Johanson and Shreeve (1989:87-88) further state:

Individuals of the *same* species can exhibit a remarkable degree of variation among themselves. A million years from now, if the proverbial anthropologist from Mars comes across the skeleton of a female pygmy in central Africa and then finds another skeleton--this one a male Eskimo--in Alaska, will he know enough to assign both to the species *Homo sapiens*? Maybe not. Even within single populations our species shows marked differences in brain size, facial characteristics, jaw shape, and countless other traits. But if this same alien bone hunter found thirteen perfect skulls together in one place, all of them very much alike, he would probably make the logical assumption that they were members of the same species, even though they were all a little different from each other.

Although Johanson and Shreeve sidestep Buettner-Janusch's initial criticism, the fact remains that anatomical differences are important in speculating about behavior, especially the capacity to reason, think, and modify the environment. Very little of the debate between Richard Leakey (Leakey and Walker 1980; Leakey and Lewin 1992) and Don Johanson (Johanson and White 1980; Johanson and Shreeve 1989) is useful in terms of determining the specifics of human behavior, the ability to create, human grouping, parent-child relationships, and so on. Their debate, however, does force us to think about our physical being and geographical origins and compels us to dig deeper in pursuit of ourselves.

Nevertheless, and, of course, depending on the sources you choose, the main characteristics of our proposed lineage (i.e., *Australopithecus* ----> *Home habilis* ----> *Homo erectus* ----> *Homo sapiens*) are upright posture, bipedalism, opposable thumb, large brain-to-body-weight ratio, facial flattening, and stereoscopic vision. Add to this, from observations and comparisons among contemporary humans, other great apes, and monkeys, decreased body hair (more so for the female), the loss of scent-emitting apocrine glands and the increase in eccrine glands for producing sweat, a layer of subcutaneous fat, and, for females, breasts that stay enlarged even if they are not pregnant or nursing (see Knight 1991, Morgan 1990).

From endocrainal casts, there is lateralization and more prominent definition of the sylvian fissure or Broca's area, which is related to speech. Worked stone tools were used by our protoancestors more than of 2.5 million years ago. There is some disagreement as to which of our ancestors fashioned these tools--an *Australopithecine* or *Homo*--but the modified or worked stone represents a significant piece of physical evidence of our ancestors, early on, using symbols and generalizations on a grand scale. Lieberman (1991:160) states, "It seems impossible to say very much about the cognitive complexity of a toolmaker's mind on the basis of the tools that he or she made." Wynn (1989), however, using Piagetian observations and theories of mental perception in child maturation, has developed an interesting analysis of tool manufacture and spatial thinking. By examining tools dated over two million years ago, Wynn has been able to say something about the knapper's ability to think, to visualize, and to develop symmetry, which is the starting point for analogous thinking with which humans are obsessed. Symmetry, though, according to Piagetian theories, is not a thought process with which one is born. It develops, instead, out of a combination of perceptual abilities that mature as the infant explores its environment (see Donald 1991). Moreover, symmetry is perceived long before it can be produced or manufactured. In other words, a certain amount of knowledge about "things" in the environment is necessary before symmetry can be realized or created in another object. As Wynn (1989:50) points out, nothing in nature is perfectly symmetrical; it is, in reality, an "almost like" phenomenon. The "almost like" represents an analogy. Yes, other animals use tools, but none modifies stone into the shapes resembling teeth and claws, which, I believe, are symmetries or analogues to these early stone tools. The other feature that conjoins with analogous thinking is analogous teaching (see Prieditis 1988). This is where language becomes an absolute necessity, especially when teaching abstract, social concepts. If the individual can make the analogous connections, then a system becomes necessary for distributing these ideas if they are to have long-term survival value.

The crucial step in understanding our protoancestors is evidence of symbolizing--for example, stone tools, which are, I believe, symbolic of extensions, modifications, improvements over physical anatomy. Stone tools, and other artifacts, represent a second stage of analogous thinking beyond the tool use of, for example, the chimpanzee, a primary stage. Such modification, moreover, represents a separation of the self from the environment--a "standing back," if you will, observing the self and the group in the environment, and opening the door wider for further modifications--and the accumulation of knowledge about these modifications and how, where, when, and why these modifications are to be used. From my perspective, and contrary to Jaynes's (1990) intriguing hypothesis, "the origins of consciousness" telescope back in prehistory to at least the moment of tool manufacture and tool transport. Existent artifacts tell us something about the behavior and thinking of our protoancestors, that is, stone-tool manufacture and their possible analogous relationship to claws, teeth, and the like. They also tell us that our protoancestors were observers of the world around them and were able to take an observation and mold it into another thing--an "entity," if you will, which separates the self from the environment (consciousness). Such tangible analogues are psychologically very powerful and can create a splitting of the psyche, an initial psychological step toward separating one's self from the environment. As we will see, such separation is dangerous if taken too far because it threatens group cohesion and cooperation and can lead to chaos. Mechanisms must be developed for reintegration, and this is precisely where myth, ritual, religion, medical systems, and eventually law come into play. Culture may be a genetic mechanism for preventing chaos by giving stability to accepted ideas, processes, and procedures. The mechanisms or institutions mentioned earlier (i.e., myth, ritual, etc.) become necessary for explaining and justifying what the people and culture are doing. They are also mechanisms for connecting behaviors back to nature and/or communitas (see Figure 1.2). This will become evident when systems of curing are considered in Chapter 4.

Figure 1.2
Connecting Nature to Communitas

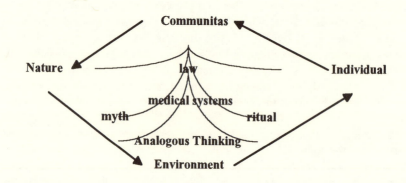

Keep in mind that analogous thinking would not be limited to the stone tools representing animal tooth or claw model, but would include analogies of animal social structures, dietary habits, and sexual behavior. These observations are the models upon which every culture was and is based. Beyond this, however, little can be said.

White (1989:98-99), referring to the artifacts of the Aurignacian period of approximately 35,000 years ago, states, "The transfer of qualities from one context to another is an essential part of the construction of metaphors." The type of thinking, I believe, that led our protoancestors out of environmental encapsulation to environmental operationalism or modification was the mental ability and physical capacity to engage analogous thinking and borrow an idea from nature and reproduce it out of nature's materials at hand, that is, stone, wood, bone, hair, and so on. The paradigm jump here is the idea of efficiency of effort; as an extension of one's self, it does the job better than could be done with one's physical endowments. And, as an extension of one's self, it symbolizes separateness from nature. No longer is the individual or group bounded by its own genetic limitations. It is my contention that this analogous thinking is one of the crucial components in the development of culture and social organization (which helps to explain the eventual regulation of sexual behavior, basic cooperative economic exchange, and home base), as well as the basis of individual and group psychology, prehistorically as well as today.

What can we interpret from the physical remains regarding individual and group psychology of the past? We can conclude that the stone tools fashioned by *Australopithecines* and/or *Homo habilis* are probably analogous representations of teeth and claws. Why can this be said? Because they are more than sharp rocks in a ditch that one steps on; they are rounded and symmetrical like teeth and claws. More important, stone tools are purposely shaped with the resulting shapes in mind (see Wynn 1989), shapes that would possibly represent observations of teeth and claws along with the experience of being bitten by animals or observing how other animals kill their prey. It would be difficult to deny the existence of such knowledge or observation in the minds of our protoancestors (see Bickerton 1990:75-87), as their physical survival would depend, in part, on behaviors that would prevent falling prey to the possessors of teeth and claws. But there is another consideration. From the beginning of the Acheulean hand axe tradition, approximately 1.4 million years ago, and lasting for about 1 million years, little change occurred in our ancestors' tool kit. Moreover, there are questions as to the purpose of these tools as they are not especially useful as hunting weapons, although there is an aerodynamic aspect to these "hand axes" which might suggest that they were made for throwing. Although there are suggestions that they could have been used for butchering scavenged animals (see Binford 1987), it is also suggested that these might have been defensive weapons, indicating a great deal of male vs. male conflict over meat and females (see Knight 1991:261). Another possible explanation is that they also might have symbolized an association *with* the predators around them, sort of a badge of reference, as the makers were likewise predators. Moreover, flint, chert, and quartz, all sedimentary rocks composed of minute quartz grains, fracture via concentric rings, which could have been seen as analogous (perhaps, and I realize the gross speculation here) to the sun and more specifically to the moon, and its crescent shape. Viewed from left to right, one may be witnessing the waxing and waning of the cycles of the moon, a perhaps useful connection if indeed females had synchronized with the moon, as Knight (1991:244-245) suggests, thus giving males some sort of guide as to when to have sex with females. However, our female ancestors, because they were probably perpetually pregnant, had fewer periods by far, contrary to our own time and culture, and it is unlikely that our lusty ancestors simply sat around counting the phases of the moon as a signal to procreate. Outside of rape, the women do indeed chose their partners, but their selections have a great deal to do with the signaling or communication efforts of the male(s) as neither is passive in the process.

A reason there was such conservation with these tools is that they may not be tools, in an overall sense, but perhaps calendars or, more likely, symbols of power, or life and death (symbols of the moon), usurped from the powerful predators with whom they had to compete. Such symbols of power, similar to the handgun of today, could have bestowed on the carriers a sense of invulnerability, a belief that they could go anywhere and survive, a push factor that led to a more rapid migration out of Africa.

Neanderthal Remains: Social and Psychological Characteristics

The Neanderthals hold a special place in our prehistory, being the subject of a great deal of speculation as to their behavior, physical attributes, and demise or absorption into the gene pool of more modern humans. Of more importance, the Neanderthals allow us a glimpse of a near ancestor who perhaps was unable to culturally and/or physically adapt, depending on one's theoretical perspective, that is, extinction or absorption.

In a review of the Neanderthal materials dated to the Upper Pleistocene period, Trinkaus (1986:205-206) concludes that the morphological charac-teristics suggest great strength and endurance for running down small animals over an uneven terrain. Neanderthals were "opportunistic hunters," without a "planned subsistence pattern," and used energy in the food quest rather in-efficiently.

The organized hunting of big game, as opposed to scavenging and the taking of weak game, is a relatively recent phenomenon, beginning only about 40,000 or 50,000 years ago. The suggestion of lack of efficiency and lack of cooperation might also imply problems in interpersonal and group commun-ication, a high rate of in-group conflict, and consequent injury, a short life expectancy, and a selection for strength or hypertrophy in order to simply defend one's self. Further, in-group fighting also leads to continued group fissioning and the spreading out of individuals and groups over a wider territory and would thus certainly inhibit the accumulation of information and in-group as well as out-group cooperation. Because of this, the Neanderthals might have found themselves in small groups (less than twenty-five) existing at the very edge of group continuance from Wobst's (1974) point of view discussed earlier. If Neanderthals, as Lieberman (1991) suggests, were not capable of articulate speech, their ability to discuss conflict, present their points of view, form "pressure-valve" rituals around it, and negotiate would be seriously restricted. This would limit group size and ability to organize on a grand scale.

If modern humans originated in Africa, as the recent DNA studies suggest, and if Africa has been the mixing pot for our ancestors' contact and resistance to disease, it is also possible that Neanderthals died out once they were subjected to novel pathogens as modern humans moved into their territories. Assuming that Neanderthals lived in small, isolated groups, disease factors, as McNeill (1989:197-200) points out, become more devastating for the smaller and more isolated groups. On the contrary, the larger the population and the closer or more frequent the communication between people, the less destructive the disease. McNeill (1989:197):

Consequently, the tighter the communications net binding each part of Europe to the rest of the world, the smaller became the likelihood of really devastating disease encounter. Only genetic mutation of a disease-causing organism, or a new transfer of parasites from some other host to human beings offered the possibility of devastating epidemic when world transport and communication had attained a sufficient intimacy to assure frequent circulation of all established human diseases among the civilized populations of the world.

During the time from the Middle to the Upper Paleolithic period and the advent of modern humans, there is a change in technology, from one of generalizations on a theme to one representing more and more specialization. Beyond these symbols of culture, information about self, group, and environment was ever increasing and evolving into what Pfeiffer (1982) has called "The Creative Explosion." As Trinkaus (1986:207) summarizes:

Among the Neanderthals there are examples of personal adornment, a probable case of artificial cranial deformation, and some simple scratches on bone that may or may not be intentional designs. However, evidence of an esthetic among these archaic humans is rare, and in no known case does it approach the art of the Upper Paleolithic. The art, regardless of whether we will ever decipher its iconographies, is best seen as a form of information processing. The representational nature of much of it and the presence of notations on bone indicate that the associated humans were recording information for transferal through time and space, probably on a regular basis. The appearance and rapid elaboration of art and notations at this time imply a major increase in the amount of information being communicated. Since shared information about the environment and the distribution of resources in it is an important part of modern hunter-gatherer adaptations, this suggests the appearance, for the first time in human evolution, of social group oriented information-based adaptive systems, ones that would rely far less on energetically expensive opportunistic foraging that appears to have characterized preceding human adaptive patterns.

It is also at this time in history that we more consistently encounter grave goods, which could imply that some individuals were accorded higher status than others or were more highly regarded by other group members, which may mean the same thing. Moreover, the average longevity of Neanderthals was approximately thirty to forty years. With the advent of modern humans this average increases to 60 plus years. Trinkaus (1986:208) further comments:

If this interpretation of an increase in maximum age at death can be substantiated with larger samples and more refined techniques, it would indicate the appearance among early modern humans, probably for the first time in human evolution, of significant postreproductive survival. That would indicate an increase in the transgenerational communication of information about variability of resources in the environment. It would also imply increased grand-parenting and associated reduction in orphaning and of the subsistence work load per adult.

Trinkaus (1986:208-212) goes on to suggest that physical strength and risks of physical trauma in modern humans had decreased from that of the Neanderthals, with a corresponding increase in social complexity. Of great interest here as well, and suggested through analysis of pubic-bone growth, are the decrease in the fetal gestation period and probable changes in hormonal secretions, with even small changes in hormonal secretions translating into large changes in neural and other physical structures. This suggests a longer infant dependency period, thus creating a longer period of parent/child cooperation and perhaps more flexibility in learning and/or creative potential. The longer the maturational process, the greater the learning potential and the more flexible the learning process.

The key element defining culture, however, is the use of symbols that transcend the individual and his or her direct observation or personal experience with events. As White (1949:22) states, "[t]he symbol is the unit of all human behavior and civilization. All human behavior originates in the use of symbols. It was the symbol which transformed our anthropoid ancestors into men and made them human." At some distant point in prehistory, our protoancestors came to the realization that one thing could stand for another, not necessarily related thing. How did this come about? It would seem reasonable to speculate, using a Darwinian model, that the dynamics revolve around the concept of utility and survival; what works toward preservation of existing genetic material survives. This becomes even more important considering Eldredge's punctuation theory mentioned earlier (what works will probably, everything being equal, work for a long time). However, this seemingly unique ability of humans to symbolize in the extreme may have been a byproduct of unrelated yet survival oriented, genetically available conditions that were brought about, for example, by our ancestors' reaction to climatic changes (Calvin 1990) and the neurological changes that followed. Also, it is possible that brain mass and consequent hypersymbolism, language, and consciousness might be a byproduct of more practical concerns, that is, as a means of cooling off the inner structures of the brain (Ornstein 1991:55-66). It is further possible that mental development evolved not in any linear fashion, but instead in a nonlinear, or chaotic manner, the dynamics of which are not self-evident (see Prigogine and Stengers 1984 and Davies and Gribbin 1992 for philosophical concepts of chaos and its relation to human behavior; see Briggs and Peat 1989:167:180 for a specific discussion of the brain as a nonlinear system; see Casti 1989a for mathematical models of chaos and human behavior).

The ability to symbolize has an all too often recognized consequence in our own age and time. Symbolizing helps to order the world, explain events, and create conformity, expectations, and the essential individual and group security, but it can also do just the opposite. It can create disorder, chaos, and oppositions which may be just as logical and "saleable." It can also result in what we term "insanity," or the engagement in thoughts or behaviors that society (or psychiatrists or clinical psychologists) considers abnormal.

Our protohuman ancestors, existing one million plus years ago, were group animals biologically designed to most effectively work, play, and essentially interact in small units of between 25 and 125 individuals. The stone tools fashioned by our distant ancestors highly suggest analogous thinking and thus consciousness which allows the individual to transcend the environment. With the advent of language (probably much more recently), the transmission of information about events becomes possible *before* the individual actually has to deal with a situation, thus allowing rehearsals, which increase survival in dangerous situations. Language, then, is a superchunking of environmental and social rules that aid in individual and group survival. Longevity also permits more information to collect in individuals, therefore allowing for intergenerational transmission of ideas. Older people become, in a sense, "libraries" or storage units. Moreover, those who could store the best or most useful information were perhaps accorded higher status because they were seen as more valuable in a relative sense.

Pfeiffer's Information Explosion

The Paleolithic period in France and Spain (40,000 +/- 10,000 years ago) offers us physical evidence, again subject to interpretation, that suggests, through a proliferation of art forms and tool specialization, an increase in population density and an accumulation of knowledge. As Pfeiffer (1982:123) comments, "What it all added up to was more to know, more to learn, more and more information. An information explosion occurred together with the explosion of ceremony and the explosion of art."

As information accumulates and is utilized, it then becomes a part of doing, that is, choices for survival. But as information accumulates, it becomes more and more difficult to transmit this information from generation to generation. I am sure that very useful information was frequently extinguished with the death of an individual and society had to backtrack on itself until the information or knowledge was rediscovered. It is like attempting to traverse a steep incline and losing the toehold, slipping back several yards, regaining the ground, and then finding that old toehold anew. This problem of information storage and retrieval created a crisis:

The crisis, as severe as the threat of famine, threatened chaos. The here-and-now emergency gave rise to measures of a different sort, measures created to transmit the expanding contents of "the tribal encyclopedia" intact and indelibly from generation to generation.

That put the pressure squarely on the human brain itself. It meant pushing things further, exploiting natural and hitherto-used storage capacities more and more fully, putting what the tribe had learned and needed to preserve into memory. The Neanderthals must have faced storage problems of their own, and worked out techniques which have left few traces. But whatever the nature of those techniques, they became increasingly inadequate for handling the new information during the Upper Paleolithic. New developments were needed in the art of remembering or mnemonics, ways of imprinting far larger quantities of information, and the cave art was part of ceremonies which accomplished precisely that. (Pfeiffer 1982:123-124)

Pfeiffer goes on to suggest how the environment of the cave, the artworks themselves, and the accompanying ceremonies would have been used to anchor information, with the caves acting as a sort of library or computer for storage.

Considered from another direction, as information accumulates, it is chunked into units that contain the underlying processes along with content. For example, flint knapping is a process that can be applied to numerous shapes and sizes (the content) of stone tools. As another example, the keyboard on which I am typing is made out of some type of plastic made from petroleum. Although I know how to use the keyboard, I would not, with my knowledge, know how to produce the plastic out of which the keyboard (and many other products, both the content and the processes) is manufactured. What the ancients, as well as current humans, attempt to do is remember or store the *processes* of doing, with such processes stored in the content of expression. The crisis associated with Pfeiffer's "information explosion" is precisely to store the processes, as these are easy to lose with the loss of personnel even though the content remains. Content often transcends the processes, and once this happens, and if there are inadequate means for storage and retrieval of the processes, the social system becomes more and more unstable. One of the problems facing modern civilization is the medium of storage, as the metal-impregnated plastic film on which information is stored by this computer, and the similar material used to store information on video and audio tapes, does have a relatively short life expectancy.

Brain Size and Archetypes

As we examine the physical evidence of our hominid remains from the *Australopithecines* to *Homo sapiens*, one feature that looms large is the ever increasing ratio of brain to body size. The brains of the *Australopithecines* are estimated to be approximately 450 cc with modern humans at approximately 1400-1500 cc. There seem to be two factors of importance, one being an observation and the other a question.

The first involves the convolutions of the brain, which increase surface area.[7] The suggested significance of this, in terms of current brain functioning, relates to information storage and increased "specialization" of brain functions.

I place specialization in quotes because the brain functions as a unit, but there are areas of the brain that function in a particular way in conjunction with the total brain, that is, speech centers around the sylvian fissure, the visual centers in the occipital area, and so on. But as we look at brain development from a comparative anatomical perspective, we note that our triune brain (spinal column/reticular formation, limbic system, and cerebral cortex) represents an addition to and an elaboration upon older structures represented by fish, reptiles, and the earliest mammals. The increasing brain-size-to-body-weight ratio, again, is clearly noted in the increase in size of the cerebral cortex from our earliest ancestors to us.

The question arises then: At what point did our ancestors begin to process information the way we do? Campbell states that there is really no difference between us and Cro-Magnon man of 35,000 years ago in terms of thought and psyche (*Transformation of Myth Through Time*, with Bill Moyers, Program No. 1, video tape). As proof of this statement he utilizes the numerous myths and the Jungian archetypal images that show similarities across the cultural lens. The myths tend to reach out and "grab" those buried symbols, so that the underlying concept is, in some unconscious way, understood, although perhaps not adequately articulated by human speech. Although Campbell's statement seems reasonable, we notice in the archaeological evidence the rather abrupt change in social organization and accumulated information from Neanderthal to Cro-Magnon. Did Neanderthals have within their archaic memories the same archetypal images, or did these symbols arrive on the scene with modern humans? Campbell does mention (1989a) that Neanderthals buried their dead and thus must have been aware of the change in state between life and death (see Stringer and Gamble 1993:158-161 for a brief discussion of the conflicting opinions regarding Neanderthal remains). However, there is really very little in the way of artifacts to suggest much about archetypes. There is debate as to the Neanderthal place on the evolutionary tree, with some saying that this variation of human morphology died out, while others say it is a direct ancestor, and others believe that they were absorbed (see Trinkaus and Shipman 1993). There would appear to be a large difference between the Neanderthal as opposed to Cro-Magnon worlds. Why such a difference? Was it a different wiring in the brain? Were there fewer crises facing the Neanderthals, as they had apparently already adapted to the cooler climate and were surviving well until they came in contact with Cro-Magnon man?

Possible Hormonal Changes

As Trinkaus suggests (1986:211), slight changes in hormones can create large physical changes, for example, slower maturation. Recent research indicates that changes in estrogen levels, for example, can alter not only mood but also thought. Research by Kimura and Hampton at the University of

Western Ontario showed

that a woman's monthly ebb and flow of gender-related biochemicals has predictable cognitive and behavioral effects. The results were not related to mood changes [or the] premenstrual syndrome that when a woman experiences low estrogen levels she excels at tasks involving spatial relationships but performs poorly at complex motor tasks, including some involving speech. In contrast, peak estrogen levels are associated with improved performance of motor and verbal tasks but difficulty with problems involving spatial relationships. (Weiss 1988:341)

The research goes on to say that there are similar cycles in men, which research will more clearly identify (O'Brien 1992:28).

Since Selye's (1956) research in the 1940s and 1950s, it has become increasingly evident that, as the individual reacts to stressors in the environment, hormone levels are likewise altered. As we move from the Upper Paleolithic information explosion and the probable associated stress as Pfeiffer (1982) suggests, such hormonal dumping would most certainly have had an across-the-board effect on cognition and perception for all group members plus the next generation still in the womb. There has been speculation, along with folk beliefs,[8] although no definitive evidence of support, that stress and subsequent hormonal dumping within pregnant females could create permanent physical changes in the developing fetal brain. Changes in diet and the ingestion of chemical agents (thalidomide, for example) and psychotropic agents (alcohol, cocaine) can have a permanent physical effect on body and brain. Research by Di Chiara and Imperato (1988) has linked addiction to drugs like alcohol and cocaine to the effect these drugs have on the neurotransmitter dopamine. Cocaine ingestion, particularly in freebase form or the more recently introduced "crack," can cause permanent changes in the number of dopamine receptor sites (Nunes and Rosecan 1987). Further, an increase in dopamine and/or dopamine receptor sites has been indicated in schizophrenia (Kety and Matthysse 1988).

Psychotropic Agents and Nutrition

We know that psychotropic agents have been associated with human culture for many thousands of years. The *Amanita muscaria*, for example, was brought into the Indus Valley of India approximately 3,500 years ago; referred to as "soma," this psychotropic agent is surrounded with religious rites that come down to us in the Rig Veda (see Wasson 1967). Allegro's (1970) rather controversial book, *The Sacred Mushroom and the Cross*, posits that Judaism and Christianity developed out of an ancient fertility cult that worshipped the *Amanita muscaria*.

Field (1960:81), through her research in Africa, suggests that Moses utilized the sacred mushroom and also nitrous oxide, created by burning ammonium nitrate on a hot dish or through the lightning ignited oil shale on Mt. Sinai, in order to commune with God.

As foragers, our ancestors must have time and time again come across psychotropic plants, for example, cannabis, and fungi, and ingested these. (Also see Matossian 1989 and her discussion of ergot fungus and decreased fertility as well as other aspects of physical and mental health.) And there must have been a certain amount of experimentation as groups moved from one ecological niche to another. Incipient drug use in the 1960s and 1970s in the United States gave rise to many new drug experiences and many deaths as well, as in the case of inhaling hair spray or injecting milk as an antidote to drug overdose.

Alcohol also has an early history in the Middle East. As Ralph Solecki has stated (personal conversation, October 1966), "The use of storage jars for grain, in the ground as they were, would have on occasion filled with water. Yeast being ubiquitous would have done the rest."

Bread making is a complicated process, and certainly you uncomplicate the process by having unleavened bread. But, what is the connection between grain and bread? None, until some experimentation. Grains, though, become palatable if you soak them, softening the glume, so that the digestive tract can digest the inner and softer part of the grain. The soaking of grain, and the release of starch, invites fermentation.

Cannabis is certainly another drug with a long history in the Old World, and, according to Schultes and Hofmann (1980:83-86), was cultivated by the Chinese 8,500 year ago. Cannabis has a worldwide distribution and is used ceremonially (and habitually by many people) in the Old and New World.

More recently, McKenna (1992:24) makes a bold and direct statement about psychotropic plant ingestion and the development of consciousness:

My contention is that mutation-causing, psychoactive chemical compounds in the early human diet directly influenced the rapid reorganization of the brain's information-processing capacities. Alkaloids in plants, especially the hallucinogenic compounds such as psilocybin, dimethyltryptamine (DMT), and harmaline, could be the chemical factors in the protohuman diet that catalyzed the emergence of human self-reflection. The action of hallucinogens present in many common plants enhanced our information-processing activity, or environmental sensitivity, and thus contributed to the sudden expansion of the human brain size. At a later stage in this same process, hallucinogens acted as catalysts in the development of imagination, fueling the creation of internal stratagems and hopes that may well have synergized the emergence of language and religion.

McKenna's (1992) statements regarding the part psychotropic plants had in building culture are reflections of Siegel's (1989:10) earlier position:

Recent ethnological and laboratory studies with colonies of rodents and islands of primates, and analyses of social and biological history, suggest that the pursuit of intoxication with drugs is a primary motivational force in the behavior of organisms. Our nervous system, like those of rodents and primates, is arranged to respond to chemical intoxicants in much the same way it responds to rewards of food, drink, and sex. Throughout our entire history as a species, intoxication has functioned like the basic drives of hunger, thirst, or sex, sometimes overshadowing all other activities in life. Intoxication is the fourth drive. It is as bold and inescapable as the drug stories that dominate today's headlines. Individual and group survival depends on the ability to understand and control this basic motivation to seek out and use intoxicants.

In the late 1960s, Timothy Leary, the guru of psychedelic experience, suggested that, in the next generation, our youth will not be putting drugs in their brains in order to expand their consciousness. Instead, they will be using electrical stimulation. He wasn't clear on how one would do this, but his statement seems prophetic. More recently ("Tuned into High-Tech Psychedelics" 1992:C1, C3) Leary points out the memory problems associated with "LSD and other psychedelics" and the fact that "they're isolating and alienating." Mirroring his statements of the 1960s, compact discs and virtual reality programs may be the media of hallucinations in the future. Hallucination-producing drugs, according to Leary, may become a thing of the past (also see Rheingold 1991 and his discussion of the "realities" created via computer imagery). Our ancient ancestors, however, in all probability did not take drugs as an isolating experience; isolation from the group would have been an emotionally devastating and physically deadly prospect initiated by other group members and not by the individual. The purpose of the drug, in many cases, was to interact with the larger world; social or recreational use of drugs was too dangerous. A person would "take a trip" and upon "returning" would be debriefed in order to share the experience with the other members.

Of course, intoxication and the ideas, visions, and sensations generated can be not only be useful for the group, but devastating as well; altering consciousness invites chaos. Dangerous behavior toward in-group members would be eliminated quite quickly in these small bands by either destroying the group (and the behavior altogether), expelling the dangerous members (this would amount, in most cases, to a death sentence), killing the offender, or forcing the group to control the ingestion of such drugs and/or place drug taking within some ritual context. Societies that regularly use psychotropic drugs and keep the drug use within a ritual context experience fewer incidents of social disruption due to drug abuse. Much of the drug use in our own society has been stripped away from social ritual; it has become secular and personalized, and the problems associated with this type of drug use/abuse are immense. However, psychotropic drug use could have enhanced awareness in terms of cooperation, for example, food sharing, technology, and so on; it is a distinct possibility.

We, *Homo sapiens*, may be equipped with a psychic energizer of our own, that is, uric acid. We know the effects of caffeine on the human nervous system, that is, excitation. Coffee, for example, is regularly used by millions of people to stay awake, the "think drink," as used by advertisers. What is of interest here is that humans are one of the few mammals that do not have an enzyme (uricase) for the complicated transformation of uric acid into allantoin thus removing uric acid from the blood; instead it is filtered out by the kidneys. In some cases, uric acid can build up in the blood, manifesting itself in various forms of gout, for example, gouty arthritis, wherein uric acid crystallizes out of solution and settles in the first metatarsophalangeal joint. Uric acid, however, has a chemical structure quite similar to caffeine, creating the possibility that humans are perpetually psychically energized. Could consciousness have, in part, been brought to the fore through the loss of this uric-acid-eliminating enzyme, thus allowing uric acid to freely circulate in the body and brain until filtered by the kidneys? At what time in our biological evolution did we lose the enzyme uricase? Because all primates excluding *Homo sapiens* have this enzyme, I would assume that this biological change occurred sometime within the last three or four million years. This corresponds, at least, with our hominid ancestors' first manufacture of tools and with the consciousness and analogous thinking that eventually led to culture as a survival mechanism. Could uric acid have played a part in this?[9]

"Food" and Altered Consciousness

Jackson (1991:505) reports the following about the ingestion of plants that are not considered hallucinogens:

Human biological variability, in conjunction with specific aspects of cultural diversity, provides a dynamic template upon which natural selection continues to operate. Contemporary human biological diversity may reflect the differential exposure of various ancestral and modern groups to diverse environmental constraints, including variable exposure to plant-derived secondary compounds. As omnivores, ancestral as well as contemporary human groups have been in regular contact with an array of plant chemicals. The usual human diet has facilitated our exposure to many of these toxic compounds. Given the ubiquity of such compounds in most of the very plants we depend upon for subsistence and the common persistence to toxicity even after extensive processing, it is unlikely that human dietary contact with plant chemicals has been without *biological and behavioral consequences*. More likely, chronic exposure to specific plant compounds has been a salient part of our species' evolutionary experience. [emphasis mine]

Disease Vectors

Brown and Inhorn (1990:188) comment:

The study of disease and human behavior in an ecological setting is a fundamental task for medical anthropology. The approach contributes to basic and applied research in the field by providing a strategy for answering some of the major questions raised by general anthropology and epidemiology. For example, it can be applied to anthropological questions concerning the interaction of biology and culture in human evolution or to question why particular cultural behaviors may make sense and be retained in an ecological setting.

They go on to say (1990:195) that

the human immune system can be viewed as the product of genetic adaptation to disease pressures. A primary biological characteristic of the immune system is its adaptability; in other words, it is a generalized mechanism capable of providing protection against potential (yet-to-evolve) pathogens. The evolution of the immune system is the product of human adaptation to disease; at the same time, the immune system has required that disease organisms adapt to their host-victims.

Although there is certainly mention of disease factors affecting physical evolution and cultural adaptations, it is of interest that there has been little mention, even speculation, regarding the effect of disease vectors as a crisis or factor that abruptly altered human neurological/emotional/behavioral evolution. We can begin, then, with Moore's (1984) discussion of parasites and how they change behavior in their hosts.

Parasites can be considered an information intrusion (or invasion), and the process of adaptation can be considered assimilation and modification to accommodation. As Moore comments (1984:108), "One of the most familiar literary devices in science fiction is alien parasites that invade a human host, forcing him to do their bidding as they multiply and spread to other hapless earthlings. Yet the notion that a parasite can alter the behavior of another organism is not mere fiction. The phenomenon is not even rare. One need only look in a lake, a field or a forest to find it."

By observing pill bugs after being infected by the parasite *Plagiorhynchus cylindraceus,* Moore observed changes in behavior *and* apparent physiological modifications. The behavior changes involved movement to areas that would allow their black color to stand out more and thus subject them to a higher probability of being eaten by birds. Moore (1984:114) states that *P. cylindraceus* itself "influences the pill bug's predation by starlings." It is also suggested that the parasite alters the pill bug's physiology, so that it is less sensitive to and can live within a lower than normal humidity; its preference, in its uninfected state, is a humidity level of 98 percent.

Here we have one of many cases where behavior as well as physiology is altered without, at the same time, immediately altering the genetics of the host, although over time genetic and/or physiological alteration would certainly accompany parasitic invasion; symbiosis would result. Once again, we may be witnessing, with respect to schizophrenia and manic-depressive reactions, for example, environmentally induced syndromes that can lead to alterations in consciousness and consequent alterations in cultural directions if such syndromes become manifest at the right time and place. As Gershon and Rieder (1992:128) point out, the thought processes emanating from these syndromes can lead to creativity with high social impact.

Consider for a moment a group of hominids, *Homo erectus*, moving out of Africa toward the Asian continent equipped with an immune system designed to deal with the African milieu. As McNeill states (1989:21), "Probably the most significant factor in blunting the initial impact of humanity upon other forms of life was the peculiar richness and elaboration of African infestations and infections--an elaboration of parasitism that evolved along with humanity itself and tended to intensify as human numbers increased." As our ancestors moved out of Africa, and into drier and cooler climates to the north and east, disease vectors, according to McNeill (1989:25-26), decreased, allowing for a population expansion with new problems of adaptation. Moving into other tropical areas to the east, however, and in the process of experimenting with new foods, our ancestors would have encountered new microbes and parasitic worms ready willing, and able to find and utilize new hosts. Do we dare speculate about possible physiological, behavioral, and/or cognitive changes that might have resulted?

From a population increase alone, one would expect behavioral changes. But what about cognitive changes occurring as a result of parasitic invasion? Information intrusion and accommodation comprise a mechanism worthy of study when considering human cognitive development. However, McNeill (1989:37) states that "exact information is lacking wherewith to create a history of human infections."

Such modification to accommodate can be seen, according to Hamilton, Axelrod, and Tanese (1990), in sexual (rather than asexual) reproduction, as a means of maintaining traits that, although presently ineffective, might be useful when encountering other parasites. They state (1990:3566):

Darwinian theory has yet to explain adequately the fact of sex. If males provide little or no aid to offspring, a high (up to 2-fold) extra fitness has to emerge as a property of a sexual parentage if sex is to be stable. The advantage must presumably come from recombination but has been hard to identify. It may well lie in the necessity to recombine defenses to defeat numerous parasites. A model demonstrating this works best for contesting hosts whose defense polymorphisms are constrained to low mutation rates. A review of the literature shows that the predictions of parasite co-evolution fit well with the known ecology of sex. Moreover, parasite co-evolution is superior to previous models of evolution of sex by supporting the stability of sex under the following challenging conditions: very low fecundity, realistic patterns of genotype fitness and changing environment, and frequent mutation to parthenogenesis, even while sex pays the full 2-fold cost.

Disease factors, then, must be added to the equation of physiological, behavioral, and cognitive changes as hominids populated the habitable world. There were crises created not only by climate, but also by population increases and decreases, disease factors, the ingestion of new foods with new chemical components, and, in all likelihood, the ingestion of psychotropics, unintentionally at first, but then purposely.

The point here is that biological and social stressors would have created periodic situations of extreme individual and social stress. Such stressors, be they disease vectors, chemical compounds in ingested plants, hallucinogens, or rapid population growth, all would have affected our ancestors' behavior, genetic constitution, and perceptions of self and the surrounding environment. Stress at the individual level (i.e., distress as one interprets the information available to the senses, especially for pregnant females) would have created hormonal dumping that might have been, in itself, an important consideration in terms of brain and cognitive development at the genetic level. Moreover, certain of the mind-altering plants or substances could also have had *permanent* effects (at the genetic level) on the neural development of unborn children. Nutritional factors (i.e., an increase or decrease in available protein, essential minerals and vitamins, and so on; the ingestion of new chemical compounds, as mentioned earlier) can also have a permanent impact on individual functioning, which can likewise affect genetics over time. But the brain, unlike a foot or a hand, has the ability to transcend the environment, the group, and the individual, and to change and to modify itself (increased brain weight through an increase in dendrites) simply by thought and the addition of new information. A leg muscle, for example, changes on a linear scale. If you exercise, muscle mass increases, positions of attachments enlarge to accommodate this, calcium in the bone increases, and so on. If you do not exercise, the muscle atrophies, calcium is lost from the bone, and enzymes decrease in capacity to handle fats. In terms of aging, the part of the cell (mitochondria) necessary for building the energy packets (adenosine triphosphate) for cell functioning slows down. The brain, however, as long as it is subject to novel information, and assuming adequate nutrition, continues to develop mass. Moreover, and more important, the brain does not change in a linear, two-dimensional manner, but, instead, has a non-linear, multi-dimensional characteristic often referred to as "plasticity."

Brain Lateralization, Language, and Consciousness

A recent and very interesting concern of the paleoanthropologists has been brain lateralization and the consequence of this for human speech and human social development. Calvin's (1983) thesis is that, when a female holds an infant in her left arm and next to the rhythmic beating of the heart, the infant more readily calms down. This is useful if the dyad is being pursued by a predator. In this position, the right hand is free to use a stone or stick to frighten away the predator. This, as Calvin suggests, is how we became predominantly right-handed. Moreover, hand-eye coordination and speech are linked in our neurological development. He states (1983:29-30):

But I suspect that pitching and talking did have something important in common, not recently but back a few million years ago. It probably all started with the invention of one-arm rock throwing, handy for hunting prey without the usual long chase scene. Throwing possibly established the first important lateralization of the function to the left brain, an ability to rapidly orchestrate muscles in novel sequences. And I'll bet that this muscle-sequencing lateralization, most noticeable these days as handedness, was what started up not only tool making but language.

As interesting as Calvin's speculation regarding brain lateralization and origins, Falk's (1987:26) remarks are instructive.

Lateralization in Homo sapiens may be viewed as a manifestation of a general rule that emerges from observations of animals as diverse as rats and birds. In rodents, direction of circling behavior is associated with fighting and sexual display. Left lateralized control of male bird song is associated with territoriality and mate attraction. Therefore, neural asymmetry may increase the efficiency of spatial analysis involved in mate attraction and territoriality. Thus, the evolutionary history of basic neurological asymmetry appears to be ancient, and ongoing research suggests that nonhuman primates, although they lack language, are characterized by lateralized brains. If so, hominid brains would already have been fundamentally asymmetrical at the time of their origin, and the extreme lateralization associated with language and handedness in extant humans would represent elaborations on this substrate.

The speculation about brain development is interesting and is discussed briefly here to show how newer structures and capacities are built upon older ones. This can be seen in both the biology and the social organization of our species; analogy is both a physical and a social process. Considering language specifically, Chomsky (1957) and his followers (see Casti 1989b:209-260 for an overview of Chomsky's position) have theorized that the language process is an innate feature of the human mind with its own generative rules. The capacity for language evolved out of the necessity (or a byproduct of this necessity) for processing and organizing information perceived in the environment, all of which was built upon earlier information strategies. Donald (1991:90) states:

The language module supposedly contains the encoding and decoding devices for speech and graphic representation (of which signing and writing are two examples), and the lexicon, or lexicons, that serve the system. Whether the same module includes grammar is debatable; but it does not seem to contain some of the basic human se-mantic reference systems, which often remain intact during clinical language loss. . . . [I]n the absence of language, it is impossible to test many aspects of meaning, especially those that are inherently linguistic; and thus it remains possible that certain aspects of semantic representations are unique to the language module proper.

It is reasonable to assume, though, that human language abilities are the outgrowth of many interlocking factors, that is, analogous thinking, the ability to vocalize, the position of the larynx, brain lateralization, brain size, and so on, which, through happenstance, came together as our ancestors were adapting to other environmental factors. The origins of language can only be speculative because there is no way of replaying the prehistoric scenarios that were selected for its advantage. In humans, language is a byproduct of earlier and not clearly understood adaptations.

Language, Rules, and Roles

As a group develops rules of organization, it creates in the individual a social reality beyond his or her individual interpretation of the world. Culture does, indeed, surpass the individual. Once established, culture orients, conditions, and pushes its group members. The sole function of language as we know it is to place the individual within a social context of rules and to give the social plane a feedback mechanism for compliance and change. Verbal (and nonverbal) language, as complicated as it may seem on the surface, serves two functions, both of which are concerned with rules: that is, the stop and start of behaviors and the meta-function of communicating about behaviors and rules. Within these categories lie the arts (poetry, storytelling, myth-making, etc.), which tell the receiver rules about the sender's likes and dislikes (personal and social values), change and social discontent, laws, technology, relationship rules, roles, and statuses (see Figure 1.3).

Stating what language does, and the purpose it serves, and using Bickerton's observation, let us expand on language, as it is humankind's most important survival mechanism.

According to Bickerton (1990:46), representational systems are not passive or accurate models of outside events, but, instead are analogues inhibited or directed by the rules of their own functioning or make-up. In other words, the structures and functions of the brain dictate what and how information is perceived. The meaning of the processed information is assigned by the individual or culture and expressed through a language. This allows for a great deal of creativity, constrained by culture, and the diversity of thought, beliefs, and behaviors that define culture. When we speak of language, then, the reference is to the genetic, deep structures, which are in some way a mirror of the environment within which they evolved, and the cultural content that is manifest in a specific language, for example, English.

Genius

One element that is missing from the discussion of human or protohuman anatomy, tool use, and other behavioral speculations is the development of

Figure 1.3
Language (Verbal and Nonverbal) as a Tool for Setting Rules

Rule Category	Relationship To
Relationship Rules (Beliefs and Behaviors Toward)--->	1) In-Group 2) Out-Group 3) Superordinate Agencies
Division of Labor ----->	1) Male 2) Female 3) Children 4) Elders 5) Specialists, etc.
Technology------------>	1) Manufacture 2) Use (How, Who, When)
Rules about Rules (Meta-Systems)------->	1) Law/Sanctions 2) Formal Teachings 3) Myth 4) Ritual 5) Art forms

genius. In all times and all ages, there have been individuals of a group who combine information differently, who see the world through a different lens-- without the use of psychotropic drugs. Many would have, no doubt, been outcasts, depending upon the values of that particular group; the genius, like the psychiatric patient, has unusual ways. Some of our early, protohuman tool inventors were probably of the genius type, with the rest of the group quite able to carry on with an idea once it emerged. There would be essentially three types of genius: (1) the technological innovator; (2) the social or rela- tionship innovator, essentially a leader; and (3) the artistic genius. All three would feed into one another.

A genius comes up with a procedure for fashioning implements out of stone. He or she passes this information on to the group, and it is an instant success--like many inventions. However, there is no sure way to pass on the outward expression of genius or creativity itself, and there is no way to store the information or procedures except within the tool or idea itself. When the individual dies, creativity continuance in that particular area can cease, especially in small groups with limited personnel. And, without a means of preserving the thinking processes of these individuals outside of the materials or artifacts created, it would be difficult to innovate further. In any culture, genius is conservative, even when we consider the many issues that lead to the expression of genius. And there is survival value in this. If everyone were a genius, then chaos would ensue. Innovation destabilizes systems; absolute creativity is absolutely destabilizing. Knowledge and innovation are dangerous to the maintenance of order, as history adequately displays (Kuhn 1967). Dramatic innovation, though, during a crisis (population pressures, disease, etc.) could be the path of choice. However, from the first stone implement to the first verb to the cave painting at Lascaux, one can envision a creative presence, someone who was there at the right time with the right "brain-stuff" and combination of social and environmental information.

OVERVIEW

There were thirteen universals uncovered in the above brief review of human evolution:

1. When considering human behavior, we have to consider groups of people and not individuals. Individuals, by themselves, are necessary elements within a much larger picture. Human psychology is, in reality, group psychology, as human brains work in tandem, just as neurons work in tandem within the brain.

2. Our hominid ancestors had the ability to observe, listen to, or perceive occurrences of significant survival value in the environment and to store and retrieve that information when needed. Consciousness, therefore, and the ability to manipulate the environment, is at least 1.5 million years old and can be detected at the moment our ancestors began to manufacture *and* transport tools.

3. Going beyond technology, the disposition to observe and understand motivation, desire, passion, and behavior, to place these within a symbolic context (i.e., roles, rules), and rituals, and to understand the advantages of cooperation through the serial aligning of human brain power to solve problems, are part of our prehistoric and current tools of survival.

4. Tool manufacture implies analogous thinking and the separation of self from the environment (consciousness), which can be expanded into all areas of beliefs and behaviors.

5. Physically and psychologically, *Homo sapiens* and our hominid ancestors would have been exposed to negative bits (stressors) of information, which, when physically and/or psychologically ingested, lead to action and can be seen as physical, psychological, and social modifiers. At the emotional, social, and information-storage levels, negative bits are generalized and stored as High Risk Messages (HRMs), upon which the individual and the group loop. This process can lead to explanations of that information and social action. At the physical level, HRM activation means an unbalanced physiology leading

to expressions of illness or disease.

6. Political culture (as opposed to technological culture) is a survival tool that evolved from existing relationships, that is, male-male, male-female, mother-child, and so on. These relationship dyads can be found in all hominid groups and thus can be seen as the stepping-off point for inventing or reinventing more complicated sets of statuses, interaction patterns, and power relationships, especially during periods of crisis.

7. Implied rules are one of the "glues" of culture; they self-generate and maintain cultural momentum. Doing and allowing or doing and not allowing establishes rules that are automatically engaged and quite conservative over time. Rules that aid survival usually stick around.

8. As humans have limits on information-processing abilities, this leads to the compression or chunking of information. Combining this with analogous thinking, one can generate symbols to represent an infinite variety of ideas.

9. Language, an outgrowth of analogous thinking and the generalizing or chunking of information, allows rules to become explicit and, therefore, more subject to renegotiation.

10. Our ancestors were able to recognize and eventually store information outside themselves in the form of symbols carved or painted on cave walls, bone, and so on, and within technology itself. Once you store information outside of the individual or the group, you increase the probability of cultural survival; ideas, concepts, and behaviors do not have to be continuously reinvented at the death of group members.

11. As a process of organizing our world, we have developed the "us" vs. "them" distinction. This had survival value in limiting access to group membership and consequent information overload on the individual's information-processing abilities and rapid cultural change. It also had the virtue of spreading groups out over a wider territory and thus limiting competition for scarce resources. "Us" vs. "them" also leads to prejudice and attack on "them" by the dominant group and usually withdrawal by the subordinate group.

12. Our hominid ancestors have had to adapt not only to the macro-world, but to the micro-world as well. Our close association with microbes and parasites has undoubtedly had an effect on our physical as well as our neurological/emotional/behavioral development. As in item 11 above, minimizing contact might have a secondary effect of allowing a slow leakage of disease vectors from group to group, perhaps allowing more time for the development of immune responses without catastrophic results. The exact opposite could also occur.

13. Our association with plants and the chemicals contained within them has likewise altered our physiology and has perhaps amplified our consciousness. As cultures collide, culinary habits modify, introducing both groups to different plant and/or synthetic chemicals, which can result in a variety of health problems.

What I have explained are factors, both biological/psychological and social, that allowed for the transition from preculture to culture and then from bands to tribes, and from tribes to more complex social arrangements, that is, nation-states. Our ancestors would have had to come up with some revolutionary ideas and processes (technological and social) that could be built upon existing frameworks for these transitions to have taken place. After the event of culture some 1.5 million years ago, I believe that more recently (30,000 to 50,000 years ago) a crisis evolving out of ample food supplies, increased population, and the stress of interaction prompted changes in the interpretation of self, others, and the surrounding environment, and thus changes in relationships or social organization. I further speculate that the existing implied rules of relationship and division of labor were built upon and chunked. The tapping into HRMs and the resulting psychological looping would have led to explanations of existing conditions (illness) and a starting point for solutions that would reduce stress (curing, religion, etc.). The dynamics of game theory and the evolution of cooperation also help us to solve part of the social aspect of this equation. However, our ability to deal only with limited amounts of information, combined with our ability to superchunk information, is at the heart of this equation for language development and the storage of information outside of the individual. At the next level, though, we need to consider the need to optimize one's gain or perceived gain, to act on one's or the group's self-interest. Any individual or group, while operating in what it terms its own self-interest, that takes too much of the perceived "pie" from other members or group, is apt to bring upon itself verbal or economic sanctions or war. Another generalization begins to emerge at this point. Individuals and groups will act in what they consider to be their own self interest, with the primary push factor emanating from the genetic fact of genes needing to survive and from the social fact (not quite in the Durkheimian sense) that, once a social system is established, the rules and roles surrounding it become self-perpetuating.

NOTES

1. Recent use of acupuncture for arthritis of the knees, by physicians in the US, has yielded some interesting results ("Acupuncture" 1994:319).

2. I reference Knight's work, *Blood Relations* (1989), because it is one of the more recent (and sophisticated) discussions of social origins.

3. According to Harris (1979:275):

Since we intuitively know that there is a rule for everything, we are easily misled into believing that rules govern or cause behavior. But the principle that rules govern or cause behavior is no more credible than the proposition that the earth is flat. Rules facilitate, motivate, and organize our behavior; they do not govern or cause it. The causes of behavior are to be found in the material conditions of social life. The conclusion to be drawn from the abundance of "unless" and "except" clauses is not that people behave in order to conform to rules, but they select or create rules appropriate for their behavior.

I strongly disagree with Harris when it comes to implied rules. Ask any married couple to list the rules of their relationship and you will receive, in most cases, a blank stare. And yet they relate day after day using a set of rules that are not immediately identifiable. The fact that they are not identifiable and yet are automatically engaged is one of the major causes of marital failure in North American, urban culture.

4. Some cultures allow for other categories--for example, *berdache* (see Williams 1992)--but it is difficult to know when in human cultural organization such distinctions entered into the language. I assume, and perhaps wrongly, that such terminology is probably quite ancient.

5. Only recently in human existence have we been afforded the illusion, created by technology and a concept of strict individualism, that we can "go it alone."

6. Chinese and Japanese are contextual languages, and I am making the assumption that there were languages wherein meaning could not be easily determined unless the individual was actually present during the event under discussion. This may be a false concept on my part.

7. The need for the increased area of the cerebral cortex, as mentioned earlier, might have been an adaptation to heat dissipation (Ornstein 1991).

8. During my research with Italians in Toronto, Canada, a popular belief involved fright during pregnancy, which could result in the object of fright becoming a birthmark on the infant. In other words, if one generated fear over seeing a mouse, then a birth-mark resembling a mouse would be found somewhere on the torso of the infant. It is therefore important to guard the pregnant female against certain types of information with which she would get upset.

9. Could this loss of the enzyme for removing uric acid from the blood also be connected to other enzyme/hormonal changes that altered estrous in females, wherein the signals communicating fertility and/or receptivity were "concealed"? (See Knight 1991:200-222 for a review of theories related to the loss of estrous.) Could such changes have been accentuated by dietary changes? As Jackson (1991:505) states, "Contemporary human biological diversity may reflect the differential exposure of various ancestral and modern groups to diverse environmental constraints, including variable exposure to plant-derived secondary compounds." Further, "dietary contact with diverse plant chemicals produces a range of selective constraints expressed as a spectrum of alterations in human metabolic biology. These, in turn, may result in differential survival of individuals and populations. This differential survival of certain individuals and groups may affect their biological fitness by altering the selective advantages (or disadvantages) of particular genetic mutations, allowing their frequencies to become fixed more quickly in the population" (1991:507). Certainly, a rapid alteration in estrous, more specifically, its identification for males, would have placed protohuman groups in an interesting crisis.

CHAPTER 2

The Origins of Culture

Chapter 2 considers some of the theories of origin, information processing and storage, the development of human consciousness in relationship to both sociological and environmental (e.g., diet and disease vectors) factors, and theories of chaos, which help to suggest elements of human information processing that maintain stability or lead to change. Such universals point not only to a model of human behavior, but also to clinical tools.

INTRODUCTION: STORYTELLING

Discussing cultural origins, as Knight (1991:68-69) has recently pointed out, has been out of vogue for many years. At this juncture in time, I believe that there is enough quality information within the social and biological sciences to paint a realistic picture as to how human culture developed, enough understanding of human behavior to outline the basic scenario(s). As I stated in Chapter 1, Knight's (1991) thesis, I believe, is based on a point of view (Marxist) of the downtrodden proletariat (females) overthrowing the ruling class (males) through the use of a sex strike. The problem, as I see it, is this: If such an overthrow occurred, it implies that culture already existed. It implies a conscious political base as well as rules regarding sexual access. To overthrow a system, the system must first exist in some shape or form. The Marxist point of reference is, in reality, a backward extrapolation from nation-states to cultural origins. I believe it does not represent an accurate picture. There was no female oppression among our hominid ancestors; males and females did what they did, behaved the way they did, because it worked in terms of a survival strategy. Saying that our female hominid ancestors were oppressed is like saying that reindeer does are oppressed by the bucks. Both males and females were active participants on the road to culture. Within the Marxist tradition, as suggested in Knight's work (1991), is the premise that culture evolved out of internal conflict, conflict between males and females. It is my contention that intense male/female conflict and internal group conflict in general are more recent in origin, possibly beginning with Pfeiffer's (1982) "Creative Explosion." I say this in light of the fact that our ancestors for many hundreds and thousands of years lived, worked, and died in small groups-- approximately 25 to 125 individuals per group, as I mentioned in Chapter 1. These groups are, however, unstable in that, if you lose group members, if you have morale problems, the whole group will suffer. In order to survive, conflict had to be kept at a minimum. As group size increased, approximately 35,000 year ago, certain types of conflict probably did increase, necessitating other type(s) of political arrangements, but this occurred, I speculate, after the basic male/female/child cooperative arrangements, sexual restrictions, and probably marriage arrangements (exogamy) came into existence.

Now, here is what I consider most significant and important in terms of cultural origins because everything else flows from this. Once information began to be stored outside the individual, one has the building blocks of culture, the group consciousness and analogous thinking. Once information about the environment and other hominids (in-group and out-group) could be separated out as things or ideas, humankind had the basic tools of culture. Culture, quite briefly, began when our ancestors were able to understand that they were a part of nature, but could separate from nature, where they could use nature rather than simply being used by nature. This represents a rather dramatic psychic split where modification of the environment and refinement of those modifications can accumulate, slowly at first. Culture, or the storage of information outside of the individual, in terms of tools (probably the first external-to-individual and -group information-storage mechanisms) and, at the same time, ideas about relationship rules and division of labor (including sexual restrictions and consistent food sharing), probably had its first spark of being (a thing or concept seemingly separate from the individual) between 1.8 and 2 million years ago (see Klein 1989:131). These ancestors were the first technological and social scientists. In this day and age, it is difficult to imagine the shift in thinking it took to pick up materials close at hand, modify them, and carry them around. We are so used to the chunks of ideas, the thousands of combined ideas, in the form of lock-back knives, compound bows, cars, and computers that it is easy to miss that original complexity of thought. The stone tools, Oldowan and Acheulean artifacts, are what remains, but surely wood and bone would have been used as well. All of these things are representations of the world around the individual, the claws, the fangs of predators, associations with life and death. These early concepts and associa- ted objects, which represent the storage of information outside the individual and the group, were all that was needed for survival in a manner that far outdistanced their nearest competitor for scarce resources, which then allowed these ancestors to "boldly go" out of Africa and into the new "worlds," toward new opportunities and the consequent ecological/biological and social selective pressures. The reason that the Acheulean-tool complex lasted so long without modification is self-evident--it worked, and it allowed our ancestors to take with them the symbols of power from which they came, that is, the teeth and claws of predators. Our ancestors usurped the power of these predators. Not only were these artifacts utilitarian, but also they were powerful symbols of strength and superiority. Just imagine the psychological advantage--call it even arrogance, if you will. But these tools allowed for another type of symbolizing, and that is the possibility of carrying or keeping an artistic part of the original maker of the tool. The tool would embody the manufacturer, perhaps a relative, or it could be traced back to some mythical manufacturer, a person, thing, or animal, allowing for the possessor to reference a mythical charter. From a utilitarian[1] point of view, again, it allowed migration into all habitable and accessible areas. But, because of the continuity of this tool type throughout Africa, Asia, and parts of Europe for 1.5 million years, one also can assume a back-flow of migration. There must have been movement out of Africa and back into Africa, with continual cultural contact. This cultural contact is extremely important because it would offer an opportunity for stress and conflict of a different and more intense nature than that experienced in a singular group of hominids. The stress and conflict would arise out of (1) in-group/out-group hostilities ("us" vs. "them," too much information to process, competition for scarce resources) and the development of methods to deal with these hostilities (e.g., warfare, gift giving); (2) the introduction of new bacteria and parasites through close, intimate contact (i.e., sex, food sharing, and so on); and (3) the exchange and collection of new information gained through experience. During all of this, and stimulated by one crisis after another, and for about 1.5 million years, information is collecting and being stored outside the individual most obviously in the form of tools and probably ritual, until finally, 40,000 to 50,000 years ago we encounter Pfeiffer's (1982) Creative Explosion. This was probably touched off by population pressures and longevity.

Reproduction and Sexual Restriction

Many researchers equate incest taboos, exogamy, the development of rules and roles, and politics with the emergence of culture. Culture is built upon existing patterns of interaction. With respect to relationships, we know that there was at least a sexual relationship between males and females. This relationship, in other organisms and prior to the existence of our hominid ancestors extending back perhaps as much as three or four million years, was based on reproduction, which is obviously a form of cooperation. But as

Prochiantz (1989:90-91) explains:

It appears today that the second very significant invention of evolution was to separate, in humans, the reproductive functions and the sexual functions. While in most species sexuality and reproduction virtually overlap, the human species makes the greatest distinction between the two. To be sure, sexuality is part of a general reproductive process, and in a recent book, Jean-Didier Vincent [*Biologie des passions* (The biology of passion), Odile Jacob, 1986] presents a very good analysis of the hormonal mechanisms that underlie orgasm during copulation; he shows that pleasure is related to the activity of cerebral structures in the hypothalamus. But the structure involved in fantasizing, the one that can control this hormonal machinery, in particular, is linked to the cortex of the individual and hence, as I mentioned before, to the history of the individual, unique in each case, which is inscribed in the cortex. The result is a multiplicity of possible pleasures unrelated to the reproduction function. The body can respond to this multiplicity in a thousand ways, all of them individual, according to an infinity of scenarios; for our purposes, it is irrelevant to what extent, if any, these ways and scenarios may in all cases be consistent with a social code. The reader may consult his or her own experience or give free rein to the imagination.

What I would like to emphasize, however, as a matter of scientific objectivity of obvious emancipatory value, is that any morality seeking to link reproduction and sexuality in human beings is a morality more applicable to monkeys. . . . [T]his invention of sexuality for its own sake, which is exclusive to the human species, is no doubt related to the exceptional potential for fantasizing and cognition of the human brain. The arts, the sciences, and thought in general are the fruits of this marvelous invention.

One way of explaining this split between sexuality and reproduction is through analogous thinking, a byproduct of an enlarged brain, upright posture, the freeing of the hands, and so on, along with a different concept of time, of cycles that represent occurrences in the future. Analogous thinking has to include a time orientation, that is to say, one thing can only *represent* another thing (it really is not that thing) if there is also a concept of space and time. Things are similar, but they are found or exist in different space, environments; the concept of time flows from this.

Considering the split between sexuality and reproduction, what is well known is that a fantasy can be more motivating than what the genes or hormones call for; thought and fantasy can override basic biological needs and urges. Fantasy also implies the "what if this had happened instead" phenomenon and the thoughts into the future or the possibilities of happenings. The emancipation Prochiantz refers to above allows the consideration of an infinite array of possible sexual relationships, from group sex to exclusive sex with a specific mate to sex with "foreigners," outsiders, or even other animals. It would seem reasonable that the type of expressed sexuality that was the most stress reducing would have had high survival value. Once again, we do not need to evoke a sex strike as envisioned by Knight (1991).

Consciousness, Food Sharing, and Cooperation

We also know that there was a relationship between mother and infant(s) that was more long lasting because of the length of dependency of the child upon the mother. If Anatol Rapoport's Tit for Tat (see Chapter 1) can be seen as a simple cooperative mechanism that has immense survival value, then the relationship between mother and children holds the key to the establishment of stable relationships between males and females in general. Of course, the scenario to be outlined hinges on human consciousness, the ability to see one's self as separate from the surrounding environment, and the ability to think analogously, which I believe was in place 1.8 to 2 million years ago with the event of manufactured and transported tools.

By feeding and nurturing children the mother would have been establishing a precedent for receiving "favors" in return. In this day and age, many families can spoil their children; they do not have to expect much work from children because, in most cases, it would not contribute to basic survival. In fact, it would be counter-productive in terms of an ethic that says one needs to play to learn, with learning and education opening the door to success. Moreover, it would dump too many people into the labor market. So most parents today do not put their children into the work force. Less than 100 years ago, however, the purpose for having children was to have hands around the farm and caretakers in old age. For most of human history, children were "hands around the farm," as they contributed time and energy in their quest to survive in that economic climate.

Two million years ago, mothers would have fed children and, early on, would have began a process of teaching these children how to find food, mainly by example. Only relatively recently did they combined this with spoken language. It is easy to shape the behavior of children; adult behavior is more difficult to alter. Our ancestors could not afford spoiled children. Because mother shared with the children, the food the children collected would, in some measure, be shared or given away: "I've shared with you, now you share with me." When a child would not share, a frown, a growl, or the "all I've done for you" message, would help to build and/or tap into a High Risk Messages. Guilt and shame are likewise part of this equation. When we consider guilt and shame as mechanisms for shaping behavior,[2] the guilt (or shame) that could be generated to obtain compliance, to begin a process of food sharing and distribution, in my mind, would be very important in protohuman social development. As the children matured, the behavior of sharing food with the mother and other siblings, everything else being equal, would be maintained. Those mothers who did the best job of instilling the concept and practice of sharing, either with guilt/shame or with some positive reinforcement, could maintain the rule and behavior of sharing between mother and child and between siblings throughout the lives of all concerned. The concept of not eating a certain portion, or even all, of one's gatherings could then be modified to fit a similar arrangement with meat or big game kills for the male children (assuming the males were the big game hunters) as they got older. We do not have to theorize a sex strike by females in order for meat or other food to be placed before them. As humans "package" or symbolize in a rather compulsive manner, giving up a portion of the kill or food in general becomes symbolized in the taboo or the totem and is actually analogous to exogamy.

Incest and Food Sharing (Economics)

When researching literature, one is struck by the fact that father/daughter incest and brother/sister incest are common. The interesting thing is that mother/son incest is rare; I can find no societies in which it is ritually sanctioned. After 25 years applying anthropological concepts in marriage and family therapy, I can count one example of mother/daughter and two examples of father/son homosexual contact, and only one example of mother/son incest. I have numerous examples of father/daughter and grandfather/granddaughter incest, stepfather/stepdaughter sexual contact, and brother/sister and stepbrother/stepsister sexual contact to the point of penetration. These are all documented cases, although I have numerous accusations of father/daughter and stepfather/stepdaughter incest, made during child custody battles, which are questionable at best.

With respect to mother/daughter, father/son, and mother/son sexual behavior, *all* parents were under the influence of alcohol (or some other drug) at the time. Why is mother/son incest so rare? The confusion here, it seems to me, lies in what we can learn as we study preliterate society, and the beliefs and practices, the rationales and reasons that have grown out of earlier behaviors and situations. I believe that mother/son incest is so rare because, as the sharing of food aided in mother/children survival, it would aid in overall survival if it was expanded out to the group in general. In order to do this, the older males, the fathers of the children, had to sever these ties between mother and son so that the son's energies could be utilized for the group as a unit. Yes, the older males might have felt threatened sexually by the close contact between mother and son. Male initiation rites (extreme rites involving mutilation, the ingestion of drugs, etc.) are economically, not sexually motivated, and such rites appear to be quite ancient, with all designed to force the male into a responsible position in terms of the total group, not just mothers and siblings. Our own society has a male initiation rite that is designed to separate son from mother. It comes in the subtler form of peer harassment, the hazing with accusations of "being tied to mother's apron strings." It is interesting to watch the average teenage boy pulling away from the kiss or "clutches" of his mother.

In Italian culture, the bond is broken in a less dramatic fashion through demanded respect by the mother who presents herself as an asexual figure, the Madonna, and by segregating men from women with a fairly clear concept of male vs. female behavior.

Within the Mexican family, there is a similar type of segregation of males and females. During the dinner hour, for example, the older women serve the men and children and only sit down to eat after everyone else has been served. Likewise there is a division of labor that further segregates males and females. When the male reaches puberty, he is accorded more respect by the mother, but he continues his respect for her, similar to the Madonna figure noted above. The mother is the controlling figure in both the Italian and the Mexican families. When the son marries, the mother's dominance is not as noticeable, and the husband becomes dominant over his new wife, influenced from the wings by his mother but in subtle ways, that is, dinners at the mother's house, and the like. When the wife bears children, however, the husband's status diminishes, and her dominance comes to the fore, repeating the process over again. Most currently existing societies have various mechanisms for severing the mother/son bond.

Looking at incest taboos in general, keep in mind Wobst's (1974) numbers for living together and survival. Twenty-five members is on the low end for numbers in a group cooperating for mutual survival. With just twenty-five members, the half-life would be 250 to 500 years. As you drop below this number, group survival decreases in a geometric fashion. Therefore, creating a situation where one can count on males and females for group sharing would have the highest survival value. If we can assume that analogous thinking was in place perhaps two million years ago, and if we can assume, as does Fried (1967), that, in these band-type groupings there are as many statuses as there are people to fill them, then, through analogous thinking, sharing would spread throughout the group by using one mechanism or another. With an equal number of people and statuses, there would have been a high level of synchronized behavior.

Returning to the concept of sexual restrictions and incest taboos, many writers, (e.g., Freud, Knight) see this as a turning point in the development of culture. So as not to confuse sex with marriage, my reference here is strictly to sexual behavior. All cultures have restrictions on sexual access to specific categories of people within and outside the group. Is there some principle of cultural adaptation here? Yes, several. First, and in principle I agree with Knight, by making sure that each person has a sexual partner, energy otherwise devoted to keeping other males away from one's "herd of females" (or vice versa) can be directed to other cultural pursuits. Second, because incest is common, although there are incest taboos, there is probably no innate aversion to sex with a sister, daughter, mother, and so on (Brown 1991:128). By cutting down access to certain categories of people, one can reduce stress and tension by structuring the interaction patterns and the expectation of group interaction. Third, familiarity, contrary to Westermark's hypothesis, does not necessarily breed contempt. As Harris (1989:198) states, "[T]he wide occurrence of incest taboos may merely show that they are extremely useful, not that they are innate." The question then is, In what other ways are incest taboos useful? Harris (1989:204) comments further:

Studies of modern-day foraging bands show that in such groups the prevention of mating within the band is essential, not because of the danger of having physically impaired offspring, but because groups of that size *are too small to satisfy their biopsychological needs and appetites on their own and risk extinction* if they do not establish peaceful and cooperative relationships with their neighbors. [emphasis mine]

Now let us combine several factors and then another statement from Harris. First, we have discussed the fact that humans are small-group animals with limits on information-processing ability. Group size has its limits in terms of stress generated on a day-to-day basis simply by having to keep track of who is who and the implied rules developed over time. Occasional contact between neighboring groups, for the purpose of sharing group members, ideas, and newness of any kind, would have great survival value and yet not outstrip the information processing abilities of the individual on a day-to-day basis. Second, the cooperative nature of the mother/child bond mentioned earlier is the template out of which, I believe, all sharing began; this develops the economics of our ancestors. Third, the very simple, yet effective strategy of "tit for tat" introduced by Rapoport is a social idea with great survival potential not only within the group, but also between neighboring groups. Fourth, the institution of implied rules would allow the process to maintain momentum through time. And, fifth, all the above factors are duplicative or rediscoverable by other groups if one group should meet with a calamity.

Harris (1989:204-205) further states:

Since exchanges of goods and services lay at the foundation of harmony within afarensis or habilis troops, it was no great innovation to create alliances between neighbors through the exchange of valued goods and services. What was the most effective form of exchange open to them? Through trial and error they inevitably discovered that it was the exchange of their most valuable possessions, their sons and daughters, brothers and sisters, to live, work, and reproduce in each other's midst. But precisely because human beings are so valuable, each group is tempted to keep sons and daughters and brothers and sisters at home, to enjoy their economic, sentimental, and sexual services. As long as the exchange of persons proceeds smoothly, the loss of one is compensated by the acquisition of another, and both sides gain from the resulting alliance. But any prolonged delay in reciprocating, especially if caused by the refusal of one group to live up to the bargain, would have devastating effects on all concerned. The dread and horror and anger surrounding incest reflect the dangers to which a breakdown in the exchange of persons exposes all members of the group, and at the same time function as an antidote to the temptation felt by people who have been brought up together to have sex together.

When I mentioned cooperation between neighboring groups, the concept of warfare comes to mind. Isn't man naturally warlike, as Thomas Hobbes would have it, attempting to gain at the expense of those around him? Our concept of violence has evolved from our recent experiences with war and, more currently, the sensationalism from the news media and cinematic irresponsibility. Our early ancestors risked extinction over conflict. It only makes sense to assume that many behaviors and attitudes were socially inspired to reduce stress, and this would have included all ingroup relations-- male-male, male-female, and so on. When there are pressures involving competition for scarce resources (i.e., food, status, etc.) and defection in the process of give and take (tit for tat cooperation), this is where intra- and intergroup conflict, feuding, and warfare begin. Yes, our ancestors had emotions and would get annoyed and angry at one another. Left unchecked-- that is, without social systems (rituals, taboos, etc.)--we would have killed ourselves off long ago.

THE ESTABLISHMENT OF LARGER GROUPINGS: SUPER-CHUNKING THE GROUP, THE CONCEPT OF POWER, AND CHAOS

In Chapter 1, I outlined a number of aspects about human mental processes and group behavior, namely, that humans organize their environ-ment; that there are limits on the amount of information that the human brain can process; and that, as familiarity and overlearning are accomplished, infor-mation is superchunked. Spoken language would appear to aid in this process of superchunking. Also, somewhere between 30,000 and 50,000 years ago, some sort of crisis (or crises) emerged that pushed our ancestors into a different type of living arrangement and forced us to use language differently. It has been suggested that extrahuman storage devices were created, for example, cave paintings. According to Marshack (1991), information was being stored on bone implements as well, making information separate from the human craftsman and more tangible and portable. There also has been an observation or suggestion that, once you separate man from himself via writing or art, you create a psychic split (disassociation), wherein the individual (or the group) resides in two "places" (McLuhan 1962:32). If, as researchers have suggested, there was an accumulation of specific information, and this information was being stored by specialists, and differences in status were an outcome, we have a number of elements in place allowing for larger groupings (i.e., the beginnings of tribelets, tribes, and nation-states), to develop. If analogous thinking was well established at the time our proto-ancestors first fashioned stone tools, and it is probable that our ancestors perceived a status difference between children and adults and certainly between males and females, it would only take some sort of crisis to push the analogy to differences among males and females based on what each person knew (special knowledge) or could do (special abilities). The biggest problem, as I see it, is not explaining the psychological and grouping mechanisms that would allow tribelets, tribes, and urban centers to develop, but, instead, determining what the circumstances were that led groups to accumulate in specific geographical areas in the first place. Was it population explosion? Was it the accidental propinquity or the movement of people into lush areas? Was it due to a vision(s) produced by the ingestion of psychotropics that foretold that different groups would come together, a self-fulfilling prophecy? Was it the invention of agriculture? Was agriculture invented after the fact? You certainly do not need agriculture to have large populations. What you do need is (1) ample food supplies, (2) low levels of disease vectors, and (3) an ideology or political invention that would allow groups larger than 25-125 to come together with a low level of conflict. Population size will increase in direct relation to available food supplies and in inverse proportion to disease vectors, but the change in ideology or politics has to emerge as an afterthought, so to speak. Humans have a tendency to solve problems as they go along, to embark on a course and only then to attempt to solve problems that arise. The larger the group size is, the more difficult it is to anticipate the types of problems that will become manifest.

Tribelets, tribes, and nation-states could never have come about without adding another dimension to the third factor above, and that is the ability to call upon people with experience, people with accumulated knowledge, that is, elders, both male and female.[3] People, for thousands of years, were the books, computers, storage places of information, and the longer one lived, the more information that individual would have stored. Women, with their ability to produce the "books," and elders, who would carry the culture, were human-kind's first specialists.

The first evidence of a people living into their fifties, sixties, seventies, or longer does not show up in the archeological data until 30,000 to 40,000 years ago. Elders, then, like a hand axe or fire, are tools of survival. They can give advice and be listened to. At times, that advice would have been very conservative and, at other times, very radical. It was not always sound, good advice. But, occasionally, it would have been both sound and radical. But, once we have a specialist given legitimacy to think up new ideas and add this information to the system, we indeed have a sense of social power (way above and beyond physical strength), mentioned earlier, which can be personalized or even vested in special groups.

The human ability to alter the environment, as a generalization, is the basis for all stages of human development. If we accept that bands, tribelets, tribes, trade centers, and nation-states can be seen as a linear evolution representing increasing degrees of social organization, then we can say that, through manipulating the environment to produce more food, conditions are met to sustain more people per acre of land. With more people per acre, and realizing the limits on information-processing abilities, new types of social organization would have to spontaneously generate or be purposefully invented. We do not need to suggest conscious invention at each new step in complexity. What we have to assume, however, is that the human nervous system is designed to go toward stress reduction. There tends to be a built-in entropy process in human information processing which can be stated as follows: When stress increases in terms of the processing and interpretation of available information and consequent behavioral reactions, continued similar information and/or behavior only serves to increase the stress to the point of (1) system breakdown (fight, flight, freeze) or (2) the spontaneous alteration of the behavioral reaction to the stressors. The first set represents physiological reactions. The second set represents social responses that stem from analogous thinking (often initiated out of desperation) and the chunking of ideas. A very simple concept in process here is this: If whatever you are doing does not work, almost anything else you do will work (it will change the outcome). In terms of human social evolution, many simple principles have been overlooked in favor of complexity. No human system is built from complex ideas, although when you bring large numbers of people together, problems result that generate complex solutions, which are, in reality, multiples of simple ideas. On the contrary, all cultures are built upon simple principles that are easily duplicated. A nation-state is a complicated idea if you have to sit down and create it from scratch. But that is not the way it happened. Organization is based upon the simpler ideas that preceded it. Those simpler ideas are quantifiable. When put all together, it is impossible to predict the outcome (the whole is more than the sum of the parts); perhaps unpredictability *is* the outcome. Being able to predict may not have the same survival value as allowing systems to simply run, thus forcing the cognitive apparatus to come up with new solutions. This leads us into chaotic behavior, which will be discussed at the end of this chapter.

Returning to spontaneous alteration of behavior, one can generate behaviors that are not especially useful, but still hold the possibility of altering a system in some other useful way. Of course, you can have purposeful introduction of novel information that can lead to novel, useful, and nonuseful behavior, which also alters the system in ways not predictable. How do we get to a point of purposefully altering a system, even though the outcome cannot be predicted? Once the idea of specialists arises, especially the elder specialist, one creates an agent who is given license to go beyond the boundaries of the system and return with special insights. Certainly, the use of trance states or psychotropic drugs could have served a very useful purpose at this point in human prehistory. By transcending the system, by becoming (achieved) or being labeled (ascribed) a specialist, the individual can purposely "depart," "return," and enter new ideas or novel concepts or suggestions into the information pool (perhaps this is the origin of the hero myth discussed by Campbell 1972). In fact it would be expected or demanded. Again, drugs could have been used to transcend the system, but transcending the system in order to set the scene for altering it does not require drugs. What is needed is the concept of legitimate power, assumed wisdom, or trust residing in an individual. My assumption is that early hominid bands were basically egalitarian, with their normal squabbling, but with internal group stress kept to a minimum--individual and group survival was at stake. How, then, do we get from egalitarianism to power vested in one or more individuals, power that can serve to increase survival potential of the group, but not necessarily the individual? Did this spontaneously come about through elementary forms of specialization? More about power shortly. First, though, we need to consider consciousness and its implications for specialization and consequent power to add new information to a social system.

Definitions of Consciousness

By reviewing the physical evidence and making comparisons to our primate cousins, band-type organizations, and current populations, we can draw some conclusions as to the physical developmental patterns and human information processing that have ultimately led to culture. Another developmental pattern, mentioned earlier and more difficult to identify, is that of consciousness, what it is and when it developed.

First, how we define consciousness will have a large influence on the theories that develop. Second, consciousness may exist on a number of different levels with resulting behaviors just as likely to push culture in a positive direction. Third, consciousness may be more pervasive across species than previously thought. And fourth, is consciousness necessary in order for culture, as we know it, to develop?

As Skinner (1972, 1974) maintains, consciousness is a byproduct of brain functions, the chemical and electrical combinations, without a causal role in human behavior and by implication human social development.

According to John (1976:4):

Consciousness is a process in which information about multiple individual modalities of sensation and perception is combined into a unified, multidimensional representation of the state of the system and its environment and is integrated with information about memories and the needs of the organism, generating emotional reactions and programs of behavior to adjust the organism to its environment. . . . Consciousness is third-order information. Many levels of consciousness can exist, in which these dimensions are present in variable amounts. The content of consciousness is the momentary constellation of these different types of information.

Pribram (1976:52) states, "Self-consciousness is said to occur when an observer is able to describe both the observed and the observing."

Jaynes's (1990) discussion of human consciousness is of interest, in that he places the event of consciousness within quite recent times. He states

(1990:55):

Subjective conscious mind is an analog of what is called the real world. It is built up with a vocabulary or lexical field whose terms are all metaphors or analogs of behavior in the physical world. Its reality is of the same order as mathematics. It allows us to shortcut behavioral processes and arrive at more adequate decisions. Like mathematics, it is an operator rather than a thing or repository. And it is intimately bound up with volition and decision.

Consciousness, then, is connected with language and the metaphors represented within. The transition to consciousness, according to Jaynes (1990:221), involved a number of factors:

In summary, I have sketched out several factors at work in the great transilience from bicameral mind to consciousness: (1) the weakening of the auditory by the advent of writing; (2) the inherent fragility of hallucinatory control; (3) the unworkableness of gods in the chaos of historical upheaval; (4) the positing of internal cause in the observation of difference in others; (5) the acquisition of narratization of epics; (6) the survival value of deceit; and (7) a modicum of natural selection.

Although Jaynes is cautious about origins, his definition of consciousness and its probable causes places it within a relatively recent time frame. Jaynes also objects to a purely biological origin of consciousness: "For if we still hold to a purely biological evolution of consciousness back somewhere among the lower vertebrates, how can we approach such phenomena or begin to understand their historically and culturally segregated nature? It is only if consciousness is learned at the mercy of a collective cognitive imperative that we can take hold of these questions in any way" (1990:340).

I agree with Jaynes that consciousness is not purely a product of biological evolution, although a number of physical processing elements must come together in order for social or environmental information to be processed in a specific manner and reveal consciousness. However, I believe that consciousness of the nature Jaynes discusses existed hundreds of thousands of years prior to the advent of nation-states and the prevailing conditions inherent within that time period triggered consciousness. But, so as not to throw away the peach fruit with the pit, the accumulation of information and information overload, as we have seen with Pfeiffer's, "Creative Explosion," can be a definite push factor to different ways of thinking about one's world and perhaps the development of a *type* of consciousness . More about this shortly.

Hofstadter and Dennett (1981:266-267) offer an instructive position regarding self-consciousness:

Could a machine have a self-symbol, or a self-concept? It is hard to say. Could a lower animal? Think of a lobster. Do we suppose it is self-conscious? It shows several important symptoms of having a self-concept. First of all, when it is hungry, whom does it feed? Itself! Second, and more important, when it is hungry it won't eat just anything edible; it won't, for instance, eat *itself*--though it could, in principle. . . . These simple questions reveal that even a very stupid creature must be designed to *behave with self-regard*--to put it as neutrally as possible. Even the lowly lobster must have a nervous system wired up in such a way that it will reliably distinguish self-destructive from other-destructive behavior--and strongly favor the latter. It seems quite possible that the control structures required for such self-regarding behavior can be put together without a trace of *consciousness*, let alone *self*-consciousness. After all, we can make self-protecting little robot devices that cope quite well in their simple environments and even produce an overwhelmingly strong illusion of "conscious purpose". . . . But why say this is an illusion, rather than a rudimentary form of genuine self-consciousness--a kin perhaps to the self-consciousness of a lobster or worm? Because robots don't have concepts? Well, do lobsters? Lobsters have *something like* concepts, apparently; what they have are in any event enough to govern them through their self-regarding lives. Call these things what you like, robots can have them too. Perhaps we could call them unconscious or preconscious concepts. Self-concepts of a rudimentary sort. The more varied the circumstances in which a creature can recognize itself, recognize circumstances as having a bearing on itself, acquire information about self, and devise self-regarding actions, the richer (and more valuable) its self-concept--in this sense of "concept" that does not presuppose consciousness. [emphasis as in the original]

The authors go on to say that, if one adds language, a representational system, and the ability to update and know about other actors in the environment, their knowledge and behavior, this does not necessarily indicate that consciousness really exists. It all could be programmed, thus creating an illusion.

Dennett, in an earlier work (1978:269-271), discusses six ideas or factors, including consciousness, that he considers dependent upon one another and necessary conditions of personhood.

The *first* and most obvious theme is that persons are *rational beings*. . . . The *second* theme is that persons are beings to which states of consciousness are attributed, or to which psychological or mental or *intentional predicates* are ascribed. . . . The *third* theme is that whether something counts as a person depends in some way on the *attitude taken* toward it. . . . The *fourth* theme is that the object toward which this personal stance is taken must be capable of *reciprocating* in some way. . . . The *fifth* theme is that persons must be capable of *verbal communication*. The *sixth* theme is that persons are distinguishable from other entities by being *conscious* is some special way: there is a way in which *we* are conscious in which no other species is conscious. [emphasis in the original]

Griffin's (1992) very thoughtful book on other-than-human animal consciousness throws a large wrench into the academic gears on the subject. His discussion on the ethical and philosophical parameters of the debate is especially instructive. He states (1992:257-258), after a lengthy review:

I have reviewed many cases of animal behavior that appears so versatile and so appropriately adapted to unpredictable circumstances that it seems likely to be accompanied and guided by simple conscious thinking. Such versatility is very often based on the application of learned knowledge, but this may be neither a sufficient nor a necessary condition in any absolute sense. Animals may "figure out" what will get them things they want even when the knowledge needed for such thinking about probable future events has not been learned in any direct and explicit sense.

More recently, Penrose (1994:407-408) concludes that consciousness is not unique to humans. However, his position is one of "degrees" of consciousness.

As the reader will quickly realize, we have a problem with definitions and attributing something "special" to humans and our hominid ancestors; the quality of consciousness may not be enough. I will refer to a more recent work by Dennett (1991) shortly and expand on his definition.

At this point, I want to turn to Gardner's (1983) definition of self as it evolved from his theory of multiple intelligences. As with Dennett, being human and having something called self-consciousness involve a number of considerations. Gardner (1983) lists what he considers several types of intelligences that make up the human mind, ranging from linguistic, musical, and logical-mathematical, to spatial, bodily-kinesthetic, and personal. With respect to personal intelligences he states (1983:242):

[A]n emerging sense of self proves to be a key element in the realm of the personal intelligences, one of overriding importance to individuals the world over. While the developed sense of self is ordinarily viewed as a quintessential manifestation of interpersonal intelligence, my own inquiry has led to a different conclusion. The wide variety of "selves" encountered throughout the world suggests that this "sense" is better thought of as an amalgam, one that emerges from a combination or fusion of one's intrapersonal and one's interpersonal knowledge. The overwhelming differences in the *senses of self* around the world reflect the fact that the merger can come about in widely divergent ways, depending on those aspects of the person (and of persons) that happen to be accentuated in different cultures. Accordingly, in what follows, I shall use the term *sense of self* to refer to the balance struck by every individual--and every culture--between the promptings of the "inner feelings" and the pressures of "other persons." [emphasis in the original]

Although Gardner does not use the words "conscious," "consciousness," and "self-consciousness" his statement does echo Pribram's definition mentioned earlier. Any definition of consciousness we utilize must, in my mind, combine the ideas of self and others because the awareness of self *within* (empathy) and *among* (cooperation for mutual survival) others would have been a necessary element in social/cultural development.

Oakley (1985) gives us some useful concepts that define consciousness or awareness by comparing different life forms. His model is based on the structure of the human brain, assigning different levels of awareness or consciousness to each part of his triune brain as represented by different species. The first level is "simple awareness," represented by animals possessing a brain stem without the addition of other structures, that is, limbic system and neocortex. This type of awareness involves the genetically generated behaviors along with conditioned responses. At his second level, Oakley uses the term "consciousness," which goes beyond conditioned responses and includes the construction and storage of information regarding experience (space and time relationships) within an environment. His third stage is "self-awareness," which includes a construction both of the outside world and of the self within that world.

Donald (1991) goes beyond Oakley's description and includes a fourth stage of "semantic" memory, evolving out of the use of language (1991:152), which he feels embodies "mimetic culture." Mimetic culture includes "toolmaking, and eventual fire use, coordinated seasonal hunting, rapid adaptation to climate, ecology, intricate social structure, primitive ritual group mimetic acts" (1991:198, Table 6.1).

With shades of Hockett (1960), Donald (1991:171-173) goes on to describe the elements that accumulate in mimetic culture and then suggests numerous social consequences, that is, knowledge sharing, conformity and ritual, games, and so on (1991:173-176).

In Dennet's more recent work (1991:166) he states that consciousness is a "*mode of action* of the brain rather than a *subsystem* of the brain." Humans, then, rather than having consciousness, display consciousness in their behaviors or actions.

I have chosen the above definitions out of the hundreds available to show the simplicity and complexity. In Skinner's case, his definition is simplistic because of his apparent need to eliminate specific variables that were a nuisance in terms of explaining or complementing his main behavioral positions. John's definition, on the other hand, is an example of complexity and just how wrapped up in words we can get--consciousness at its best, I suppose.

Pribram offers a practical example that can be more easily validated and is more useful, to my purposes, in determining when self-consciousness became more important or more exploitable by our species. This would place the display of human consciousness within the time frame attributed to the emergence of portable tools. This implies the separation of the symbols of one animal and the attribution of those characteristics to another (i.e., the symbols of a predator's power being transported by our protoancestors) and the emergence of protolanguage, that is, the appearance of *Home erectus* approximately 1.6 million years ago.

I could go on and on with definitions, each of which is specific to the author's goal in presenting an interpretation. My goal is to formulate a definition that will allow us to bridge the gap in behaviors that separate ourselves and our hominid ancestors from other life forms. To begin, then, all life forms have consciousness; all life forms are in some way conscious of their surroundings. Consciousness and the individualized self-consciousness must, therefore, be seen within the mosaic of other human traits, that is, bipedal locomotion, opposable thumb, increased brain size, primary and secondary representational systems, a descended larynx for more exacting verbalizations, and the recognition beyond the self--a recognition of being part of a larger unit, the group, which is itself part of a larger unit, the environment or nature. As Scott (1995:159-160) states: "We must construct consciousness from the relevant physics *and* biochemistry *and* electrophysiology *and* neuronal as-semblies *and* cultural configurations *and* mental states that science cannot yet explain." [emphasis in the original]

Without considering consciousness within a mosaic that spreads out from, rather than toward, the self, combined with the taking of the symbols of "that which exists out there" and incorporating them into group survival, we then have to debate the consciousness of my dogs, cats, and other barnyard species. We, therefore, have to understand the difference in consciousness across species not as a singular feature, but as a cluster, with one factor enhancing or amplifying the other. The difference between our hominid ancestors and other species would seem to be, in conjunction with the outward-projected mosaic just mentioned, the addition of protolanguage, wherein consciousness and protolanguage become a feedback loop. Consciousness, then, becomes a tool of protolanguage, a tool for expanding awareness about self and the environment, which then allows for language to develop and utilize this awareness through efficient transmission to others. Although we cannot, at this time, describe what consciousness really is, we can say something about what it does. When I refer to human consciousness, I am referring to not only a type of thinking about self, the group, and the surrounding environment, but also the ability to efficiently and metaphorically communicate that awareness to others via a shared code, first through protolanguage and then, more re-cently, through language.

Home Base

Paleoanthropologists have paid close attention to four behavioral factors when analyzing hominid cultural development. These are economics, sexual restrictions, politics, and home base. The first two have been considered; home base and power (politics) deserve further consideration.

According to Knight (1991:190), "It will have become apparent by now that the core concept central to all the models which we have surveyed is that of the 'home base'."

He goes further.

Although in technical terms it rests on many factors including the domestication of fire. . . , what has all too often been overlooked is that the home base as an institution is equally rooted in a fact of sexual politics--the fact that human females do not "chase after" males out hunting in the bush. In effect, hunter-gatherer women stand their own ground. Even if they gather over a wide area, they do so usually quite separately from men, typically in all-female groups. Their activities and solidarity may give them considerable autonomy and power. Female status among hunters and gathers varies widely according to conditions. . . , but whatever the precise mode of foraging, women almost invariably organize their lives around "their own" space, whose focal point is the hearth and campsite. (1991:191)

Knight goes on to say that the home base is central to all activities, that division of labor between men and women is part and parcel to this concept, and that contrary to the feminists, home base has little to do with the "'home' in its western cultural sense as a privatized space peripheral to the centers of social and political power" (1991:192).

But let us consider home base from another perspective. First of all, a home base is a space or territory defined in some way by how the members use it. Second, a home base offers the individuals a sense of familiarity "marked" by behaviors and activities, including sounds, allowing other conspecies or predators sufficient information for avoidance (or attack). A home base, essentially, is a defensible territory or a place more likely to be defended violently against assault.

Third, a home base allows individuals to gather and communicate, to share and invent, to clarify and instruct. It also allows for conflict; any time you bring numbers of people together, you increase the probability of conflict. this is where many implied rules are generated which then establish more explicitly of defined relationship behaviors. Over time, this assigns predictability and eliminates a great deal of possible day-to-day conflict. In accordance with Knight's statement above, home base is synonymous with community or family, men's work, women's work, and children's work. It is also synonymous with safety and reciprocity. I personally do not believe that the concept of home base has changed much over the millennium; the content has changed to fit the social complexity. This being the case, home base, like language or an Acheulean hand axe, is the use of space as a tool. Can we then, like Bickerton's protolanguage, speak of a proto-home base?

Sept, in her recent article (1992:196), asks some intriguing questions with respect to home base among Ishasha chimpanzees: "What are the effects on them of territoriality, group size, and population density?" and "How does predation risk influence the choice of nesting localities?" It seems reasonable to assume (and it goes without saying) that nesting sites will relate to food sources in some direct way. And, as Bickerton (1990:95) has pointed out, "mental maps" are certainly not unique to chimpanzees, but are necessary for any creature, insect or mammal, once the behavior develops and a secured location or locations are selected. Perhaps chimpanzees exhibit proto-home base behavior, as perhaps do wolves and wild dogs. As Sept's critics amply point out at the end of her discussion, more research is needed.

Power

According to Barnes (1988:1), "Power is treated as an entity or attribute which all manner of things, processes, or agents have. Natural forces and phenomena may have it, as we speak of powerful currents or powerful magnets; artifacts may have it, and with some artifacts, engines and machines, their power may be their most important single feature; animals may have it, or even plants--as when tree roots undermine buildings."

At its simplest level of abstraction, and using a definition that will allow a bridge into social power, power is the ability of an organism to have some sort of control over its environment rather than the environment having total control over the organism. By control, I am referring to the ability to sustain its own life, to derive nutrients from that environment. Obviously, this definition is inadequate once we begin to discuss other than single-cell organisms. As mentioned earlier, not only can parasites obtain nutrients from the environment, but also they appear to have developed complex and often synergistic methods of manipulating or controlling their host, their environment. The concept of power becomes even more complicated as organisms begin to cooperate as a means of adapting to a specific environment. We can see the roots of social power reaching deep into our organic and inorganic past, and it would be difficult to dismiss genetic push factors that move toward more and more control over environmental, both organic and inorganic, influences. Discussions of power, however, regardless of whether they lie within the description or content analysis of social or political power (see Banton 1965), or a broader treatise on the evolution of social power (see Mann 1986), or special issues of power considered from the perspective of knowledge and power (see Parkin 1987; Riches 1987), must consider the *limits* of power. Power does corrupt because it can be destabilizing; absolute power is absolutely destabilizing and leads to chaos unless there is a contract (supernatural or otherwise) between government and subjects. Chaos is the signaling of a process point, indicating that the system is about to change into something else, and it is just as applicable to social systems as it is to physical and biological systems, for example, the weather, metabolic functioning, and so on.

At some point along the biological continuum from the *Australopithecines* to *Homo sapiens,* power became less and less wrapped around physical abilities and became more and more centered in mental/psychological abilities or ideas and concepts, beliefs, and practices designed to more efficiently manipulate the environment. Some of the thought processes have been considered earlier. Power, in short, moved away from physical strength and toward knowledge, and, more important, the application of that knowledge. But how does the realization that knowledge is power come into being? There is no single way that this realization came about, but, instead, there are many avenues. One of the first involves a symbolic usurping of power from a powerful predator, that is, the construction of tools, such as hand axes, that represent the animal's power. Initially, this power was only seen as power gained from or over the predator itself and useful for the group through the individual. However, this symbolic power was never absolute, which is to say, even though there was the symbol of this power, the predator sometimes took back its power--when the predator would injure or kill one of our proto-ancestors, for example, during a hunt.

By attributing the power of observation and perceived outcome to our ancestors, there must have been a realization that power also evolves from cooperative effort. Observing the cooperative efforts of other social/predatory animals, and through analogy, perhaps helped to engage the connection. Continuing with this, and in a more abstract form, the concept of power derived from doing things for others and then obtaining something in return, that is, the reciprocity of the mother doing for the child and then the child reciprocating at a future date. This holds all the elements that could lead to the obligations accrued and favors received with respect to the specialist mentioned above. Power was ascribed to those who had a knack for doing certain things, to elders because of the knowledge they had or to women for their special ability to bear children. In short, the features of power that we currently witness in contemporary societies, from personal, physical power to power through cooperative effort and tyrannical power that forces people to kill for their country, were all available to our protoancestors through observation of the individuals within the group and the behaviors of other animals. But there are limits. Mann (1986:37-38), after considering the rather standard and linear evolutionary processes in social development, and the power bases applied to each, makes an interesting statement (1986:39):

[G]eneral evolutionary theory may be applied to the Neolithic Revolution, but its relevance then diminishes. . . . [B]eyond that, we can discern further general evolution as far as "rank societies" and then, in some cases, to temporary state and stratification structures. But then general social evolution ceased. . . . I . . . suggest that the further general processes were *"devolutions"*--movement back toward rank and egalitarian societies--and a *cyclical* process of movement around these structures, failing to reach permanent stratification and state structures. In fact, human beings devoted a considerable part of their cultural and organizational capacities to ensure that further evolution did *not* occur. They seem not to have wanted to increase their collective powers, because of the distributive powers involved. As stratification and the state were essential components of civilization, general social evolution ceased before the emergence of civilization. . . . This argument is reinforced by a second. . . .This emphasizes boundedness, tightness, and constraint: members of a society interact with one another but not, to anything like the same extent, with outsiders. Societies are limited and exclusive in their social and territorial coverage. Yet we find a discontinuity between civilized and noncivilized social groupings. . . . Few families belonged for more than a few generations to the same "society," or if they did, this was constituted by such looseness of boundaries as to be quite unlike historic societies.

Most had choices available to them in their allegiances. The looseness of the social bonds, and the ability to be free of any particular power network, was the mechanism by which the devolution mentioned above was triggered. In noncivilized societies escape from the social cage was possible. Authority was freely conferred, but recoverable; power, permanent and coercive, was unattainable.

Mann goes on to state that, because civilization only burst forth independently on limited occasions, its emergence can be attributed to factors other than that of a normal evolutionary stage. For Mann, it emerged as a consequence of systems of power that overlapped, an agricultural and herding base, and relations between others in an area of diverse ecological exploitation (1986:102). Bringing all these elements together over time creates dependency. This is different from allegiance and the power that so derives.   At the civilization or nation-state level, allegiance often has to be forced; one has to submit to the power of the state.   Once the state has to threaten its citizens to pledge allegiance, the system is unstable in direct proportion to the amount of knowledge the individual or group possesses relative to the governmental activities, and the ability of the populus to intervene in those activities through either election or force. The less the people know, the easier they are to control; the less personal power the individual or group controls (be this in the form of printing presses or guns) the more control the ruling body can wield through taxes or   torture.   In short, the more power the citizens have by contract, the more stable the society is.   Stated another way, the more fearful the government is of its citizens, the less likely the government is to act in its own self-interests.

The message here is that humans are small-group animals who have great difficulty maintaining allegiance to an impersonal government.   A world government, as such, can only be effective in special-issue situations, that is, environmental concerns, hostile warfare situations that threaten civilians (but, even here, there is reluctance to engage in combat where there is no special alliance or economic interest, as is the case in Bosnia and Rwanda; Iraq was a different situation because oil, money, and political positioning were at stake). One of the reasons that governments are strained to maintain allegiance from their people centers on the legitimacy of their power. Remember, we are a small-group animal, and it is only when people are willing, agree, become so entangled economically you have to play along, or are threatened with abandonment and all its ramifications (i.e., the fear of physical or emotional punishment through jail or the psychiatric ward, fines, confiscation of property, hurting/tourturing loved ones, being told to get off the planet, etc.) that they stay in the system. Large systems, through the efforts of small groups of people--special interest groups (remember Miller's number!)--tend to enact more and more rules designed around their self-interests which actually serve to destabilize the system. Why would this be? Well, it is uncertain what effect each new rule will have on the rest of the system.[4] This brings us to the concept of chaos.

Chaos

The concern for order and the prevention of chaos appears frequently in the beliefs and practices of numerous cultural groups. However, by chaos, I do not mean disorder so much as a move toward another, perhaps antithetical type of order. Chaos, as we will see, is anything but disorder, but what is it exactly? Dentan (1988:860), in his study of medical beliefs of Senoi Semai, who inhabit areas of the West Malaysian hills, found that, although there is an inconsistency and "untidiness" of their beliefs, this very untidiness can be seen as embodied in metaphors about souls represented by birds, butterflies, and so on, and "lent credence to the notion that some birds were not real, *mtul*, but rather embodied forces of chaos that continually threatened the tidy Semai world." He states further (1988:868), "The world of disease was a natural symbol for the chaos Semai said can follow lapses of self-control. Descriptions of pain-spirits were lessons in how not to live, a counter-culture." Chaos, in this sense, is not disorder, but a point for the establishment of another type of order, perhaps threatening to the Semai. This point can be seen as an attractor, or as Edward Lorenz described it, "one behavior that prevails when the system settles down, and it is a chaotic attractor" (Gleick 1987:233).

This is a common theme. If ritual is not observed, if you speak ill of others, take more than your fair share, or essentially break the rules, chaos (the return to an attractor or another state or order which is perhaps feared) or, at the very least, disaster will ensue (see Gottlieb 1988; Kunitz 1989:128; Ohnuki-Tierney 1984:31-40; Sullivan 1988:70-71, 103-105, 292-293; Marwick 1964; Gluckman 1944; Saler 1964; and Beidelman 1963:79-94, to offer a few of many examples). A witch, for example, is the antithesis of society, chaos in human and other forms, who resides usually on the fringes of the group or is symbolized by disloyalty or lack of affiliation (Rush 1974:37; Mayer 1970:62-63; Macfarlane 1970:196-197). But the concept of maintaining ritual order is very old indeed, as suggested by the covenant between man and animals as depicted by Paleolithic cave paintings (see Campbell 1990:18). In other words, to exist, one has to kill, and killing may be offensive to those killed, thus leading to resentment and lack of renewal. In order to avoid the potential of chaos, appropriate rituals need to be enacted. Thus, if Campbell and other writers (see Bahn and Vertut 1988:151-176) correctly interpret these paintings, then the need to maintain order or balance in the world reaches back at least to the Paleolithic. Pfeiffer (1982:123), as mentioned earlier, suggests that it is at this time period in prehistory that the problem of information storage and retrieval threatened chaos. There is a special implication here that relates to the totality of what we call culture. That is, culture appears to be information structured to prevent random thoughts and actions, no matter how creative or potentially useful, from too rapidly entering the knowledge base, destabilizing group organization (psychological and social), and resulting in chaos. Culture is, in some ways, comparable to an enzyme designed to inhibit certain types of information from entering the system or to remove them from the system. First, though, let us examine the modern concepts of chaos to see what they have to offer the social sciences.

Chaotic theory is mathematically based on non-linear propositions, "meaning that they expressed relationships that were not strictly proportional. Linear relationships can be captured with a straight line on a graph" (Gleick 1987:23). It may be the case that "chaos is a science of process rather than state, of becoming rather than being" (Gleick 1987:5). Although the precedents to the science of chaos can be seen in the works of Henri Poincare (topology) and certainly in the influence of the mathematicians who came before (see Stewart 1989:59-72), one of the first mathematical expressions of chaos was accidentally discovered by Lorenz in 1961. Before considering Lorenz, let me point out that, according to Stewart (1989:96), it was Pierre Simon de Laplace, in the eighteenth century who locked mathematics into the use of formulas, rather than pictures, for the expression of concepts. Poincare, however, altered that by bringing the visual image, pictures, legitimately back into the field of mathematics. I am personally more comfortable with this, as it allows me to "see" the process in total rather than to digitally and abstractly make sense out of a formula (see Abraham and Shaw 1983 for numerous visual depictions of attractors, saddles, and repellors).

Returning to Lorenz's discovery in 1961, in order to save time, but to see the outcome of a model of a weather system, Lorenz made some calculations regarding where a system would be in a certain length of time, allowed the system to run for awhile on his computer, collected those figures, and used them as a new starting point, again allowing the computer to run. Upon returning and expecting to find a duplication of his earlier run, he noted, instead, that an entirely different pattern emerged, what he called "the butterfly effect" (Stewart 1989:141; Gleick 1987:15-31). Essentially, Lorenz had rounded off numbers when he reentered the data, and the outcome was that, with small initial differences, you can end up with large, unpredictable results. The results do not represent linear relationships.

When it comes to prediction, the complexity of weather is directly related to the number of factors involved over a specific time period and the ability (or inability) to specify initial conditions. As that time period increases, so does the number of factors that have to be taken into consideration. Moreover, weather or atmospheric conditions are not stationary, but move and are thus continually being influenced by changes in geography. Herein lies the problem of predicting future events in dynamic systems. As Glass and Mackey (1988:6-7) state:

Mathematics offers us two distinct ways to think about the irregularities intrinsic to physiology. The more common of the two is *noise*, which refers to chance fluctuations. . . . Although "chaos" is often used as a popular synonym for noise, it has developed a technical meaning that is quite different. Technically, *chaos* refers to randomness or irregularity that arises in a deterministic system. In other words, chaos is observed even in the complete absence of environmental noise. An important aspect of chaos is that there is a sensitive dependence of the dynamics to the initial conditions. . . . This means that although in principle it should be possible to predict future dynamics as a function of time, this is in reality impossible since any error in specifying the initial conditions, no matter how small, leads to an erroneous prediction at some future time.

Glass and Mackey (1988:19-21) further comment:

Theoretical analyses of physiological systems attempt to develop equations that describe the time evolution of physiological variables, for example, blood gas concentrations. . . . The physical sciences place great emphasis on obtaining solutions to differential equations, with a consequent emphasis in applied mathematics courses on mathematical techniques to integrate differential equations analytically. Since biological systems are generally described by *nonlinear differential equations* . . . . for which no analytic solution is available, alternative techniques to the analytic integration of differential equations must often be sought in the study of biological problems. Moreover, biological systems are so complex that it is generally impossible to specify exactly the dynamical equations describing the system. Thus the dynamical equations must generally be considered as approximations and may not have the same validity as differential equations in the physical sciences.

As discussed in Chapter 1, the formula $(N_2 - N)/2 = D$, is one of those linear (actually quadratic) equations that can be used to determine numbers of dyads and the potential for conflict due to information overload. It tells little about the dynamics of conflict and, hence, has only a limited value for predicting real situations, which have to take into consideration the many factors that apply in face-to-face interaction, that is, age, sex, status, time of the year, numbers of people present, and so on.

Concerning ourselves with biological problems, which might enlighten us as to chaotic complexes in social systems, what, then, are the alternative techniques for solving nonlinear differential equations? Although the main focus of understanding chaotic complexes would be the predictability factor in human behavior, my concern is not so grandiose with respect to economics and the social ramifications of political decisions. My concern is on how social systems or elements of social systems prevent chaos and collapse of existing social institutions through conservatism, but, on the other hand, invite chaos by attempting to fix something that, on its own, seems to be moving toward an attractor, or chaos, which is seen as objectionable. It is like a spinning top. One can keep it spinning in a conservative manner, that is, keep doing the same thing. On its own, you can let it slow down and change to another state, or you can give it a different spin, also inviting a whole bunch of new consequences.

As Glass and Mackey (1988:135) point out, after exploring some rather simple factors of biological systems, they turn out to be so complex that they cannot be observed in a system, let alone be understood. They have taken into consideration phase-locking of different biological rhythms (i.e., cardiac rate and respiration), sleep arrhythmias as phased with circadian rhythms and diet, and disease factors and periodic behavior, to name a few. The mathematics has not been adequately worked out, mainly, and again, because the issues are too complex.

A phenomenon that is often considered representative of chaos is strange attractors. As Gleick (1987:134) writes:

The strange attractor lives in phase space, one of the most powerful inventions of modern science. Phase space gives a way of turning numbers into pictures, abstracting every bit of essential information from a system of moving parts, mechanical or fluid, and making a flexible road map to all its possibilities. In phase space the complete state of knowledge about a dynamical system at a single instant in time collapses to a point. That point *is* the dynamical system--at that instant. . . . The history of the system time can be charted by the moving point, tracing its orbit through phase space with the passage of time.

Gleick (1987:134) goes on to ask, "How can all the information about a complicated system be stored in a point?" This is an intriguing question, which is beyond the scope of this discussion. However, information, when it reaches some order of complexity, seems to compress or fall in on itself; it chunks, perhaps in a similar manner that words, as symbols, are chunks of ideas. The apparent difference is that human symbols, constructed in language, are subject to interpretation. But does nature continually reinterpret its chunked symbols? If we exist within a pulsating universe, is this what happens with the "Big Bang," a reinterpretation of natural laws?

Returning to Gleick's statement above, the more variables you have, however, the more attractors that are possible [let's add to this saddles and repellors as well (Abraham and Shaw 1983:13-25)], and, of course, the more complexity and diversity of systems.

So far I have considered non-linear systems, attractors, and the complexity of biological systems. The mathematics of predictability for future events in large systems is a long way off. However, and as I mentioned earlier, conflict (or disequilibrium) seems to be an inherent part of human systems just as disequilibrium seems to be part of biological systems in general. Systems, through feedback mechanisms, are never at an optimum or balanced state for any long period of time. They are either at one position or another with respect to that point. This seems to be the case for social systems as well as biological systems. So questions are in order: Is a strange attractor the point at which a rule is broken (essentially the alteration of an expectation)? And is a rule the embodiment of social order? The answer to these questions, I believe, is, yes. And if this is true, one is struck with an interesting possibility. Once an organism is able to generate ideas and concepts about

itself and the surrounding environment, and once this information is stored
outside of a genetic framework (in artifacts; cave paintings; notations on
stone, wood, or bone; books, etc.), the door opens for random thoughts,
random behavior, and random altering of basic group processes that lead to
cooperation and survival. Culture, the process, would seem to be an attractor,
chaos,[5] if you like, designed to inhibit newness and maintain a steady state.

As Briggs and Peat (1989:19-20) state:

Ancient peoples believed that the forces of chaos and order were part of an uneasy
tension, a harmony of sorts. They thought of chaos as something immense and
creative. In his *Theogony*, Heisod assured his audience, "First of all things was *chaos*;
and next broad-bosomed Earth." Cosmologies from every culture imagined a
primordial state where chaos or nothingness pervaded, from which beings and things
burst forth. The ancient Egyptians conceived of the early universe as a formless abyss
named Nut. Nut gave birth to Ra, the sun. In one Chinese creation story a ray of pure
light, yin, jumps out of chaos and builds the sky while the remaining heavy dimness,
yang, forms the earth. Yin and yang, the female and male principles, then act to create
the 10,000 things (in other words, everything). Significantly, even after they have
emerged, the principles of yin and yang are said to retain the qualities of the chaos
from which they sprang. Too much yin or yang will bring chaos back.

They go on to discuss other creation myths; for example, in Babylonia,
chaos was personalized (Tiamet and "the hidden") and, rather than being without form, had different "faces" or characteristics, suggesting another type of
ordering of elements. In short, modern thinking has simply rediscovered what
the ancients had conceptualized. Indeed, is there anything new under the sun?
Although the content of current beliefs has altered to fit our concepts of
science, the underlying processes were realized long ago. The explanation of
this can be seen in innate mental processes, that is, analogous thinking and
polarity. In other words, one can envisage similarities between objects and
events, but, if one can conceptualize an event, then the opposite or antithesis
likewise exists--culture, like human physiology, swings between these two
poles with metaphorical expressions constructed in terms of health and illness,
both physical and social.

What we have is this appreciation of order and disorder existent since
ancient times. But what we have are not statements about what *was* or
the coming into existence of humankind and culture; we have, instead, a
statement of what *is* and already exists, and the problems that obtain when
order is broken or change occurs. Chaos, in short is not the beginning; it is the
point when something new is added to or extracted from the old, thus leading
to a new order. The origins of culture lie within the stabilizing, and thus
limiting, realm; all we experience around us represents the actions and
reactions to an initial and, at times, stable protostate. Chaotic moments led to
the development of institutions designed to further preserve stability in the
face of change initiated by varying types of information input and loss, both

socially and environmentally inspired.

Culture is in a constant battle against the backsliding or even jumping forward through strange attractors--our symbiotic relationship with our environment, our biological sexuality, Miller's number in terms of information-processing ability, alliances (the give and take of social intercourse) that do not extend past certain limits, conflict and violence, our analogous thinking and ability to generate novel ideas--that, if left unchecked, would not allow interpersonal and group problem solving to occur, thus leading to some other type of order/chaos relationship pattern. Following from this, culture itself may be a strange attractor depending upon which end of the process you are examining. In the next two chapters, I will return to this concept of chaos as it is delineated by "disease" and "dis-ease" or "illness" states or symptoms, which embody those strange attractors mentioned above.

CONCLUSIONS

Our hominid ancestors were information processors quantitatively and qualitatively different from any other animal in the environment. Through our unique information-processing abilities, we were able to engage in analogous thinking and build onto relationships and behaviors that already existed prior to cultural development. We can see implied rules as primary mechanisms in the development of rules, roles, and cooperation. As we have information-processing limits (Miller's number), we carry with us a built-in conflict/stress generator which can be useful for inducing positive change as well as destructive conflict within and between groups.

Consciousness, as defined above, and inherent analogous thinking lead to a need to organize and to put meaning to the information processed that far exceeds that of other animals. Consciousness and analogous thinking are of little value unless some meaning can be attached to the raw data indicating where they fit into the scheme of things. With the necessity of organizing data into meaningful concepts, a concept of reality is born--a philosophy, if you will--regarding cause and effect. Out of this springs a meaning to cycles observed in nature, traditions, associated ritual behavior, and myths or explanations of why and how. And because of the nature of human information processing and the inherent need to organize, *everything* is subject to an explanation. Things left unexplained lead to uneasiness, a lack of expectations and threatened security, and strange attractors that invite new ideas, behaviors, and change. It is this need to explain to one's self and others (i.e., the interpretations we place on the data we process) that will occupy the remainder of this work, for it is our interpretations of information that lead to much of the conflict experienced by individuals and groups. When our interpretations are unsettling, we loop on the data, attempting to arrive at a more comfortable interpretation. And sometimes these new interpretations are not forthcoming.

When this happens, individual and group stress goes up, leading to numerous behavioral and emotional results. At this time, then, it is necessary to approach human information processing in more detail and essentially describe how people get to be the way they are from both emotional and social perspective.

EPILOGUE

As interesting and provocative as origin theories are, they are still "just so" stories. In fact, all origin stories, like "how the leopard got its spots," are probably true or could have happened. With analogous thinking of the extreme variety attributed to our hominid ancestors, it makes no difference what the exact content or steps were that led to the development of sexual restrictions, politics, or even the use of fire, although defining the initial conditions might be helpful in terms of predicting our future. It is the processes themselves (i.e., analogous thinking, information chunking, etc.) that explain the outcome, but not the content of the future. The eventual use of fire, for example, from seeing the effects to experiencing fear or wonder to then removing fire from an environment and containing it for some future use, was not necessarily a linear process, but it came about through analogous thinking. A non-linear process, a spontaneous happening, could just as well have been possible. A child could have picked up a burning stick and brought it to one of the adults which, could have led, in different groups, to the use of fire. What we need to understand and appreciate are the under-lying mental and social processes that set the stage for doings or behaviors that could be reinvented. To assume that the use of fire as a tool, for example, or the sharing of meat was only invented once and then spread by culture contact and diffusion underestimates the underlying mental processes.

NOTES

1. There is debate as to the exact use of these Acheulean hand axes (see Binford 1987; Knight 1991:261; Klein 1989:217; Jelinek 1977:16-21), and they, again, may have incorporated more of a symbolic use.

2. Guilt and shame appear to go hand in hand with group living and relate to a biological fear of rejection that has been with us, I speculate, for millions of years; you do not have to be human to experience guilt or fear of rejection. However, you have to be a group animal in order for fear of rejection or guilt to make any sense.

3. Longevity may be a necessary back-up system in case technology fails. Being able to have living representatives of people who used an earlier technology and who could rebuild it would have immense survival value.

4. For example, no one could predict what effect Prohibition would have on law enforcement and the establishment of organized crime. Moreover, no one could predict

the consequences of laws outlawing specific drugs, that is, marijuana, cocaine, and so on. The belief was that, with laws, the problem of drug abuse among a *small* portion of the population could be corrected. The motive was good--to protect members of the public from themselves (I am being sarcastic here)--but a very large portion of the "criminals" who overflow the jails are there because of these laws. However, in order to maintain the laws, you have to enact *more* laws, build *more* jails, and hire *more* police personnel. When you take a look at the North American social environment, drug use or abuse is not even the problem but, instead, a symptom of a problem. As the reader will understand in Chapter 3, drug abuse is a form of withdrawal from information that taps into HRMs. This translates into lack of acceptance in primary groups, especially the family--Miller's number again. Enacting drug laws (as well as anti-gun legislation) is like trying to fix the fuel injection unit on the car by changing the tires. Such laws target symptoms, very much like Western biomedicine targets symptoms, and such symptoms are usually the system's best choice in solving or curing a problem. By targeting the symptoms, in either the social or physical system, you actually inhibit the solution and move toward chaos. Violence and drug abuse can perhaps be seen as strange attractors, and in their own way tell us what to do. When you target symptoms and attempt to remove them from the system, you also eliminate useful information that tells you possible courses of action. It is like throwing away your phone book and guessing at the numbers.

5. This might seem like a paradox (i.e., culture representing order *and* chaos at the same time); it depends upon whether the observer is standing inside or outside the system under investigation. Self-assembling systems (human culture self-assembled, as mentioned, through implied rules which then became explicit) develop by extracting information from (information loss) or adding information to (information intrusion) surrounding systems. If this is done too rapidly or if the information cannot be replaced, this behavior actually moves these other systems toward chaos. The greatest example of this can be seen in our own technology and our ability to extract more and more from the environment and, at the same time, pollute with chemicals, thus pushing ecological relationships toward a chaotic state. Our technology, on the one hand, is an example of sophisticated order. On the other hand, it disorders the environment. Another example would be a cataclysmic event--for example, a meteor striking the earth--which adds too much information (information intrusion) over a short period of time; order creates disorder. When self-assembling systems do not remain in synergy with surrounding systems, chaos or a new order will surely follow. However, systems do not remain forever in synergy with other systems. If they did, change at the physical and social levels could not occur.

CHAPTER 3

Humans as Physical and Social Information Systems

Chapter 3 represents a theory or model generated from the anthropological literature that serves to define a human being as a group animal. The model, using the universals presented in Chapters 1 and 2, will take the reader, in a general sense, through a physical and social interface culminating with a number of conclusions. Such conclusions include human dependency upon the group for survival; the concept of rejection that evolves from the genetics of group living and the need to keep the individual oriented toward the group; and the concept that socialization involves the learning of social rules, tools for setting rules with others, a personal style of tool use, and the accumulation of history or memory. A fourth factor involves what I term *High Risk Messages* (HRMs), or genetically inspired (stemming from rejection) and anchored-in social content that the individual's group-self acquires as he or she learns the rules, both social rules and those imposed by the environment. HRMs are a problem to the individual because they represent both physical and psychological death, and are prime movers, along with the need for food, air, and water, to human action. Moreover, HRMs are universal and are an extremely important part of individual and group information processing.

This model explains much of human behavior and motive, and stands as a pivotal point in the developmental process (not necessarily the content) of all human systems. Out of this model the reader is able to begin to build a procedure of diagnosing social and individual illness and disease issues in any culture, or subsystem of that culture, using a rather neutral information processing model that avoids the value judgments inherent in Western psychological and medical practice.

REVIEW OF HUMAN UNIVERSALS FROM CHAPTERS 1 AND 2

At this point, and with the information presented, there are a number of generalizations that can be made.

(A) Human neural function (and this probably applies to all other animals as well) uses emotions in the process of organizing, storing, and retrieving information (LeDoux 1994). Emotional reactions are, in part, culturally conditioned and specific or appropriate (or less appropriate) according to the circumstances.

(B) Humans are a small-group animal and thus develop a concept of who they are relative to the group(s) and group members surrounding them.

(C) The fear of rejection by group members and/or significant others is a human universal. It serves to keep the individual oriented toward the group and is a push factor in cooperation. The fear of rejection seems to be built into our psyche; rejection equals physical and psychological death. The fear of rejection and the experience of rejection are very important and necessary factors in human social development and stability. This contradicts Maslow's needs theory, in that self-actualization may have more to do with the experience and fear of rejection, the resulting emotional pain, and actions (i.e., cooperation, sharing, inventing, accomplishing, etc.) designed to move toward stress reduction. Cooperation, the next step above fear of rejection, is also a human universal, but specific social triggers need to be in place before cooperation will occur and/or be sustained.

(D) Humans have a long dependency period, which allows for the teaching and accumulation of knowledge, group bonding, and formation of identity or references to a group.

(E) Human brains are designed to deal with only small amounts of potentially available information at any one time. The process of chunking, compressing, generalizing, or categorizing allows the individual to keep or store vast numbers of concepts.

(F) Humans have a tool called language, which allows information to be transmitted from individual to individual via a shared code. Language is essentially a device designed, in large measure, to communicate rules.

(G) Humans superchunk information, with language representing an expression of this process. Language represents compressed data, which are "unzipped" by others as the information is delivered. Feedback aids in clarifying accuracy of interpretation. All information is subject to interpretation.

(H) Humans relate to ideas, beliefs, behaviors, and technology through analogies, similar to the generativeness expressed by Chomsky (1957, 1968, 1975, 1980, 1985).

(I) Humans, through their technology (existing for at least 1.5 million years) and art forms (cave painting, clay tablets, books, storytelling, etc.), store information about culture and cultural processes outside of themselves for future use by both contemporary group members and future generations.

(J) Humans have a need to explain everything. Language allows for the explanation of any event. The explanation need not represent fact, but only serves to explain or give reasons for behaviors and events, to generalize or categorize, and thus to order one's world and to aid in the process of reducing stress, exiting information, and getting on with basic survival processes.

(K) All human groups have specific rules regarding relationships between group members (politics, rights, and obligations), incest taboos (sexual restrictions), marriage rituals (marriage restrictions), economic systems, and concepts of territory (home base). All human interaction exists within a matrix of implied rules or behavioral sequences that can be mapped and studied in much the same way that language can be mapped and studied.

(L) Continuing with this, all human groups have concepts of power among individuals and groups and symbols that connote power including brute strength, achieved and ascribed statuses, and mythical charters, as well as natural expressions of power (i.e., the wind, a river, etc.) and supernatural causative influences.

(M) Not only is culture a mechanism designed to organize the environment for purposes of group and individual survival, but also culture is designed to inhibit the rapid influx of new information. It is essentially an anti-chaos mechanism comparable to an enzyme designed to remove information or stop/inhibit it from entering or leaving the system.

(N) Beliefs and practices regarding cause and effect in all matter of social and environmental relationships are designed to reduce individual and group stress.

We need then to place these above universals within a clinical context. That is to say, looking at humans in groups, what are the processes that lead to crisis handling and stress reduction at both the group and the individual levels? This might seem like a large undertaking; however, as will be revealed, the processes involved are really quite simple. First, I will start with the birth of a human being and then place that human being within a social context. The reader should keep in mind that *how* the individual translates his or her world, aided, of course, by the interpretations of others, is a key feature in individual and social stress. It is individual and group stress that generates action. How we get to be the way we are as individuals and as groups of individuals is a product of information, first of genetic information and then, as an extension, of the way we send and receive information. Stated another way, personal identity is a product of our genetic predispositions coupled with the way we translate our worlds and the information within them. As Glass-Coffin states (1992:33):

Personal identity is constructed, we are told, as it is "displayed (enacted, expressed, or performed) both to other aspects of itself and to others through language, gesture and appearance, at a particular time and in a socially organized context" (Weigert, Teitge, and Teige 1986:49). Discourse, as language usage or performance--shaped by the agendas of human intent (Ricoeur 1971)--must be integral to identity construction. Discourse also shares an intimate relationship with threatened identity and the experience of illness. . . . Discourse, in short, has the power to wound and to heal.

Building the Human Being

At birth, all human infants come into this world with some genetic givens. One is that all human infants are born with slightly different brain chemistry and neural wiring. Each is born with perhaps a little more or less of, for example, the neurotransmitter dopamine and a little more or less of serotonin, and so on. This sets up the individual for being more or less sensitive to the world in general; some infants are calm, some sleep very little, some are more hyperactive, and so on, with much of the behavior a result of how that unique individual processes information, that is, light, sound, heat, touch, smell, taste, and the like. This neurochemical predisposition, as we will see, is extremely important when considering the genetic theories of schizophrenia or manic-depressive psychosis, both of which, in most cases, are not purely genetic in etiology. They are a product of neurochemistry genetics, metabolic issues, injury, diet, and the information presented or available to the individual as he or she matures as well as the individual's interpretation of that information.

The infant also comes with other behavioral predispositions, which, at this state of genetic understanding, are difficult to qualify and quantify; he or she does not enter this world with a blank slate, as there are certainly innate factors relative to language and emotions discussed earlier.[1] Moreover, in the womb, the fetus is subjected to the diet and drugs ingested by the mother as well as the hormonal dumping when under stress and the metabolic issues arising from normal changes as fetal maturation occurs. The fetus is also influenced by the mother's heartbeat and probably voice tone, touch, and surrounding light intensity.

There are, at birth, these more or less differences in immune system responses, again, usually a genetic issue, which can affect brain chemistry and bodily functioning in general. Allergic reactions (e.g., to foods, molds, pollen) over time can lower immune responses, leading to depression and anxiety, to "not feeling well"; alterations of the immune system will place demands upon brain functioning. Nutrition is certainly an issue during gestation, at birth, and as the infant matures. Coming in contact with pollutants in the environment (e.g., lead, mercury, and other heavy metals), is likewise a consideration. But all infants everywhere share one identical problem in common, and that is the problem of physical survival after parturition.

This biological information package, this infant--a genetic experiment, if you will, will not survive unless he or she is plugged into a social information system, that is, a family or some other similar social support system. The social system, or culture, takes over where genetics leaves off, but it is more than that. Culture is a mechanism for turning genetics inside out and creating an information storage system that can be directly manipulated by the possessors. Only recently, and this would certainly have been impossible without culture, have we been able to work in reverse, to manipulate the genetic code as well.[2]

Once the infant is placed within that social system, that system inherits the problem of survival because it cannot allow the infant, the toddler, the adolescent, or the adult, to do what he or she wants to do. To do so defeats the purpose of culture and the process of cooperation and survival potential. In short, the caretakers are compelled to establish conformity, which leads to expectations, which leads to a sense of security and ultimately, everything else being equal, to survival. What we have, then, are caretakers protecting the infant from outside elements (i.e., cold, heat, predators) and, at the same time, protecting themselves from anarchy and chaos by establishing rules. The question, then, is, How do the caretakers set the rules? They do so with a tool kit called *language,* which contains a cluster of tools for setting rules. These tools include ordering, warning, threatening, hugging, kissing, praising, using logic, nagging, withdrawing, frowning, yelling, and other more complex verbal and nonverbal messages, that is, storytelling, initiation rites, and so on. Such tools are usually combined in clusters, so that numerous receptor systems (visual, auditory, kinesthetic) are activated in the receiver at one time, thus increasing the probability that information will be received.

By seven, eight, or nine years of age, the child has acquired a set of rules for "doing" and "not doing" and relating to others in a particular environment or environments. He or she has also acquired tools (or a tool kit, that is, language) for delivering rules to others and a style of presentation acquired from caretakers and significant others. And, as each of these significant others has a slightly different style, the child negotiates between them to create his or her own unique presentation. The individual's tool kit and style of delivery combine to define what anthropologists, sociologists, and psychologists call personality. Because of the diverse factors involved (i.e., the individual differences in brain chemistry, the circumstances within which the individual finds himself or herself, and so on), there are as many personalities as there are people on the face of the earth. Personality testing, as conducted by psychologists, although interesting, is questionable in terms of meaning. Pigeonholing people into personality types, however, tells us more about our innate need to classify than about the reality to such type-casting. Personality types are presented to courts, for example, as "things," real entities, when, in fact, what is being presented is a slice of time and the individual's interpretation of self, others, concepts, and images at that time. And, like Werner Heisenberg's uncertainty principle, one cannot measure position accurately without sacrificing accuracy regarding momentum (in social terms, read this as contextual mental set and actual behavior). As indicated by flying reindeer and the pot of gold at the end of the rainbow, the human mind and its linguistic ability have an unlimited imagination and an innate need to label or categorize (compression or chunking of data).

Along with a set of rules, tools, and style of delivery, he or she also has a history of events, a memory of past events and interactions with others. When I use the term memory this is not to imply or suggest that stored information represents exact happenings, as if events were being video- or audiotaped. This is not the time to delve into the concepts of short-term vs. long-term memory, and the processes of memory storage in general, but it is important that we understand a crucial feature of memory, without which psycho-therapeutic measures in all societies would not exist. This crucial feature is that memory can be altered. If this were not the case, perceived negative events would overwhelm the mind in endless loops without resolution. This would eventually lead to emotional and behavioral dysfunction and total system (social as well as biological) shutdown.

The fact that memory can be altered suggests, then, that memory is an ongoing creation, sort of a piecing together of events, using symbols from history as a model, as the individual experiences his or her world. It does not represent fact so much as an interpretation using the past as a template. And, as the past is intimately bound to specific cultural beliefs, memory represents a specific cultural continuum.

HIGH RISK MESSAGES

At this point, we have determined that, by the age of seven, eight, or nine, the individual has acquired a set of rules, tools, a style of delivery, and a personal history or memory of events. But also by this time, the individual has acquired a bonus. This bonus is what I term a cluster of High Risk Messages (HRMs) which become very important in terms of stress reactions. All humans have an innate fear of rejection, which is part of the general grouping mechanism as seen in all group-oriented animals. Rejection, in the large sense of the term, equals physical and/or emotional death. Over the millennia, group animals have evolved a complex set of behaviors that decrease the survival of individual members--and possibly the group itself--if the individual members, are left or forced outside the group. Instead, the group survives only when individual needs and group cooperation fuse, for example, in the food quest, birth process, mutual protection, and so on. (see Bonner 1980; Hinde and Groebel 1991). Being physically driven out of the group equals death. Keep in mind that our ancestors of 100,000 years ago, and earlier, existed in small groups. Forced to leave, the individual would not long survive, and, of course, procreation would be impossible once outside the group unless the individual made contact with other groups. Certainly, individuals did join other groups, but if they were forced out because of antisocial tendencies or extreme rule infractions, they might not fare any better in the new group. Also, there is the "us" vs. "them" attitude, which would have been a barrier to joining a new group. In any event, being forced outside the group of origin was life threatening and emotionally devastating.

Analogous to the fear of being physically rejected from the group are the HRMs, or the social expressions that are analogous to being outside the group. Symbolic rejection, through the use of rule-setting tools (e.g., "Shut the door, stupid!"), is, from the mind's perspective, equal to physical rejection.[3] The social symbols that represent the HRMs (i.e., "not good enough," "stupid," "lazy," etc.) to which I am referring are acquired as the individual learns the rules. An HRM is any internally constructed message activated when that individual perceives certain types of information emanating from the environment, or at times from associations of internal thoughts, as threats to the maintenance of physical/emotional or social integrity. The term I use for such information in the external environment is negative bit (Rush 1976, 1978). I have combined the physical and the emotional because the separation of mind and body, as is often expressed in Western biomedicine, is not universal, and, in fact, as far as the brain is concerned, there is no difference between mind and body. By environment, I mean predators, natural disasters, accidents, assaults, and, more important, social information or input while caretakers and others are attempting to set or maintain social rules. However, in some cultures, evil lurks within; sometimes we hear voices from forces that have invaded our being, as would be the case with spirit possession. Even in our own culture, for example, someone suffering from amphetamine psychosis is usually convinced there *are* entities or individuals within that are giving instruction, suggestions, and critiques.

As the infant is exploring its world, the caretakers are establishing rules through voice tone, facial gestures, touch, phrases, explicatives, and so on, to which the child eventually puts meaning and is able to feed back to caretakers and others. Further, as the infant or toddler is exploring his or her environment, he or she will come upon situations that are dangerous to his or her physical integrity. This could be a poisonous snake, a fast-moving river, water boiling on a hearth or stove, or bleach under the sink. In a scenario enacted 30,000 or 40,000 years ago, physical injury could mean death; without antibiotics, the specialist to mend the fractured leg or stop the bleeding of a severed artery, or the techniques of artificial respiration, the victim would not survive. From what was stated in Chapter 1, regarding numbers necessary for survival, a great deal of energy is expended on the infant who survives the birthing process. The purpose of the individual, contrary to our own times in Western culture, where having children is centered around the need to love and to be loved in turn, is to eventually aid in group survival, to contribute "another set of hands around the farm," so to speak. Until quite recently, children were an investment for the future (in some cases and at some times male children were more important than female children or visa versa--see Harris 1989:311-315), and a physical injury to a child would have been costly indeed. It is reasonable to suggest, then, that there were many rules for maintaining physical integrity. Some of these rules, no doubt, were relayed through myth and ritual. However, if an infant were about to place himself or herself in jeopardy, an immediate, life and culture-sustaining mechanism would be to abruptly and even harshly anchor in a rule through the use of negative bit(s), which might include physical aggression. Yes, nature provides its own feedback-being slightly burned or perhaps bitten by a fire ant. My reference is to potentially life-threatening situations.

In our own culture, my wife and I recently saw a perfect example of a mother protecting her children from a life-threatening situation. The mother had parked her car, during rush hour, next to a baseball diamond. Traffic was heavy to her south and east, and it was safe to walk only to the west, to a path connecting the grandstand with the diamond. Her two small children, perhaps ages three and five, opened the doors to the car, exited, and immediately began running east toward the crowded highway. The mother screamed, and the older child stopped in her tracks. The younger, male child, laughing and perhaps thinking this was good fun, continued to run toward the road. In hot pursuit, the mother caught up with the child, yelled, picked the child up by the arm, and gave him a good swat. What was most interesting was that the child, crying, began to wobble back to the car; he did not attempt to continue on toward the road. Now, can you imagine the mother calmly saying to the child, "I would really be pleased if you didn't run toward the road," *a la* Thomas Gordon (1970). In this situation, and many like it, there is no survival value in an initial positive approach. There is no way to explain, in a logical positive-bit fashion, to a three-, four-, or five-year-old that playing in the traffic is dangerous and know that the child received and understood the message. It is necessary to create anxiety and just enough trauma to anchor in the message of danger. Certainly, one can overdo it, which is sometimes the case in our society, as in our hypothetical group of 30,000 to 40,000 years ago, but it is unlikely that brutality in and of itself would have been the rule. It is highly unlikely that our ancestors were the brutes depicted by Hobbes. On the contrary, brutality would have been just as devastating as permissiveness. I suspect that a good portion of the content of proto-language (Bickerton 1990) was designed to set rules for maintaining physical integrity, rules that needed to be anchored immediately and harshly. Negative bits used in current languages, and extending into all areas of rule setting, are an extension of this.

We must distinguish between behaviors/messages designed to maintain physical integrity and those designed to maintain social solidarity or cooperation. These are important distinctions, although the latter are an extension of the former.[4] Both are designed to instruct. Out of these, over time, the individual learns and operates on self-directed messages, some conscious and some unconscious. The breaking of a learned oath or a religious or sexual taboo will usually bring about a guilt or shame reaction in the perpetrator.

High Risk Messages (HRMs)--Where Do They Come From?

In our own culture, many rules are set up, as the child matures, in a negative manner.[5] This could be because that style was learned from the parent's parents, because stress levels are high and the parent feels threatened by the child, or because such models are presented by the mass media; there are many reasons. At any rate, with the setting of a rule, the child is potentially learning many things--not just the rule of a behavior wanted or not wanted. As words, phrases, and gestures represent compressed data, the potential interpretations placed on them as they pass through the reality of the receiver are specific to the receiver.

Let us say, for example, a child is playing in the living room, and he leaves his toys scattered all over the place and decides to go outside and play. Father comes home from work, hoping to sit down and relax, only to be inconvenienced by having to remove little Bobby's toys from his favorite chair. Being frustrated, he goes to the front door and yells out, "Bobby, come here! What do you think this is, your own private pig pen? Pick up these toys, put them in your room, and stay there until further notice!" What message, what rule is the father trying to get across? Well, the most obvious is "Pick up your toys," but there are other potential messages; the rules that "when Dad gets home from work, especially if he has had a bad day, don't get in his space," "big people can yell at little people"; and so on. The tools used to deliver these rules include sarcasm, ordering, voice tone, and accompanying facial gestures. This covers, at least in part, some of the more obvious rule(s) or information delivered and the tools used. But what other messages are available for Bobby to pick up about Bobby and others? This is a difficult question, and the answer depends upon how he has been communicated to in the past by his father (past context), whether or not others are present and who these others are (current context), Bobby's mood to begin with, what activity was interrupted, and so on. But the main factor here, because it is difficult to qualify and quantify all the variables, is that the meaning of a message is always determined by the receiver. The possible meaning or meanings that could attach to this message are that he, Bobby, is inconsiderate, thoughtless, stupid, incompetent, not good enough, unlovable--the list can go on and on. It might be even that Dad is a jerk, "always stressed out," and so on. There is also the inherent message that, if the father believes that he can communicate to his son this way, he must believe that he is superior and the son is inferior. Or, if there are other siblings to compete with, "Dad always picks on me." There is an almost endless stream of possibilities. But the child, for more or less arbitrary reasons related to past messages, will consider some of this information as more important than other parts. Keep in mind that parents have a style of rule delivery, which they use, regardless of whether or not the techniques work in specific situations. They are on autopilot.

Moreover, children have a tendency to accept messages literally, with the moon being made out of green cheese, Santa Claus, and the Tooth Fairy being obvious examples of this literalness. They believe such things because their information base is limited and they have a tendency to trust (until that trust is lost, at least) the judgments of people of significance to them whom they perceive as powerful. Messages like "stupid," "not good enough," "ugly," "fat," and "unlovable" become just as believable, and because they are unprovable judgments (we *can* prove Santa does not exist) they can become part of the individual's HRM package. An HRM is essentially a loop that the individual goes over and over, attempting to retranslate. Keep in mind that HRMs are conjoined with the innate fear of rejection. Resolution is not available because an alternative, acceptable message is not always accessible. This is especially true in the family origin where the styles of communication are held in place by implied rules. Retranslating, altering, or eliminating HRMs, or the effects of HRMs, as we will see, is the key to all successful individual/physical and social healing.

Thus, as the child is learning the rules, he is learning the language. He is learning styles of language use. He is learning about the idiosyncrasies of those around him. He is also learning about himself, and who he is in the group.

In North American culture, many, many rules are set using such strategies as ordering, warning, threatening, making logical arguments, withdrawing love, and nagging, which are all high risk for communicating negative bits, implying rejection, which are then converted, over time, into a person's HRMs. Such rules relate to proper relationships between people, moral issues, religious/supernatural issues, and so on. We can see this process of HRM development in all cultures; learning the rules is both necessary, for reasons of individual and social survival, and potentially traumatic in an emotional as well as a social sense. Rules cannot be set haphazardly, nor can they be set arbitrarily. When an individual breaks a rule, social order is halted and a door opens; this is a dangerous time, as we shall see. Rule infraction is also accompanied by feelings of what we, in Western culture, term *guilt,*[6] which in some cultures can bring on fears of not only social reprisal, but supernatural sanctions as well. Guilt can be defined as extreme emotional flooding followed by a culturally defined and stereotypical response, that is, depression, neurasthenia, other somatic complaints, acting out toward self (suicide, alcohol abuse) or others, and so on. All the behaviors in our society generated as a result of guilt are stereotypical; they are not abnormal but, instead, represent expectations of society or primary group members. In our society, as in all societies, the psychiatrist, the psychologist, the shaman, and the witch doctor diagnose stereotypically and according to that culture's beliefs about cause and effect. This should not be confused with truth or reality.

Keep in mind that all members of a culture, in the process of setting rules, are also communicating about *who the receiver (and sender) is in the group,* both positive and negative. A person's cluster of HRMs, combined with the positive elements, represents this "who" (or personal identity), with the cluster of HRMs representing a person's pain, his or her negative self-worth or, as I term it, *group worth*. To digress for a moment, the terms *self-worth* and *self-esteem* are psychological constructs that have evolved from a particular cultural perspective that values and accentuates individualism. In fact, there can be no self-worth without a reference point that moves toward the larger group. As Stein (1987:36) states, "The psychogeography of society is. . . . mapped outward from the body and family, not--as most social scientists argue--inward from culture." The term *group worth* is a preferable term, as it avoids the ethnocentrism inherent in Western psychology. In other words, you cannot have a concept of who you are without information input from the larger environment. The issue is not how you feel about yourself, but how you think others perceive you.

The larger and more dense the cluster of HRMs, the greater the person's pain, and the lower the person's group worth. It is almost as if we point an antenna at the world, an antenna that is ever on the lookout for information that represents rejection. Why is this so? My belief is that picking out the negative in the field of available information had great survival value to our protoancestors (as it would for any species); the unusual, the out-of-place was potentially dangerous (the polarity of this, of course, is curiosity and pro-pensity to find out about the out-of-place information). Although we do not have to contend with being eaten by the animal predator, we are now more concerned, by analogy, with predatory words, those real or imagined messages of rejection.

This pain generated from HRMs is motivating; it is motivating because it is unresolved and it can motivate the individual to greatness, or into the gutter, as the symbols of rejection become attached, through analogy, to other diverse information. We speak of dysfunctional families in North American psychology, and yet out of so-called dysfunctional families emerge individuals who achieve greatness by our cultural standards. One must question, therefore, this notion of dysfunctional as a negative construct. Dysfunctional may simply be a metaphor for a strange attractor which leads the system, and those within, to another organizational style.

STRESS AND HRMs

When a person's HRMs are "tapped into," so to speak, and this can be through the translation of incoming information from natural environmental events, friends, relatives, teachers, or so on, or from the individual's own loop-ing on internalized information over time (i.e., reflections on past and current behavior), that individual's stress goes up, and then his or her ability to communicate with self and others (communication potential) decreases. This process is illustrated in Figure 3.1.

Figure 3.1
Stress Diagram

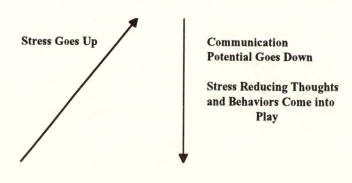

When stress goes up, the individual (or group) engages one or a combination of about five universal mechanisms that are actually designed to reduce stress, but they can likewise increase stress. The mechanisms that come into play will be discussed shortly. By universal, I mean that not only do *all* human groups revert to these mechanisms, but other species do as well. Moreover, much of human behavior can be seen flowing out from and as analogous to these five universals.

Let's consider these in detail, keeping in mind the reference point of a message entering the person's senses that taps into the individual's cluster of HRMs. When stress goes up, Miller's number of 7 +/- 2 becomes important (see Chapter 1). Under stress, the individual's information-processing abilities decrease, with the higher the stress, the lower this ability becomes. In an average, moderate stress situation, the individual can pay attention to 7 +/- 2 chunks of information. As stress increases, the individual can pay less and less attention to new information input, and, at the same time, internal information compresses further. This is where automatic responses come into play.

Stress Reducing Mechanisms

The overall design is to reduce stress by getting rid of or avoiding the stressor. With the advent of language and the symbols that serve to activate memories, ideas, rights, and duties and the overall complexities of social living, avoidance is difficult because events can be replayed over and over. Basic mechanisms are engaged to stop the loop. Keep in mind that all of the basic mechanisms listed below have analogous counterparts, which, in some cases, may seem more socially acceptable. Again, most if not all of human behavior can be seen as first-level, second-level, or even third-level analogues of the five mechanisms listed below. For example, verbal fighting (second-level) is analogous to physical fighting (first level), structured debate and/or civil and criminal court proceedings are analogous to verbal fighting (third-level), with satire of the court proceeding representing a possible fourth-level, and so on.

Verbal and Physical Fighting

The strategy or mechanism of *verbal fighting* is potentially life saving or at least stress reducing in many situations. Yelling at a child because the child almost gets hit by a truck, and having the child associate the yelling (an unpleasant experience) with danger (being hit by a moving vehicle), can be life saving in the future. A girlfriend verbally fighting with her boyfriend because he drinks too much can be stress reducing for her because she has expressed her feelings, or taken action about a behavior, and even more stress reducing if she obtains compliance. Keep in mind that a shaman might use verbal fighting to ward off evil spirits. Certainly, verbal fighting can be stress enhancing-- becoming verbally abusive to someone larger and stronger than you with poor impulse control could lead to physical violence. The design with verbal fighting is to either scare off the "predator" with voice tone or threats, or, using logic, side trips, and other confusion techniques, to deliver a message so that the other backs down or compliance is obtained.

The analogy to human verbal fighting among other animals would be, for example, two dogs growling at each other. But in any case, dog or human (or superhuman), the problem is resistance encountered when the person/predator does not back down and, instead, fights back. During human verbal aggression, stress often increases, with both parties sending out a lot of information that is highly compressed with a low level of specificity. The escalation to physical violence is always a possibility at this point, depending upon the history of the participants, impulse control, being under the influence of drugs, being observed by others, and so on. Verbal fighting includes the defensive reactions of lying, bluffing, rationalizing, arguing, and debating.

Physical violence is likewise used to reduce stress by defending one's emotional and physical integrity.

The goal with physical violence, again, is to reduce stress by winning or getting away, and this would be the case whether the attack was coming from a saber-toothed tiger, a mugger, or one's wife. Physical violence is a useful strategy in some situations, but as an overall strategy for dealing with conflict, it only breeds more conflict over time.

Withdrawal

The second strategy on the list is *withdrawal,* which is also known as flight, and, in terms of the predator scenario, it can be the behavior of choice. Withdrawing physically from an uncaring husband or a nagging wife might likewise be useful, although other strategies could be more effective. The shaman who withdraws from the social setting in order to commune with spirits is reducing stress for the patient and the group simply because some sort of action is being taken that represents an appropriate type of activity in a crisis situation. With physical withdrawal, for example, in marital situations, the message communicated is often, "I don't love you," "I don't want to be around you," or "I don't care." In this case, withdrawal can be stress enhancing over time.

Menstrual seclusion might, in some cases, be seen as physical withdrawal for purposes of stress reduction both from a social taboo situation (or avoidance of evil possibilities) and to a sanctuary situation, allowing an escape, so to speak, from the rigors of day-to-day living (Buckley and Gottlieb 1988:11-13).

There are two other ways to withdraw. The first is through emotional withdrawal, as when a wife is disinterested in her husband's day; she continues to make eye contact, but her mind is somewhere else. The extremes of withdrawal are certain internal states, like depression and/or neurasthenia (which is noted among many cultures--see Kleinman and Good 1985), or psychotic states (catatonia) that render the individual socially non-functional. Flights into fantasy, or age regression, would also fit into the realm of emotional withdrawal, as would be trance states in order to commune with the spirits. Television programs, the cinema, and listening to music are likewise forms of emotional withdrawal.

A final way to withdraw, especially in our culture, is through the use of drugs--alcohol, marijuana, cocaine, amphetamines, DMT, LSD, Prozac, Valium, and the like.[7] By altering the brain chemistry, the individual withdraws from a social reality and reverts to another level of awareness or reality, which is created from moment to moment while on the drug. In other cultures, such withdrawal is often ritualized and socially sanctioned. It is perhaps a method of communicating with spirits for the purpose of obtaining a guardian spirit (Harner 1984) or, as among the Fang of Africa (Dobkin De Rios 1990:170), a means of obtaining information from spirits. The design, though, is not simply the drug experience itself but to obtain something and bring it back for the benefit of the group.

Freezing Up

The third strategy is to *freeze up,* which is similar to a fawn in the woods who freezes and allows the predator to pass by. By freezing, you cut down on information output, and thus, in a sense, "hide" yourself from the enemy. Freezing up and not adding information in a social situation can indeed be useful, as, for example, when the innocent bystander during a bank robbery. Freezing up and remaining motionless could be life saving.

As another example, the catatonic (which can also be a process of withdrawal mentioned above), remaining motionless month after month, is probably in a protective stance, protecting himself or herself from further onslaughts of negative bits. According to our cultural values, such behavior is neither socially productive nor approved.

In other situations, freezing up can be embarrassing and even traumatic for the individual who has to go in front of a group and speak. Where taking some sort of action *is* necessary, freezing up can be costly. By freezing up, the mind does not stop so much as loop without being able to problem solve and take action. As stress is high, it is difficult to pull together information that is necessary to make a decision. Thus, not doing anything is the result.

Emotional Conversion

A fourth strategy is *emotional conversion,* wherein one emotion is substituted for another. For example, a person feeling frustrated could convert this frustration to anger and lash out at others. Stress is potentially reduced by taking action relative to frustration. Or a person could be feeling frustrated and convert this into another internal state, depression. Depression is potentially stress reducing by cutting down information input, although the internal looping can only be stress enhancing in itself.

In non-Western curing situations wherein the shaman establishes contact with spirits and a diagnosis is forthcoming, the curing ritual serves as a mechanism for individual and group emotional conversion. The conversion goes from, perhaps, frustration and anger to hope and relief.

Further, emotional states can be converted into somatic sensations, as when there is anger or frustration which is not outwardly expressed but, instead, converted into a stomachache, headache, and the like, which are actually analogous to emotional states. Such conversion and expression are very common among Asian and Southeast Asian populations and can be seen as a process to avoid social confrontation or the blaming of emotions and behavior on others. Moreover, the brain does not seem to care whether it is an emotion-to-emotion or an emotion-to-somatic conversion. We have an extensive language that reflects this metaphoric conversion: for example, "I can't stomach it," "My heart isn't in it," "This is a pain in the neck," "This situation is just one big headache," "I can't handle this anymore," and "I can't stand this." By listening to the individual's metaphors of this type, you can often detect where someone has experienced or will experience a physical illness.[8]

Again, when such metaphorical statements are processed too literally by the mind, they can lead to physical illness; this is essentially the general mechanism involved in psychosomatic illness or linguistic-somatic illness and psychological death, a very important concept when considering stress and physical disorders in all cultures (Tobin and Friedman 1983). Thus, emotional conversion can go from one emotional state to another or from an emotional to a somatic state, as the brain apparently does not make a distinction between emotions (mind) and body; to the brain, they are one and the same.

Sexual Behavior

Finally, the fifth strategy designed for stress reduction is *sexual behavior*, which could be masturbation, sex with one's partner, voyeurism, frotterism, and so on. Beyond the usually pleasurable nature of the act, and the fact that it can be physiologically reregulating (like any exercise) if the time frame is long enough, it can represent feelings of power and control or mastery over one's self or another or feelings of acceptance by another. Rape for the rapist, although an act of violence, is stress reducing for the rapist (not for the victim). One of the reasons that sex offenders are difficult to treat in Western culture is that sex is stress reducing (see Harvey and Gow 1994 for an interesting cross-cultural perspective on how sex and violence can fit into society to maintain balance and reduce stress). Few therapies consider rape in this manner and do not anchor in alternative stress-reducing mechanisms that are equally as effective (perhaps because there are no substitutable behaviors). Most of the therapeutic approaches consider the motives behind the behavior, while some attempt to alter the fantasies that lead to the acting out. Still others explore recognition of sexual urges and objects of references so that behavior can be short-circuited. Sex as stress reducing can be inferred in all cultures (but not necessarily for all members of that culture) on a physiological basis alone; sexual expression or preferences, however, are not a constant.

Individual and Group Stress

The above discussion of group survival, rule setting, and the development of HRMs can be seen as a building platform from which thought problems, and dyadic, intragroup, and intergroup conflict stem. Although intergroup conflict will be considered in more detail in Chapter 5, its connection with HRMs will be discussed briefly.

Most individuals develop loyalties toward primary groups (family of origin, procreation), and secondary groups (church, village, state/province, nation), which act as reference points for organizing time and space. The group of primary reference, at any time, depends upon who is sending a message and who is receiving. A quarrel between neighbors is really between families, and a quarrel between two rival gang members is really a quarrel between the two gangs; the one represents the other. If a wife, for example, is having difficulties with her neighbor, she will expect her husband to take her side. If he does not, he had better have good diplomatic skills. This is why it is easy to develop national loyalty through the use of well-placed words that hit at the HRMs of the individual, using the enemy's statements or actions as a perceived attack on the individual, his family, his livelihood, and so on. The mass media have been used in this capacity at least since the Civil War. National attacks, then, are made to appear as attacks against the individual, an analogous representation of the state.

HRMs thus are the keystone for understanding individual social stress reactions and, through analogy, group stress reactions as well. Moreover, individual stress reactions are not individual phenomena, but evolve out of the actions and reactions of others. The strategies individuals use when distressed, if not projected onto others, are certainly learned from others. Further, through the process of synchronicity, individuals react to other individuals at the subconscious level with stress "spreading out" through a group.

Returning to the biological level, HRMs can be seen as the interface between the genetic, predispositional givens, for example, schizophrenia (Fowles 1992) and drug addiction (McGue et al. 1992). HRMs, remember, can come about through the social learning of rules and choices of behavior. The individual's or the group's reaction under stress is a choice in the sense that the individual models the behaviors of others; he or she sees and hears what one should do in particular situations (verbal/physical fighting, withdrawal, etc.), with these choices engaged automatically through overlearning. Alcoholism, a form of withdrawing, is only inherited in the sense that it becomes a choice through modeling or experience. This is not the same as inheriting blue eyes from a parent. In fact, those that subscribe to alcoholism being inherited are actually engaging a form of Lamarckian Inherited Characteristics, along with giving individuals who choose to abuse alcohol (and other drugs) a label to justify their history and current behavior, as is apparent in the words Alcoholics Anonymous. When alcoholism is seen as an incurable disease that is exactly what it becomes. Alcoholism is a social/behavioral description or concept, not primarily a genetic issue. The physiological reactions to alcohol, in terms of metabolism, are genetic (see Stinson 1992:149-151 for a brief review of this issue). It is difficult to predict the behavioral manifestations connected to the ingestion of alcohol in each case, although they are highly conditioned by cultural expectations (Hsu 1955:53-56; Douglas 1991a, 1991b; Heath 1991). Even within these cultural expectations, however, behavior has a lot to do with previous levels of toxins in the body, how recently a person has eaten, who the person is with, and the context or setting within which the behavior is engaged.

Long-Term Effects of High Risk Messages

The universal stress reactions listed above (i.e., withdrawal, verbal/physical fighting, freezing up, etc.) are also the building blocks to long-term reactions or responses often diagnoses as dysfunctional or abnormal in many cultures. Alcohol (and other drug) abuse can be seen as a long-term reaction to stressors, a form of withdrawal, although, on the surface and in some situations, a procedure to enable social interaction (Douglas 1991b; see also Helman 1994:209-215). I use, "on the surface" because, although drinking alcohol can be seen as a social activity, the alcohol, because it alters brain chemistry, moves the imbiber more and more into his chemically constructed or influenced reality and away from an agreed upon social reality.

Different societies use alcohol and other drugs for different purposes, but these purposes fit into two general categories: (1) non-ritual withdrawal/distortion or a strategy for coping with information (how alcohol is generally used in our culture, for example); and (2) ritual social integration, for example, the use of wine during communion in the Catholic Church. This is likewise the case when the shaman takes a drug, hallucinates the evil force/entity possessing the patient, does battle with the entity, instructs the entity to go away or pays homage to it is in some way, and then returns to society, the patient cured (an example would be the Reindeer herdsmen of Siberia--Dobkin De Rios 1990).

When one consults the 1994 edition of the *Diagnostic and Statistical Manual of Mental Disorders (DSM-IV)* the reader is confronted with many categories and subcategories of behaviors currently considered abnormal, or socially dysfunctional, which are then placed on different axes for purposes of diagnosis. In my opinion, most of these categories or behaviors are brought on by long-term looping on HRMs, combined in some cases with genetic predispositions of the type mentioned earlier, nutritional issues, and metabolic problems; a holistic approach is necessary for any realistic diagnosis of these conditions. Keep in mind that every time you think, you alter your brain chemistry. Looping on the same problem over and over and over, for many months and years, creates a learning wherein the person's thoughts automatically return to the loop when certain information is encountered in the environment. Although the *DSM-IV* would appear scientific, this hairsplitting serves more to create labels and some sort of artificial organization or classification than it does to then refer the label to a specific therapy designed to cure the condition. Such labels[9] are not the same as a broken leg, appendicitis, or bacterial infection, with a specific procedure for repairing or eliminating the pathogens. These labels represent symptoms of underlying issues or causes many of them social in origin. The use of drugs as a method of cure is misdirected. Curing is something the body/mind does, not the doctor or shaman, with the input (removal and/or alteration) of specific types of information representing the cause. As long as Western biomedicine deals mainly with symptoms, rather than underlying causes, symptoms are suppressed and new or similar problems simply surface at a later date. By suppressing symptoms, the physician invites total metabolic breakdown, that is, chaos, and a movement of metabolic processes to another order or level of functioning. [10]

The *DSM-IV* is a very useful research tool for understanding Western psychiatric beliefs as an extension of Western medical thought in general. However, it is not atheoretical as suggested by some researchers (see LaBruzza and Mendez-Villarrubia 1994:85-86), nor is it possible to be devoid of theoretical perspectives of cause and effect. As Clarke et al. (1995:147) comment, "In the long run, of course, the most clinically useful system will be one that has maximal predictive power regarding course and treatment because it is based on a scientific understanding of the relevant parameters." Let me add to this that the "most clinically useful system" will be the one that understands the underlying cause/causes and, for the most part, Western biomedicine, which includes psychiatry, does not take a holistic approach when it comes to cause, but, instead, is concerned with suppressing of symptoms and managing behavior for economic, security, and liability reasons.

ILLNESS CATEGORIES: GENERALIZATIONS

By examining the psychiatric perspective through the *DSM-IV* and Western biomedicine in general and the way other societies categorize "illness" or "disease," one is struck by the fact that medical, psychiatric, psychological, and social categories can be grouped under the following headings (keep in mind that this represents placing all illness/disease into a Western model, using Western concepts, and assuming that they can be applied to all cultures--Gaines 1992b:4-5):

Category A--Physical Damage--Injury, Viral and Bacterial Infection, Helminths, DNA Damage, Exposure (sun, cold, heat);
Category B--Metabolic Function, Dysfunction, and Aging;
Category C--Nutritional Problems;
Category D--Organic Disorders (Neurochemical Predispositional/Genetic Issues Amplified by Social Learning and Other Environmental Factors).
Category E--Interpretation of Environment, Stress Reactions, and Alterations of Physiology thus Altering Brain/Body Chemistry (Psychosomatic/Linguistic-Somatic Issues);
Category F--The "Evil," Moral Model.

Certainly, categories can spill one into the other. For example, cancer can have its origins in free radicals (Categories A and B) that damage tissue and/or disrupt metabolic functions and in inadequate nutrition (Category C). Most people who die of cancer usually die of malnutrition. An injury (Category A) could lead to metabolic problems (Category B). And all of the above likewise involve emotional as well as physical stress (Category E); therefore, Category F could be considered as a causal factor, for example, in the case of AIDS.

Murdock et al. (1978), considering a worldwide distribution of illness, have developed a more inclusive classification system containing two general categories of illness causation, that is, "Natural," which includes infection, stress, organic deterioration, accident, and overt human aggression, and; "Supernatural," which includes fate, ominous sensations, contagion, mystical retribution, soul loss, spirit aggression, sorcery, and witchcraft.

What I find most interesting about the analysis by Murdock et al. is the statement that, "theories of illness tend strongly to remain constant among the societies belonging to any particular linguistic family" (1978:459). The suggestion here is that the beliefs are very old and have remained within the reality of a language and the metaphorical expressions of that language, even though there has been social isolation and thus language divergence. This also suggests that language and the consequent expression of illness are intimately bound together, and, thus, it is impossible to separate illness or disease and their expression from the culture and language in which they are studied. Therefore, illness is bound to the culture in which it is expressed. The *DSM-IV* is thus bound to North American urban culture. From another point of view, the fact that the *DSM* is continuously being updated obviously indicates changes in thinking about illness and the expressions of these conditions; illness expressions and conceptualizations are not constants.

Language and information processing, therefore, are a key to cross-cultural analysis of illness. I will present another model shortly ,which includes most of Murdock's categories, but from an information processing standpoint. What evolves is a picture that shows that, by removing some of the emotionally charged concepts, non-Western beliefs in illness causation can be seen as analogous to many features of the Western biomedical belief complex. More important, the model to be presented uses a language and concepts that can be seen as constant when conceptualizing, describing, and dealing with illness and disease from a cross-cultural perspective.

Illness Categories: HRM Specifics

Category A--Physical Damage--Injury, Viral and Bacterial Infection, Helminths, DNA Damage, Exposure (sun, cold, heat). With respect to dealing with medical issues, such as broken legs, lacerations, and penetration wounds from arrows, knives, and so on, there are usually straightforward techniques that have evolved over time in all cultures. And, although there is always a social/emotional component, ranging from the pain and emotional trauma involved and nutritional issues to the questions and/or beliefs that can increase anxiety (i.e., "Why me," "Who have I offended," Karma, Lack of a guardian spirit), definite techniques have evolved for dealing with the physical conditions proper. These would include setting the bone and closing up the laceration, along with the use of proper nutrition, herbs, and antibiotics.[11] As knowledge increases we have become more effective at physical repair, especially within Western technology. Within the Western biomedical model, and mainly dealing with traumatic injury, is the explicit pursuit or explanation of cause and effect; that is, information (arrow, bullet, knife, freeradicals, etc.--through aggressive acts) enters the system via outside sources, causing damage. With respect to the germ theory of disease, or DNA damage resulting in cancer, this is still information penetration that is perhaps a little more tangible than, depending upon one's point of view, sorcery, witchcraft, or other evil outside forces. However, both curses and malignant spells are analogous to viruses and bacteria and the general belief is the same; that is, outside forces have entered into the body (information input) and caused "illness." All physical problems, certainly, can be exacerbated by emotional issues and poor nutrition, and vice versa. Illness is a dangerous time; one's world is disordered, and explanations of cause and effect and appropriate rituals come into play for bringing the system back to order (balance). Moreover, this balance might incorporate changes in the previous order.

Category B--Metabolic Function, Dysfunction, and Aging. For numerous reasons--perhaps from physical injury, diet, prescription drug use, emotional stress, bacterial or viral infections, or tumor formation--metabolic processes are disrupted. Liver or pancreatic tumors can, for example, have devastating effects on total body functioning. Bacterial infections of the pericardium can lead to serious heart conditions. As time goes on, free radicals are not as adequately counteracted by cellular enzymes, cell damage accrues, cancer is probable, and aging is certain (see Rusting 1992). Diet and digestive problems have a definite effect on metabolic functioning, with the consumption of too much fat and oil leading to obesity and strain on the heart and not enough vitamin C leading to scurvy. From a Western point of view, information sending between cells is incomplete or inadequate, and, therefore appropriate responses break down (see Pennisi 1993).

The ingestion of heavy metals and the consequent disruption of metabolic processes likewise fall into this category. In industrial societies, where heavy metals (i.e., lead, arsenic, mercury, etc.) are used in certain manufacturing processes, such problems are quite widespread. Certain other chemicals (e.g., methyl-ethyl-keytone, used as a solvent in the shoe and plastic industry) also interfere with metabolic processes, as do other petroleum-based oils and solvents. Considering soft-tissue tumors from a paleopathological perspective, Gerszten and Allison (1991:259) comment: "The most important factors for this low incidence of neoplastic lesions in mummified materials include the facts that almost all of the known carcinogenic agents prevalent in today's world have only recently been brought into contact with humans,' and that the immune system of ancient populations may have been different."

Aging is a concern in our society, as we are living longer and essentially becoming a society of "older people." But as Murdock et al. (1978:452) point out:

Surprisingly, this seemingly obvious cause receives scant support from the ethnographic literature, being mentioned for only 29 societies and never as an important determinant. The explanation doubtless resides in part in the widespread removal of defective infants by infanticide, and in the slow and unspectacular nature of the aging process. In any event, it would seem as though most of mankind considers itself potentially immortal and is unable to conceive of the infirmities of old or middle age in terms other than through the intervention of some hostile agency or force.

Category C--Nutritional Problems. Nutritional deficiencies can lead to numerous metabolic disorders, such as pellagra, scurvy, and cancer, as well as socio-emotional problems (Stinson 1992; Chafetz 1990; Schoenthaler 1991; Pfeiffer 1987a, 1987b, 1978, 1975) and, in a general sense, are defined by the quality and quantity of nutritional information entering the body. Again, as we are considering information input of an insufficient variety, the analogy, as found in many non-Western cultures, could be represented by a curse, witchcraft, or spirit attack (a type of information input). This is not to say that a culture would not see a direct connection between a famine and ill health without resorting to a belief in witchcraft. The famine itself, however, would deserve explanation. In Biblical times, a famine was interpreted as the "wrath of the Lord" (II Kings 8:1).

Category D--Organic Disorders (neurochemical predispositional/genetic issues amplified by social learning and other environmental factors). Organic disorders, including certain developmental disorders, which in Western culture include the various psychoses (schizophrenia, manic-depression, catatonia), are found in many cultures. This has led various researchers (e.g., Torrey 1980) to conclude that schizophrenia is a genetic problem leading to a stereotyped behavioral outcome. In an earlier work, Torrey (1986, orig. 1972) reviews the literature on curers in different societies; one of his goals is to show that witchdoctors are not crazy misfits who somehow are integrated into society to then become useful members. In order for Torrey to prove that schizophrenia is inherited, he has to disprove the idea that schizophrenics can be integrated and thus, themselves, can alter their thought problem to fit the needs of society. Torrey has some interesting conclusions, but I have difficulty accepting his thesis. First, although there are the "more or less" factors in neurochemistry (e.g., too much dopamine) which can predispose some individuals to schizophrenic reactions, the interpretation of the information in the environment tends to be the "straw that breaks the back" factor that ultimately determines the final outcome in most cases (Fowles 1992; Bloom 1989:141).

Second, and connected to the first, the thought disorder itself is manifest in the language of the afflicted. The language, although it sounds like the speaker's native language, is actually an adaptive mechanism, which protects or helps isolate the individual from others. Keep in mind that psychic hurt (emotional hurt), an analogy of physical pain, is just as painful as (in many cases, more so than) physical injury. By developing one's own language *within* a language (a meta-language), the person can stop the influx of negative bits which slam into his or her HRMs and result in looping on information and the consequent emotional pain. The process for developing throught disorders, like schizophrenia, is outlined in Figure 3.2.

Figure 3.2
Stress, Looping, and Thought Disorders

A) Genetic predisposition (dopamine?);
B) Social/environmental information input ---------> Stress goes up (continual stress over time) disrupting physiology and altering brain chemistry (nutritional issues likewise come into play);

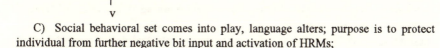

C) Social behavioral set comes into play, language alters; purpose is to protect individual from further negative bit input and activation of HRMs;

D) Social Feedback:
    1) Culture allows abnormal behavior; Places meaning onto it, that is, a calling to become a shaman, priest, politician, and so on. Reframing/reinterpretation allows social reintegration and functioning within a socially prescribed role set;
or
    2) Culture passes judgment and assigns the role of "sick," resulting in a process of distancing from that individual.

Our culture does not have socially prescribed, useful roles for schizophrenics other than "sick." They are castaways caught up in the morality and judgments of Western psychiatry.

The universal factor in schizophrenia or manic-depressive psychosis is not simply the genetic one; it is how one interprets incoming information and the consequent stress reaction and further alteration of brain chemistry and neural wiring, and it often involves nutritional issues as well (see Pfeiffer 1987b). As illustrated in Figure 3.2, under stress from continual looping on HRMs due to frequent input and translation of negative bits, brain chemistry is altered, eventually leading to thought disorders and the alteration of language (and thus an alteration of meaning), with a locking in of thoughts, sort of a thought habit. Stress is thus reduced. In order to maintain the stress reduction, the thought disorder needs to be kept in place, which likewise keeps the neurochemistry at an appropriate level to maintain the thought disorder; it becomes a vicious cycle. Drug therapy is an attempt to reregulate the brain chemistry, with the goal of lessening the thought disorder. However, it is like closing the door to a messy room; the mess still lies behind that door, and that mess usually involves information, both historical and current, impinging on the individual from the surrounding social milieu. When the drugs are withdrawn, the thoughts return because they have not been reframed or reinterpreted. Without the drug(s), the individual is often faced with the same external information, but without a new meaning, method of reinterpretation, or social support system because of the attached stigma. Cure is never realized.

On the other hand, the use of drugs, like alcohol, cocaine, and marijuana, that alter brain chemistry can create the psychosis or thought disorder that the "true schizophrenic" does on his or her own. The use of such drugs over time is addictive in a similar manner as the thinking associated with thought disorders. That is to say, the drugs alter brain chemistry, and, over time, the neurons demand the chemical information in order to maintain the condition or thought disorder. Withdrawal is not only a chemical problem; returning to social reality means returning to deal with negative bits, the perceived rejection. Much of what we in Western society consider to be withdrawal symptoms from drugs are merely beliefs that the physical and emotional symptoms will occur. I have personally used hypnosis with numerous drug addicts to remove these beliefs, these symptoms of withdrawal. Thus, even withdrawal symptoms are culturally conditioned.

Certainly there are genetic conditions that lead to behavioral problems that have little to do with HRMs or looping at the emotional level. These would include Down's syndrome, and fetal alcohol syndrome, the one being a deficiency of information and the other the addition or intrusion of information that interferes with growth and developmental patterns.

Category E--Interpretation of Information in environment, Stress Reactions, and Alterations of Physiology, thus Altering Brain/Body Chemistry (psychosomatic/linguistic-somatic issues). As proposed by Cannon (1989, orig. 1915;1942), and as systematically researched by Selye (1956), distress without resolution or action can lead to illness--from depression to physical manifestations, for example, peptic ulcers, arthritis, and, as the immune system is more thoroughly depressed, cancer as well (see Kaplan 1989 and Oken 1989 for an overview of the history and theories connected to this concept in Western medicine; also see Eden 1990 for a discussion of stress and the long-term effects as manifested in "strain"). As Oken (1989:1160) states, psychosomatic medicine is not a field in itself, but "cuts across all medical specialties and their basic sciences." A broken ankle, for example, painful in itself, can lead to fear, which can accentuate the pain, and so forth.

In Category E, however, my interest is in how the individual interprets information from the environment (e.g., a message from a relative, being laid off from work, an expression of envy); the accompanying stress reactions and resulting illness, be this depression, anxiety, an upset stomach, a headache, extreme fatigue, or the like; and interpretation of that illness. Adding to Oken's statement, this category can cut across all the other categories above.

Most illness is self-limiting; headaches, stomachaches, sprains, cuts, and many other more serious conditions simply go away in time (Magner 1992:10). Parasitic or bacterial/viral invasion may not (especially if there are poor nutrition and digestive problems); broken limbs need to be set; a projectile wound will need to be dressed, or infection may set in. But, again, most physical complaints will simply heal by themselves. However, when someone is ill with a headache, stomachache, diarrhea, a sprained ankle, or the like, the world stops; disorder or another order (chaos) has descended upon the individual and, in most cases, the group. Steps must be taken to eliminate the illness. For this to occur, some explanation of cause must be determined, and appropriate steps, any steps, must be taken to bring back order. These appropriate steps lead to stress reduction through hope and group involvement (reintegration), less depression of the immune system, and thus accentuate "healing."

Considering Category E from another direction, the vast majority of individual and group stress reactions leading to illness problems, and/or behavioral problems in Western medicine, are the product of the learning of rules, associated internalization of negative bits and development of High Risk Messages, looping on HRMs, consequent stress, and utilization of the five universal mechanisms (mentioned earlier) in an attempt to reduce stress. In Western culture, these include the eating disorders (a process of emotional conversion), anxiety and phobic disorders (freezing up), depression (withdrawal), personality and sexual disorders (encompassing parts of all five), gender-identity problems (withdrawal), attention deficits (can include withdrawal and metaphorical verbal fighting in order to get attention), and oppositional defiant disorder (verbal fighting to get attention), essentially many of the conditions outlined in the *DSM-IV*. Not all of these conditions are going to show up in all cultures, the reason being stereotypical responses to stress within a specific culture (see Appendix I, *DSM-IV*).

Reviewing Category E, we learn rules and who we are in the group (enculturation). As this process is occurring, we are acquiring a history, rule-setting tools and a style of tool use (which serve as expressions of our personality), and a cluster of HRMs. We also learn the rules of nutrition, health habits and life style, and illness causes and associated behavioral manifestations. It is, in my opinion, the looping on these HRMs, as the individual is confronted with negative bits that tap into HRMs, and the resulting stress that lead to a large portion of the abnormal behaviors, syndromes, illnesses, and so on, that cultures then attempt to cure in their own unique ways. All curing is designed to reestablish "sociostasis" and consequent homeostasis. Curing is accomplished through a reinterpretation or retranslation of life events and individual HRMs. This interpretation or reinterpretation occurs within a ritual setting (i.e., hospital, physician's office, shaman's tent, etc.), complete with props and appropriate behaviors and responses to behaviors. The most effective procedure, then, is the one that can accomplish this reinterpretation. Reinterpretation is possible because of the way our brains apparently store information and remember events. As Ornstein (1991:180-191) states, we generalize, delete, and distort information and essentially make up our memory as we go along. We live within a socially accepted hallucination most of the time. When we diverge from that socially accepted hallucination, we are then labeled as having a syndrome and in need of therapy. But, because memory is made up as we go along, what we believe to be true is always subject to reinterpretation. With the right input under the right conditions, we reinterpret our worlds, the events that occur in our life-space. As a generalization, our nervous systems desire, for the most part, to maintain low stress. Looping on HRMs, although leading to higher and higher stress, is designed to go over a problem in order to solve it. Because the brain/mind desires lower stress, a door is constantly open for reinterpretation of life events. If our brain/mind was not constructed in this fashion, we would all be socially dysfunctional, and society, if it could exist, would be very different.

Category F--The "Evil" Moral Model. People engage in anti-social acts because they are born evil or are under the evil influence of "others." People get sick because of karma, or something they have done in the past (even in a past life). Illness occurs because of inappropriate (purposeful and/or inadvertent) social behavior, that is, not paying attention to ancestor spirits, curses or spells evolving out of social antagonisms or vindictiveness; capricious spirit attack; and the like.

The "bad seed" concept of aggression and associated antisocial behavior goes back to Biblical times (at least--see Luke 6:45). More modern concepts involve the 47-XYY syndrome which relates to a chromosome abnormality (this has been shown to be inconclusive--see McGuire and Troisi 1989:277), and other genetic anomalies, including Sanfilippo syndrome, Spielmeyer-Vogt syndrome, and PKU (phenylketonuria), all of which, at least in terms of Western biomedicine, would fit into Categories B, C, and D.

In reference to my research in Toronto, Canada (Rush 1974, 1994), in the Italian epistemology, a person will be bad or evil if born on Christmas Eve; a male becomes a werewolf (*lupo mannaro* or *pumpannaro*) and a female becomes a witch *(strega)* (see Rush 1974:34). What is of interest here is that March and April tend to be "dry" months sexually, and this is likewise when there are many somatic complaints by females; interpretations of possible social misconduct, usually on the part of males; and accusations of the evil eye, spells, and activities by witches.

Other cultures likewise perceive an inheritance of evil behavior. Evans-Pritchard (1937:21), for example, was one of the first to suggest that witchcraft was an inherited set of antisocial behaviors. This category extends beyond simple inheritance to include illness as a product of the evil of others, vindictive spirits or others within one's social group. The Devil's influence, a part of Christian theology, is taken quite literally by many Christian sects.

REVIEW

Separating the social/language aspects of illness and disease from the physical aspects is problematical at best. Western biomedicine, right or wrong, makes this distinction more clearly than many cultures. From my point of view, most emotional problems and culturally expressed illness behavior can be seen as a direct product of (or, in some cases, exacerbated by) learning rules of social behavior and consequently learning about self in society, that is, one's group worth and life style, which includes use of alcohol and other drugs, contact with environmental toxins, nutrition/health habits leading to cellular toxicosis and decreased immune functioning, and, at least in North America, norms (selfishness, brutality, a weakening of sexual restrictions, etc.) projected by a very irresponsible small group of people (Miller's number again) who run the mass media (including motion pictures, television programming, and news reporting). Normative attitudes as studied in other cultures--that is, male-female relations (see Finkler 1994a, 1994b), government brutality, and so on--can likewise enhance overall stress. All of the above factors are initiated in the family of origin. Emotional problems, and consequently many physical problems (but certainly not all),[12] are the result of the individual's looping on HRMs in an attempt to reinterpret them, exit, and reduce stress. As the individual interprets messages in the environment (or already-in-place, internally generated material) as personally threatening (emotionally and physically), looping intensifies, stress increases, and socially stereotypical reactions, designed to reduce stress, are engaged. Others in the group are called upon to interpret these behaviors. In our society, the interpretations might be depression or manic-depressive psychosis, but, in other societies, the diagnosis might be witchcraft, evil eye, object intrusion, malevolent spirit attack, and the like.

Further, under stress, the immune system is taxed as specific nutrients (zinc, for example) are expended, reducing one's ability to fight off bacterial or viral infections. Bacterial infections likewise make demands on the immune system, robbing the body of needed nutrients and thus contributing to feelings of malaise. Such emotional stress further depresses the immune system: an endless circle. Add to this the nutritional habits (see Chapter 4) and other socio-economic issues, and this rounds out the picture of ill health. The vast majority of illnesses are self-limiting; curing rituals represent forms of action that lead to emotional and social comfort, lowered stress, and more rapid healing. Even in the case of parasitic attack, which may not be self-limiting, many cultures have developed herbal remedies (Etkin 1986; Mowrey 1986: 229-232), dietary habits (Johns 1990), or toiletry procedures (see David and Tapp 1993:137-138 for a discussion of procedures for removing Guinea worms) to limit the more devastating side effects.

The human organism, like a rat, mouse, or cockroach, over a period of time comes to be relatively well suited to or in balance with its environment at a specific time. Balance is altered when the information structure surrounding the group is altered past some limit; we move toward chaos. All of a sudden certain illnesses (symptoms of this information alteration) begin to take their toll. Western biomedicine looks for a cure by first diagnosing the physical symptoms and then finding a method of removing them. For example, someone has breast cancer, so we attempt to kill the cancer cells with chemicals or radiation or to excise the tumor. At another level, Western biomedicine searches for the illusive cancer gene, ignoring (or only paying lip service to) intrusive information from environmental factors (carcinogenic chemicals, electromagnetic radiation) and cultural life style (poor nutrition, alcohol and other drug abuse, lack of exercise). In other medical systems (the traditional Chinese, the Naturopathic physicians in practice in North America), the general diagnosis is imbalance, with the attention and techniques devoted to cause and prevention or to move toward some conception of cultural or physical balance, in an attempt to avoid such radical measures. This is not to say that other medical systems are better than Western biomedicine, but, certainly, Western biomedicine has diverged from the concept of balance. In doing so, Western biomedicine has taken illness out of its social/ environmental context, and, with the paradigm of scientific method, distorted cause and effect relationships.

Humans are a relatively new species, and, certainly, living in urban, industrialized complexes is newer still. We simply do not understand the consequences (physiologically, psychologically, and sociologically) of living with plastics, hydrocarbons, processed foods, and electromagnetic fields, among other factors (Raloff 1993:10-13). This is all information input; it will have some sort of effect. This is not a tentative thing; it is a fact. Disease and illness are issues of diverse information processing and how this information affects physiology and behavior.

AN INFORMATION MODEL OF CAUSE AND EFFECT

Stepping outside of the Western biomedical model, and integrating the concepts presented thus far, all illness,[13] physical and/or emotional, can be placed under the headings of Information Intrusion (the vast majority of injuries and illnesses fall under this category), Information Loss, Insufficient Information, Inherited Information, Information Alteration, Disguised Information, and Information Imbalance. Although many cultures can incorporate all or most of the above, I will discuss each of these categories separately, giving specific cultural examples. Some of these categories overlap in that cause may be expressed, for example, as information intrusion resulting in information imbalance or information loss. The usefulness of establishing such categories will be discussed at the conclusion.

Information Intrusion

As mentioned, this is the largest category by far of casual factors leading to illness and disease, with the subcategories of this broken down as follows:

A) Negative Bits
  1) Rule Setting
  2) Breach of Taboos
  3) Other Social Sanctions
B) Curses/Spells
C) Malicious Spirits
D) Bacteria/Viruses/Parasites/Dirt
E) Aggression, Utilizing Arrows, Bullets, etc.
F) Broken Bones, Natural Accidents, etc.
G) Alcohol, Other Drugs
H) Too Much Information or Information Overload (Including Obesity with Physical and Social Consequences, Mental Information Processing Overload, Ultraviolet Radiation, Heavy Metals, etc.)
I) Contact with Others or "Them" (Strangers Who Are Not "Us")

Using the Khanty (Balzer 1987:1090) of Siberia as a example, information intrusion is represented by evil spirits, curses, or malicious foreign objects causing injury, or by "too much contact with Russians" (strangers) leading to syphilis or smallpox and breach of taboos. The reason that I include breech of taboos under information intrusion is that these are community taboos existing in the culture and transmitted to the individual as he or she matures. The memory of these taboos, and their breach, intrude on the individual and thus causes the discomfort. In Western culture, we call this guilt. The Khanty also recognize natural accidents, that is, falls causing broken bones, soreness, and so on (1987:1090).

With respect to spirit healer-mediums in Brazil (Greenfield 1987: 1102), information intrusion, in the form of "perturbations," are caused by different levels (from low to high) of spiritual influences. First-order influence can cause "mild depression, inhibition, fear, malaise, complexes, jealousy, sadness, irritability, nervousness, and domestic misunderstandings." The most serious "perturbations" result in "uncontrolled outbursts of crying, apathy, or extreme pain at the top and frontal regions of the head" (Greenfield 1987:1102).

Among Andean peasants (Bastien 1987:1113), "wind and cold cause diarrhea, called *wayran catjatha* (caught by the wind) and *thayanpasjatha* (caught by the cold). . . . In addition to these empirical factors, they often attribute diarrhea to *castigo* (punishment) by *Pachamama* (Mother Earth) for failing to feed the earth shrines, participate properly in the community, and to care for the animals. *Castigo* is associated with other diseases as well."

Among the Wana of Sulawesi (Atkinson 1987:343), "intrusive objects" cause illness as well as soul loss.

Indirect Information Intrusion

This category differs from the first only in interpretation of the why or purpose of illness, and explains why innocent people get ill. The Jalaris, who live on India's southeast coast (Nuckolls 1992), explain that spirit attack and the resulting illness of the client's family members, especially women and children, are caused by a refusal to make offerings to a specific goddess. The offense is usually lack of attention to a family goddess, who then makes her displeasure known by attacking the individual's immediate family members or someone in another family, thus using "shame" in order to initiate the appropriate ritual behaviors toward the offended goddess or toward living humans who are disrupting family relationships (Nuckolls 1992:86).

Loss of Information

Information loss is represented among the Khanty by "soul loss from ancestral or spirit theft" (Balzer 1987:1090).

In Glass-Coffin's (1992:38) study of a village in north coastal Peru, a person, "because of jealousy, envy, or revenge contacts a wizard (*brujo*) in order to intentionally hurt or kill the chosen victim." Envy, usually from close relatives, results in *dano* (1992:39). Methods used to cause *dano* involve information intrusion, that is, by drinking a potion containing the bones of the dead or by having the victim step on ground-up bones. *Dano* can also occur by speaking the person's name or through sympathetic magic (e.g., the use of the victim's clothing or nail parings). *Dano*, itself, is loss of health but, it can also be suspected in cases of "interpersonal difficulties such as marital infidelity, promiscuity, domestic violence, incest, stressful in-law relationships leading to conjugal separation, or adolescent-disobedience/ rebellion" (1992:38).

Similar to *dano* is *susto*, soul loss or "loss of the victim's vital substance" (Rubel et al. 1991:45) due to fright, witchcraft, and spirits (Atkinson 1987:343; Dentan 1988:859). Other explanations offered by Rubel et al. include role stress and organic disease (1991:13), hypoglycemia (1991:8), and, depending upon whether you see certain psychiatric terms as having an organic/genetic base or a social stress base, schizophrenia (1991:9).

Among the Bororo of central Brazil (Crocker 1985:42), connected to information loss is the concept of *raka*, or "blood."

Raka can be diminished in a host of ways so numerous that the Bororo catalog them in terms of their effects rather than their causes. That is, sickness, the infirmities of age, and death itself are attributed *ipso facto* to the temporary or permanent loss of *raka.* . . . Each person is born with a certain finite capacity for the development of *raka*, determined generally by the relative and absolute amounts possessed by the parents during conception and the early months of life. One of the few unquestioned elements in the Bororo *raka* dogma is that every individual must expend his or her limited stock of *raka* after adolescence: in copulation, in physical labor, in dancing and singing.

In our own culture, loss of blood, through bleeding ulcers, wounds, hemophilia, and so on (with hemophilia also fitting under the heading *Inherited Information* due to genetic errors), represents loss of vital information. Such loss can lead to anemia, hypovolumic shock, and death. [Also see Skultans's (1988:142) discussion of menstruation in South Wales and Harner's (1984:149) mention of blood loss being equal to soul loss among the Jivaro].

In a colloquial sense, we speak of "losing one's mind," to be, "out there," "with only one oar in the water," "not playing with a full deck," "not having it together," "the lights are on, but no one is home," and so on. We likewise experience an information loss when a loved one dies or during divorce, especially if you are the one who is left or abandoned. Critical-incident stress and post-traumatic stress also represent loss of information, either directly by seeing a loved one die, especially violently, or indirectly or symbolically. This would be the case when a paramedic or police officer goes to an accident scene and sees, for example, a dead child that the officer can symbolically identify with personally or with his/her own child. Oftentimes those diagnosed as schizophrenic with flat affect are in trauma; to protect themselves, they enter a trance state, that is, flat affect.

Insufficient Information

This can be represented by nutritional deficiencies brought about by famine, eating habits that involve deficient nutritional elements (the fractionated processed food as encountered in much of North American) and the like.

Lack of oxygen would also fit into this category. Insufficient love or nurturing has been implicated in psychopathology in our culture. Insufficient touching can lead to emotional and social problems and even death. I have heard over the years an anecdotal reference to an experiment "many years ago" wherein, while attempting to determine what language infants would develop if they were not spoken to, they were not held/touched to any significant degree. Result: The infants died. In order to become social animals, we need to have our senses (sight, hearing, touch, taste, smell) engaged socially. Being touched is as important as being spoken to or looked at, and maybe more so, depending on one's personal needs.

The Ingestive Rites, among the Sambia of New Guinea, as discussed by Herdt (1987:227-239), are performed to add what is lacking in order to make males masculine.

It is urgent for boys to ingest semen to "grow big." Unless they do so, their bodies will stay "small" and ugly. "A boy who doesn't drink semen still has a *kwulai'u* skin," Tali said. And here is Juvu, talking about the functions of fellatio as he was taught them, and as he teaches them now that he is an elder.

> If you boys don't drink semen, you'll stay in the fire [metaphor for vagina]. You won't grow big. Your nose will be completely black; you'll die quickly. Black ashes on your nose will completely cover your face. If you don't drink semen, your penis will stand up and bump your own chest. When I first heard this talk [at *moku* initiation], I was very scared . . . That very night I went and did it [fellatio].

Inherited Information

In Western culture, inherited information is most clearly expressed in genetics, with some inherited characteristics leading to disease states (Devor 1993; Kosek 1990; Bloom 1989). In other cultures, there are inherited tendencies toward being a witch (Evans-Pritchard 1937; Mair 1969; Rush 1974). Perceived outsiders often are considered to be genetically inferior, for example, the racial attitudes that prevail in the United States, Africa, and Australia. In Japan, temperaments can come about by being born on inauspicious occasions (Ohnuki-Tierney 1984:71). Illness can be inherited by being born with a particular "constitution" (1984:54-55) and can likewise be inherited from a past life (1984:68). Inherited information, in some respects, could be lumped together with too little as well as too much information or altered information leading to metabolic problems, too much or too little of a specific neurochemical, and so.

Information Alteration

In years past, bleeding was considered a therapeutic measure for getting rid of altered or "bad" blood in Western culture. Currently, we bleed people in order to run tests on blood to see if there are alterations from the norm, with alterations signaling infection, metabolic or nutritional problems, and so on. Also, from a current Western biomedical perspective, information alteration can occur at the genetic level, leading to mutations. Not all mutations are lethal; many have no effect at all. Crossovers would also represent information alteration. In a general sense, the breach of any taboo alters a system, requiring ritual behaviors. In Catholic ideology, for example, a sin alters the social-spiritual balance and requires confession and penance. Generally speaking, illness perhaps could be defined as a symptom of individual and social system alteration.

Disguised Information

Within the Western biomedical tradition, and popularized by Freud, is the belief in the subconscious, which, according to Freud and others, tends to disguise information in order to protect the conscious mind. Such disguised elements represent themselves in dreams as well as symbolic association, leading to behavior in which the individual may engage and yet not understand the why? or purpose. Psychosomatic illness appears to be precipitated by unconscious thoughts, emotional conversion, and a targeting of organs often represented through metaphors, (e.g., "I can't stomach it anymore") which can lead to ulcers or other gastrointestinal problems (Ohnuki-Tierney 1984:57-60).

As Atkinson (1987:346) points out for the Wana, enlisting the spirits' aid in curing can involve, during the *mabolong* or "drumming "ceremony, dealing with disguised information in the form of riddles. In a general sense, and as represented in many societies, illness caused by spirits, because of spirit neglect, for example, can be seen as disguised or indirect. There is never a direct correlation between the illness and the spirits or witches; this cause and effect has to be sought through divination. This is also similar to the psychological and personality testing (MMPI, Rorschach, etc.) done in Western society. Of course, in Western society, most psychologists and psychiatrists (and the courts as well) see such testing as scientific and not as the divination procedures that they truly are.

Information Imbalance

In Western culture, we make reference to people being mentally unbalanced or unstable, meaning that it is difficult to predict behavior. In terms of illness, the concept of balance is widespread (Myerhoff 1976; Ohnuki-Tierney 1884; Crocker 1985; Sheikh and Sheikh 1989; Beinfield and Korngold 1991; Scudder 1994, orig. 1874). Bolivian peasants, for example (Bastien 1987:1113), refer to imbalances *(aika)* as "caused by change in food, lodging, and climate." From a general perspective, illness represents danger not just for the individual, but for the culture as well. Shamans, as well as Western medical personnel, are attempting to bring the individual into some balance. At the same time, balance relates to a larger metaphor, that is, social balance. When an individual is ill, regardless of the cause, that individual can no longer participate in normal, everyday behaviors. This has an effect on everyone. As Myerhoff (1976:100) states:

And in carrying out his cures, he accomplishes social equilibrium as well as establishing balance between the individual and his group, by reweaving the social texture that has been ruptured by illness and frequently by some violation of group norms that causes the sickened individual to be seen and treated as a deviant.

The Shaman, then, is recovering and reestablishing equilibrium in many ways at the same time. As a connecting figure, he is at once the restorer of balance and the symbol of the possibility of balance. In his cosmic undertakings, his personal destiny mirrors his profession, and the microcosm and macrocosm are reunited by his activities.

Keep in mind that this concept of balance keeps showing up in mythology (often in the duality principle) and in medical systems around the world, and this cannot simply be a coincidence. A sense of, and action toward, balance is necessary for individual and social health.

All of the above informational categories have to occur within a social context.[14] This context can be understood from within any and all of the social institutions of a specific culture. However, in order to facilitate illness description, and, at the same time, using the information categories above, the concept of rules, roles, and cooperation will serve as a stepping-off point for a more detailed look at illness in Chapter 4.

IMPLIED RULES AND THE EVOLUTION OF COOPERATION

In Chapter 1, the concept of implied rules was introduced. This is a very important concept that helps to explain how social animals create social bonds that last generation after generation without having to resort to a strict genetic model of cause and effect (see Oyama 1989). It also explains how individuals and cultures develop stereotypical expressions of illness. Before elaborating on this, it is important to come to terms with what might appear to be the arbitrary and mysterious nature of human complexity. Ross (1987:7-8) states:

If, as some have suggested (see Sahlins 1976:171), contemporary cultural patterns are, in the end, the arbitrary or random variants of mysterious structures in the human mind, then change too must be arbitrary, and the avenues by which certain definite desired ends might be achieved are beyond effective reach. . . . An anthropology that, by one methodological device or another, reduces such features of any social system to arbitrary reflections of the human mind only entraps itself in a self-indulgent relativism that precludes all likelihood of raising a coherent critical voice.

Although Ross's statement has as a reference point dietary patterns, his statement is important to human behavior in general, to our understanding of how things happen. Although the content of many behaviors that led to existing behavioral and system sets may never be known, it is possible to understand processes that generate the content. What may seem arbitrary and mysterious becomes less so when processes can be revealed. Certainly, there are genetic push factors that are of equal importance,[15] but they do not account for the complexity noted in human societies, wolf packs, and so on. Moreover, because there is a problem of determining when human language, with its phonemes, morphemes, and syntax, first arose, we need to explain the grouping behaviors of our protoancestors without pointing exclusively to a genetic model.

First, let us examine the idea of a written or verbal contract in our society. In order for such contracts to exist, one must presuppose a verbal and written language. In societies where there is a great deal of anonymity, where relationships are fleeting and with little or no duration, the emotional glue, the personalized social-control mechanisms between certain levels of organization are absent. Making contracts explicit between individuals and/or between individuals and groups or institutions, such as banks, that are not related to you through kinship, proximity, and duration, becomes a necessity, or large social conglomerates cannot exist. Individuals would optimize their gain, and perpetual conflict would ensue. John Von Neumann's Game Theory becomes a useful model in this regard (Poundstone 1992). The system would break down into smaller and smaller, more personalized or tribalized units. But, even in urbanized society, most contracts are verbal and between individuals known to one another through kinship, proximity, or duration. In highly mobile societies like our own, existing proximity and duration can become non-existent overnight leading to a great deal of conflict over perceived rights and obligations. Written contracts between even close relatives are always advised, but usually such agreements are not formally written up because of the message of distrust that accompanies such a demand. This in itself could terminate the relationship.

One of the most important elements that allowed city-states to develop in Mesopotamia, for example, was the ability to establish contracts between those in power and the rest of the people. This idea of contracts between one level of society and another probably had its early beginnings in the sacred relationships established between bands and supernatural agencies, or animal spirits. As time went on, contracts were often instituted through force or fear of force, but originally stemmed from ritual contracts between humans and the natural forces that were assumed to control their lives. I agree with others who suggest that this contractual idea is what lies behind some of the cave paintings found in France and Spain. By placing a representation of the animal on a wall in the deep recesses of the earth, the individual contracts to keep that animal safe and ensures that its numbers will increase; that is, "You keep me safe and secure by providing me with food, and we will keep you safe by entombing your essence or spirit, by making sure your image does not fade from our memory, and that your numbers multiply" (Campbell 1969: 282-312; Bahn and Vertut 1988:149-190).

It is my contention that this idea of an explicit contract, however, emerged from these consciously instituted agreements between humans and natural or supernatural forces and through the awareness of *implied* contracts that develop between individuals. Because they serve a purpose (have survival value), implied rules are continued and handed down from generation to generation as a model of appropriate behavior. Implied rules are very powerful things because they are taken for granted, just like the moon, the sun, and the changes in weather patterns. They have always been and will always be. Such rules are instituted by actions and reactions; they do not necessitate language or complicated symbolizing. All that is required is that someone do something and others allow (or not allow) the action. The action is then repeated, and then it becomes expected; an implied rule emerges. Grooming behavior can stand as an example. A parent grooms a child, and the child allows this. The parent does it again, and the child expects it. Combine this with any secondary health benefit (e.g., getting rid of disease bearing parasites) and you increase the likelihood that the behavior will remain. As the behaviorists have shown, it does not take a great deal of time to condition actions and reactions. Such behaviors become implied rules that orchestrate social organization. The levels of rule development can be found in Figure 3.3.

Implied rules are at the bottom of the list and are the template out of which the rest evolved. Implied rules, what might be termed testing behavior, however, are ever present between individuals and groups who have to interact on a daily basis. The longer the perceived duration in the relationship(s) is, the more power implied rules have in terms of maintaining relationships in automatic behavioral sequences. We can clearly see this in our society with respect to family relationships. Even when divorced, many couples tend to continue to interact, using the rules that led, in part, to the breakup in the first place. The court systems are kept quite busy trying to filter through the lying, backbiting, and petty grumbling over child custody, all of which is simply a continuation of the implied rules of verbal (and sometimes physical) combat the couple used throughout the marriage.[16] Once such rules and negative behavioral sequences are uncovered and presented, for example, to the courts

Figure 3.3
Levels of Rule Development

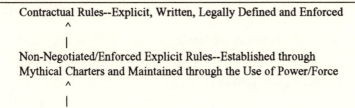

Contractual Rules--Explicit, Written, Legally Defined and Enforced
∧
|
Non-Negotiated/Enforced Explicit Rules--Established through
Mythical Charters and Maintained through the Use of Power/Force
∧
|

Social/Natural/Supernatural Explicit Rules/Contracts--Enforced through
Ritual, Myth and "Religion"
∧
|
Implied Rules--Evolved from the "Doing and Allowing (or Not Allowing)"
Social Interaction Patterns That Serve to Order Behavior and Relationships
and Reduce Stress

during child-custody and visitation evaluations, the couple can less easily engage the old rules. This stops a great deal of litigation, which is good for the couple and especially the children.

As illustrated in Figure 3.4, implied rules likewise condition illness symptoms--we *learn* how to express our pain, our illness, which then triggers more explicit social action patterns (family interaction, work, curing patterns, etc.). There is, therefore, a feedback between the implied and the explicit rules, again, with more explicit action patterns (rituals) coming into play to restore health (individual and social balance).

Illness can be conceptualized as a break in the rules (both implied and explicit) at both the genetic and, by analogy, the social levels. Bacteria (e.g., *E. coli*) entering the bloodstream interrupt the rules of homeostasis and force other rules into play, including death. A breach of a taboo brings into play explicit rules/procedures for mending the breach, and so on.

ROLES AND THE DEVELOPMENT OF STATUS

As anthropologists have suggested for years, early human groups did not have the numerous and complicated roles and statuses that are found in tribal organizations and nation-states. The reason for this is simply necessity. As Fried (1967) points out, in band-type organizations, there are as many statuses as there are group members to fill them. In nation-states, there are few available statuses, yet many people desiring to fill them. Moreover, specialization breeds statuses, with specialization being limited in pretribal groupings.

Figure 3.4
Implied Rules Triggering Explicit Social Action Patterns

    A) Implied Rules--Actions and Reactions are Automatic and expected
         1) Social Relations
         2) Relationship to Spirits

           |
           v

    B) Illness equals Imbalance

           |
           v

    C) Explicit Rules or Procedures for
    Rebalancing System ------------- > System returns to A, or alters to A^1, A^2,
    etc., If System Is Modified in the Rebalancing Process--Illness and Crises
    Open the Door to Change

Let us start with roles available in a band-type organization. There are four general roles available: child, male, female, and adult or elder. Certainly, we could make subcategories of these, but, in reality, a group would not split roles unless it served some useful purpose. Keep in mind that our early ancestors did not sit down and plan their societies (neither do we, although we suffer from the illusion that we do; behaviors generate unforeseen consequences and/or possibilities around which we have to generate other behaviors). What purpose do roles serve? Perceived roles represent markers for indicating, in a general way, a pattern of interaction and expectations for behavior. Although we, in Western culture, perceive ourselves as individuals, we are actually parts of groups; the human brain was designed to operate not on its own, but, instead, in a tandem fashion with other brains. Roles serve the purpose of aiding initial interaction, of superchunking general patterns of expected behavior, so that each time we are in contact it is not necessary to define who we are and what we are doing. It really makes little difference how we define each other and the expectations we attach to these roles. Without roles, everyone would be, in a sense, a stranger. Cooperation is best served if general expectations about behavior are predefined. This is accomplished through the concept of roles.

Kinship terminology is an extension--a splitting and refining, if you will--of the four basic roles mentioned above, that is, child, male, female, young, old, and, of course, who a specific individual (or group) is relative to you. The kinship terminology of any culture represents a cluster of symbols that allow interaction in stereotyped fashion; this creates an efficiency of interaction because the actors are not, at all times, attempting to define who they are and associated behavioral sets. When people learn the rules for doing and not doing, from parents and significant others (including the media in our society), they likewise learn roles and statuses. This is anything but a new revelation

(Durkheim 1933; Fortes 1969; Nadel 1957). The importance here is to remind the psychological and psychiatric/medical communities of the importance of roles in ordering relationships and defining interaction. The individual, and illness manifestation, cannot be understood outside of a socially defined context, and much of that definition comes by way of linguistic terms and the consequent interaction of people.

Kinship terms, or rather the behavioral expression of such terms, are often not explicitly stated. Instead, the child *observes* what people do, *overhears* verbal communication patterns, and then *models* the behavior. In our culture at least, the terms *mother, father, parent, husband, wife* are not explicitly defined. The individual learns a rendition in his or her family of origin. This is accompanied by observing/listening to the interaction patterns of the parents of friends, and, of course, the mass media leave an imprint. This is contrasted with, for example, family dynamics in Saudi Arabia, where there is great consistency from family to family in the behaviors associated with these roles. Althen (1988:87) refers to such consistency as either "high context" or "low context."

In traditional or "high context" societies, such as Arab ones, it is relatively easy to describe the patterns in male-female relationships. People in the society have agreed-upon ways in which young males and females can be together--or cannot be together, as the case may be. There are agreed-upon ideas about premarital sexual relations, appropriate wedding ceremonies, and proper behavior for husbands and for wives. Everyone knows what it means to be a good husband and a good wife.

With respect to male-female relationships, American society is exceedingly low context. Almost nothing is agreed upon; everyone's list of characteristics of a good wife or husband is different. The range of behaviors is remarkable.

Althen's observations of American society were not always the case, or at least to the extreme degree noted today. However, role confusion tends to be one of the diagnostic features of a sick or dysfunctional family in America. Social roles that are low context lead to confusion of behavior or expected behavior. A great deal of delinquency evolves out of this confusion, the searching for identity, recognition, or power. And, although we encapsulate these issues within psychological terms like personal identity and self-worth, these are social relationship issues. We talk about them, but there is no clear therapy for dealing with these issues. When we evaluate individuals engaged in delinquent/criminal behavior, we tend to evaluate the individual rather than the family, gang, or significant others with whom the individual interacts. If we treated people as parts of groups rather than individuals with drug problems and other behavioral concerns, our criminal justice system would be much different in terms of dealing with social units and sentencing.[17]

Using another, related example, individuals enter into marriage, after dating and playing the roles of friends and lovers (roles that *are* more clearly defined), and then assume the roles of husband and wife without, in most cases, a clear idea of the behaviors expected or desired. The result of this is role confusion. For example, prior to the marriage, the male was a "silver-tongued fox," using talking, discussing, and listening, behaviors that will help lead to his main goal, that is, sex. It is not uncommon, however, after marriage, for the husband to develop amnesia for speech. Why? The answer in most cases is role confusion wherein the husband, in searching for a set of behaviors to "play out" the role, takes on the characteristics of his father, who, perhaps, spoke very little in his role as husband. I will return this issue in Chapter 5.

Illness roles have behavioral sets, and they define who is sick and who will cure. Moreover, in many cases (but certainly not all), it is *not* up to the sick person to determine when he or she is sick or well; this is determined by the curer and only after certain rituals are completed.[18] The roles of "sick" and "curer," or "caretaker," are so polarized in the Western biomedical complex that an individual cannot be admitted to a hospital unless he or she is sick as determined by a medical doctor. In fact, once in the hospital, if a person acts too well, the nurses do not have a procedure for interacting other than to wheel him or her *out* of the hospital.

Now, all of this may seem like "So what!" type stuff that everyone knows. The point is that all of these behaviors (i.e., husband, wife, parent, sick, well, curer, etc.) evolve out of socially constructed symbols that are more auto-matically engaged than one might expect until you "jump out of the fish bowl" and take a closer look at things. Roles, as well as rules and HRMs, tend, in large measure, to define the social side of what I have been calling illness. Moreover, acquiring information regarding HRMs (and the informational categories they represent), rule setting, and role relationships, in my opinion, is a necessary element for diagnosing illness and disease as well as the overall communication problems that evolve in social living. Stress reactions enter into all three, as we will see, with stress reactions leading toward behavioral problems and individual and social disequilibrium, that is, illness. With this said, let us turn to specific examples of diagnosis and curing.

NOTES

1. See Ridley (1993) for a very interesting discussion of sex/reproduction as the predisposing factor of human nature.

2. Culture is not what the early cultural anthropologists (e.g., Boas, Mead, Kroeber) thought it to be. It is not simply a superorganic, something existing above and separate from the individual. Culture, again, is a product of genetics, but potentially capable of altering itself; culture is a meta-genetic system, a system within a system. The ultimate form of adaptation would be a genetic process that produced a feedback mechanism with itself via a mirror of itself (i.e., culture) so that it could learn enough about how it self-organizes within the environment in order to alter itself almost instantly, through genetic engineering, when necessary. Seen in this light, culture may

have its own agenda, and that agenda may be to ultimately serve genetics and break the slavery to the environment and mutations. This would allow adaptation to any contingency, that is, utilization of different food sources, space travel, life on other worlds, and so on.

3. It is possible, through specific language use, to reject behavior without necessarily rejecting the individual proper; "I think that you are a wonderful person, and that behavior is inappropriate." Because the meaning of a message is determined by the receiver, the receiver, in this case, might not make the separation in his or her mind.

4. Getting "growled at" for not taking out the garbage has little to do with physical survival.

5. When I say "negative," I do not mean that the message was bad or inappropriate. A negative manner means that an act or behavior is disaffirmed, not that the process of being negative is bad in itself.

6. Guilt is a Western term and is often considered a socially generated phenomenon in individualistic cultures, while shame is more commonly used in collectivistic cultures. As there is some question regarding the use of these terms, as if they existed on a continuum (Ho 1993), my interest involves the sociological expression of whatever these psychological terms imply.

7. The psychiatrist in Western biomedicine prescribes numerous and powerful mind-altering drugs for what are considered individual-centered emotional problems, which creates the illusion of bringing the individual back into balance and reintegration with society. Because we live in a society that expects instant results, little attention is paid to diet and/or a reinterpretation of life events. In fact, these drugs target symptoms that are expressions of underlying issues, symptoms that represent an adaptive response to problems in social living, metabolic problems evolving out of diet and malnutrition (macro- and micronutrition), and so on. The question, "What purpose do these symptoms serve for the individual (and possibly society)?" is rarely asked. I speculate that some of these symptoms are strange attractors which are actually pushing the individual toward some resolution, a resolution that is impossible once the symptoms are masked or suppressed with drugs. No one in the medical community would ever suggest simply suppressing the pain of a fractured leg without, at the same time, setting the fracture. If you had a toothache, and if the dentist, as a curing procedure, simply prescribed Novocain shots twice a day, this would be considered ludicrous.

8. Ohnuki-Tierney (1984:57-60) states that there are many expressions in Japanese that relate to the abdomen (*hara*); that is, "*hara go tatsu*: the abdomen stands up (get mad), *hara o iyasu*: to heal the abdomen (to wreak one's anger on someone)," and so on (1984:58). It is interesting that "stomach cancer is the most common form of cancer among men and women" (1984:57) in Japan. On the other hand, in the United States, heart attacks are a predominant killer. "As noted earlier, the stomach in Japan is symbolically the equivalent of the brain and the heart in the United States" (1984:60).

As another example, Finkler (1994b:123) suggests that Mexican women experience "[p]ain in the ovaries," which is "a 'typical symptom' women present in reference to generalized issues related to sexuality and motherhood."

9. Labeling, as Goffman (1963) points out, is potentially stigmatizing and, at the same time, self-fulfilling. Less loaded terms like High Risk Messages, although not as

colorful, offer a diagnostic process that is less likely to be stigmatizing and, at the same time, leads to a procedure of allowing the body and mind to heal.

10. Iatrogenic disorders (metabolic problems caused by medical procedures and prescribed drugs), such as tardive dyskinesia and Parkinson's disease, are evidence of this chaos. Many thousands of people are metabolically injured each year through the use of not only drugs prescribed by psychiatrists, but also prescription drugs in general. What is also of interest is that the news media quickly reported (in June 1994) metabolic problems experienced by *one* individual and caused by inappropriate or overuse of chaparral (*Larrea tridentata*), and (October 1995) warnings about vitamin A use during pregnancy, but there is little mention of the ongoing, everyday metabolic damage to *thousands* of people caused by the prescribed (not abused or overused) drugs of Western biomedicine (see footnote 19, Chapter 4).

11. See Mowrey's (1986) review of the literature regarding the validity of herbs as well as Morton's (1977) consideration of medicinal plants still in use. Also see Kinghorn and Balandrin (1993); Steiner (1985). Although the efficacy of many herbs is well documented, that of other herbs and components is not. [See Naeser's (1992) overview of Chinese herbal patent medicines, some of which contain "Os Draconis," "Os Tigris," "Snake Bile," and the like, which represent powerful symbols, but would not necessarily be considered effective within Western biomedicine. Also see Magner (1992:48) for a discussion of Chinese "dragon bones."]. Also, the herbal remedy might be ingested not by the patient, but by the medicine man instead. With respect to antibiotics, Thorwald (1963:84-85), in reference to Egyptian medicine, states:

However, we may shed some of our respect when we come upon prescriptions calling for the following ingredients: fly droppings, pelican droppings, human urine, lizard excrement, a child's faeces, a gazelle's dung--and most frequently of all, the excrement of the crocodile. . . . Nevertheless, in the nineteenth century and the first half of the twentieth, they too fell under the heading of 'sewerage pharmacology.' . . . . When Dr. Benjamin M. Duggar, Professor of Plant Physiology at the University of Wisconsin, presented the world in 1948 with the new drug aureomycin, he certainly had no thought of the effect of his discovery upon our evaluation of ancient Egyptian medicine.

It turned out that aureomycin was highly effective in the treatment of trachoma. Aureomycin was the newest among the antibiotic 'wonder drugs.' It was extracted from a type of soil found particularly in the vicinity of cemeteries--and it was just one among some thirty thousand soil specimens Dugger and his colleagues had examined between 1944 and 1946. This soil produced fungi which had an annihilating an effect upon some disease bacteria as did moulds from which penicillin was derived.

Certain waste products that result from the metabolism of these moulds have an inhibiting effect on the growth of bacteria. Investigation soon showed that bacteria living in the human body release their excretory products into the faeces and urine, which therefore are rich in antibiotic substances.

According to Cohen (1989:44-45), food storage in emerging civilizations "may discourage transmission of some parasites" and "fungal or bacterial contamination of stored foods also may provide unexpected health benefits. Mold growing on stored foods can produce such antibiotics as tetracycline and penicillin as well as toxins; archaeologists are just beginning to realize that intentional fermentation, which may also produce antibiotics, is an ancient and widespread means of preservation.

12. I would have great difficulty convincing anyone that the influx of micro-organisms into the Americas had little to do with the sharp, rapid demise of native

people irrespective of purely psychological stress factors related to the presence of these European disease vectors. Physical violence was certainly another factor that led to population decline (McNeill 1989).

13. With respect to illness and disease I will refer to Obeyesekere's (1985: 135-136) distinction. "(M)alaria is the *disease* since it has an operationally identifiable etiology whether it is found among Yoruba or Sinhala, while the *illness* is the cultural conception surrounding the disease. In physical medicine the disease can be extracted from the illness, and this makes a great difference for control and treatment. In the realms of the so-called mental diseases, however, a different situation prevails. I doubt that the illness-disease distinction is applicable since the cultural conception of the disease is intrinsic to its character: it is both illness and disease at the same time. A determinate biological/genetic mechanism is absent in mental illness, or, if present, is accompanied and superlaid by social-psychological conditions that are products of human experience in different sociocultural settings. In this situation the manner in which so-called symptoms are put together and given cultural meaning or symbolization is intrinsic to their nature as illness/disease. The *conception* of the disease (i.e., illness) *is* the disease. Or to put it differently, there are only illnesses and no diseases."

We might likewise say that illness is the experience (individual and/or social), and the disease is the name assigned to this experience. Both disease and illness are holistic concepts, but moving in different directions. That is to say, the illness is an unpacking or description of the experience using both language and nonverbal symbols, while disease, through the process of diagnosis, is the compressing of these symbols into some culturally derived terminology. Also see Mascie-Taylor (1995:1-2).

14. The Western biomedical establishment might take exception to this by saying that bubonic plague is socially neutral. However, all viruses and bacteria are altered or alter their hosts, the biological-social filter through which they pass (McNeill 1989). Thus, the social context is not irrelevant. Moreover, culture will develop a terminology and pattern of action in an attempt to deal with the disease.

15. With respect to nutrition, see Chafetz (1990) and his discussion of the neurobiological basis of food selection, which is, apparently, far from arbitrary or mysterious.

16. Such domestic verbal violence, considered by the courts as abusive to the children, becomes legitimate (legal violence) once it enters the world of courts, lawyers, and the cadre of experts (e.g., the court appointed psychologists, Family Court Services, etc.) who are given license to engage the worst form of parental and child abuse in order to divine the truth, that is, who is the best parent. The stress generated by both parents and children from these activities leads to behavioral problems, emotional problems, and, oftentimes, economic ruin for the parents.

17. The courts need someone to blame, as it is inconvenient to blame whole systems, and the Western psychological/psychiatric perspective, through an emphasis on evaluation of the individual, fits neatly into this process. I respectfully question the validity of this approach.

18. More recently in Western culture, it is the insurance companies who are defining when someone is sick or well. Hospital stays, for example, have been shortened because insurance companies refuse to pay past a certain time unless there is real justification. What is also interesting is that this action does not seem to put most patients at significant risk.

CHAPTER 4

Diagnostic Procedures

Chapter 4 is a more detailed look at applying the concept of High Risk Messages to the diagnostic process, along with a brief analysis, using several cultural groups as reference points, of what appears to happen during curing procedures.

Western biomedicine, including psychiatric concepts, is not immune to the application of this model; this chapter includes a critique of specific paradigms that have been used in the anthropological literature for explanatory purposes and that continue to influence what is termed the *psychodynamic approach*. Such paradigms include the Oedipus complex and archetypal images.

Western psychological concepts and procedures used in the clinical setting are likewise briefly reviewed to compare similarities and differences with the model presented in this work.

HIGH RISK MESSAGES IN DIAGNOSTIC PROCEDURE (MY DIVINATION PROCEDURE)

In the previous chapter, I discussed, at length, the concept of High Risk Messages (HRMs), and how HRMs tend to orient the individual to the group (the person's group worth). I also showed how HRMs are derived from social (ordering, warning, threatening, and so on) and environmental (projectile wounds, poor nutrition, and viruses, helminths, and other lessons from Mother Nature) rule setting processes, and how HRMs are perceived metabolically and by the individual within a cultural context, that is, as information intrusion, information loss, and the other information categories.

Diagnosis of emotional and social stress, as manifest in illness behavior, begins with a process of isolating a person's personal, cultural, and environmental HRMs and then determining into which information category(ies) they fit. This is then compared to social expectations/reactions to behavior. Through a process of reframing or retranslating the meaning of historical HRMs, the individual can then exit from loops that lead to stress reactions and many types of illness behaviors and, at the same time, bolster immune and healing responses. Finally, education regarding prevention, which includes how the individual interprets his or her world, nutrition, and so on, rounds out the picture.

At an analogous level of analysis, pathogens in the environment, viruses and bacteria (another type of information intrusion) are reframed in terms of how the mind/body reacts to their invasion. Cure, then, is a process of paying attention to eliminating or minimizing the effects not only of the virus/ bacteria, but also the associated emotional/social stress factors.

Behavioral manifestations are obviously important, as this is how problems are brought to the attention of the group members. But the emotional and behavioral manifestations (the symptoms) alone do not necessarily lead to therapeutic procedures, but, instead, are considered initially in a cause and effect manner, usually through some ritual, divination, or diagnostic procedure.

HRMs cannot stand alone (i.e., in terms of a process of curing) but, instead, are connected to social rules (and their infractions), culturally specific ideologies regarding the nature of illness, and appropriate social roles. Before elaboration, the concept of cure needs to be defined.[1] By curing, I am referring to (1) the return of the system (individual/physical system, individual/ emotional system, *and* individual/social system, i.e., the group) to its original, before "illness" conditions, and conceptualized as such by the individual and/or culture; (2) a rebalancing of the system, which may mean an alteration of the individual and social relationships (e.g., a rejoining of family members); and (3) an alteration of the system along with the individual(s) in question, as would be the case when the patient recovers and goes on to become a shaman.

Death, rather than cure, is always a possibility. The death of a high-status person in the social system often involves more elaborate rituals because order must be returned to the system quickly or there is a risk of anarchy (chaos) and *social* death. In short, when people do not survive the cure, society *must* be cured (funerals are for the living), and this opens the door to change. In our own culture, when death is not placed by significant others (community) within a substantial ritual context that signals both the meaningful (reframing) end to a relationship and the beginning of a new challenge, those left behind will continue to loop on the event until they find closure. Such closure sometimes never occurs and may result in what Western psychiatry calls post-traumatic stress syndrome, very common to combat veterans.

Ritual Process

Ritual is part of all curing, in all cultures, be this physical, as in the preparation procedures involved in setting a fractured leg, or social/emotional, as when the proper social information and personnel are brought together to effect the cure. Ritual cannot be avoided because it initiates, at a basic level, person-to-person or person-to-group contact and likewise serves as a marker indicating the termination of contact. Ritual establishes expectations without which a person cannot begin or end any interaction. Rituals, in fact, will create themselves and, in this light, can be seen as evolving out of implied rules. In short, and in regard to illness, ritual signals when curing begins and ends. With one notable exception, to be discussed in the next chapter, all curing has a termination ritual and social reintegration phase, or the cure is not complete.

The signal of an illness also involves some sort of personal or cultural ritual, as when a person gets the flu. Each person will have his or her own initial expression or ritual opening to the flu; this could be seen as a ritual expression of symptoms, that is, groaning, coughing, complaining, depression, anger, and so on. If a person states that he or she is sick, then culture demands that he or she sound and act "sick" in some general way. We find, then, rituals *within* rituals. I will elaborate on this, as it is extremely important in that ritual process helps to define stages of the social curing process.

In its simplest configuration, a person-to-person ritual process proceeds as follows, keeping in mind that all curing procedures are elaborations or analogues:

A	*B*	*C*	*D*	*E*
Ritual------>	Small Talk------>	Content------>	Small Talk------>	Ritual
Initiation				Termination

At part *A*, rituals initiate interaction and communicate socialness; this allows a door to open so that further interaction can proceed. Initiation rituals also allow us to collect information about one another through our visual, auditory, olfactory, and kinesthetic senses and can inform us about emotional state, drug use, group affiliation, and so on. For example, a client is walking up to my office door and this is her first session. I say, "Good morning. My name is Dr. Rush/John Rush," and I extend my hand. If the person extends her hand and says, "Hello. My name is Susan Smith," this sets the scene for further interaction. It also tells me that this person is aware of part *A* ritual behavior, which suggests an appropriate social response. If the person does not say hello or shake hands, but, instead, immediately jumps to content (i.e., tells me her problems), this perhaps suggests a disturbed communication pattern relative to our cultural expectations. It may be simply a part of her behavior under extreme stress (an element of her sick role), but it could be an indicator of deeper problems relative to communication patterns with others.

During this initiation phase, I smell for cigarette smoke, marijuana, alcohol, and other scents that can indicate metabolic problems. I look for pupil dilation and indications of jaundice in the eyes and skin, as well as skin texture, discoloration, acne, ear creases, scars, tattoos, and so on. I also observe the manner of dress, body shape, and comportment. Curers in other cultures collect different types of information and often know a great deal about the client or patient prior to the initiation ritual.

For part *B*, Small Talk, I might ask, "Did you have any problems finding my office?" or, "How was the traffic getting over here?" As she answers these questions, I learn about this person's ability to engage in small talk, keeping in mind that different cultural groups spend more or less time at this junction of the process. This represents a sociability index, if you like, and/or relative stress.

Content, part *C*, is the initiation of the reason(s) for seeing me in the first place. The length of time taken up with content depends upon the rules of the setting. Usually a client is in my office for fifty minutes, perhaps an hour, and sometimes two hours if I am doing hypnosis or if it is requested, depending upon the health issue involved; the therapeutic procedure may last over many weeks, but I always inform the client of a time frame for therapeutic termination. In a similar fashion, the content delivery time of a shaman's curing procedure could last several days, with such content being wrapped around numerous ritual procedures, sometimes more apparent to the anthropologist than the shaman. In a large majority of non-Western settings, however, and as far as I have been able to determine, there is always a termination ritual and reintegration into society. This process likewise appears to be analogous to life, death, and resurrection. Thus, in many situations, there are ongoing rituals involving coming together and going away all wrapped around a macro-ritual process that includes termination and reintegration.

Often the health practitioner and client do not understand the rituals that actually go on during therapy. As the practitioner uses similar therapeutic procedures with each client--that is, reframing the symptoms around problems

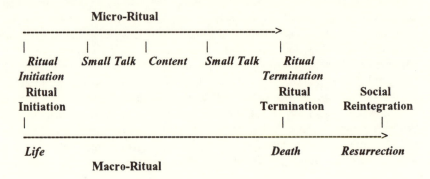

with the digestive system; suggesting (reframing) that the arguments between husband and wife indicate trust, spirit or object intrusion, and so on--these could also be considered as ritual procedures, that is, a means of approaching the client's content (problem) or the reason that the client sought out the therapist in the first place.

Interaction usually approaches termination with more Small Talk, and ends with a Ritual, that is, setting up an another appointment, statements of "Good-bye" or "See you later" (micro-ritual), or, in the macro-ritual, including a message or marker that signals that cure is complete and then making the transition to "normal" (not sick) social activity.

Why is an understanding of ritual process important? Importance has to do with intent. If my intent is to reduce stress and create a sense of familiarity, where general expectations are in place, then I would need to stick to a social formula representing each of the above parts. If my goal is to create a certain level of confusion, confrontation, or stress, then I alter the above. For example, instead of saying, "Good morning" (if it is before noon), I greet the person with "Good evening," or other such incongruent statement or behavior. Confusion is often used in many non-Western curing settings, as in my own practice, in order to initiate trance states.

If, on the other hand, I am in an emergency room with a broken leg, available information should be minimized, appropriate rituals (rituals with which I am familiar) should be used, and an explanation of the curing process should be adequately expressed so that I can begin building appropriate expectations. This is extremely important, for example, when a woman in labor enters the hospital. More than likely, the higher her stress is, the longer she will be in labor. Moreover, it is less stressful if personnel (i.e., nurses, doctors, and so on) agree that she *is* in pain rather than trying to minimize it; when you deny a person her reality, this is stress enhancing.

But there is a larger issue. For reframing of symptoms and curing to be successful, a termination ritual, signaling a completion of the curing process, and a reintegration into the social sphere are necessary. Just as analogous thinking, limits on information processing, and the of rejection are mental processes, rituals are social processes that have evolved from our psychological need to develop order and expectations. Illness interrupts social continuity, and rituals serve as basic rules or starting points to reorder relationships and reintegrate society. I will return to more specific rituals in time, but for now let us consider HRMs as a diagnostic feature.

HRMs, Rules, and Rejection: The Emotional Connection

As you will recall from the last chapter, HRMs represent loops in a person's thoughts, or the going over and over of a particular situation, concept, attitude, and the like. All HRMs represent rejection (emotionally as well as physically) or fear of rejection, which is analogous to physical and emotional death. As explained earlier, the brain/mind does not make a clear distinction between the two. Death, as far as can be determined, is experienced by the living (those remaining after a significant other dies), and it is experienced as a loss of information. Although some cultures conceptualize death as merely part of a process, it is still difficult to contemplate one's own death. Losing others (death), leaving other's behind, experiencing separation anxiety, being alone, and being socially rejected by others are analogues.

At the emotional level of HRM analysis, fear of social rejection is a very critical factor, as such fear is continuous in a person's life. We are concerned about what others think about us, especially those "significant others." We are concerned about how we look to others. We are concerned about the accepting or rejecting remarks of others. We personalize information as acceptance or rejection. We learn early in life the values of those around us, of those behaviors that serve to include us in the group and those that exclude. For example, a person could begin to believe that he or she is stupid, or considered stupid by others, after being told so during the process of communicating a rule about appropriate behavior in the home, for example, "Close the refrigerator door, stupid. Don't you know that costs money?" As the rule about shutting doors also includes the personal attack of "stupid," the individual could collect this as an HRM. It is not the intent of the sender, but it could be the interpretation of the receiver. Or cultural HRMs can be activated when a learned cultural ideal is confronted. For example, in North American culture, we, for the most part, instill the ideals of individualism, equality, freedom of speech, freedom of choice, and so on. Being told what to do by those in authority (legitimate or otherwise) is high risk because it overturns the ideal. We are also told that, to be an individual with freedom of choice, one must act in a responsible manner and obey laws that are for the social good. If the person knows he or she has transgressed some social norm/social good (i.e., went through a stop sign, stole something from work, injured someone, committed adultery, lacked proper rituals in reverence of ancestors, etc.), such behaviors (in many cases, but certainly not all) activate the cultural HRMs. A thought loop represents a process or attempt to solve the problem by finding information that explains or justifies the behavior in a way that is stress reducing. Being told that you are stupid over and over by a parent has no logical explanation, other than it being the style used by the parent. But, because parents are imbued with power, both the power of knowledge and physical power, many children accept the message "I am stupid." In other words, the child does not have enough information to know if he is stupid or not and may, on the one hand, accept the interpretation. On the other hand, being called stupid can be interpreted as rejection of self by the group because "If I were smart, then others would not say such things." Most people feel uncomfortable with this and consequently attempt to find an alternative interpretation, through looping behavior, in order to relieve the emotional discomfort. In fact, the individual will very readily pick up on the rejection in any message that relates to his or her particular HRM categories. Individuals do not do this because they want more pain; they do this in an attempt to obtain a new interpretation.

Using another culture as an example, a person who does not pay the appropriate homage to household or ancestor spirits, as is the case with the Jalaris villages (Nuckolls 1992), is not engaging in appropriate social behavior. The Jalaris can be considered a collectivistic[2] cultural group and, according to Triandis (1987), experience anxiety in the form of shame rather than guilt.[3] The internal message "I am unworthy" is one of those cultural HRMs that originates from a social rule that says, "You will pay homage to ancestors. If you do not you will be attacked by those spirits." Emotional distress over repeated looping can lead to behaviors and attitudes designed to reduce stress or, in a metaphorical sense, draw attention to the individual through various types of illness or behaviors that represent some social antithesis. In no society does curing simply represent a concern for *only* the behaviors or symptoms associated with an illness (i.e., a headache, fatigue, etc.) or the person's position in society. There is always the question of cause, which is a social construct. Even in Western biomedicine, where treating symptoms takes precedents over prevention, the beliefs about cause are directly related to a socially constructed reality surrounding economics.

Expanding the Categories of HRMs

The basic concept of diagnosis involves uncovering HRMs. There are three general categories of HRMs: personal or emotional (as discussed above), social, and environmental.

By way of clarification, environmental HRMs belong to Mother Nature (i.e., accidents, pathogens, etc.), but they tell the person something about self in the group; these HRMs are always interpreted through a reference to the personal and social. For example, if a person gets burned on the stove, the causal factor of "carelessness," or "stupid," can begin looping behavior. The reference to "careless" or "stupid" is a *social* implant that gets attached to Mother Nature's lesson.

In another example, being burned on the stove could result in thinking about one's social transgressions, thus activating a cultural HRM and possibly illness behavior if that is a social prescription for transgression. Further, a bacterial or viral infection, as conceptualized in our society, manifested in the destruction of skin tissue or immune suppression, represents pathogen-activated HRMs.

Personal and social HRMs come about in a social fashion, that is, through rule setting at that level of analysis. Keep in mind, however, that sensitivity to the rules and sensitivity to the messages of rejection in general, involve both biological aspects (the "more or less" brain chemistry, etc., as mentioned earlier) and social aspects (how one is conditioned to feel and respond to negative rule setting).

In all cultures, once cause and effect is established through some ritualized diagnostic procedure, a ritualized curing process is set in motion, which may last a few minutes and sometimes several days, weeks, or months. Again, the ritual divination or diagnostic process represents the specific culture's analytical statement of cause and effect.

Discovering Personal/Emotional HRMs

How does one discover a person's emotional or personal HRMs? One method, especially in our culture, is to simply ask, "What are your High Risk Messages?" The usual response is "What do you mean?" This would be a typical response in all cultures, as HRMs and illness are not, for the most part, consciously thought out and put into play. In our own culture, asking for a list of HRMs can lead to a discussion that not only explains HRMs, but also sets the scene for reframing or retranslating history, a main ingredient in all psychotherapy. Simply put, an HRM is activated anytime the individual interprets a message as negative toward himself or herself and/or others who represent the group-self, that is, mother, family, and so on. Once activated, the individual's stress goes up. I call the incoming message a *negative bit*, which, at the social level, is an intended/unintended message that is interpreted by the receiver, in part or in whole, as rejection (the intent is to set a rule about something, and the unintended result--not the intent of the sender-- is that the individual picks up a message of rejection from the sender).[4] In our culture, as in many others, personal HRMs include messages that imply not good enough, stupid, unworthy, and unlovable. Add to this certain universal cultural and even programmed HRMs, for example, voice tone, facial gestures, and violation of body space. With respect to specific cultural HRMs, in Thailand and in Japan, for example, verbal aggression of any sort is high risk, as the cultural goal is to limit conflict between individuals; conflict upsets order. Individuals who become verbally aggressive, show affection in public, or dress provocatively would experience a great deal of shame,[5] knowing that others are watching. In our culture, when American workers were accused of being lazy by representatives of the Japanese government, Americans became irate and retaliated. I recently saw a very outspoken T-shirt, showing an atom bomb exploding; over the top were the words "Made in America by Lazy Americans, Tested in Japan."

Another method to determine HRMs, then, is in terms of categories of relationship with individuals and groups. For example, in Vietnamese culture, what is the cultural attitude regarding the ideal nature of the relationship between father and son or father and daughter? If the "on the ground relationship" follows closely a cultural norm, the clinician can expect to find great fear of rejection and HRMs in this area. Transgressions are seen as abnormal, with social and perhaps supernatural sanctions. In other words, a great deal of energy will be expended in personal thoughts regarding this relationship (looping), which acts as an antenna for interpretation of information that resembles, in some direct or symbolic manner, the HRMs associated with this relationship. If there is a gross distortion of the cultural norm (i.e., a great deal of disrespect and insensitivity in son to father interaction), then this is an area of low risk focus for the individual, perhaps signaling social change and a social statement that such behavior is warranted or even expected. Again, uncovering HRMs can involve looking for the expected interactional behaviors in a culture and determining how closely individuals adhere to the expectations.

A third method of discovering emotional HRMs involves observing and listening to the individual's verbal and behavioral expressions of rejection. Expressions of anger, frustration, confusion, depression, and neurasthenia--all the emotions that are considered negative[6]--are the "royal road" to HRMs. By understanding the person's interpretation of events, one can uncover that individual's HRMs. When collecting a person's history, the focal point is the *content* of what was communicated[7] to the individual, verbally and non-verbally, and the individual's interpretation of those events. Oftentimes it is the individual's literal translation of statements from significant others that leads to the development of his or her HRMs.

It is in the areas of high-risk focus, or the looping on HRMs, that the diagnosis of emotional or social-emotional illness takes place, keeping in mind the place that physical illness and disease occupy in the total stress reaction. In my opinion, the social aspects of emotional illness outweigh the physical and/or genetic predisposition toward illness, although the physical or genetic aspects cannot be left out of the equation. People are born with temperaments, at the very least, due to the "more or less" in neurochemistry, as discussed in Chapter 3. Some people are indeed more sensitive to negative bits and the consequent high-risk focus because of at-birth (either genetic or introduced during gestation) neurochemical issues.

Discovering Other Social HRMs

When considering illness in any society, it is important to consider nutrition, life style, and other factors that lead to ill health. Nutrition and lifestyle are social constructs, created by a culture and/or introduced through cultural contact. When considering nutrition, the clinician needs a background in human physiology and how nutrients are utilized. This needs to be combined with an understanding of the often unique metabolic issues as represented by specific cultural groups as well as individuals within any group. For example, as stated by Alcena (1994:6), "It is important to note that hypertension in the Caucasian population is quite a different disease from hypertension in the black population. Therefore, the approach to treatment has to be different."

Alcena goes on to say that the type of hypertension representative of blacks is due to genetic transmission with, "[t]he kidneys of black individuals. . . . unable to get rid of salt in sufficient amounts because of a genetic abnormalicy" (1994:6). Although Alcena locates the beginnings of this "abnormalicy" in events in Africa a few hundred years ago surrounding working in the fields, experiencing dehydration due to lack of access to water, and developing a mechanism to prevent dehydration, this condition probably predates that time period by many thousands of years and refers mainly to in-land living peoples who had a limited salt supply. In any event, placed in a culture that almost worships salt, as evidenced by the North American fast-food establishments and processed foods, the result is a high prevalence of hypertension among African Americans. Salt, then, is a negative bit at the physiological level and activates HRM potential, and not just for African Americans.

Taking this a step further, cultural behaviors centering around food consumption often tax the environment, leading to cultural extinction. Weiss's article (1980:148-189) on the extinction of an important food source (the green sea turtle) among the Miskito Indians of eastern Nicaragua, is a case in point. Closer to home, Lappe (1991) states that our use of natural resources to produce meat and the politics of food consumption result in a raped environment and overconsumption of protein, which can lead to kidney disorders. Like the Miskito Indians, and in time, our cultural attitudes toward food consumption not only lead to poor health, but also could result, through depletion of natural resources, in cultural collapse.

Discovering Environmental HRMs

Environmental HRMs, keeping in mind the close interplay of culture and environment, include micro-predators (i.e., bacteria, viruses, helminths, etc.) and macro-predators (i.e., humans, snakes, etc.). Add to this ultraviolet radiation, earthquakes and other "natural" disasters, and the intense amount of chemical and microwave toxins. These, for the most part, represent information intrusion, are high risk, and precipitate biological and cultural responses.

It is within the human interaction/communication patterns that the vast majority of day-to-day and immediately recognizable stress is generated. This stress can lead to many socially defined illnesses, be these migraine headaches, fatigue, stomachaches, or more serious somatic problems like peptic ulcers and, through a lowering of the immune system,[8] cancer. These patterns are not the total answer and must be seen in a holistic fashion with the other factors, for example, nutrition, drug abuse, and so on. However, it is important to understand that, just as one can disregulate metabolic functioning through stress leading to these somatic problems, one can, through the same stress mechanisms, generate thought problems and/or disturbed communication patterns. There is always a biochemical/neurochemical aspect to disturbed communication patterns, as indeed the neurochemicals are altered by stress. In my professional experience, physical healing is always halted or impaired by emotional distress.

Taking this a step further, every time you think, you alter your neurochemistry. Schizophrenia, although there may be a genetic predisposition, evolves out of internalizing negative bits and looping on HRMs. Looping alters brain chemistry, and, if looping goes on long enough, thought and associated behavioral patterns become anchored in. Manic-depressive psychosis is simply another possibility evolving out of social stress. In fact, looked at closely, manic-depression resembles, in the first stage, a regression to an earlier, more animated time in the person's life, while the depression resembles a trance state. All cultures have their culture-bound syndromes that are, for the most part, stress related. These would include *susto* in Latin America (Rubel et al. 1991), *latah* in Thailand, *amok* in the Philippines, *windigo* among the Indians of northeast Canada (see Yap 1977 for a brief description of these conditions), and *piblokto* (Foulks 1972) of the Eskimo culture.

Wallace (1961) was one of the first to associate biochemical issues--more specifically, hypocalicemia and vitamin D deficiencies--with *piblokto*. During a conversation with Dr. Yap (1969), he made it quite clear that, although biochemistry and neurochemistry are a factor, "the social factors are a predominant consideration" because they: (1) accentuate bio- and neurochemical imbalance and (2) condition the socially learned behavioral outcomes. Manic-depression may be one of our culture-bound syndromes. In fact, all illness is culture bound to one degree or another. The psychiatric community, in conjunction with the pharmaceutical companies, is still searching for that "magic bullet" to deal with what are essentially social-information-processing issues in most cases. Many of these prescribed drugs, especially when used long term, *are* "bullets" that tend to further unbalance neurochemistry, leading to Parkinson's disease, tardive dyskinesia, and other, yet to be diagnosed conditions.

There is another possible category of HRMs, certainly connected to social stress and analogous to the day-to-day interpersonal and group interactions, and that is one's relationship to superordinate agencies. For example, in cultures that practice ancestor worship, as is common in many Asian cultures, one sees analogous thinking in play representing a continuation of day-to-day interpersonal interaction. The family member who does not pay proper respect to deceased ancestors risks spirit possession, which is analogous to not paying appropriate respect to elders or accepting their advice; this invites sanctions. Knitting together, then, the intrasocial, intersocial, extrasocial, and environmental agencies of illness, the following examples clearly illustrate the concept of HRMs, rules, roles, personal and group stress, and the culturally prescribed illnesses that manifest themselves.

PROCESSES IN EMOTIONAL-SOCIAL INTEGRATION: CROSS-CULTURAL SYSTEMS OF CURING

The immediate problem faced when considering curing (physical and emotional-social) in other cultures is orienting one's self to a particular culture's point of view. Other points of view disrupt our order of things, and, thus, we attempt to organize their order using our models. Our models have been represented through Freudian, Jungian, or biomedical lenses (see Tyrer and Steinberg 1993 for a brief look at numerous Western concepts), which, although interesting and provocative, do not allow freedom of movement in our understanding. As I stated in Chapter 1, in a shrinking world, we have to be careful of the models we develop--they do not represent facts. Instead, they represent concepts and ideas. However, as we (*Homo sapiens*) seemingly become, through culture contact, more and more similar in thought and behavior, we believe the models as fact. There are many models, and they all contain common elements. These include (1) an expression of illness behaviors; (2) a belief about cause and effect (a diagnosis or framing of the illness); (3) an ideology about the patient's place in society, with being out of place or balance relating, in some way, to illness (here we approach morality, life style, etc., or a confirmation of the original framing); (4) a curing procedure; and (5) a ritual process for rejoining the individual with or to his or her social milieu. The framing or reframing and cure can occur simultaneously. All of this is accomplished with symbols and ritual behavior, including verbal language, non-verbal communication or behaviors, and associated props (herbs, vitamins, antibiotics, scalpels, bed-pans, clothing, etc.), all designed to create a bridge between inner thoughts (e.g., depression) and/or physical disease or injury (e.g., amebic dysentery, broken leg, etc.) and the outer social reality. The symbols used are the key to understanding culture and its values and preferences for social action.

Curing and healing represent society. If a society or culture does not develop procedures for healing and curing, in a general as well as a specific sense, it cannot exist. Healing and curing are metaphors that represent all the ills, problems, and dilemmas faced by a culture. Sickness and illness, and/or behaviors that represent illness within a culture, are the representations that relate to pain, fear, uncertainty, and confusion--powerful sensations/emotions that lead to action. Religion, mythology, science, and medical systems all proceed from these emotions. These systems attempt to make sense out of human misfortune and then allow a procedure(s) for reorganizing or realigning the world. No science, religion, or medical system is correct in that it represents an irrefutable reality. As long as we think change is a good thing and systems evolve, what passes for science today will seem naive and primitive in 100 years.

The following cultural descriptions are couched in a language and understanding peculiar to each investigator. However, in coalescing this information, I will be necessarily placing my reality and model on the interpretation.

Cultural Philosophy

A useful starting place for understanding curing systems involves a specific culture's philosophy of cause and effect or how individuals get sick. Such philosophies, then, lend themselves to an understanding of the metaphors of healing. As we consider a number of different cultural groups, it will become clear that there are essentially three general philosophies of illness (see Chapter 3 for a more detailed discussion of these philosophies): (1) that some sort of agent, be it supernatural, biological, or chemical, has entered (*information intrusion*) or been imposed upon the body or an organ of the body (such intrusion can be intentional or unintentional, but it has disrupted the natural order of things; for example, the individual or group has, through some impropriety, sacrilege, sin, affront, or poor timing, offended nature or supernatural elements, and the ensuing illness is a message, or warning, to bring the system back to harmony by stopping the act or behavior; or, from a Western biomedical perspective, a virus has entered the body via the mucous membranes, and the ensuing symptoms are the results of that intrusion, a warning perhaps, that "It's that time of the year; get out the chicken soup, Kleenex, and Pseudoephedrine HCL"); (2) that the individual has a pre-disposition or a genetic or "born with" condition that will lead to or invite illness or "immoral," "bad," dangerous" behavior (*inherited information*); and (3) that there is *insufficient information* or *information loss* (a nutritional problem or stress that burns up vital amines, i.e., vitamins, minerals, etc.), that there is something lacking that needs to be put back into the body, or that something has exited from the individual, thereby disrupting homeostasis. *Information alteration* and *information imbalance* can be seen in all three categories or philosophies.

The cultures discussed below will be categorized under one or more of these philosophies. As I continue, I will also be indicating generalized procedures recognizable in all cultures--when, *framing* or *reframing* (the process of reinterpreting or entering a different interpretation of a cause or effect) is occurring and when a behavior represents symbolic *action* intended to bring the system to some sort of *balance* or *order*.

THE MENOMINI OF THE GREAT LAKES

The Menomini occupy an area west of Lake Michigan and south of Lake Superior. The first written reports are to be found in the *Jesuit Relations* (see Thwaites 1896-1901) with subsequent data collected by Hoffman (1896), Skinner (1915), Keesing (1939), G. Spindler (1955), and L. Spindler (1952, 1989).

To the Menomini, illness or disease is an unnatural condition that demands explanation. To this end, the *Cese.ko*, or "Juggler," was called in to consult the spirits and determine the cause of the illness, often attributed to losing one's soul (*information loss* or *deficiency--framing*) or being wounded by a witch's arrow (*information intrusion--framing*), both conditions resulting from witchcraft (a *reframing*, analysis, or description of cause). In terms of soul loss, the *Cese.ko* would convince the soul to return and entrap it in a wooden cylinder (*action*). This cylinder would then be held on the patient's chest for four days (*action*), thus allowing the soul to return to the bewitched person's body. Such actions are designed to bring the body back into *balance*.

In the above, the initial *framing* or *analysis* is the interpretation based upon that culture's concept or philosophy of cause, with the *reframing* representing an accusation or statement of cause and effect. *Reframing* places a new meaning on the symptoms, a meaning that can be translated into *action*. *Action* is the intervention process, but it also defines the *Cese.ko's* role or status, that is, the power to influence in the face of illness. Once the soul is reacquired (as a result of the *action*), this procedure of returning the soul to its proper place *balances* the system (homeostasis).

In the event that the illness was caused by a witch's arrow (*reframing*), the *Cese.ko*, using a bone tube, would suck the arrow out of the patient's body and then spit out or vomit up the small offending object in the form of a fly, maggot, or the like (*action*). From my reading of the literature, there was apparently no distinction between psychological vs. physical illnesses, for both involve loss of power, through bewitchment, with such attacks usually thought to be brought about by some social transgression or deviant behavior (cultural HRMs).

Hoffman (1896:146), referring to the "shaking tent" ceremony, a form of ritual *reframing* and *action* performed by the *Cese.ko*, states:

He usually performed after dark, in a wigwam just large enough to admit of his standing erect. This lodge or wigwam is tightly covered with mats, so as to entirely exclude all light and the prying curiosity of all outsiders. Having no light within the lodge, the acts and utterances of the medicine man or conjurer are regarded as mysterious, and credulously received by the wondering crowd surrounding the tent. He first prepares himself in his family wigwam by stripping off his clothing. Then he emerges singing, and the Indians outside join him in the sun with their drums, and accompany him to the lodge, which he enters alone. Upon entering, the lodge commences shaking violently, which is supposed by the Indians outside to be caused by the spirits. The shaking of the lodge produces a great noise by the rattling of balls and deer's hoofs fastened to the poles of the lodge at the top, and at the same time three voices are distinctly heard intermingled with the noise. One is a very hoarse voice, which the Indians are made to believe is that of the Great Spirit; another is a very fine voice, represented to be that of a Small Spirit; while the third is that of the medicine man himself. He pretends that the Great Spirit converses in a very heavy voice to the lesser spirit, unintelligibly to the conjurer, and the lesser spirit interprets it to him, and he communicates the intelligence to his brethren without. The ceremony lasts about three hours, when he comes out in a high state of perspiration, supposed by the superstitious Indians to be produced by mental excitement.

It is also important to state that the *Cese.ko* was well paid for his efforts in the form of tobacco, calico, steel traps, and so on.

In order to better understand attitudes toward illness and curing, one must explore the idea of personal power and how it is obtained. Power is obtained through a number of sources, procedures, or objects. First, explicit in the belief system of the Menomini is the idea that life and death is a cycle, with the probability that a child may inherit personal power from a deceased elder or relative (positive predisposition or acquired/genetic power). Such power would be an intangible, invisible force reincarnated in the child. Second, power is obtained through a vision that occurs during the puberty fast *(positive information intrusion)*. Such visions are reported to the shaman, who interprets them in terms of their symbolic content. From this, he determines which guardian or tutelary spirit(s) now resides with the individual in terms of a guide, force, or power.

Power can also come from owning or possessing a medicine bag. Owning a medicine bag, however, is, in itself, dangerous because one has to "feed it" through yearly acts of murder. Another method of obtaining power is simply through age. Age usually implies that the person has the wisdom to survive, and elders are often attributed with power simply through living a long life.

Perpetrators of witchcraft were never directly singled out because this could lead to further conflict or violence. One of the tenets of this culture was self-control and limiting open expressions of aggression toward others. Because there were few explicit social control mechanisms for limiting conflict (such as police) the fear of being bewitched, of having one's power magically usurped, and of facing the resulting illness served to limit social aggression.

The Menomini, then, seem to fit into all of the above three categories, that is, illness being caused by losing some psychically acquired substance translated as power (*information loss*), by having magical arrows penetrate his/her body (*information intrusion*), with various personal powers--for example, the power to heal--being acquired from a deceased elder or relative (a predisposition or acquired characteristic--inherited information). The illness (a *frame*--the symptoms), or its physical manifestations are *reframed* as an expression of power loss. Let us take a closer look at this system, using an information-processing model.

First, we are not required to believe or disbelieve in the Menomini's epistemology. Whether or not there are guardian spirits, and whether or not people can magically take away power or inflict injury with magical darts, is irrelevant. The Menomini believe it; it is true to them. This being the case, how one acquires power, how it is lost, what the results of this loss are , and how individual and social equilibriums are reestablished can be seen as information being added to or subtracted from the system.

Second, looking at the Menonini system in terms of generalized HRMs, the highest risk is the loss of power, with the antithesis being the gaining of power through the mechanisms listed above. One loses power, again, through some social transgression or deviant behavior.

This brings on the fear of rejection and, through looping on the behavior and associated stress, the culturally prescribed illness behavior.[9] In reverse, there is a certain amount of anxiety and anticipation involved in the incorporation of power (with such symbols representing positive information input in a general sense), that is, in the curing ceremony itself. Both the loss of power and the gaining of power, as in a curing ceremony, are times of stress, as they open a door to change.

Third, individuals acquire a social realization at an early age, of what constitutes tapping into cultural HRMs, that is, being disrespectful of elders, openly expressing aggression to others, not engaging appropriate social rituals, and the like. Personal illness or deviance, then, is not really a personal matter. It is a statement about interpersonal relationships and social dynamics in general (the overall health of the system), including relationships with the outside, yet dominant cultural groups.   Illness, emotional/physical, is a metaphor, a statement about social relationships in general and the need for social action to be instituted, that is, interpretation and curing by the *Cese.ko*.

Disease organisms are not recognized by the Menomini, but the intrusion of information (magical arrows, for example) stands as a metaphor for this concept, just as in Western thought, the removal of the organism/"arrow" is part of the process leading to health.   However, the ritual procedure in both systems is perhaps just as important in establishing the emotional/ symbolic set necessary for the cure.

The belief that illness is the result of a psychic attack perpetrated by a witch, or that one has not performed the appropriate social rituals is not unique to the Menomini. In fact, it is common belief not only among North American Indian groups, but also around the world.[10] For example, the Apache (Basso 1989) believe that illness is brought on by the individual's aggression toward others, while the Iroquois who falls ill first applies a traditional herbal cure, and, if this does not seem to work, he or she questions interpersonal relationships or the neglect of some ritual obligation (Shimony 1989). HRMs, then, center around learning the rules regarding socially appropriate behavior, breaking of the rules, and facing the personal recriminations as well as the social sanctions applied by others.

THE IU MIEN (LAOS AND SACRAMENTO, CALIFORNIA)

Among the Iu Mien refugees (originally from Laos) residing in Sacramento, California, antisocial behavior is diagnosed as spirit attack (*information intrusion*, a *framing* statement of cause), as no one except an outsider would purposely create conflict. The diagnosis leads to the prescription of herbs intended to stop ancestral spirit attack (*information intrusion*) and cure consequent soul loss (*information loss*). Paper money is burned and food is prepared (*action*) as an offering to appease the offended spirit. If this is insufficient, a shaman will be summoned, who, through spirit possession of his mentor spirit, will attempt to determine the identity of the offending spirit (*further reframing*) and the appropriate payment, that is, a sacrifice, the burning of paper money. If soul loss (another *framing*) is the problem, then a ritual procedure involving elaborate symbols of building a bridge from the soul to the person is enacted (a *reframing* and *action*--see Moore-Howard 1989:46-47). Coin-rubbing is also a practice among the Iu Mien as a counterirritant (*positive information intrusion*) to relieve various illnesses (Moore-Howard 1989:47; see also Sue and Sue 1990:253-254 and Yeatman and Dang 1980 for their discussion of Vietnamese coin rubbing).

Again, the concept of offended spirits represents some violation of a cultural HRM, although sometimes spirits are simply capricious; children have to be guarded from such capriciousness. As the Iu Mien are a collectivistic culture, where controls are outside the individual (i.e., the individual is controlled by others through their observations, attitudes, and behaviors), personal HRMs are tapped into anytime the individual engages in a behavior that is perceived as contrary to group values. The individual will be name-called, keeping in mind that name calling, unlike in our culture, is a statement against the group and not just the individual. For example, if I call my child stupid, that is a reflection on the child. If a Iu Mien calls his child stupid, that is a reflection on all the group members. Although the term stupid is used as a *negative bit*, thus tapping into personal and cultural HRMs, stating that a young female will not be an adequate wife is a rather extreme form of rejection, which can lead to depression and somatic complaints (Beiser 1985; Westermeyer 1983). However, even such a strong statement is not simply a statement against the individual, but reflects inadequacies in the group as well.

THE HMONG (LAOS AND SACRAMENTO, CALIFORNIA)

Among the Hmong, also refugees from Laos residing in Sacramento, California, the belief in spirit possession and soul loss is prevalent, although not necessarily subscribed to by first-generation children born to refugees who are exposed to competing systems of explanation for specific physical conditions or illnesses. For example, soul loss (*information intrusion* and *loss*), resulting from not paying attention to ancestor spirits (*reframing*), is thought by Hmong shamans to cause nightmare death or nocturnal death syndrome. Other causes, of a similar nature, involve the possession of or involvement with new, unrelated spirits (another *reframing* or diagnosis) left behind in houses or apartments occupied by others (Tobin and Friedman 1983:441). Divination and curing procedures, using symbols to redirect spirit activity, or to confuse or appease spirits (forms of *action*), are similar to those of the Iu Mien. The Western biomedical system, however, seeks answers to nocturnal death syndrome in terms of war and other related traumas in history (post-traumatic stress syndrome) that can result in stress severe enough to halt biological functioning (Moore-Howard 1982:38-39).

Considering cultural HRMs, not paying attention to ancestors, which symbolizes not paying attention to social duties and responsibilities, is represented, from an emic perspective, in illness.

Also, from a cultural HRM perspective, openly confronting someone and creating conflict is interpreted as spirit possession, as one would not do this on his or her own. Confronting people in private, such as a mother-in-law making unkind statements to a daughter-in-law or a husband verbally abusing his wife or vice versa, certainly occurs and is considered more appropriate, but is difficult to specifically document. It would be important to know more about these verbal exchanges and emotional and behavioral reactions. In any event, when personal or cultural HRMs are activated, and certainly when they are mixed with conditions such as dysentery, nutritional deficiencies, and so on, this leads to (or accentuates) various types of illness expression, that is, depression or somatic complaints (Beiser 1985; Westermeyer 1983).

Again, what can appear to be put-downs of children, however, have more to do with not singling out the individual's positive attributes over those of the group. For example, if a child is praised by another parent, the praise will be minimized; that is, "He is just average." This could be interpreted as a put-down and thus high risk. Because not singling out the individual is an expected cultural trait, it is doubtful that this has the same impact as for a North American child. On the other hand, stating that a young lady will not be a good wife has a different purpose and implication; it reflects on the whole group in a negative fashion.

Not all illness is attributed to the possession of spirits and necessitates shamanic ritual. In Laos, as Westermeyer (1982:268) points out, many conditions result in "symptoms such as pain, cough, and diarrhea for which opium provided excellent symptomatic relief." As many of the refugee Hmong in the Sacramento area are suspicious of and reluctant to apply Western biomedical approaches to illness, traditional interpretations, herbs, and shamans are still utilized. Opium is likewise grown by many Hmong and

Iu Mien elders (helped by other family members) and is used for medicinal as well as recreational purposes.

THE HAUSA (WEST AFRICA)

For the non-Muslim Hausa, "[T]o be sick is to be in the grip of a spirit. Spirits can grab a person by the arm or squeeze his chest; they can shoot him, but the weapon is merely an extension of the spirit. To make the spirit let go is to cure the disease" (Last 1976:145). Again, the spirit represents *information intrusion (framing)*. And with respect to emotional problems, "[m]ental sickness is rare among Maguzawa (though it is on the increase through the use of amphetamines); when it occurs, it can be seen variously as a soul or spirit taking over the person or as the result of 'poison'. In general it seems that soul-attack results in depression, spirit-attack in what appear to be toxic confusional states, but the possibility is publicly recognized that women (particularly Fulani women) may mimic soul-attack/depression to obtain their own ends" (1976:146). As Last further states (1976:146), "Diseases are more or less capricious, but as there is in theory a disease for all forms of abnormal (including antisocial) behavior or results, the threat of disease may enforce some aspects of morality."

Males conceptualize illness differently than females, as more impersonal (*framing*), and usually resort to herbal remedies. Women, on the other hand, more often see illness as caused by spirit attack (*information intrusion--framing*) and resort to different types of spirit appeasement in order to avoid "long-term troubles" (Last 1976:147).

One of the keys to understanding cultural and personal HRMs also lies in understanding the different exposures to information, about self and group relationships, as presented to men and women as they are enculturated. How one is disciplined in terms of specific information sent and how it is interpreted becomes an important component not alluded to in Last's discussion. From my point of view, it is difficult to comprehend illness and the expression of disease without an understanding of cultural and personal HRMs. I mention Last's article in order to point out that any discussion of medical beliefs, illness, and disease from a cross-cultural perspective that leaves out this consideration becomes only a list of conditions, emotional reactions, and/or behavioral sets without an understanding of factors precipitated by information input and interpretation, that is to say, cause. This would entail collecting a great deal of communication content, and that certainly was not Last's intent. In short, the content of interpersonal communication as the child is enculturated is extremely important; most of the literature refers mainly to enculturation processes. From a therapeutic standpoint, content becomes very important.

THE GNAU (WEST SEPIK DISTRICT, NEW GUINEA)

Of the Gnau of New Guinea, Lewis (1976:81) writes:

The causes said to produce [illness], such as spirits, destructive magic and sorcery, are explicitly and conventionally held to cause lethal illness, not just illness, and the outcome will be death unless appropriate and effective treatment can be performed. Once ill, the sick person is more vulnerable to further attack and compound illness. His isolation and withdrawal from normal life contains an important element of prudence.

Lewis's study is useful because of his interest in terminology, that is, what constitutes illness as opposed to disease. Illness is the person's or the culture's description of a particular disorder, while a disease represents certain types of physical changes occurring in an organism. "In global perspective such changes may be seen to result from varied causes such as genetic change, maladaption to environment, environmental change, the predatory, parasitic, and competitive habits of different organisms--bacteria for instance. The concept of disease is focused on the individual of the species" (1976:89).

What is of interest here is that in preliterate societies, as reported by ethnographers, usually find spirits, witches, and sorcerers as the causative agents of illness (*information intrusion*). As Fortes (1976:xiv) points out:

[W]e see the same orientation in the proliferation of studies of social and cultural responses to illness and death defined as affliction or misfortune, from the emic point of view of a particular culture, as in the classic studies of Evans-Pritchard and, more recently, those of V. W. Turner. This reduces the study of health and disease to studies of witchcraft, sorcery, magic, and in general curative or socially re-adjustive ritual practices, with herbalist and empirically rational diagnosis, treatment and prophylaxis as residual categories.

Again, what seems to be lacking in most of these studies is how the individual is communicated to, how HRMs develop, and what their relationship is to a culture's expression of illness, whether it is precipitated by the invasion of microbes, stress and a lowering of the immune responses, nutritional issues, or some other factor.

It is not until we approach complex state societies--for example, Egyptian or Chinese--that we approach belief systems that mirror what in the West would be considered a scientific approach. But this is a recent position. Fortes (1976:xii), commenting on Sigerist's (1951) observation, states "that to 17th century European observers American-Indian medicine would not have seemed 'strange or primitive'. Not only were such treatments as cupping, bleeding, purging, herbal remedies, some forms of surgery, and even exorcism, common to both, but so also were some of the associated beliefs and mystical theories about the causation of illness and the rules of healthy living."

THE JAPANESE

Ohnuki-Tierney's study of illness in Japan (1984) offers us an instructive picture of how illness is a metaphor of society, of how individuals are categorized within and outside of a system. Japan, by anyone's standards, is a modern, technologically sophisticated society, with vast exposure to Western medical ideology. Western concepts of sickness and cause and effect, of health and cause and effect, of what is clean and what is dirty have not been accepted in the same way as the microchip, the television set, and the automobile. One then has to ask, "Why not?" If Western medical diagnosis and practice are scientific and an accurate description of reality, why have the Japanese not fully indorsed this ideology? In order to offer an explanation for this, we first have to understand concepts of inside, outside, and boundaries.

As Ohnuki-Tierney states:

When Japanese come inside the house from outside, they wash their hands. This practice stems from the notion that the outside is categorically dirty. The accepted Japanese explanation for this behavior is the germ theory--that there are many germs outside. However, there are germs inside too. Thus, the germ theory, as Levi-Strauss notes, becomes a screen to hide the real model--that is, the symbolic equation of outside with pollution and inside with purity. (1984:17)

To keep oneself clean and healthy "inside," in one's own living quarters, one must get rid of this dirt through cleaning. The symbolic equation here is of the inside with purity and the outside with impurity. (1984:21-22)

Therefore, upon entering a house one must remove one's shoes, wash his or her hands, and gargle. Boundaries between clean and dirty are also recognized in that the exterior side of a wall is subject to dog and human urination. As death is associated with pollution, purification rituals, with the use of salt, are engaged in when people return from funerals (1984:25). "[D]aily hygiene is closely correlated with Japanese spatial classification. The outside, or more specifically, outside one's home but still within the cultural sphere, and the below, as represented by footgear, feet, floor, and ground, are dirty. 'Outside and below' are where germs and pollution, especially 'people dirt,' are located" (1984:27).

She further comments: "The ultimate etiology for all these forms of illness is *kaze* itself, or all types of air current. More specifically, it is the chilling effect of wind, rain, and other climatic conditions that produces the humoral imbalance in the body that is considered to be etiological. "(1984:32).

She goes on to state that humoral imbalance is most likely during seasonal transition (i.e., from spring into summer), as it is during these times that there are natural imbalances.   Because the Japanese see themselves as intimately connected to nature, such imbalances will have a corresponding effect on health. However, because these transitional periods are dangerous, they possess great power that can be actively used to generate health (1984:32-33).

She sums up by saying that outside elements are dangerous and causal factors in ill health; this includes strangers. This being the case, culturally constructed measures have been developed to control these outside powers or threats (1984:33-34).

The concepts of inside, outside, and boundaries represent or are analogous to the condition of *information intrusion*, although inside doesn't necessarily mean penetration as in the case of bacteria entering into one's body through an orifice. Illness is caused by an intrusion of information on the inside which represents culture or balance, with physiological imbalance being the result. Outside, although representing another type of order, is dangerous because it is extraordinary or strange. The boundary between inside and outside is most dangerous, and it is here that order is blurred and for the potential intrusion of information and the activation of cultural HRMs that are intimately bound up in "us" vs. "them," ethnocentrism, and avoidance of interpersonal conflict.

The recently deceased are likewise in a transition phase, similar to weather patterns mentioned earlier, and represent, according to Ohnuki-Tierney, "cultural germs in a concentrated form," existing at the boundary between society and nature (1984:70).

As illness represents an imbalance caused by outside germs, curing such illness is brought about by procedures that *balance*. The concept of cause (physiomorphism) and cure of illness, then, can be placed within a social context wherein there is an emphasis on physiological, as opposed to psychological, treatment procedures (Ohnuki-Tierney 1984:84-86).

Their culturally constructed etiology of disease allows the Japanese, as is the case in all cultures, to create a ritualized process of control and cure of illness that includes dietary and medicinal measures. Excluded from this culturally constructed etiology is psychological causation. In other words, physiomorphism is the antithesis of sorcery or witchcraft accusations, which personalize or assign blame to specific individuals (although witchcraft accusations in other cultures--e.g., Italian--can be interpreted as impersonal). This would seem to limit the conflict, both psychological and interpersonal, that would derive from such accusations.

The concept of boundaries[11] is of interest, in that, although there is the danger, the "dirt," and the impurity, there is also the possibility for healing. This is the case of marginal people in Japan, the *burakumin,* who perform a number of tasks that deal with dirt or impurity (i.e., butchers, undertakers), and who are "the symbolic equivalent of the ancient deities of the *marebito*, deity strangers with positive and negative power who were introduced to the community through seasonal rituals" (Ohnuki-Tierney 1984:44). Here, again, we find the concept of "us" vs. "them," or inside vs. outside, that is, natural elements and foreigners, especially Westerners.

There are other aspects of illness besides *information intrusion*, and these are *jibyo*, or "my illness," and *taishitsu*. The first corresponds to "an illness that a person carries throughout life, and suffers at some times more acutely than at others," and the second, to predispositions (*taishitsu*) or constitutional states, which is analogous to genetic conditions or inherited information (Ohnuki-Tierney 1984:53-54).

It is within the concept of *jibyo* that we most clearly see illness as a group phenomenon represented in individual actors. Illness, then, is a non-verbal statement designed to evaluate and reinforce social bonds. Carrying this to its logical conclusion, we can see the collective nature of Japanese society through illness behavior, where the individual is conceptualized as an essential part of a group, quite the opposite of the individualism in Western society. Cures, then, are an act of bringing the body into *balance* much the same way that you bring social relationships into *balance*.

The concepts of negative bits and HRMs, when applied to the Japanese situation, can be described as follows. Negative bits equal dirt or outside forces; negative bits are likewise any information that upsets the *balance* between people and/or between nature and people. HRMs, both cultural and personal, center around the idea of *balance*. Any behavior that upsets that balance--that is, engaging in confrontation in public, lacking respect for relatives (or even having private thoughts that fantasize such confrontation or lack of respect), and not engaging appropriate rituals (i.e., removing one's shoes upon entering a house, not washing one's face and hands after entering a house)--demands attention, explanation, and ritual procedures. Although all are individual behaviors, and thus individual phenomena, they are a group or collective concern. Unlike in Western culture, illness and its expression are a group rather than an individual phenomenon. From a Western perspective, the individual's reaction (stress) to cultural and personal HRMs, the resulting bodily imbalance, and thus the expression of illness, are not, for the most part, considered a group focus. Individual stress reactions, as originally outlined by Selye (1956) and more recently discussed by Pasnau and Fawzy (1989) and Oken (1989), however, are always a component of illness and disease, sometimes preceding the onset, and certainly a contributing factor after the fact, in both Japanese and Western cultures. The difference lies in each culture's focus of importance, that is, the group vs. the individual.

Looked at from a different direction, suicide statistics offer a glimpse of HRMs and violence toward one's self. As Tatai (1983:28) notes:

The rates given above reflect the social stresses of Japan's vertically structured semifeudalistic society. Those with the least status and fewest options, such as laborers and fishermen, show the highest rate of suicide, whereas administrators, professional men, and technicians suicide much less frequently, probably because their lives are less stressful in such a society.

Among recently compiled data on suicide rates, the most marked feature is an increase in the male early teen group and among middle-aged males. The former may be affected by severe competition in school entrance examinations; the latter, by economic pressures.

It is not difficult to make educated guesses regarding the specific cultural and personal HRMs that are wrapped around status, economic pressures, and thoughts of failure and how the stress can result in the expression if physical illness as well as suicide.

THE ITALIANS (TORONTO, CANADA)[12]

There are two polar messages recognizable in all cultures when considering behaviors (i.e., acceptance and rejection), and, in most cases, little distinction is made between rejection of the behavior and rejection of the individual. This is a universal process, with the content of rejection or acceptance changing from culture to culture. Put into a specific context, my Italian informants use love, or messages of intense adoration, sent on all channels (i.e., by word, by visual statements, and through touch), to condition the child to expectations of acceptance. But, just as intensely, they use the fear of rejection through the withdrawal of love--that is, not speaking, avoiding, using sarcasm, ridiculing, and making martyristic statements ("all I've done for you")--to bring the child's behavior back into some acceptable pattern. There are general areas of behavior wherein rejection is most noticeable. These include when the child shows disrespect (especially for an elder), when the child refuses to follow a rule (arbitrary or otherwise), when the child is detected exploring genital areas, when the child does not finish food put on his or her plate, and when the child "forgets" to hug/kiss his or her mother, father, or other relatives upon departing or arriving.

Then there are specific behaviors fostered in males and females. Males, who are considered to have "uncontrollable sex urges" (see Rush 1974:73), are expected to pursue women; if they do not, they are suspected of being homosexual. Women, on the other hand, are supposed to be chaste. In recent times, the concept of equality between the sexes has filtered into all groups found within the North American urban milieu. The former double standard now represents a contradiction and creates a certain amount of confusion regarding sexual identity in females, and is a starting point for the expression of certain illness behavior.

Information about sex and sexual behavior is, for the most part, withheld from the female, who is often informed of the basics by an aunt or, more than likely, a girlfriend. Males in their peer groups talk more freely about sex. Currently, and in reference to females, much of the information regarding sexual behavior is acquired at school in family dynamics classes. Issues of sexuality, and the anxiety surrounding attitudes and behavior, are not a phenomenon specific to Italians in Toronto, but are representative of an honor and shame complex found throughout Mediterranean societies, as discussed by numerous writers (Peristiany 1970; Cohen 1991). For example, Cohen (1991:112-113) writes:

As a heuristic device, three principles can be distinguished that frame the sexual ideology associated with honor and shame in many traditional Mediterranean societies. First, a strong emphasis on female sexual purity, in particular, the virginity of girls as a prerequisite for an honorable marriage, and the exclusive possession by the husband of his wife's sexual and reproductive potential. Second, the community judges a man's honor to a significant degree according to the sexual purity of the women to whom he is related. Failure either to protect that purity or to avenge its violation is generally regarded as a humiliating failure of masculinity. Because of its capacity to bring ruin to a man and his house, woman's sexuality is seen as a dangerous force that men must guard and restrict. Third, although active and dominant male sexuality is positively valued, there is some ambivalence about unbridled exercise. The adulterer is a man who robs other men of their honor by seducing their wives, and although he enhances his masculinity by doing so, the socially disruptive force that adultery represents leads, particularly in certain contexts, to a negative valuation of men who destroy the homes of others.

As Cohen further comments, we need to go past the ideal and understand "the larger context of practice, purpose, and ideology of which they are a part" (1991:112). As communicated by my Italian informants in Toronto, the women are the controlling force in terms of sexual access. Males, for the most part, have little say in the matter. This leads to male-type expression of illness, wherein the wife is transformed into a mother figure and the males assume the position of children to be taken care of.

Although one can obtain an impression that males dominate in family dynamics, this is not the case. Males make a lot of noise, but it is the women who really set the tone and usually control from the bedroom (see Barzini 1965:210, and Parsons 1969:67-97 for discussions of authority in the Italian family).

Certainly, this is a generalization, but it seems to hold true for the vast majority of my Italian informants. HRMs from both males and females tend to center around acceptance by their mother. For the female, acceptance by her mother and other females is extremely important, as it is through such acceptance that her femininity is established. For the male, acceptance by his mother and other females is likewise very important, for it is through females that his style of masculinity is established.

Fathers, on the other hand, with respect to the daughter, tend to be seen as less of a threat because they are not as likely to withdraw love as a means of manipulation. Punishment is more direct and complete, in the sense that once punishment occurs, history fades. For the mother, events of the past, regardless of punishment, apology, and good deeds since, will be retrieved in a current situation in order to compound the sentence of rejection (this is not specifically an Italian trait). Both mother and father will encourage their son's sexuality, especially if there seems to be a lack of it, with the mother being more subtle in her comments and the father engaging in a more joking style of approval (or disapproval in the case of lack of involvement), for a son's sexuality is a direct reflection on the father's historical prowess.

Concepts of femininity and masculinity, however, are at odds with one another. For the female, this can be noted during the various stages of establishing a relationship with a male. The first step, which is dating, is usually a chaperoned relationship. Such chaperoning can be quite formal, where the couple is not out of sight of another, usually female relative. Males usually visit at the female's home (matri-focal dating). Informal chaperoning is where the kin of the female verbally acknowledge that the couple desires to be alone, stated as if the couple desires "only" to talk (*una conversazione a quattr'occhi*), but with facial gestures and body language implying that they are doing more than talking. However, such privacy is more a recognition of the need rather than privacy in fact. During dating, there is much show of affection and various degrees of petting behavior; premarital sex for daughters is openly discouraged.

Engagement is more of the same. Once married, however, the female's behavior begins a gradual shift away from that of lover to that of caretaker, and, once children are born, she can almost overnight assume the role of the Madonna figure of Catholic epistemology. In this role, she is an all-caring, martyristic, asexual being, where sex is now a chore and engaged in for the benefit of the male (pleasure) and the benefit of religious faith and conviction (procreation). Among females who strongly believe in the existence of the witch (*strega*) and the werewolf (*lupo mannaro*), sex is avoided altogether between the first week of March and the end of April, for should conception occur and the child be born on Christmas Eve, he or she will become a *lupo mannaro* or *strega,* respectively (see Rush 1974:34).

The female initially experiences rejection from her mother; fathers tend to spoil their daughters, although they are very protective as well. The main disciplinary figure is the mother, who, again, controls through various forms of rejection. Now, the reader may encounter a contradiction here in terms of the mother's all-loving, all-forgiving Madonna status. Actually there is little contradiction, for once the child's behavior returns to that expected by the mother, the mother is all-forgiving. However, this does not mean that historical events are forgotten. When mother and daughter are stubbornly at odds, there is always a crisis situation (i.e., an illness, a death, or some other life crisis event) that allows the two to make up. However, the daughter usually has to admit fault, or the conflict will continue; daughters usually admit fault.

However, there are other times when mother and daughter can be brought back into contact and their conflict reframed in a way that explains events and directs blame. This can have the effect of mending the relationship or further destroying it. This is where the daughter experiences chronic headaches, stomachaches, fatigue, or depression. Such illnesses can be interpreted, in some indirect phrasing, by the Italian curer (*fattucchiera*) as ill will (*information intrusion*) coming from the mother to the daughter, as a curse placed on the daughter by another family member, or from a boyfriend or other male who has amorous desires. Most of the interpretations I witnessed were derived from observing blobs of olive oil as they disperse on water (see Rush 1974). These blobs represent relationships between individuals both inside and outside of the family network as well as impersonal forces--a witch, for example, bewitching randomly or for historical reasons usually involving some social antagonism.

If the *fattucchiera* interprets the illness as being caused by the mother (again, the accusation is not, in my experience, a direct accusation), the rift between the two widens. If the interpretation involves other family members or an outsider, then blame for the illness and the rift can be conveniently placed on the shoulders of others, allowing mother and daughter to resume communication, which equals social reintegration.

Illness can likewise stem from anxiety over sexual desires and the cultural demand that the female maintain virginity. Headaches and stomachaches are common and are usually interpreted by the *fattucchiera* as the result of the evil eye (*malocchio--information intrusion*) stemming from the evil intentions of some male. This helps to further anchor the ideas of male intent and female resistance and of her need for control in order to maintain family honor or family well-being. Control of her own sexuality (a social rule) is, in reality, control of the male, for as she controls her sexuality and male access, she can utilize sexual access to control male behavior in general.

Illness also becomes manifest once married. There are two aspects of this. The first involves the sick headache or stomachache that is endured so that family needs are met. Some of my male informants saw this as a birth control device. But there is more to this. Her illness behavior draws attention to herself and what she has to endure for the family. Her amount of illness is often directly proportionate to the health of the relationships and economic conditions of the family unit. In this sense, she is a metaphorical barometer. If relationships are not good, if economics are less than expected, this is a statement about her failing. Poor relationships and economics activate HRMs and translate into somatic complaints. Males usually do not enter into this type of illness expression. The most common complaints of males are colds, flu, backaches, and leg aches. When they are ill, however, they become incapacitated, with their wives and/or mothers looking after their needs.

Moreover, as the mother role is the Madonna role, there is anxiety over sex and its proper place in the relationship, as sex is not necessarily something to be enjoyed. As many of my female informants have stated, "Men enjoy sex, women endure it."

Sex is also used as both a reward and a punishment for behavior. In other words, if the husband's behavior is not appropriate (i.e., being condescending to his wife, especially in front of others), sex will be withheld. Illness behavior, therefore, can be specifically related to the health of the husband-wife relationship, and family relationships in general, with health being defined by the female through her symptoms. Illness behavior after marriage, although expressed in headaches and stomachaches, is also evidenced by a high percentage of dysmenorrhea and yeast infections. I am not aware of either of these two conditions ever being brought to the attention of a *fattucchiera* or considered to be associated with the bad will of others. (Although I have no statistics across cultural groups, there seemed to be unusually high percentage of dysmenorrhea, yeast infections, and hysterectomies among the Italian females in my research sample.) Yeast infections could be explained by continued reinfection by the husband, who may or may not be seeing or having sex with other women, or by immune deficiencies evolving out of stress and digestive problems due to culturally based eating habits. The dysmenorrhea could be from nutritional deficiencies, that is, a deficiency in vitamin B6, calcium, linoleic acid, and so on. The hysterectomies, although highly symbolic for the females, have more to do with the "slash and burn" ideology inherent in Western biomedicine which regards female emotional and physical health as being somehow connected to the uterus and ovaries, as many of these operation were unnecessary as is the case for North American women in general.

From a mind-body perspective, the possibility of emotional conversion (i.e., confusion or guilt over sex being converted to somatic problems thus targets the urogenital area) is likewise a possibility. As the Japanese tend to target the stomach and intestines, North Americans tend to target the heart and breasts (Ohnuki-Tierney 1984:56-60), and Italian females may target urogenital organs (also see Finkler 1994b for a similar targeting among her Mexican informants).

The social dynamics and communication patterns, the establishing of rules of relationships between parents and children and between males and females, is clearly the key to understanding the expression of illness among my Italian informants. Without an understanding of the above dynamics the beliefs in the evil eye and the Madonna figure, and the connections among HRMs, rules, and roles, any interventions, of a medical or marriage counseling/psychotherapy nature would be approached blindly. My experience has been that the indigenous curers, the *fattucchieras,* were far superior in dealing with depression, headaches, extreme anxiety, and other somatic complaints then Western biomedicine because there was a termination to the curing procedure and a social reintegration process. An interesting example will help clarify this.

In 1970, Dr. P.M. Yap asked me to review a case with him. Dr. Yap wanted me to give my opinion on the diagnosis (paranoid schizophrenia) assigned to an elderly Italian female recently admitted to local psychiatric institute. Although she had been medicated, she was still quite agitated and adamant that a witch (*strega*) had put a curse on her. After both Dr. Yap and I listened attentively and indicated belief in her story, I suggested that we bring in a traditional Italian curer (*fattucchiera*). Although it is more common for a victim of a curse to resort to a member of her own family network, the lady agreed. Two days later I brought a curer to the hospital; a divination procedure was performed, the curse was removed, the lady's anxiety abated, and she was released from the hospital. The conclusion of the medical staff--"misdiagnosis" (certainly not a change in paradigm).

Although I was not able to spend a great deal of time with other family members in this case, I did learn that the lady's husband had recently died of a sudden illness and she, understandably, had become quite depressed. Moreover, her daughter and son-in-law had moved to Buffalo, New York, the previous year, and she, according to her son-in-law's sister, "must feel all alone" (*information intrusion*--impersonal rejection). The son-in-law's sister, I might add, met us at the hospital when the lady was released and, I believe, symbolically represented social reintegration. My analysis of this situation, although with great caution because of only limited data, was that the belief that a *strega* (*information intrusion*) had put a curse on her reflected the very impersonal and rather anonymous circumstances within which she found herself.[13] She had difficulty explaining her husband's death and, at the same time, was fearful of the future. The *strega* gave her a focus of explanation (*framing*), and, of course, her behavior brought her from anomie to a recognized status or role of "patient." The HRMs cautiously assigned in this case involve finding herself more and more an outsider, someone who has been abandoned and left on her own, so to speak, due to natural (or supernatural) events, that is, the death of her husband and the fact that her daughter was not in close proximity. Feeling rejected and alone prompted an emotional conversion of depression to fear and the accusation of being cursed by a *strega*.

Certainly, not all the Italians in the network subscribed to the indigenous beliefs and practices, and even those who did often turned to Western biomedicine for certain types of complaints--that is, heart problems, allergic reactions, skin problems, and certain types of intense and unrelenting pain (e.g., arthritis), and so on, most of which can be directly connected to dietary patterns, although in no case did Western biomedicine offer this as a cause of these conditions. But for those who utilize the older beliefs and practices, illness can be seen as *information intrusion* in most cases. Witches and werewolves represent *information alteration* analogous to pathogens that *might* be a problem, like any member of the social network, but, because they have "mutated," pose a real threat. On another symbolic level, they represent the impersonal forces in one's life, forces over which one has little control. On the other hand, the evil thoughts and looks from relatives and outsiders, with their expression in illness, are also *information intrusion*, although of a more personalized nature. And, much like the Japanese example discussed earlier, such expressions of illness, and the *framing* or *reframing* in terms of cause and effect, communicate a great deal about the health of family and other relationships. Illness is more than the personal condition and can be seen as a metaphor of a larger arena of social experience.

WESTERN MEDICAL PHILOSOPHIES

Psychiatric Issues

Beginning with Western psychiatry, the current handbook of diagnosis in Western biomedicine is the 1994 edition of the *Diagnostic and Statistical Manual of Mental Disorders (DSM-IV)*. Essentially, it is an example of a behavioral catalog. It does not supply the reader with statements of cause and effect, but, instead, is a labeling of symptoms and tends to stand as a moral statement, a cultural judgment, as to inappropriate behavioral manifestations.[14] By cataloging and labeling behavior, the physician, psychologist, or social worker would then have a therapeutic procedure to apply, much the same as with the diagnosis of a broken leg (simple fracture), where there is a standard procedure for dealing with the trauma (see van Praag 1993 and his very interesting critique of the *DSM* as well as the biological model in psychiatry; see Ross and Pam 1995 for a critical review of biological psychiatry). With a broken leg, the average physician believes that knowing how it happened has only minor importance, although listening to the trauma story has therapeutic benefits in and of itself.

With behaviors resulting from psychological stress, it is necessary to understand the events preceding the behavioral manifestation, and this would include brain trauma, drug abuse, diet, and so on. Preceding events, which are provided in a life history, are matched or pressed into the categories presented in the *DSM-IV*.

Looked at as a process, then, one encounters behavioral manifestations that are out of balance with accepted or socially appropriate behaviors. A specialist is consulted, and these are matched, while considering communicative behavior, against the *DSM-IV*. A diagnosis is made (a *frame*), and then a therapeutic procedure (a *reframing* technique) is chosen to deal with the behavior (see Reid 1989). This is precisely the process that one encounters in every culture I have studied to date.

As stated in previous chapters, Western psychiatry sees many psychological problems as a product of genetics that result in neurochemical alteration (*information alteration*), successfully eliminating social issues in terms of cause. This approach matches our individually centered culture and is applauded by the government and courts because to consider psychiatric problems as socially caused is messy business indeed.

The "ill" individual comes to the attention of the psychiatrist via two general routes. First is the referral by the family practitioner, which is probably the most common. Second is through a court order, mainly for purposes of evaluating risk factors to society, competence to stand trial, or disposition before (and sometimes after) sentencing. My main focus here will involve the first or voluntary contact with the psychiatrist.

Diagnosis begins by observing and listening to the patient, taking a life history, and perhaps engaging in psychological testing, a popular type of divination procedure, which includes the MMPI, Rorschach, and so on. In a relatively short period of time, the individual's behavior is slotted into specific diagnostic categories as listed in the *DSM-IV,* with syndromes placed on axes and accompanied by appropriate numbers, which give the illusion of being scientific. Depending upon the psychiatrist and his or her training, and the diagnosed severity of the situation (i.e., ability of the individual to function in the home environment, perceived danger to self or others) hospitalization may be recommended or ordered, psychotherapy of one brand or another might be advised, or, in a large number of cases, drugs are prescribed.

When hospitalization is the case, length of stay is correlated with occupied bed space necessary to pay the bills (usually about 80 percent capacity will pay the bills) and insurance company rules; treatment ends when insurance runs out, in many cases. The type and length of psychotherapy are also an insurance issue unless the patient can or is willing to pay the bill. With respect to medication, this continues (although dosage or type of drug may change) "as long as necessary," which, in many cases, means many years.

Considered from a ritual process perspective, one notices an interesting deviation from most non-Western systems. Although the ritual process as outlined on pages 129-131 is engaged at the time of each visit to the psychiatrist, this can be seen as the micro-ritual--the larger context, the macro-ritual, is almost always incomplete. That is to say, there is no ritual termination of treatment or social reintegration. The reader might say that termination is represented by release from the hospital and social reintegration occurs when the patient returns home, but this is not quite the case. If drugs have been prescribed, and as long as the individual is drug dependent, the ritual is incomplete, and social reintegration is impossible because the individual is not "cured." Although the individual's behavior has changed, due mainly to the drugs, he or she, and the social unit to which he or she returns, knows that the "problem" is still there.

Again, termination and reintegration are absent. The question then is, "Why?" Is it because our theories are inadequate to adequately reframe the individual's problems and allow an exit? Is it because the drugs administered only mask symptoms? Is it because we have no adequate methods of reintegrating the individual into his or her social group (i.e., family, community)? Or is this a signal that cure, in many cases, means altering the social fabric within which the symptom developed? I would say "yes" to all four.

Part of the cure in non-Western examples involves reintegration as a social recognition of rebalancing the system. In Western culture, however, having a psychological or psychiatric condition is stigmatizing, and, thus, reintegration, in the large sense, is not available. Instead, reintegration is usually accomplished by the patient, who then tends to gravitate toward other individuals encountered in the psychiatric ward, drug rehabilitation center, halfway house, out-patient clinic, and the like. This creates an inbreeding of the syndromes, which, instead of going away, moderate only in the fact that they become interfaced with the syndromes of others. In short, the individual synchronizes with others who are more or less accepting and learns other symptoms. This is especially true of those who end up on welfare and government housing because of their psychiatric symptom.

I will come back to Western psychiatry, but I now want to take a brief look at Western medicine in general in order to expand on the above picture.

Medicine in America

It would seem that modern medicine in the United States is a product of an adaptation to unhealthy life styles, along with the ability to sell the idea that technology will come to the rescue.[15] Many of the modern miracles of medicine have developed from saving the lives of people who eat too much, smoke too much, drink too much, exercise too little, stress themselves from the pressures of living in this society, and so on. Such behaviors accumulate and, with respect to physical symptoms alone, find their expression in our digestive systems, which then affect the total metabolism. In short, if the digestive system is not working properly, this will affect the total physiology, including mental functioning. However, digestion and elimination, as conditioned by diet, stress, and so on, are probably the most neglected factors of Western biomedicine. In fact, the leading moneymaker of the pharmaceutical companies in the United States is antacids, signaling that digestive problems are a major issue in overall physical health. The issues of diet, digestion, and elimination are discussed later in this chapter and in a companion volume (*The Holistic Health Practitioner*).

With respect to psychological/psychiatric issues, many of the diagnoses offered represent reactions to life style as well. Anorexia nervosa and bulimia, for example, are offshoots of the fashion industry and ideals as to female attractiveness. They are also the byproduct of athletic competition, wherein coaches cajole their students into losing or maintaining weight, thus frequently leading to the above psychiatric conditions; many of these coaches (and the parents as well) should be brought up on charges of child abuse. Such conditions, however, are usually placed solely on the shoulders of the individual for the individual to correct "when he or she is ready for treatment," thus mirroring our ideals (and illusions) of individualism and free choice.

Another philosophical construct evolves from the fact that the medical establishment, aided by the federal government and the Food and Drug Administration (FDA), has convinced the average citizen that his or her health is in the hands of the Western biomedical establishment. We have the Surgeon General, who speaks for the establishment, and the FDA, which, in the past few years, has attempted to suppress (see Hammell 1995), and even purge libraries of any and all information relating to the efficacy of vitamins, minerals, and herbs. Preventive medicine has yet to be sold with the same vigor as consulting your doctor. Practicing preventive medicine or engaging in a healthy life style is more of a fad, to be capitalized upon by current commercial advertisers.

Again, the vast amount of physical healing that goes on can be attributed not to the medical community at all, but to the natural healing abilities of the individual, coupled with the empathetic support from others.

Western biomedicine, then, is an adaptation to a life style that is unhealthy and to a public that demands instant relief from the physical and emotional problems that evolve from this style of living. Within this philosophy, the metaphorical aspects of illness and its reflection of social functioning are lost to an illusion of the scientific method.

However, Western biomedical philosophy, including psychiatry and regardless of efficacy,[16] still fits within the information categories outlined earlier, that is, *information intrusion, information alteration,* and *inherited information.*

The Continuity of Medical Beliefs Through Time

If we look carefully, there is a detectable thread of continuity of beliefs or philosophies, concerning health and illness, that can be seen connecting humankind since the beginning of recorded history. Earlier parts of this chapter have given an overview of contemporary preliterate and literate peoples and their beliefs, which probably resemble, in many ways, those ancient, prehistoric systems. Rather than noting how these systems differ from Western beliefs, I have, instead, shown that there are great *general* similarities in curing processes.

With respect to this continuity, the idea that systems evolve at least begins formally with the Darwinians. For example, as one reads Sigerist's (1951, 1961) two-volume work, one can appreciate the continuity and exchange of ideas between cultural groups (also see Edelstein 1987:402-439 and his discussion of the Greek world and current philosophy). As Grmek (1989:1) comments:

Notions of disease and even of particular diseases do not flow directly from our experience. They are explanatory models of reality, not its constitutive elements. To put it simply, diseases exist only in the realm of ideas. They interpret a complex empirical reality and presuppose a certain medical philosophy or pathological system of reference. . . . The history of Western medicine, as well as the comparative study

of medicine in diverse societies, shows clearly that diseases are not inevitably conceptualized as they are now.

In short, and considering information discussed earlier, the concepts or the
content changes as we acquire more detailed information. However, much of
the process of cause and effect (*information intrusion, inherited information*,
etc.), and thus diagnosis (i.e., determining cause and effect), has remained
quite constant.

And as Grmek further comments, ideas change with the "sophistication of a
society" and "the pathological realities of a given historical moment in a
specific geographical area" (1989:1). Ohnuki-Tierney's (1984) research in
Japan, however, refutes the conception that social/technological sophistication
inevitably leads to the Western biomedical model. One reason for this is that
illness is an analogy and a representation of processes in social-biological
feedback.

WESTERN PSYCHIATRIC/PSYCHOLOGICAL
CONCEPTS OF CAUSE AND EFFECT

Myth and Illness

Much of psychiatry practiced in the West is chemical oriented, which
seems to be an attempt to emulate Western biomedicine in general. How- ever,
not all psychiatrists and psychologists subscribe to prescribing drugs, but,
instead, use varying psychotherapeutic methods in order to cure psychological
problems. At this juncture, then, it is important to look at some of the general
concepts that knit together the Western philosophy of cause and effect.

To begin, and according to May (1991) in his latest endeavor, mental illness
was/is not a problem in societies where myths are intact and are lived by the
people. He states, "Indeed, the very birth and proliferation of psychotherapy
in our contemporary age were called forth by the disintegration of our
myths" (1991:15). He goes further and concludes (1991:16) that "when the
myths of classical Greece broke down, as they did in the third and second centuries, Lucretius could see 'aching hearts in every home, racked incessantly by
pangs the mind was powerless to assuage and forced to vent themselves in
recalcitrant repining'."

I suspect that Lucretius was reflecting upon social waning in general and
not just the loss of the myths as a guide. May's position of the importance of
myth for mental health is an echo of other writers, Joseph Campbell being the
most recent and outspoken on the subject (Campbell 1990). I strongly question
this position as factual, with all due respect to the works of these scholars, and
consider it, instead, a *reframing* (not truth) within which to engage therapy.

First, I question the interpretation of many of these myths. For example,
and I will expand on this, even Oedipus, within that myth, states, "I must

find out who I am and where I came from!" (taken from May 1991:30). Myths, in fact, state the problems already existing, and indicate common themes that, perhaps, people can take solace in; myths do not solve anything, although they can be used to *reframe* specific life circumstances.

Second, I question the interpretation and license somehow granted to psychologists and psychoanalysts who enter their own interpretations as if fact. May, for example, utilizes his psychoanalytic artistic license in his interpretation of a dream of one of his patients named Ursula.

Near the end of her first month of psychotherapy, she had the following dream:

I was cut in the forehead. I searched around for a bandage. All I could find was a Kotex. I put that on the cut. It's all right if you don't mind. (May 1991:35)

Now, just what does that dream mean? May's first interpretation was

that the cut referred to her coming to see me; we were "cutting" into her head. Since it was a cut in the forehead, it could also tell us that she had a tendency to intellectualize, which we knew anyway but it did not interfere with our doing productive work. The Kotex seemed to refer partially to her sexual seductiveness toward me, although this was not in a degree as to be troublesome. Other associations with the Kotex were procreation: since Kotex is used for menstrual periods she could have a baby (which could refer to her expecting a positive outcome in our therapy, though I thought it was too early in the treatment to verbalize that). The "if-you-don't mind" remark seemed to be simply the statement of a middle-class person of "good" upbringing (1991:35-36).

And then he asks, "But is this all?" According to May, "It is the narrative of the birth of Athena, who leapt out of a slit in Zeus' forehead fully armed. It is the famous birth of Athena who was androgynous" (1991:36). Here, I think May has taken a quantum leap (i.e., artistic license in the largest and longest sense), although it is a beautiful *reframing* for introducing a new interpretation to the patient. The Greek myths come from a different reality, a different frame of reference, which today we can only intellectualize upon, but not adequately understand. His reference here, of course, is to Jungian archetypal images, images buried deep within the subconscious (see Campbell's 1988b discussion of this in *The Way of the Animal Powers,* vol. 1).

Psychoanalysis cures by offering alternative interpretations (*reframing*) to childhood conditions that are unsolvable to the individual with his or her current beliefs about those childhood memories. These memories are not fact, but, first negotiated as the information is experienced (incoming data) and, second, renegotiated over time.[17] Analytic statements represent not truth but only a different perspective, a different frame, or a way to see things from a different, perhaps more comfortable, angle.

When the therapist works almost exclusively with our culture's concept of troubled people or dysfunctional families, he is *not* subjected to the formulas for living generated by nontroubled individuals or functional families. Is May saying that all happy and well adjusted individuals possess myths of the nature discussed by Campbell, Freud, and others? Or is being well adjusted mainly an outcome of simple assumptions that work for the individual within his or her social milieu? I think that the latter is the case. Ancient Egypt ran on extensive myths (their truths). Are we to assume that all ancient Egyptians were happy and content? I think not, and there is documentation and historical reconstruction to back this up.

All the misery we see in the world, which comes to us through personal and group experiences and is combined, in our culture, with the filtered and selective messages of the mass media, helps to build attitudes and myths that we do eventually live by. Myths are, as Campbell has adequately expressed, metaphors of basic concerns, that is, birth, life, death, illness, time, and so on.   These are the progenitors of myths, ideologies, science, and religion. Without these progenitors, society, as an adaptive mechanism, has no direction, science has no goal, and religion has no purpose. Misery is the grist for the development of the best in the human spirit, and sometimes there would seem to be more grist than desirable.

Misery, wonder, contemplation, and all these psychic events precede myth and force its happening. But large social systems like "America" do not change evenly. That is to say, certain attitudinal and behavioral changes will lag behind others. For example, we have the technology to feed everyone in the United States, but our sociopolitical attitudes and behaviors prevent this from happening. These socio-political attitudes are wrapped around myths that we live and cannot see. Our highly ritualized lives are the enactment of these myths. Oftentimes it takes a large crisis to push the society in a direction that alters the myths and ritual, thus reducing stress for the majority of the inhabitants.

Myths, yes, are guides, but believing that we do not have myths of the same import in our society as, say, the American Indians did is false. To say that, if individuals had myths to live by, there would be less emotional misery in the United States is likewise false. In fact, the myths are already in place and have been in place all the time; we just do not see them--we are currently living them.   For example, there are the fiercely independent hero myths (see Campbell 1972), as depicted in cartoons (see Savage 1990), movies, and the like. These are usually coupled with romantic love ideologies, violence, intrigue, and tests, with some moral message presented at the end of the presentation, that is, good triumphs over evil, political and economic statements, and so on. Medical doctors, and thus the Western biomedical community, likewise fit into the hero myth typology. The images and story lines are analogous to the Arthurian legends of the Middle Ages (Campbell 1989b). The differences that I see contained within our contemporary myths involve a current inability to avoid temptations during the quest and to accept the responsibility for one's behavior.   Moreover, without a clear objective or quest, along with the concept of responsibility for actions, one ends up with an overabundance of tragic heroes in real life, that is, fiercely independent types, in search of something undefined, laying waste to the land. These myths are just as alive as the myths of the Middle Ages. The problem encountered by Campbell and May, in my opinion, is that their personal morality, or ideal behavioral set, is of a different nature than the morality as presented in our contemporary myths. As morality changes so does the constellation of the mythical elements.

But there are other types of myths, for example, that technology equals power with the possibility of saving humanity. Technology, in this sense, is no different from God, or Zeus, or even the Devil. Once more, such beliefs are self-fulfilling. And we act out our myths through our rituals, but we do not comprehend our own rituals. And just like those cultures with "real" myths, we do not really think we are acting out a myth. These are not myths; they are facts. Myths explain, through elaborate metaphor, a social and spiritual climate at a particular time.   As Macrone (1992:XII) comments, "Myths weren't invented to please scientists, historians, or philosophers. . . .   Most myths were simply attempts to imagine, in terms of common religious beliefs, how the natural world took shape and why it behaved as it did."

Because of the position that the guiding myths are gone, and this has led to the psychological misery around us, let us examine some of our myths connected with psychotherapy in Western culture and critique their interpretation. From this, we can see how these interpretations have led to the philosophical position espoused by the medical, psychiatric, and clinical psychological establishment.

Oedipus Wrecked

The character of Oedipus was revealed by the Greek dramatist Sophocles (496-406 B.C.). His works about Oedipus (i.e., *Oedipus Tyannos, Oedipus a Colonus*, and *Antigone*) were written over a period of forty years. The essential plot of this trilogy is as follows: Oedipus was born the son of Laius and Jocasta, king and queen of Thebes.   A prophecy is revealed that their son would later kill the king and marry his mother, and, to avoid this possibility, Oedipus is handed over to a shepherd, who then gives Oedipus to Polybus, the childless king of Corinth. Oedipus grows to manhood, leaves his adopted parents because he hears the prophecy, unwittingly kills his real father, solves the riddle of the sphinx, becomes king of Thebes, and, in turn, marries his own mother, Jocasta. When Jocasta learns who Oedipus is, she hangs herself, and Oedipus plucks out his eyes.

From this work, Sigmund Freud developed his famous Oedipus complex:

The principles of the Oedipus situation are regarded by psychoanalysts as characteristic of all persons. During the phase of late infancy, the child shifts a quantum of energy into sexual interests in his parents. Normally the boy becomes chiefly attached to his mother, the girl to her father. The solution of the struggle determines the character of the child's later reactions. During the latency period the Oedipus complex is normally relinquished in favor of extraparental activities and interests. With the advent of puberty the original, infantile Oedipus situation is again aroused, and is normally dissolved by the centering of interests in others.

However, the average psychiatric patient never successfully manages his Oedipus complex. Schizophrenia serves as an excellent example. A schizophrenic patient believes implicitly that he was not the child of his parents, that his mother was his wife and that his brothers and sisters were his children; he maintained that his father did not exist. The same patient also insisted that he was blind; on other occasions he spoke of having been castrated. The schizophrenic patient relives the Sophoclean tragedy often with minute precision, even to the point of claiming royal birth.

The same theme is common to psychoneurotic patients, but it is often highly symbolized as a fear, compulsion, or a conversion phenomenon.

Freud is responsible for the introduction of the Oedipus concept into psychiatry. "One says rightly that the Oedipus complex is the nuclear concept of the neuroses, that it represents the essential part in the content of the neuroses. It is the culminating point of infantile sexuality, which through its after-effects decisively influences the sexuality of the adult." (Hinsie and Campbell 1976:144-145)

One might ask whether or not Freudian theory or, more specifically, the Oedipus complex, is an important feature in current psychological or psychiatric thinking. The answer is most definitely "Yes." As Leak and Christoper (1982:313) state, "There can be little doubt that Freudian psychoanalysis is the 'first force' in 20th-century psychology. Psychoanalysis as a personality theory is the most comprehensive one available, detailing the structure, dynamics, and development of personality to a degree unsurpassed by its competitors."

Paul Kline (1981:28) comments, with respect to the Oedipus complex, "[B]oys and girls do have sexual feelings toward the opposite sex parent of which they are largely unaware [but this does] not establish the Oedipus complex as the central conflict of mental life or show it to be the kernel of neurosis." Kline, of course, is acting as a critic. The reality is that the Oedipus complex is alive and well and, although the terminology has changed to "protect the innocent," is a basic premise in intellectual discussions of cause and effect in the psychiatric and clinical psychological communities. The primary question often raised in such discussions involves the universal application of the complex. A second, and perhaps more important question, involves Freud's original interpretation of the Oedipus plays as written by Sophocles. I will respond to the universal issue, but let us first look closely at the interpretation Freud placed on the Oedipus trilogy.

The Meaning of the Oedipus Myth

The best way to look for meaning in these ancient plays is through the eyes of those thoroughly versed in the subject of these ancient myths. Jean-Pierre Vernant (professor emeritus of comparative study of ancient religions at the College de France in Paris) and Pierre Vidal-Naquet (director of studies and professor of sociology at the Ecole Pratique des Hautes Etudes in Paris) will act as guides through the difficult journey of meaning.

According to Vernant and Vidal-Naquet (1988:85-140), the meaning of the Oedipus trilogy can only shine through a lens that is made up of the problems of linguistics, history, social and political factors, and the mental context of that particular time period. Freud did not include this in his analysis. As they clearly state, one must have a knowledge of the social and political factors in play during that time period (i.e., Athens during the fifth century B.C.) in order to deduce any psychological issues represented in these plays. The Athenian audience of that period, in comparison to a contemporary audience, would surely have attached a different meaning to the presented symbols (1988:87-88).

Referring to the social and political climate of that time, Vernant and Vidal-Naquet (1988:88-89) go on to comment that the philosophical questions of responsibility for behaviors (i.e., "intentional" vs. "excusable" offenses) were beginning to be addressed. City living, and the associated autonomy, forces a close look at crime and responsibility. Where does group control and responsibility end and individual blame begin? Does man, in fact, have a say in his own destiny? According to the authors, this is an "experiment" of sorts, developing as human groupings are evolving. They go on to say that the art form, the construction of the tragedy, comes and goes in a very short period of time (100 years), suggesting that the need to explore such concerns had waned in importance. The historical significance of the Oedipus tragedy is overlooked, or considered insignificant, by Freud. The question the authors have for Freud, and others who still see a universal psychology within these plays, is, Why did they have such a short life span, and why was tragedy as an art form not found in other civilizations? (1988:88-90).

The keys of importance for Freud are the murder of one's father and sex with one's mother, accompanied by revulsion and self-punishment. But, as Vernant and Vidal-Naquet point out (1988:90), in the earlier versions of these plays, which Freud was apparently unaware of, there was no self-punishment; Oedipus simply dies still king of Thebes. Moreover, there are many tragedies from that time period by Euripides, Aeschylus, and Sophocles which have nothing to do with Oedipal themes.

Finally, Vernant and Vidal-Naquet (1988:93-94) state:

Freud's interpretation of tragedy in general and Oedipus Rex in particular has had no influence on the work of the Greek scholars. They have continued their research just as if Freud had not spoken. . . . True, a psychoanalyst might suggest a different explanation for this lack of recognition or rejection of Freudian views. He might well see it as the proof of a psychological barrier, a refusal to admit to the role of the Oedipus complex both in one's personal life and in human development as a whole. Debate on this point has been reopened by the article in which Didier Anzieu set out to repeat the work undertaken by Freud at the beginning of the century, this time on the basis of the new data available in 1966. If, armed only with the insight afforded by psychoanalysis, Anzieu can venture into the field of classical antiquity and there discover what the specialists continue not to see, does it not prove that the latter are blind or rather they want to make themselves blind because they refuse to recognize their own image in the figure of Oedipus?

So we must examine the value of the universal Oedipal key, the secret of which is known to the psychoanalyst and that is supposed to enable him to decipher all human works without any further preparation. Is it really the key to the doors of the mental world of the ancient Greeks? Or does it simply force the locks?

Vernant and Vidal-Naguet also comment on Freud's confusion about social obligations prevailing in ancient Greece--the reference here is to Antigone's attachment to Oedipus, with innate sexual desires, that is "philia" rather than "eros" (1988:100-102). In short, Antigone's relationship to her father was dictated by social mores rather than innate erotic desires.

I think that the points made above, in themselves, would force an air of caution, if not refutation, regarding the universal nature of the Oedipus complex. But the fact that the Oedipus complex is still considered as fact by many in the psychoanalytic, psychiatric, and psychological communities says more about the persistence of theories (Kuhn 1967) and ideas, and their fit with Western concepts of individualism, than it does about whether the theories are factual. The Freudian position is elegant in its complexity and ability to explain everything about mental functioning; both, as well, are its downfall. Put quite simply, there are more verifiable ways of explaining mental functioning and human behavior in general without resorting to the Freudian position or analysis of a myth ripped away from its social context.

Oedipus and the Anthropologist

Spiro, an anthropologist who likewise finds the Oedipus complex to fit within a universal framework, deserves mention (see also Paul 1976). His work, *Oedipus in the Trobriands* (1982), centers around the original anthropological work in the Trobriands, conducted by Malinowski, commencing in 1914. Out of this field research, Malinowski wrote several books, one entitled *Sex and Repression in Savage Society* (1927), in which he refuted Freud's claim that the Oedipus complex was universal. Spiro's book is an attempt to vindicate Freud and place the Oedipus complex back on the universal shelf, or at least to indicate that the Trobriand islanders did indeed exhibit the Oedipus complex or a variation of it.

First, Spiro begins with the assumption that Freud's understanding of the classic Greek myths was correct. If Freud's analysis of the myth is incorrect, then Spiro's discussion operates on a false premise in the first place. But let us consider Spiro's argument further. Spiro states (1982:164), "Although the structure of the Oedipus complex, while variable in principle, seems to be universal in fact, this is not the case in regards to its two other attributes--its intensity and outcome--in which cross-cultural variability is not only a theoretical expectation but an ethnographic fact."

Part of the basis of his statement revolves around the belief that, "[s]ince libidinal desires for the mother may be present, as we have seen, in the nursing infant, the implementation of the incest taboo may be said to begin with weaning, which is also the time when the child is usually banned from the mother's bed." (1982:164-165) To begin with, no one that I am aware of has been able to determine that children have libidinal desires, and, until we determine that they do, the mere *belief* that such a drive exists in infants does not make it so. This is reminiscent of the "We all know that there is a God, now let's prove it" position which leads to circularity, not proof. Low libido, I must add, is a metaphor for lack of sexual desire, but stating that someone has low libido does not really mean that there is a thing called a libido that is low. This is not the same as being low on gasoline or money.

The second consideration, and the last one I will address here, is the variability factor of libidinous expression from society to society, which is conveniently handled with the analytical term called repression. Let me quote Spiro (1988:167):

Operationally defined, a "weak" or "incomplete" repression of the Oedipus complex is one in which repression is insufficiently powerful to preclude the conscious arousal of the boy's incestuous wishes for the mother (and hence his hostile wishes toward the father) under conditions of incestuous temptation. Hence, those societies in which incomplete repression is the dominant outcome of the Oedipus complex are societies in which the implementation of the taboos on mother-son incest and father-son aggression by the enculturation and socialization techniques described above is not entirely successful in achieving their internalization. This being the case, rather than relying on the boy's own psychological resources--extinction, repression, and reaction formation--to insure compliance with those taboos, many of those societies achieve compliance by means of social and cultural resources, as well.

With all due respect to Spiro, in the above statement, there is the assumption that the Oedipus complex is a real and verifiable thing.[18] Vernant and Vidal-Naguet, mentioned above, cast real doubt on this. Using Kuhn's (1967) concepts of paradigms, it is not too difficult to understand that, once the belief is established and accepted (i.e., "the Oedipus complex is universal"), data coming into the senses are channeled in that direction whether they fit or not. This is what I call the "cookie cutter effect," where you take the excess dough that lies outside of the mold, the dough that "doesn't fit," roll it up, flatten it out, and press the cookie cutter down another time. There is another, simpler metaphor to explain positive mother-son relations, as well as antagonistic mother-son (mother-daughter, father-daughter, father-son, etc.) relationships, and this has to do with acceptance and rejection and the connection between rejection and emotional/physical death (see Chapter 1). Briefly, what is trying to survive here is genetic information, and, because of our evolutionary heritage (our group-animal status), being outside the group equals death. Emotional death, through rejecting comments by a fellow group member, and physical death through being abandoned to die, are, in my opinion, synonymous, with the former being attached to the latter as culture and consciousness evolved. I do not want to belabor the point regarding Oedipus. It has little explanatory value, although when it was first presented by Freud, it served a useful purpose of altering the previous paradigm and creating a new understanding (metaphor--*reframing*) of our humanity. Whether it was correct or not is less important than the fact that Freud's conceptualizations made us look at ourselves differently.

The Id, Ego, and Superego

Freud's elegant use of metaphor led him to postulate the idea that the human psyche contained an id, an ego, and a superego. In order to fully appreciate these things, we first have to come to terms with human consciousness, our biological/behavioral heritage, and whether or not the ego is a "more or less" concept depending on social dictates. In other words, North American urban culture upholds the idea of individualism and free speech to such a point that narcissism (often viewed as a personality disorder) and self-centeredness tend to be the rule or even an ideal. Traditional Japanese and Chinese culture, on the other hand, extol not the rights of the individual, but, instead, the individual's place in a group. In this sense, if everyone has an ego, it surely varies in importance in terms of social interaction and psychological well-being from culture to culture.

Essentially, and according to Freud, the id represents the animal instincts possessed by man and woman. Sulloway comments (1979:411):

The id, or seat of the unconscious, is said to be the original repository of life (Eros) and death instincts in this tripartite scheme. Within the id, the death instinct aims at tension reduction and thus at an eventual state of Nirvana. Eros, by contrast, continually introduces new tensions into the id, tensions that take the form of instinctual needs required for the preservation of life and for the continuance of the species.

The ego and superego evolve from the id, according to Freud, as I will discuss shortly. For now, what can be said about the id? First, it represents a wonderful metaphor for explaining, or at least connecting, humankind with our biological and animal heritage. Second, with the benefit of almost 100 years of probing the concept of consciousness, the id is seen as the raw material with which the human organism attempts to make sense out of the information that surrounds it. Let us consider for a moment concepts of human consciousness that are intertwined with current Western therapeutic processes and around which the id does its work. (The reader can review concepts of consciousness as presented in Chapter 2 for more general considerations.)

Archetypal Images

Evolving from Jungian psychology, originating from theories of the subconscious, and utilized currently in psychoanalytic thinking are the concept of and the belief in archetypal images or symbols. These symbols, theoretically, are imbedded within the psyche and are the product of elements in the environment, that is, responses or triggers to perhaps life-threatening features that impinge on the individual. These could be predatory animals, life, death, or the like, that have "attached" themselves to our nervous system in some fashion. This could be of the nature of Lamarckian Inherited Characteristics or perhaps through some sort of "topobiological" (Edelman 1988) factor not well understood.

The questions I have regarding archetypes are these: Are they accumulative, and, if so, why am I not afraid of hawks the way a baby chick is (this was an example used by Joseph Campbell, discussed below, to "prove" their existence)? What is the life expectancy of an archetype? Are they species specific?

Campbell (1988b:47-49) in vol. I of *Historical Atlas of World Mythology*, referring to "Innate Releasing Mechanisms," a concept put forth by Nico Tinbergen, makes his case for the existence of archetypes. According to Campbell (1988b:48), "[E]ven if all the hawks in the world were to vanish, their image would still sleep in the soul of the chick--never to be aroused, however, unless by some accident of art." It would follow from this that my psyche should contain all and any archetypal images that my ancestors somehow acquired, perhaps even going back before the age of the dinosaurs, which would include birds.

Other questions come to mind: Are archetypes species specific, and are they acquired in perhaps a species-specific manner? If this is the case, then how a bird might acquire such archetypes, such "Innate Releasing Mechanisms," might have little to do with humans because of the differences in the character or make-up of their respective nervous systems.

More questions. If the environment outside of the individual is responsible for initiating the building of these releasing mechanisms, why do not the diverse cultures living in diverse environments have different archetypal

images? Or perhaps archetypal images only happened during an early slice of
hominid development, perhaps when our distant ancestors lived within a
similar environment, for example, East Africa? Are we still evolving
archetypes?

The answer here is that, because there are such similarities between
mythical themes, this tells us precisely that archetypes of the nature discussed
by Jung, Campbell, and May, at least for humans, do not exist. Myths relate
to real, *conscious* (not collective unconscious) concerns that everyone is forced
to face and explain in the process of organizing events. And what are these
basic concerns that every human faces? They are life (and the elements that
sustain it--birth and/or rebirth, acceptance, sex, acquiring food, male, female,
light, etc.), death (and the elements that are analogous to it--dark, rejection,
eating and killing to sustain life, killing for self-protection, illness, loss of
group members, and the restructuring of groups, etc.), conflict between
individuals and groups, and peace and order. Thus, there are general themes
that can be found within the world's myths. But we do not need the concept of
archetypes to explain their existence and our responses in such a specific
manner.

What I have found to be a more useful way of organizing available information (although it is still a "story") is what Bickerton (1990:16), as discussed
earlier, calls "representations." Again, the organism perceives its environment
not as an environment as such, but as a representation, with specific aspects of
the environment being detected by sensory receptors and then interpreted.
Each organism perceives and responds to those aspects of the environment
most relevant to that organism's needs for survival, which includes "lines at
various angles, motions of varying kinds, different qualities of light, and so on.
. . . Creatures get the senses they need for the behaviors they are capable of. If
they cease to need them they lose them."

Representations are built from basic elements perceived in the
environment. At this point, I will briefly consider images, keeping in mind
that there are other senses (i.e., auditory and tactile) that cross over into one
another. According to Marr (1982:41):

There are four factors responsible for the intensity values in an image. They are (1)
geometry and (2) the reflections of the visible surfaces, (3) the illumination of the
scene, and (4) the viewpoint. In an image, all these factors are muddled up, some
intensity changes being due to one cause, others to another, and some to a combination.
The purpose of early visual processing is to sort out which changes are due to what
factors and hence to create representations in which the four factors are separated.

Although this is not a book on vision specifically, let me consider some of
the assumptions that Marr (1982:44-68) makes that serve to construct representations. These include existence of surfaces, hierarchical organization,
similarity, spatial continuity, continuity of discontinuities, and continuity of
flow. Getting more specific, Marr lists edge or boundary, bars or parallel edge

pairs, and zero-crossings "where the value of a function passes from positive to negative" (1982:54). Within these, he lists position, orientation, contrast, length, and width. Each one of these can be seen as a part of higher-order representations. All of these, from the complex geometrical composites to the individual units, are far from anything that would represent an archetype. Figure 4.1 illustrates how I conceptualize these representations. Once again, and in my opinion, archetypes are cultural representations that are analogous to common human concerns that are expressed not only in myth, but also in all human activity and/or the rituals that represent or enact the myths, with myths spontaneously forming and then unfolding in front of our eyes.

Archetypes, then, have been invented to explain an innate consciousness, one that is ever present and guides our experiences, much the same as the id proposed by Freud. From a therapeutic perspective, archetypes are useful as a metaphor for reframing a belief and then creating a potential for reaching some goal. This is essentially what Estes (1992) performs in her recent writings. She states (1992:15-16):

Stories are medicine. I have been taken with stories since I heard my first. They have such power; they do not require that we do, be, act anything--we need only listen. The remedies for repair or reclamation of any lost psychic drive are contained in stories. Stories engender the excitement, sadness, questions, longing, and understanding that spontaneously bring the archetype, in this case Wild Woman, back to the surface.

Archetypes are another form of analysis, a metaphor, that has to appeal not to testable problems in human relationships, but to innate strengths and weaknesses. All one need do is convince the patient that archetypes do indeed exist. This is a elegant form of reframing using archetype consciousness as a focal point.

Behavior Modification

Behavior Modification (Pavlov 1941; Skinner 1972, 1974), which consumed much of the research time, dollars, and classroom space during the 50s and 60s, had difficulty with the Freudian concept of unconsciousness motivation. In short, neurotic behavior is learned; there is no deep problem to uncover. Simply get rid of the symptoms, a mirror of Western biomedicine in general. This explanation, in itself, is a reframing that takes the individual away from the belief that it is only through depth psychology that issues can be resolved. The process, then, is to use conditioning procedures to modify one behavior by substituting another. In fact, all therapies do this during an educational process, that is, learning about one's self in society or simply learning and implementing new choices. Such learning does not have to be fact, only believable and thus self-fulfilling. The difference lies in how the person is convinced to do something different, that is, how the unwanted behavior or thought pattern is reframed or conceptualized.

Figure 4.1
The Development of Representational States from Simple
to Complex (Based on Marr 1982 and Bickerton 1990)

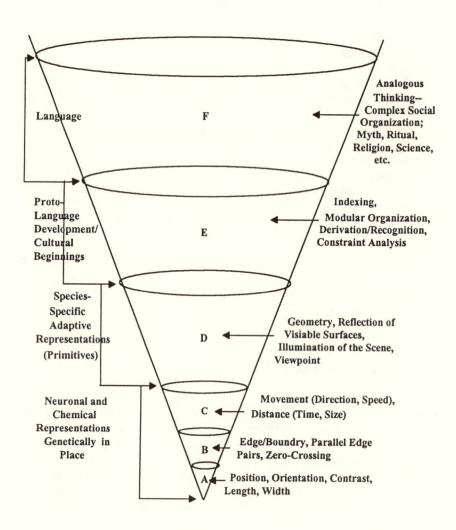

Behavior modification, however, could not do away with the unconscious altogether, as certainly we are not consciously aware of our conditioning and are not consciously aware of everything we do. The reaction of Skinner and others was a movement away from concepts that were metaphorical and unprovable and toward a "scientific method," which, in large measure, was in tune with the then-current methods being employed by Western biomedicine in general.

Humanistic Models of Therapy

The Humanistic school of psychology, a reaction against the mechanical, mechanistic, and rather cold position of the Behaviorists, once again finds its roots in unconscious motivation, Freud, and psychoanalysis (see Watson 1977). Encompassing many different methods or brands of therapy, all, once again, lead to a reframing of the client or patient's cognitive problems. Many, like "Client-Centered" or Rogerian therapy (Rogers 1965), involve letting the client "talk" about issues. As trust is built, deeper issues are revealed. All of these therapies imply that consciousness and personality are alterable and that nurture has the biggest hold on social functioning irrespective of archetypes, ids, egos, libidinous desires, or conditioning.

Others, like those engaging in Gestalt Therapy (applied in group as well as individual, client-therapist sessions), use the innate process of generalizing on themes, or Gestalts, in the therapeutic process most notably expressed in Gestalt Dreamwork (Perls et al. 1951; Polster and Polster 1973). In the Rogerian process, the goal is to externalize a story. Once the story is out, so to speak, the speaker and the listener are in a better position to apply alternative interpretations (reframing) to the content. Gestalt does the same thing, but perhaps in a shorter period of time. By combining or adding elements in dreams, one can very quickly acquire a different perspective (reframing) as to meaning, which can then be applied (interpretation or another reframing) to current situations.

Transactional Analysis (Berne 1973), a very popular individual and group therapy approach in the 1970s, looked at the structure, and what I call the implied rules, of interpersonal and group communication patterns in order to make them explicit. By making behavioral sequences explicit, the individual is in a better position to alter them. The reframing occurs in the fact that the interaction patterns are blamed for the problem rather than the individuals who are automatically engaging learned patterns. The recognition of unconscious patterns, then, is the key to change.

But, even though there is a recognition of unconscious motivation, people were often conceptualized as wanting to be in power, being manipulative, planning moves, as if we are all engaged in a social chess game. This is far from the truth; most people are on autopilot. So, although there is an unconscious base to these therapies, the unconscious is not carved in stone. Personality is alterable. Spinoffs of these approaches have led to assertiveness and parent-effectiveness types of training. However, not one of these therapies can claim a better cure rate than another, and, probably more important, termination, signaling cure, and social reintegration are, for the most part, absent. Moreover, the originators of these processes (e.g., Perls and his Gestalt Therapy) often had greater success in curing than did their students. What does this say about charismatic leaders, akin to Franz Anton Mesmer, and the faith people simply have in a specific individual's ability to "cure," that is, self-fulfilling prophesies, the placebo effect, and so on. None of these aspects of curing has anything to do with scientific method, so desperately sought after by the psychological and psychiatric communities, because they are unpredictable and are not subject to controlled studies.

Many of the approaches involve a once-a-week therapist-client interaction pattern for many months and sometimes years, with termination often left up to the client. Further, there seems to be a correlation between length of therapy and depth of problem. In other words, the longer the person is in therapy, the sicker he or she is (or gets), which is good for the therapist, but not for the client. Moreover, continually talking about an issue can be retraumatizing.

In my opinion, the position of authority of the psychiatrist and psychologist (or MFCC, LCSW, etc.) in the "emotional curing industry" needs to be questioned. Because they tend to focus on individuals and not systems, there is little understanding about the curing process in general and how it has to fit into the social milieu. For the most part, these are well meaning professionals trapped in models regarding individual functioning with little regard for social dynamics.

Group Therapies

Group therapies, including self-help, encounter groups, psychodrama, Gestalt, Transactional Analysis, and the various "cult"-type group therapies (i.e., EST, QUEST, LIFE SPRING, etc.), once again, all center around reinterpreting a person's behavior, that is, reframing. Some therapies approach this in a gentle fashion, without confrontation, and others, like EST, tend to be rather forceful in pushing a new interpretation onto individuals.

Some self-help groups (e.g., those dealing with sexual abuse) often and unwittingly end up retraumatizing individuals through talk about events *without* reframing or placing a meaning onto the event that is more acceptable to the individual. Instead, many of the participants are left in the status of "victim." Without a reframing of the events, without a different and more satisfactory meaning, without a termination ritual, and without a reintegration into society, the person cannot exit from the event(s) and continues to loop.

There are many other types of therapeutic approaches in the marketplace, for example, Primal Scream, Milieu Therapy, Rational-Emotive, and so on, all of which are simply different ways of doing the same thing, that is, reframing life events. Again, all have evolved from Freudian theory and use reframing as their basic therapeutic technique, that is, giving a new and more satisfactory meaning to life events. From that point, solutions are generated in terms of new options or new choices. And, again, this is the process applied in cultures throughout the world. The two features that are almost always lacking involve the termination ritual and reintegration into society. Western psychology, like Western biomedicine in general, is a system worthy of study, but it should not, in my opinion, be the belief system or template by which to measure other methods of curing (see Berry et al. 1992:2-3).

THE WESTERN BIOMEDICAL CONCEPT
OF DISEASE AND ILLNESS: AN OVERVIEW

In Western culture, we tend to make a distinction between emotional, or psychological illness, and physical illness, a distinction that is not as clear-cut in other cultures. At this point, we need to build a bridge between these two concepts.

Current Western biomedicine is not traditional medicine, and, although a continuum was noted from ancient times, it contains many features that are a recent outgrowth of advances in chemistry (inorganic, organic, biochemistry, analytical), cellular physiology, and surgical techniques. Research in these areas is carried out not only in the hospital arena, but also by pharmaceutical companies, with pharmaceutical companies attempting to meet the current and long-term needs of the medical establishment. Western biomedicine deals mainly with the suppression of symptoms, thus matching a life style. Other, more traditional systems (i.e., eclectic and naturopathic) include the use of herbs and more group-oriented, symbolic/emotional mechanisms for counterbalancing individual and consequently social imbalance and look for causes rather than treating symptoms. These latter systems seem to be reemerging and resemble, in large measure, the Darwinian and evolutionary positions that are gaining popularity (see Lappe 1994; Nesse and Williams 1994).

Although many prescription drugs used herbal bases until the early 1980s, a large number of the herbal components have been synthesized by the pharmaceutical companies and the natural forms are no longer a part of the pharmaceutical industry.[19] The reasons for synthesizing these extracts are expedience and money. Ownership of an extract, especially if it is altered in some perhaps non-essential way, translates into money in the marketplace. It is important to realize that in the United States, like no other country in the world, money is very much a part of what we call "illness" and "disease." Who diagnoses, who cures, who lives, and who dies are intimately sewn into the economic fabric of this country.

Western Biomedicine, Power, and Economics

Further, in order to comprehend human biochemistry, the researcher or physician must understand the part nutrition plays in the process of health and disease. And yet very little time is spent in this area during formal medical training. This brings us to a basic biomedical philosophy, which can be seen in our concept of individualism and the law. That is, we react to things rather than "proact"; you fix rather than prevent. Although there are many physicians who preach prevention, who have a good grasp of nutrition, the medical complex cannot economically prosper with a preventative system, with a system that freely disseminates information on health and methods of longevity. From a purely economic perspective, it is more sound to have the individual dependent on the medical establishment, to keep the populace ignorant of health, and to convince all its citizens that it has the "truth," or the proper method of health care; that Western biomedicine should always be consulted; and that other philosophies, or alternatives, are fraudulent or quackery. Moreover, the American Medical Association has been granted legitimate (state-authorized) power to coerce and force people to accept treatments; they have the power to prescribe and have the exclusive use of specific words or symbols, for example, "cure," "diagnose," "treat," "patient," and "medicine." Moreover, and mirroring the legitimate powers of the state, the Western biomedical specialist can gaze at, touch, and intrude into the orifices of your body thus overturning all the social taboos associated with that behavior. And they can do this "in your best interest." The medical establishment can even remove tissues from your body, and consequently the genes within, and patent them for its own use; the courts have upheld this in the name of science. Any genetic engineering from these tissues can be converted into vast sums of money, which is then out of reach of the original owner of that information. The medical community is establishing precedents that have real shades of *Frankenstein* and *Blade Runner*.

The Western biomedicine complex, in order to stay in business, has to fight against several of the cultural ideals (i.e., individualism, free choice, equality, and a dislike and fear of centralized authority--see Lupton 1994:105-130) that can lead, and have led, to poor nutrition and overall poor health. These ideals, however, could be turned toward health. For example, when the individual enters the "sick" role he or she, through labeling, becomes the illness; individualism, free choice, and equality cease. But, when these cultural HRMs are tapped into, as when the physician places himself or herself in some position superior to the patient through word and action, over time, some patients seek advice and care elsewhere. Although this may seem like politics on my part, the manifestation of the doctor-patient relationship (i.e., how this relationship proceeds) tells us a great deal about overall medical philosophy. Most physicians run their offices like airlines; they overbook, which results in long waits at the doctor's office. The message is that the doctor is more important than the patient, and the only reason such arrogance goes on unabated is the fact that they are "the only game in town." That may be changing as rapport between doctor and patent erodes and more information regarding alternative and/or preventative health procedures, enters the market-place. The FDA, which appears to be more of an extension of the medical establishment than a government agency established "by the people and for the people," has done its best to prevent information about alternative procedures from becoming common knowledge. This has been done by using SWAT teams to raid health food stores and by censoring and prohibiting the truthful health claims by the manufacturers of vitamins and other supplements. There is a great deal at stake in terms of keeping the power to prescribe in the hands of Western biomedicine, and it will be interesting to see how current lawsuits (see Hammell 1995) against the FDA unfold.

The medical establishment has also created an illusion that we enjoy better health and longevity due to medical efforts. This is not true. As Larsen (1995:204) states, "The shift from foraging to farming led to a reduction in health status and well-being, an increase in physiological stress, a decline in nutrition, an increase in birthrate and population growth, and an alteration of activity types and loads. Taken as a whole, then, the popular and scholarly perception that quality of life improved with the acquisition of agriculture is incorrect."

Larson's position is equally relevant to our current circumstances. Medical knowledge has had its greatest impact on trauma injuries, but has contributed little to longevity and overall health, and, in my opinion, is a contributing factor to poor health and decreased life span.

Several aspects stand out in the philosophy of Western biomedicine: (1) the approach involves treating (suppressing) symptoms; (2) disease is seen as a scientific, clinical matter, with a strong emphasis on diagnosis and naming (word magic), and treatment centering on removal of the pathogen (Ohnuki-Tierney 1984:92-102); (3) the patient is always in a subservient relationship to the doctor; and (4) Western biomedicine has the "truth" (and power) over all other systems, with other systems being labeled "less than," "alternatives," or even "quackery" and Western biomedicine being labeled "traditional"--questioning a doctor's diagnosis or procedure is tantamount to sacrilege.

Stress and Disease

There is agreement in the Western biomedical community that any disease has an emotional component. It is a matter of how important that component is with respect to the disease/illness state. Are the symptoms merely a product of the disease, or is there a less appreciated, culture-bound aspect involved? Do we conceptualize healing as a natural process of the human body, and is this process initiated by the physician, the patient, or both?

The general thinking is as follows (and this can be added to the philosophical points mentioned above): If you cure the disease, the emotional component will evaporate, and, therefore, analyzing the emotional aspect of illness is not as important as treating disease. In short, illness equals symptoms, while disease is what one really treats. This is why, in many cases, a patient's complaints are considered "only in your head." As Mills (1991:14) states:

One of the most frequent complaints made about doctors by patients turning to alternatives, at least in Britain, is that they do not take enough notice of the patients' stories.

It is not just the usual argument that the doctor has so little time: it really seems as though the doctor is not interested in the details of the story. Even more disquieting, and this is a complaint most often made by women patients, the doctor will actually discount features of the story that do not accord with the expected presentation. The following example might not seem unfamiliar:

Patient: *My stomach swells up straight after eating, especially after eating acid foods... I feel as though I cannot lose this weight even though I eat only a tiny amount... I also get a lot of headaches and feel very tired all the time...*

Doctor: *The blood tests show there is nothing wrong with you; it is probably your nerves... the only real way to lose weight is to cut back on your calories - of course, you could also try and do a little more exercise... I can give you something to help you relax better. ....*

Apart from the obvious slight to the patient, in such conversations the implication is that the doctor knows what goes on in the patient's mind/body better than the patient. This is not surprising.

Targeting Symptoms Rather Than Preventing or Balancing the Body

Information intrusion in the Western biomedical model involves having bacteria or viruses enter the body through the varying orifices or through puncture wounds. Diverse types of bacteria and viruses have been isolated, and biochemical descriptions are available as to their effect on the body. Numerous helminths have likewise been isolated and, through epidemiological studies, numerous disease vectors have been detected (Singleton and Sainsbury 1993).

Various drugs (i.e., antibiotics) have been developed which target bacteria or the environment (e.g., skin abrasions) within which the bacteria exist. The Western biomedical system also has identified metabolic dysfunctions that lead to disease, dysfunctions that can be caused by injury, and genetic issues leading to metabolic/disease states. Advances in anesthesia and surgical techniques have allowed for invasive surgery on cases previously deemed inoperable, as well as non-invasive techniques using ultrasound and chemotherapy. A proud tribute to technology. All these techniques emphasize a targeting of a specific pathogen or condition, rather than looking for cause and a holistic balancing of the body, which belongs to past medical philosophies in this country (i.e., eclectic, naturopathic) and certainly to non-Western systems as well.

Prevention in Western biomedicine is conceptualized as testing for symptoms before they fully mature into illness (see Leutwyler 1995). In other words, when operating within a social model of free choices and then reacting to the long-term effects of exercising these choices, life style is not targeted in terms of prevention. Instead, the individual is free to engage in high-risk behaviors (i.e., use of alcohol and other drugs, tobacco, fractionated foods, etc.), and the family physician, aided by other medical specialists, will use expensive tests to determine "if you have gotten away with it." This is not, in my mind, prevention so much as Russian roulette.

Nutrition and Illness

As Helman states (1994:37), "Food is more than just a source of nutrition. In all human societies it plays many roles, and is deeply embedded in the social, religious and economic aspects of everyday society. . . . Food. . . . is an essential part of the way that any society organizes itself--and of the way that it views that world that it inhabits" (see also Levi-Stauss 1970; Simoons 1994). One should not be surprised, therefore, when encountering food in Western culture as intimately bound to social symbols and to specific political and economic philosophies and practices (see Lappe 1991; Robbins 1987).

There are many misconceptions about nutrition both within and outside of the Western biomedical complex. And to narrow vision even more, most medical schools do not mandate courses in the subject area, but, instead, center on drugs and monitoring technology (testing, as mentioned above). Moreover, those who are expert in the field of nutrition often, and inadvertently, lead the average physician away from questioning the importance of consuming fractionated foods (processed foods). For example, Veldee (1994:1237) reports, "Specific nutrient deficiencies have been largely eliminated in the United States owing to a number of developments." She follows this with the observation that foods are "fortified" and "enriched," that food technologies have advanced to the point of creating a consistent, nutrient-rich food supply, and that the general public has been educated with respect to proper nutrition intake. First of all, our knowledge of vitamins and supplementation has, for the most part, eliminated scurvy, pellagra, and related issues. However, when we take a food, like wheat, process it, remove many of the essential vitamins and minerals, and then replace or add a few, this is *not* enrichment; the concept of enriched foods is a misconception. The food is still fractionated. Moreover, the nutrients removed (e.g., the bran) are sold as other commodities suggesting that the food processor or manufacturer is looking after the health of the nation by offering fiber-rich food. Malnutrition, as Veldee (1994:1237) states, is still a problem, although she overlooks the outcomes of eating fractionated foods with preservatives as well as the consequences of combining specific foods.

Second, adding preservatives to foods serves mainly the manufacturer in order to increase shelf life. Preservatives stop food spoilage. What spoils foods? Usually bacteria and molds. In short, either the bacteria will not live on the food, and/or it takes them longer to extract nutrients. The question is, If bugs cannot eat or metabolize this food, can you? Answer: No, and for the same reasons that bacteria cannot metabolize it.

Third, North Americans have not been educated in a meaningful way with respect to appropriate nutrition. Being told to lower fat, salt, and sugar intake is not adequate knowledge, assuming that people will act on this information in the first place. Moreover, and due to the fact that there are vast amounts of convenient, processed foods, as well as fast-food establishments on every corner, it is often difficult to maximize one's nutrient intake and not incur digestive problems without doing extensive research, and most people are not knowledgeable and/or motivated enough to take this step.

An essential point is that the established Western biomedical position often colors the Western anthropologist's perception of what information is important when collecting data on nutrition both within our own culture and in others. If we use the FDA's or the medical community's opinions, this may structure our questions and base our perceptions of nutrition, or of what constitutes good or adequate nutrition, upon a faulty paradigm.

Digestion, Malnutrition, and Illness

Veldee (1994:1237) goes on to state, "[T]he application of clinical nutrition principles is hindered by a lack of evidence demonstrating that nutrition support will reverse the morbidity and mortality associated with malnutrition. Prospective clinical case-control trials of the late 1970s and 1980s failed to show consistently a beneficial effect of postoperative TPN" (administration of nutrients intravenously). Many of these studies were criticized for various reasons. However, giving a patient nutrients via I.V. assumes that the medical establishment knows what nutrients to give, that these nutrients are matched to the patient's prevailing needs, and that giving fractionated nutrients via I.V. really imitates the process of digestion, utilization, and elimination. But a larger consideration is neglected. Most people have digestive problems as evidenced by the mass consumption of antacids (antacids also disrupt digestion and deplete vitamins A, D, E, and K). With digestive problems one cannot properly metabolize foods, essential nutrients are not efficiently absorbed, and toxins are added to, rather than removed from the body. Moreover, with the

I.V. patients, if digestion and elimination were problems before the operation, giving nutrients via I.V. does not correct those problems, and toxins continue to accumulate, thus slowing healing potential. If a patient goes into surgery with digestive problems and is encouraged postoperatively to eat fractionated foods without proper sequencing (most hospital food is notorious for being highly fractionated, overcooked, and of low fiber content), that guarantees continued digestive problems and a slower recovery. Not paying attention to preoperative and postoperative digestive problems will have an effect on any research in this direction.

Moreover, a vast majority of catastrophic medical conditions can be directly tied to poor nutrition and to digestive and elimination problems. Constipation, for example, defined as "the passage of less than 3 stools per week," accounts for 2.5 million physician visits per year (Dugdale and Eisenberg 1992:14). What is considered a normal number of bowel movements is an average from asking patients, not what is really healthy. Because the average North American diet is composed mainly of fractionated, fiber-deficient food, constipation, which is a signal of digestive problems in general, is almost guaranteed.

Dugdale and Eisenberg (1992:15) give a list of metabolic and endocrine disorders that "cause" constipation (i.e., diabetes, hypercalcemia, pregnancy, and so on), without any suggestion that digestive disorders, with constipation as a symptom, may *cause* or contribute to the cause of metabolic and endocrine disorders. Pregnancy, for example, does not cause constipation; the ingestion of fiber-deficient foods and dehydration from inadequate water intake are the main causal factors. Bowel compression, as the fetus matures, only hinders elimination if there are digestive problems, which are often a direct result of a low-fiber/low-moisture diet.

From a medical anthropological standpoint, why are digestion and elimination not factored in as causal factors of malnutrition and illness? Pellett (1987), for example, offers a wide perspective for assessing human nutrition, but the part digestion plays in overall nutrition and health (i.e., the absorption of nutrients and the elimination of toxins) is lacking.

Milton's articles on primate diet and gut morphology (1987; 1993) are instructive, especially in her observation about fiber intake and the fact that the human digestive tract is better suited for degrading vegetable fiber, rather than cereal fiber, with cereals being a food source not fully exploited until the beginnings of sedentary agriculture around 9,000 years ago. Moreover, "[o]n average, for example, individuals in Western societies are estimated to take in no more than 10 grams of fiber per day, whereas members of some rural African populations may take in more than 170" (Milton 1987:101). One of the conclusions she draws from this is that there may be differences in gut proportions in living populations, a very important consideration when dealing with migrant or refugee groups entering urban complexes and being exposed to energy-dense, low-fiber foods. However, although Pellett (1987:163) does not consider fiber a nutrient because it is not absorbed, fiber, rather than simply being part of the foods consumed by our protoancestors and ancestors, becomes an absolute necessity when consuming large amounts of energy-dense foods like animal protein, pasta, bread, and so on. Macronutrients, like protein and starch, can add significant amounts of toxins to the body as they are metabolized. The dyes and preservatives in processed foods and the hormone and antibiotic supplements administered to or consumed in the feed of cattle and chickens add other toxins. Fiber, then, becomes an adjunct and necessity to, rather than a byproduct of, the balance of nutrient input (information input), digestion, and elimination. Lieberman (1987:245), on the other hand, states, "[I]nfants and children on primarily low-processed vegetarian diets may have difficulty obtaining the RDAs for protein and other nutrients because of the high fiber content of the diet, their small digestive tracts, and their relatively higher nutrient needs." Breast milk would certainly overcome protein deficiencies, but for older infants and children, as long as they are consuming a *variety* of fresh fruits and vegetables (preferably raw) and raw nuts, and are avoiding processed cow's milk, I have never encountered a deficiency. On the contrary, such children look healthier and sound healthier and have fewer or no ear infections and dental problems, and, when they have colds and flu, they experience rapid return to health.

But the larger issue in Milton's paper is that "the hominoid gut is similar throughout the superfamily," with humans having more volume in the small intestine, indicating an increase in required energy without a necessary change in nutrients consumed (Milton 1987:101; 1993:86-93). In looking at the evolution of the human gut, we not only have to pay attention to what types of foods were consumed (until quite recently, mainly plant), but also from what ecological niches they were derived. Through cooperative hunting and food sharing, humans are able to exploit many niches at once, thus increasing nutritional availability and stability (Milton 1987:108). However, these niches are not exploited at the same instant, as our ancestors would travel long distances to make use of different nutrient sources--the positioning of all types of foods in one place is a relatively recent human predilection, with its extreme expression found at the local supermarket. What this means is that the human gut has evolved over time to utilize *specific* foods and in a more or less *sequential* fashion. In other words, a diet low in fiber and combining animal protein, starchy vegetables, fractionated grains (bread), and lots of liquid (milk, water, beer, wine, pop, etc.) together at one meal will result in indigestion, malabsorption of nutrients, and elimination problems through time. Regardless of the quality of the nutrients consumed, if they cannot be properly digested and toxins eliminated, a balance is not achieved. Moreover, the cooking of food is of relatively recent origin, and cooking destroys many of the enzymes necessary for absorption and utilization--although cooking and processing is absolutely necessary in other cases (e.g., the preparation of manioc root because of its prussic acid content, combining corn with lime, fava bean preparation to lower toxicity, etc.--see Katz 1987; Rozin 1987). Instead, our digestive systems seems to function best with raw fruits, raw vegetables, nuts, and seeds, (with all the former derived from a variety of available sources and types and consumed in a sequential fashion), with pure water (about two liters a day under average conditions and consumed mainly between meals), and with a minimum of animal protein.

From an evolutionary perspective, the illnesses that derive from poor digestion and nutrition (except in those cases involving famine, dysentery, etc.) take years to become manifest. Thus, established dietary habits (environmentally inspired, but socially driven) should not significantly affect gut morphology and function (unless Lamarckian Inherited Characteristics can be resurrected) because reproduction usually has occurred before catastrophic health issues interfere with reproductive capabilities.[20] There is, as Milton (1987:101) suggests, gut "plasticity. . . . in terms of its responses to changes in diet." However, there is a limit to this plasticity, and, without genetic "refitting," most humans are still operating with a digestive system that was in place at least 100,000 years ago, and, from a comparison between human dental characteristics and those of *Australopithecus afarensis, africanus, and robustus,* has probably been in place for several million years. In short, gut morphology and function is not suited to Western and other cultural culinary practices in terms of long terms (post-reproductive) health.

How do the politics surrounding the production and sale of foods contribute to a lack of interest in digestion and elimination? What is the cost with respect to illness, loss of life, and the larger economic picture, which could include less food processing (this should make foods less expensive), more healthy foods, and fewer visits to the family physician? The politics of, and the power surrounding, food and medicine are by no means an exclusively Western phenomenon and can be found within all cultures, as food and medicine symbolize life and death and relationships within and between groups (see Brodwin 1992; Lupton 1994; Morsy 1990; Palacio 1991; Pellett 1987). As Western biomedicine has come into competition with other practices (e.g., the public's interest in vitamins and herbal remedies), a broader perspective, simply for economic reasons, may be taking hold.

Naming the Disease or the Disease of Naming?

The Western disease model spills over into conditions or behaviors that are largely social in origin (Peele 1989). For example, we speak of alcoholism as being a disease, even though there are many studies that question this (McGue et al. 1992).[21] Also, the various learning disabilities are similarly seen as diseases, or inherited conditions. In fact, most children labeled as learning disabled are looping on rejection received at home (and at school), have digestive problems and associated nutritional deficiencies, and are the victim of "teaching disabilities," especially in situations where a teacher, because of shrinking school budgets, has to administer to the needs of thirty children in a classroom and essentially ends up spending most of his or her time on classroom management. It is impossible for him or her to adequately meet each student's special learning needs (Coles 1987). We do not all learn in the same manner, but those who are matched with the teacher's style of instruction have less of a problem in our current formal educational system.

The disease model even extends to individuals who, like a bacterium or virus, lack conscience and simply predate on others without concern for their well-being. We speak of psychopathology or sociopathology[22] metaphorically the same way we talk about cancer or any parasite that simply takes without concern for the host. And, much like our medical system, we react to crime, wage war on crime, with only lip service to prevention.

In imitation of current medical practices, the psychiatric community sees emotional problems as medical conditions. Because of the advances in biochemistry, molecular biology, and pharmaceuticals, psychiatry has, in large measure, moved away from psychotherapy and more toward a biochemical approach to behavioral management (Winokur and Clayton 1994). Here, again, one can see the philosophy of a disease separate from the individual, and, if treated with the right drug, the disease evaporates, and health is restored. This is an illusion (see Helman 1994:220).

This biochemical perspective also mirrors our cultural need for instant solutions to behavioral issues of long standing, for chemical solutions to the numerous social stresses, and our preoccupation with mind-altering drugs, both prescribed (and therefore legal) and "off the street." There is one aspect of prescription drugs that is often overlooked in the literature, and that is the placing of drug taking within a ritual context. In other words, you go to your family physician, obtain a prescription, and take the drug at regular intervals essentially without an attached stigma. It is legitimized *and* ritualized. This is not quite the same with street drugs, although there are certainly ritual components. Because the procurement and ingestion are illegal, this colors the mental set, and, because availability (unless you have almost an unlimited supply of money) is not on par with going to the local pharmacy, ingestion is less ritualized and geared to availability. Mental set and setting, as recognized in the 1960s, is important to behavioral outcomes. The more legitimate and ritualized the drug use, the fewer the socially negative behavioral outcomes.

However, as stated earlier and in reference to prescription drugs, the individual is "ill" or "sick" as long as the drug is being consumed; without a ritual termination of the drug, and with long-term use, such prescriptions may kill or create metabolic imbalance, which the individual will pay for with other varieties of ill health as time goes on.

Emulating the Medical Model: The Psychological
Analogy of Medical Testing

Analogous to the process of testing for biochemical problems in the human body is the belief that one can test for psychological/psychiatric problems. The MMPI (Minnesota Multiphasic Personality Inventory) and the Rorschach, for example, are frequently administered in an attempt to diagnose numerous syndromes. What is of interest here is that, unlike many medical tests, such psychological testing has no predictive value, and I would respectfully challenge anyone to explain what these tests *actually* measure. Although the MMPI attempts to weed out faking, I have yet to meet anyone (and I have met hundreds of people who have taken the test) who was totally truthful in his or her answers.

Such tests likewise only deal with at-the-moment "realities," which are conditioned by current stressors in the person's life, the setting within which the tests are taken, the purpose of the testing, and the way the test is explained/administered. What is of great interest, especially for court evaluation purposes, is that, if the results of the testing come up "not significant" (in short, if the person "passes"), then the test results are no longer referred to, and other data (the person's actual behaviors and/or information from significant others) are pointed to as being more significant. If, on the other hand, the test results indicate problems, then these are paid attention to, even though there may be little information from other sources to suggest problems in social functioning. Testing, therefore, is only significant if negatives are detected.

But, to *not* pay attention to the tests when they come out normal says little for the validity or ability of the test to suggest an accurate picture of the individual's functioning. Why are the results useful when they come up significant, and of little interest when they do not reveal abnormalities? To even consider such testing as representative of the individual is grossly misleading, and yet the courts will indulge in this type of fantasy because it appears to be tangible evidence. Again, testing individuals outside of a social, interactive context betrays the discipline and deludes the public. Such tests actually depersonalize the individual and reduce him or her to a set of statistics frozen in time. People change from one moment to the next, and to think that such tests even represent some average of day-to-day thinking and behaving is, again, a misrepresentation. Moreover, much of the testing was never designed for assessing parent-parent or child-parent relationships in child custody evaluations, and yet it is common practice, is readily accepted by the courts, and is, in my opinion, a misrepresentation by the psychological community (see Melton et al. 1987:330). These tests, in fact, are analogous to behaviors engaged in by other societies, and these are the divination procedures for assigning cause or blame (see Evans-Pritchard 1937; Turner 1968).

Psychological testing is a divination procedure because the outcomes of the self-reports are not in any way a direct correlation to what the individual actually thinks or does, but are, instead, what I call fourth-level compressed data no different from the I Ching, astrological forecasting, scapulamancy, or reading the entrails of a guinea pig. As Park (1967:234) states, "Divination is always, I think, associated with a situation which from the point of the client or instigator, seems to call for decision upon some plan of action which is not easily taken." This is precisely the condition that prevails in child custody and other civil and criminal cases; the judge needs help making a decision and calls upon the expert for assistance.

With respect to levels of compression, the symbols represented in spoken and written language represent symbols or compressed data. The first level of compression occurs when the individual brings information into the senses for interpretation and storage. Second level compression can be represented by the mental coding process of symbols for delivery, that is, the formulation of what we intend to send. As we talk and listen, code and decode in face-to-face interactions, we use a process of feedback for clarification, and we are involved in a process of generalizing, deleting, and distorting the information in order to fit the unique realities of the sender and receiver. This process of coding, decoding, and feedback hopefully leads to some level of mutual understanding, understanding which is difficult in even the best of situations.

When the individual takes a psychological test, such as the MMPI, he or she has to decode someone else's meaning and then compress that meaning and render a response, without benefit of feedback for clarification. This represents third level-type compression which assumes accurate presentation of meaning, again, without feedback. The belief is that, by allowing the individual to come to his or her own conclusions, the psychologist can reach into the depths of the psyche and locate the real person or the personality of the individual. This belief is questionable and denies the dynamics of individual thinking which is dependent on the context within which the questions/testing is administered, the mood of the individual, other thoughts that are generated as symbols remind the individual of other symbols, and so on. As Graham (1987:74) states:

That scores on tests of ability, interest, and aptitude should have high temporal stability is quite accepted by most psychologists. *What should be expected from personality tests is not as clear.* Although personality test scores should not be influenced by sources of error variance, such as room temperature, lack of sleep, and the like, *it must be recognized that many personality attributes change over relatively short periods of time.* [emphasis mine]

The fourth level of compression is engaged when responses are number-crunched by a computer. Interpretation of the numbers is a process of decompression. As the numbers crunched are compared against responses from others, the interpretations can only be represented by suppositions such as "most of the time this means X," "sometimes this means Y," "possibly A," "the data suggest Z," and so on. They can never adequately reveal anything close to the information processing that goes on in the mind of the specific individual being tested, from second-to-second, minute-to-minute, hour-to-hour in a multitude of contexts, and can never be used to predict actual behavior. The suppositions from the tests, usually without adequate interviewing in a variety of contexts outside of the psychologist's office, are, through artistic license, converted into facts. Converting suppositions into facts, a process that the courts actively discourage, is allowed by the expert. This is a questionable methodology at best and, again, is simply a divination procedure. In child custody situations the psychologist, in most cases, never sees the roles and associated behaviors and emotions that he or she is attempting to evaluate, that is, parent, husband, or wife. What he or she does see are the roles of respondent and petitioner, and these roles do not represent those of husband, wife, and parent. To assume that the behaviors and emotions that unfold in the psychologist's office can be pasted unto the multiplicity of roles engaged in by each individual on a day-to-day basis, indicates a lack of understanding of the dynamics of human behavior, the very licensed expertise that the psychologist is supposed to possess when rendering an opinion to the courts.

In my opinion the clinical anthropologist should shy away from testing. From a therapeutic point of view, testing does not necessarily lead to therapeutic procedures and can end up simply being a sophisticated method of name calling. Even if consulted to conduct an evaluation for an attorney or the courts, you are on much sounder ground if you engage in extensive interviews with the individual over time and observe interaction patterns within wider social environments outside of the office setting, that is, home environment, peers, work, and so on.

DIAGNOSTIC CONCLUSIONS

The use of the informational categories (i.e., information intrusion, inherited information, information loss, etc.) is a beginning point for developing more complex models for approaching more specific clinical problems. Moreover, these categories are simple, are actually an unconscious starting point in building models, and help to keep initial data collection as neutral as possible.

From Chapters 3 and 4, the following conclusions can be summarized. Illness is a culture-bound phenomenon regardless of the information category into which it falls, that is, information intrusion (a curse, a bullet, a virus), information loss, and so on. Moreover, there are always emotional stress factors (information intrusion) connected to the informational categories presented in Chapter 3. Emotional stress can often be seen as predating and certainly ante-dating disease, with the expression of distress, both physical and emotional, equaling the recognizable symptoms (culture bound) of illness expression. Crisis develops out of this, and action patterns come into play.

All of the informational categories trigger emotional and physical responses. In short, all trigger HRMs, regardless of whether this stimulus comes from an environmental vector, such as a virus, or a social vector, such as an arrow or an unkind word. It is a matter of how the mind and body interpret this information. How one's physiology interprets syphilis or influenza is analogous to how the individual interprets being ordered, warned, threatened, name-called, or hit by a bolt of lightning.

Diagnosis of an illness cannot be made solely on a behavioral checklist of patient symptoms, as this removes the symptoms from the social milieu to which they are intimately bound. For example, antisocial or criminal behavior is not simply the result of growing up in a dysfunctional family, individual weaknesses, and being immoral, but involves an understanding of how the individual interprets family communication and interaction patterns over time (acceptance and/or rejection--this includes issues of poverty, discrimination, etc.), prevailing social attitudes that indicate acceptance and/or rejection of the individual and/or his perceived group affiliation, environmental factors (toxins, pathogens, etc.), social responses to illness and/or criminal behavior, and nutrition and digestive problems. Arthritis, as another example, is more than inflammation and pain of the joints; arthritis is usually symptomatic of underlying and long-term nutritional and digestive issues, all representing information intrusion, information loss, and information alteration. When diagnosis is synonymous with symptoms, any information input (i.e., painkillers, cortisone shots, etc.) is likely to further unbalance body metabolism because you are targeting symptoms (indicators that the body is attempting to protect or heal itself) rather than causes. The probability of creating metabolic chaos is almost guaranteed.

As another example, understanding how the body interprets *Dracunculus medinensis,* along with the social behaviors or social activities that bring individuals into contact with this parasite, and how it response to this parasitic nematode defines the illness. When health issues (emotional, physical) are diagnosed as occurring within systems, proper therapeutic procedure is more likely to be revealed. Once again, the starting point would be defining or uncovering the informational categories and the body's or system's HRM activation. HRM activation is then the target of therapy or rehabilitation through environmental alteration, nutritional changes, and a reinterpretation/reframing of significant events in history. One must understand the flow of information within the individual, and between the individual and the environment, the culture and the environment, and the individual and significant others and also understand how this is interpreted by the individual physically as well as emotionally and according to some social template.

Again, one of the key aspects of individual stress, and thus system stress, is the acquisition of HRMs as the individual learns the rules and generates stress in an attempt to come to terms with these essentially sociolinguistic issues. As stress goes up, a number of mechanisms come into play in an attempt to reduce stress. All reactions to information in the environment alter brain and body chemistry. Certain types of emotional reactions, according to the individual and the culture, can, over time, disregulate body functioning. The results of this can include all matter of somatic complaints (headaches, stomachaches, fatigue) and, over time, more serious conditions brought on by depression of immune functioning. Moreover, under stress, we alter our brain chemistry, and, combining this with the "more or less" in neurochemistry as discussed in Chapter 3, severe psychiatric conditions become manifest, that is, schizophrenia, manic-depressive psychosis, *latah*, *amok*, *windigo*, and so on. The diagnostic feature that fits all clinical settings, both in our own culture and cross-culturally, is the cluster of HRMs to which the individual and the group react emotionally and physically.

The vast majority of illnesses are self-limiting; they simply go away. If action is taken, this is stress reducing for the individual, allowing a heightened immune response. Good nutrition is likewise a part of the self-limiting feature of system healing. But illness is also symbolic and representational of social functioning in general; illness opens a door to social intervention and thus a rebalancing of society as well as of the individual. Finally, two features that are usually lacking in Western biomedical, psychiatric, and psychological procedures are a recognizable termination ritual and a ritual that moves toward social reintegration. These factors are usually left out of the equation because Western biomedicine treats symptoms, looks for singular causal factors, and attempts to utilize a scientific method that treats the symptoms as separate from the individual and the surrounding social milieu. This, then, brings us more directly to clinical anthropology.

NOTES

1. There is ongoing debate in Western society, between Western biomedical specialists and alternative health practitioners, regarding the concept of *cure*. Western biomedicine uses a very powerful array of drugs to suppress symptoms and thus takes credit for the cure to the point of "copyrighting" the right to use the term in medical practice. The debate centers around the accumulation of toxins in the body and whether suppressing symptoms really approaches the cause of the problem. Many alternative health practitioners believe that suppressing symptoms leads to the accumulation of toxins in the body, with an end result of more rapid aging and a repetition of specific illnesses on a periodic basic, leading to an eventual catastrophic event. The use of specific powerful drugs can actually create more and more imbalance (e.g., the use of insulin for diabetes and cortisone for arthritis), although symptoms are momentarily alleviated. Suppressing symptoms, however, does match the Western, (especially North American) need to achieve instant cure or instant relief, to return the

employee to work, and to free the individual to maintain a personal life style (nutrition habits, tobacco use, alcohol and drug abuse, disrupted sleep patterns, indiscriminate sex, etc.), believing that the medical establishment will come up with a magical cure for a lifetime of abuse. This is a reactive, rather than a preventive philosophy, which is very expensive to maintain. I will examine this philosophy in more detail in Chapter 5.

2. See Ho (1993) and his statements regarding problems of a continuum of "collectivistic" to "individual centered" concepts of culture.

3. Although shame can be seen as the individual's reaction to group censure (i.e., a person sees his or her behavior as a group infringement, and, thus, shame is something that comes or is imposed from without), the experience of guilt, an inner experience, is always part of the process. Shame and guilt are part of the same process, with shame being instilled as a control mechanism for maintaining group values and guilt being generated as one breaks more abstract laws or values. Guilt is imposed from within as the individual breaks away from personal responsibility, and so on.

4. See Rush (1976:31-33).

5. Prostitutes in Bangkok, however, do dress provocatively and do show affection openly in order to attract clients. But this is not the norm.

6. I do not mean to imply that negative emotions are bad or good. Emotions seem to be tags for storing and retrieving information and thus are connected to generalized experiences. They are necessary components of information processing.

7. The actual content is lost forever, in most cases. However, it is the individual's recollection of the content that is important, along with the client's associated meaning.

8. See Bower (1993:153 for a recent discussion of immune system functioning and family relationships.

9. There are times, certainly, when the person has not transgressed or subverted some social norm. Here is where malicious spirits or ancestor spirits, perhaps getting even with someone else, represent a reframing of the illness proper.

10. See Watson and Ellen (1993) for Southeast Asian cases, Middleton and Winter (1963) for East Africa, Sullivan (1988) for South America, and Kalweit (1992) for the Arctic and other areas of the world.

11. The concept of danger and healing located at boundaries is not the private domain of humans and culture, as it can be recognized in other animals as well. Dogs and cats, as is well known by their owners, establish territories, outside of which it is dangerous. Equally interesting is the behavior of animals going to boundaries (i.e., fences, demarcation points, etc.) to eat grass and other plants. At these boundaries, moisture accumulates and allows for grass, for example, to grow greener and more hardy. Usually, this behavior is engaged in order to purge, or empty stomach contents. Horses seem to usually prefer new grass shoots, as they are sweeter, but they, too, will go to boundaries and ingest taller, less sweet grasses when they are ill.

12. Research conducted by the author from 1969 through 1981 involved a large Italian kinship network in Toronto, Canada. Much of the data is still unpublished, but certain aspects of the theme of the research objectives (i.e., curing rituals) can be found in Rush (1974, 1994).

13. See Rush (1994:60-61) for another example of a *strega* being accused of causing a terminal, impersonal illness, that is, cancer.

14. The process of finding new diseases for Western psychiatry to treat is indicated in the new edition of the *DSM*, that is, the *DSM-IV*. One of the latest "mental illnesses" is "Disorders of Written Expression" (Code 315.2--see Leutwyler 1984:17-

18). However, there is a category of disorder that is missing from the *DSM*, and that is educational disorders. M.D.'s, Ph.D.'s, and others, essentially educate themselves out of society. They think differently than the average person, behave differently, and usually feel more estranged, anonymous, and in a world of their own. Are highly educated people normal? I would say, "No." In all seriousness, if we can invent "Disorders of Written Expression" then surely we should have "Educational Disorders." Educational disorders have their extreme expression, for example, in those individuals who design munitions for the military. These individuals surely have found a niche to express their emotional disorders and, at the same time, reap high rewards.

In a similar fashion, screen writers, movie directors, and special effects teams, who "entertain" us with the abundance of blood, guts, and gore, are surely exercising more than artistic license.

Small numbers of police personnel, especially those on SWAT teams, engage in antisocial behaviors in order to deal with others engaged in antisocial behaviors; such behaviors cannot simply be turned on and off. In short, not everyone who *would* fit into the category of having a disturbed communication and/or behavioral pattern is considered psychotic; it depends upon the government's need for such individuals at any point in time. When you can arbitrarily apply these categories, depending on social need, this certainly leads one to question the overall purpose of the *DSM*. In short, the psychiatric community has become the moral watchdog of society, and, for this reason alone, any scientific validity is suspect.

15. There is a bit of fate connected to the development of Western medicine as practiced in the United States. According to Ody (1993:21), and speaking of eclectic physicians, "At its peak, Eclecticism claimed more than 20,000 qualified practitioners in the United States and was a serious rival to regular medicine. The challenge ended only in 1907 when, following a review of medical training schools, philanthropists Andrew Carnegie and John D. Rockefeller decided to give financial support solely to the orthodox medical schools." If you read up on Carnegie and Rockefeller, it is quite evident that they did not like competition in their own empire building, and to invite competition in the medical community would have been outside their paradigm of "sound business practices."

16. See Anderson (1991) for an interesting discussion of research into the efficacy of ethnomedicine. The efficacy of Western biomedicine is itself questionable, traumatic injury notwithstanding, and even using the biomedical model as the template upon which to judge other systems, I believe, is an arrogant position. The use of powerful pharmaceuticals is proving to create chaos in human metabolism over time, antibiotics are proving to be less and less effective because of overuse (see Nesse and Williams 1994; Lappe 1994), and, as mentioned above, the scientific method that Anderson suggests (see Kent 1994b for a discussion of design flaws in control studies) eliminates the social elements and other factors that relate to the holistic aspect of illness, disease, and curing.

17. In a recent article in *Science News* (see Bower 1994), discussing child sexual abuse, researchers suggest that "instances of such trauma may interfere with the brain's conscious recall system while leaving intact conditioned fear responses stored as visual images or physical sensations in other brain regions [and] that adult memories of confirmed childhood sexual abuse invariably appear first in perceptual fragments that get woven into a coherent story over weeks, months, or even years"

(1994:365). The researchers go on to say that prolonged and early exposure leads to "the most fragmented perceptual memories of the trauma," and that "people seem to need to remember the details of their trauma to deal with it effectively." I seriously question the conclusions of this research. First, not all childhood sexual abuse is traumatic, as it is only abusive from a cultural definition (see Herdt 1987; Williams 1992; Bornoff 1991). As Erickson (1966:6) states: "Deviance is not a property inherent in any particular kind of behavior; it is a property conferred upon that behavior by the people who come into direct or indirect contact with it. The only way an observer can tell whether or not a given style of behavior is deviant, then, is to learn something about the standards of the audience which responds to it." Second, as humans are analogous thinkers, second to none, and we have the ability to connect symbols that, at first sight, are seemingly unrelated, it is impossible to know if an event that occurred many years ago is faithfully reported in the present; information distorts over time. Period. Even an event reported seconds after it happened is still a distortion of what happened; it is not the actual event and can never be the actual event. Even video cameras do not capture the event, as there is always a context within which things happens, and this can never be in total "view." The Rodney King trial was a clear example of this. And, third, it is not necessary for people to remember the "exact" details (they may have invented these) to deal with trauma. In fact, getting into detail can sometimes make the trauma worse, as occurs in court cases where a victim is interviewed or interrogated by police, psychologists, and attorneys. A psychologist can be just as "brutal" (inadvertently) as any defense attorney.

18. I am well aware of the fact that HRMs and negative bits are metaphors as well; while dissecting the human brain, you will not encounter such things. HRMs and negative bits are ideas and, like the Oedipus complex, are used to explain behavior and outcomes in social interaction. I do believe, however, they offer a more understandable, less complicated, yet verifiable cause and effect approach to human interaction.

19. What must be kept in mind is that the vast majority of visits to the Western biomedical doctor's office are for complaints that are self-limiting. The aches and pains, and the colds, flu, coughs, and so on that are the economic mainstay of Western biomedicine are self-limiting. That is to say, these illnesses simply go away and, in many ways, mirror problems in social relationships; that is, they simply heal themselves. Because of this, and because of the economics of owning patents on medicines, the use of alternative healing philosophies and herbs, instead of patented, doctor prescribed medicines, can only be seen as competition to the pharmaceutical/ medical complex. Alternative medical philosophies and procedures, therefore, must be purged from the landscape. This is done with the aid of the Food and Drug Administration (FDA) which is essentially a policing agency for the medical and pharmaceutical companies. At the current time, there is no competition within the health industry in the United States, and this has culminated in long waits at the doctor's office because of overbooking, an extreme inflation in the price of prescription drugs, conflicts of interest among doctors and the pharmaceutical companies and the laboratories that the doctors own, and a tenfold increase in health insurance costs (see *Amazing Medicines* 1993 for a scathing report on the American medical complex). Health maintenance through nutrition, including herbs and vitamin/mineral supplements, is as effective and, by all statistical data encountered so far, a couple of thousand times safer than prescribed, FDA-approved drugs--every year over 186,000

people die from iatrogenic (directly related to medical rather than disease factors) causes, many drug related, and 659,000 hospitalized with serious side effects from taking prescription drugs. For example, as of June 1992, 1,313 died from taking Prozac *(Amazing Medicines* 1993:27, 71; Dean et al. 1993:126-129; Quillin 1994:48-50; Carper 1993). Compare these startling figures to the approximately 10,500 people killed in 1994 with handguns (*The Bureau for At-Risk Youth,* 645 New York Ave., Huntington, NY 11743--1-800-99-YOUTH). The implication here is that it is safer to walk the streets than to go to your family doctor. If certain life-style changes (i.e., appropriate nutrition, avoidance of toxins, emotional stress reduction, etc.) became the norm, the medical community would have to do business quite differently.

20. See Knowler et al. 1983, and Knowler et al. 1990 , for their discussion of the Pima Indians' predilection to diabetes. During periods of decreased food resources or starvation, a selection for a slow metabolism with a high resistance to glucose utilization allows for the accumulation of fat reserves. Once such a metabolism is subjected to calorie-dense, low-fiber foods (i.e., the average North American diet) diabetes is the result. The point is that hormonal functioning has altered not to accommodate calorie-dense, low-fiber foods, but to adapt to a diet that is low density in nutrients, with high fiber, and scarce in the environment. Our gut morphology and function are still geared to low density, high fiber foods. Also see Lappe (1994:166, Table 4) for the prevalence of diabetes in gatherers as opposed to industrialized Westerners.

21. As McGue et al. state (1992:15), "In any case, our findings suggest that in the headlong rush to identify molecular genetic processes, researchers may be ignoring the significant influence that the environment has in the origins of alcoholism."

22. The current terminology is antisocial personality disorder (*DSM-IV*).

CHAPTER 5

Elements of Clinical Anthropology

The preceding material allows for a more specific consideration of clinical anthropology by first developing a model and a process of diagnosis through an analysis of informational categories.

Chapter 5 now moves toward the actual application of the model in clinical settings, that is, marriage and family counseling, health issues, court evaluations, and so on. Those familiar with the marriage and family setting will notice a distinct difference between a psychological or psychiatric approach and the one presented in this work.

The reader will also note the difference in approach to Western biomedicine when dealing with health issues.

The anthropological approach, as discussed in this work and related to a Western setting, describes to the client(s) the model used in therapy, including the procedures and communication tools the client is expected to put into practice. The clients, then, become active participants in the therapeutic process rather than patients waiting to be "healed" by the therapist. The anthropological approach is one of immediately reframing beliefs about cause and effect, educating the clients in a number of areas, and avoiding a passive posture in the educational process. Reference points in information delivery center on human information processing, which involves dyads and small groups; individual psychology can only be understood within a group context. In the light of this, psychological testing, and its validity in diagnosis, is questioned.

Information on nutrition and life style is included in the therapeutic process, with nutrition, for the most part, being neglected by the Western biomedical and psychological complex.

Cross-cultural counseling, in desperate need of anthropological input, is briefly discussed, with details more appropriately outlined in a separate volume.

This chapter also explores the legitimacy of the anthropologist as an expert witness in civil and criminal issues, as well as licensing.

INTRODUCTION: A SELECTIVE HISTORICAL REVIEW

Applied anthropology can be considered the general reference to using anthropological concepts and procedures within human systems, with clinical anthropology, an offshoot of medical anthropological, more specifically relating to health care settings. I recall hearing this terminology, *clinical anthropology*, while a graduate student during the late 1960s, and was pointed in the direction of Caudill who, in the early 1950s, feigned psychiatric problems, was admitted to a psychiatric hospital, and consequently wrote extensively about that experience.

In a more encompassing analysis of the psychiatric hospital, Caudill (1958) indicated, for example, how a "psychiatric hospital is indeed a social system" (1958:318), with inherent "ground swells," and "blocked mobility"; how this influenced communication patterns and differences of opinion as to patient behavior; and how entering the "sick" role conditions an attitude on the part of staff to justify and even maintain that role. Diagnosis proceeds from a theoretical perspective, and, with respect to a patient named Mr. Esposito, " the diagnosis seemed to function less as a useful classificatory tool, and rather more as a security operation on the part of staff by means of which they could feel there was little the hospital could do further for the patient. This very possibly had the reciprocal effect of bringing the patient to sense that he was now considered more as a case than as a person" (1958:54). Further, "[w]ithin the hospital, diagnosis may be thought to serve two functions: on the one hand, it is a useful way of classifying a patient in terms of etiology and symptoms of his illness; but, on the other hand, it also is a way of disposing of a patient by labeling him. For example, if a patient's behavior comes to be continually explained by the 'fact' that he 'has' schizophrenia, then the chances of the patent's being relegated to a chronic hospital career are increased. In this later case, diagnosis may be thought of as a security operation, meaning that uncertainty about a patient is removed by labeling him and that many communications from him may now be safely ignored" (1958:62).

Engel more recently (1977) stated that a new medical model is necessary, and that the vested interests and economics of the current perspective force a delay in its development. Anthropologists play a crucial role in this because, although biased by their own observations and needs with respect to collecting and clarifying data, most are acutely aware of the ethnocentrism of Western biomedicine.

According to Alexander (1979), the term *clinical anthropology* evolved out of a concern for what was already happening, that is, anthropologists applying anthropological concepts to clinical settings. Further, she outlines some of the problems in duplicating the models already present in clinical medicine, the problem of observer bias, and the difficulties evolving out of the realities inherent in language. In short, model building is a problem. As Chrisman and Johnson (1990:104) state:

One of the most significant issues facing clinically applied anthropologists is the matter of theory. Theory may be considered in two ways: as anthropological concepts and their relationships that constitute the core of the discipline. . . . and as perspectives on how to use these concepts in clinical settings. We are able to take the first for granted since anthropological concepts and theories, along with methodology, define much of what anthropologists do. The second, how to apply the discipline, is underdeveloped and requires much more thought and practice among clinically applied anthropologists.

Although I disagree with taking their first premise for granted, I do agree with their second. Anthropological concepts span both time and space and have more to do with the purpose of the collected information. For example, much of the data collected by British social anthropologists in the early part of this century served to aid administrative practices in their colonies (Africa, India, etc.). Information collected with a view to administrating (controlling) will have a different flavor than that collected to prove or disprove a pet theory for Ph.D. dissertation purposes. Moreover, theories are necessary not only for collecting, but also for explaining--such theories have changed greatly since the turn of the century.

Models and Theory

In Western biomedicine, as well as in all curing systems, there exists a model of cause and effect. Without some reference point, the observer knows neither what to observe nor the significance of the observed information. This is not to say that the reference points represent truth of some empirical nature. As the human being is doing the observing, it is impossible to avoid the bias and/or the effects generated by the observer on the observed. As Greenwood and Nunn (1992:25-26) state:

[O]rthodox science has major limitations. It arises from cultural assumptions--such as the possibility of objectivity--that have been shown, over the past sixty years or so, to be inadequate. . . . To understand the paradox of our medicine and of our cultural illness, we must grasp the assumptions on which we base our lives. We must understand the fundamental error implicit in the practice of objective scientific inquiry, an error which has by now become all-embracing in its implications.

Psychiatric diagnosis in Western biomedicine likewise proceeds from a model or theory that justifies the inclusion of specific types of information when a formal diagnosis is offered; a theory or bias cannot be avoided. However, LaBruzza and Mendez-Villarrubia's (1994:85-86) recent statements regarding the *DSM-IV* are instructive in that there appears to be a continuation of this belief, by some, in objectivity. They state:

DSM-IV deals with mental disorders occurring in individuals rather than in families, groups or society. *DSM-IV* is also theoretically atheoretical--that is, it tries to stick to empirical evidence and to avoid theoretical speculation about causes of psychiatric disorders. To this end, it focuses on objective signs and symptoms while avoiding inferences about unconscious process or content. *DSM-IV* avoids dynamic formu- lations, not because unconscious factors are irrelevant to clinical work, but rather because psychodynamic diagnosis is based on a specific theory about mental life that is not part of the official *DSM* classification. *DSM-IV* seeks to make diagnoses based on a Kraepelinian approach of objective, empirically verifiable signs and symptoms of mental disorders.

Individuals do not occur in a vacuum, and, therefore it is impossible, in my opinion, to isolate the individual from the group and assign a diagnosis. Moreover, some theoretical bias will always surround the collection of data, or why else would you single out some information and ignore the rest? Further, as data are placed within a diagnostic category--as they make the transition from "objective signs and symptoms," they (the data), of necessity, acquire some theoretical emphasis. For example, the diagnosis of post-traumatic stress disorder (*DSM-IV*, 309.81) assumes that the manifest behaviors are the result of something important to social functioning, or why pay attention to the symptoms in the first place? The assumption or theory is that either events traumatize people or people traumatize themselves with the information coming into their senses. Implicit in *all* the diagnostic categories in the *DSM-IV is* a model or theory; all the lists of behaviors refer to some *unstated* cause and effect. The *DSM-IV* is not atheorietical.

The *DSM-IV* likewise attempts to pay attention to cross-cultural issues. Suggesting that there is a difference in illness manifestation or categories in different populations, again, opens up a theoretical (and very important) bias in information collection. However, the *DSM-IV* does *not* properly address the issues of illness categories in other cultures, especially if it is maintained that the *DSM-IV* is atheorietical. Having a category (see *DSM-IV* Appendix I:843-849) entitled, "Culture-Bound Syndromes" *supposes* a model in which illness manifestations *will* differ from society to society. Moreover, most of the culture-bound syndromes mentioned are presented with a theory of etiology. This total of seven pages in a volume 886 pages long is certainly a start in expressing the relevance of cross-cultural issues, but it also implies that what preceded it is likewise culture-bound.

In terms of a model for classifying illness--a system relevant to all cultures--Clark et al. (1995:147), in their critique of the *DSM-IV*, state, "In the long run, of course, the most clinically useful system will be one that has max-imal predictive power regarding course and treatment because it is based on a scientific understanding of the relevant parameters." "Relevant parameters" must, of necessity, include a model or theory of cause and effect, which, unlike much of Freudian or Jungian theory, should be verifiable through repeated observation.

Model Building

We need a model or theory because it aids in the type of information gathered, and the only objective manner to collect data is to understand that the data *are* wrapped around a theory or model, and that the model may not necessarily be correct. Moreover, the observer/participant will bias the collection of information, and the language used to describe the observations will impart a reality of its own to the data. Once again, being aware of these factors allows one to proceed with caution, with the data and connected model subject to constructive critique.

With respect to a model surrounding clinical anthropology, it should be drawn from the domain of anthropology, describe human behavior in systems and as a product of systems, and be verifiable by others using a similar theory or model.   Out of this will evolve generalizations, a "work-speak," and, hopefully, tools or a methodology for application to clinical settings. Data collection must go beyond description; data collection must be connected to application. Most data collected by anthropologists are descriptive and not geared toward application, and, thus, no model has emerged in clinical anthropology that integrates collection/description *and* application.

The Practice of Clinical Anthropology

Clinical anthropology can be defined as the use of anthropological concepts and ideas within a clinical setting. Such ideas and concepts can come mainly from the field of anthropology, that is, physical anthropology, linguistics, psychological anthropology, and so on. The clinical setting can be within a hospital, jails and detention settings; forensic[1] evaluations for the courts especially with respect to cross-cultural issues, evaluations of dangerousness; and individual and marriage and family counseling/therapy.[2] Moreover, it is doubtful, contrary to Chrisman and Johnson (1990:96-97), that anthropologists in a counseling or therapy role would be merely duplicating that which already exists in psychology and the other counseling professions (also see Alexander 1979:83). In fact, as I have indicated in previous chapters, anthropologists can add many new dimensions to the profession. It is my experience that most psychologists, counselors, and therapists in North

America present an ethnocentric view regarding self in society, which does not open a door to other therapeutic possibilities. As Shiloh (1977:443) stated some years ago, and referring to specific issues (i.e., "alcoholics," "mentally ill," etc.):

All of these may well be manifesting problems whose etiology originated not necessarily in themselves, but in American culture, and my position is that it is therapeutic anthropology that can assist significantly in improving the degree of successful treatment, the reduction of recidivism, and the establishment of economically viable prevention. All of these problems, and many others, are manifestations of fundamental culture disorders, and therapeutic anthropology can play a critical role in their resolution, particularly on the personal level.

One of the reasons that they have not been resolved is that other so-called specialists have attempted to grapple with them in a vacuum, or a partial social grounding, rather than to recognize them as specific manifestations of culture disorder.

Moreover, as most problems in social living evolve out of interpersonal communication patterns (see Campbell 1982:186; Ruesch and Bateson 1968:168-227, 273-289), it is surprising that clinical psychology, for example, has not been relabeled "clinical communication," and, although a great deal of lip service has been paid to the importance of communication in the development of psychological/psychiatric and marital problems, there is no clear model available as to how this comes about. This present work is an attempt to build that model, which, in my mind, clearly separates what anthropologists can contribute clinically from what already exists.

CLINICAL ANTHROPOLOGISTS AS
COUNSELORS AND THERAPISTS

Traditionally, a distinction has been made between counseling and therapy, although the one seems to blend into the other. Moreover, what are the difference among counseling, therapy, and education? Counseling, for the sake of having a reference point, can be defined as giving advice regarding social living. Therapy can be defined as dealing with more severe problems in social living. *Both are educational*; neither needs to be construed as mystical or magical, although the magical and mystical factors can be therapeutic in certain settings in that they set up an expectation of action and thus success.

Both counseling and therapy are designed to impart new possibilities (framing and reframing), and, in that sense, *they are educational*. As counseling and therapy usually deal with the individual's relationship with others (problems in social living involve dyads and groups), interpersonal and group communications are focal points of therapy/counseling and/or education. How the individual interprets information is a key factor in personal and social stress reactions. Thus, we are dealing with information input, the meanings assigned, and the therapist's ability to educate the individual (or family) with respect to alternatives or more comfortable interpretations that allow the individual to take positive, socially approved steps to resolve conflict with self and others.

Health History

The clinical anthropologist must acknowledge certain limitations. First of all, she or he does not practice Western biomedicine, psychiatry, or psychology. What he or she practices instead is a comprehensive, holistic approach to individual, family, and system health. This may require referring a client to a biomedical specialist, especially in cases where a person has paid little attention to personal health and the body is so unbalanced that cancer, liver disease, kidney failure, or heart problems are suspected. A health history is important to collect. This would include contacts with Western biomedical practitioners and knowledge of any medications given or invasive procedures performed. It is important to know about childhood illnesses (i.e., chicken pox, measles, mumps, tonsillectomies, etc.), as well as their durations and outcomes. It is important to know about skin problems (e.g., acne), as this gives information about diet, and possible deficiencies, and about social functioning, that is, how the individual dealt with problems of body image and rejection--a potential source of High Risk Messages (HRMs) that may be ongoing.

It is likewise important to have specific information regarding lifestyle, that is, if the person smokes and/or uses alcohol and other drugs. In my mind, there is no such thing as the recreational use of drugs; they always serve other purposes, some of which have a direct connection to problems in social relationships and expressions of illness. Another direct connection to social relationships and image of self relates to the use of food and exercise. Nutritional deficiencies (a lack of biochemical information) are extremely important and are directly connected to mood swings, PMS, and many symptoms of disease, that is, enlarged prostate or prostate cancer, chancre sores, heart problems, diabetes, hypoglycemia, and so on. Exercise can be compared to a feedback mechanism that tells the body how to store and utilize energy. Without exercise, the body cannot operate efficiently. Our brains and bodies were designed many thousands of years ago not to sit on a comfortable couch and drink beer and eat bonbons, but to interact with the environment in a fairly strenuous fashion. Preventing future metabolic and catastrophic illness is directly related to nutrition and digestion. Giving important information on nutrition/digestion can be used as a reframing technique to bridge over to family functioning and health as well.

Information about the family of origin (i.e., mother, father, siblings, divorces), and family members' use and abuse of drugs (including tobacco and prescription drugs, especially tranquilizers and anti-psychotic medications) is important, as the family of origin presents the first model of "social doing" and general life style that the individual refers to when engaged in his or her family of procreation. Information on exactly how significant others communicated with him or her is very important. How rules were set, what tools were used (i.e., sarcasm, name-calling, etc.), how discipline was achieved, and how the individual felt about discipline are important questions. The life history should be designed around issues of health, how illness is expressed, and the individual's HRMs. If you are dealing with a marital problem, it is important to understand how the individual perceived the roles of husband, wife, and parent in his or her family of origin. Much of this information can be conceptualized as information intrusion.

The Tools and Information Base of the Clinical Anthropologist

Within the context of individual, marriage, and family counseling, the key is to uncover the negative bits that activate HRMs in the system. These include the nutritional, environmental, and life-style negative bit/HRMs complex (eating fractionated foods and digestive problems, contact with environmental toxins, use of alcohol and/or cigarettes, etc.).

The next step is to understand the social HRMs (poverty, discrimination, employment factors, etc.) of the individual or members of the family system and the mechanisms of stress reduction when HRMs are activated. From this, the clinical anthropologist offers and solicits alternative translations (reframing) to both early and current life events that aided or aid in the development and/or maintenance of the individual's HRMs. The clinical anthropologist avoids assigning blame, as this is unproductive and halts the therapeutic process.

A third step is to develop an understanding of the implied rules that run the system and to then move toward altering specific relationship rules by discussing and using new communication tools. Again, blaming husband or wife for controlling or wanting power, current procedures in Western psychology, shows a lack of understanding of system functioning. A fourth step, in marriage and family counseling, involves a clarification of the roles of husband and wife.

The basic elements of this procedure--that is, identifying, retranslating, or removing HRMs (social/ emotional, nutritional, and environmental); understanding how implied rules run the system and then instituting new, explicit relationship rules; clearing up role confusion; and conducting appropriate rituals for the termination of curing process and social reintegration--are the key elements in establishing individual and system health. Cross-cultural issues, discussed below, contain the same elements, but presentation is usually accomplished in a manner that respects a specific culture's values and curing procedures, that is, cultural content.[3]

In the marriage and family setting the clinical anthropologist educates with respect to family communication dynamics and uses skills to teach skills. With respect to family communication patterns, this is the social anthropologist's stock in trade. From the classic writers--for example, Morgan (1870, 1877), Radcliffe-Brown (1922, 1952), Malinowski (1929), Levi-Strauss (1969)--to more recent scholars, that is, Fortes (1969), Firth et al. (1970), Bott (1971), Boissevain and Mitchell (1973), and so on--kinship dynamics have been a focal point of study. Considering tools or skills for delivering information or reframing events, attitudes, beliefs, and practices, all can be found in play in one culture or another during curing ceremonies around the world. These skills or tools include storytelling or *metaphors*, the use of *analogies* in order to bridge one symbol to another, and *bridging experiences,* which include, in a more specific and elaborate form, metaphors and analogies (Atkinson 1992a; Lewis 1992; Howard 1990; Lakoff and Johnson 1980; Levi-Strauss 1967:197; Eliade 1972). In fact, just as all illness is metaphorical, all healing ceremonies, in themselves, are metaphors that can be seen as relating to social balance (Atkinson 1992a; Powers 1986; Bean 1976; Turner 1970b).

The use of *dream analysis*, another type of metaphor, is not a Freudian invention, but is commonplace in many cultural groups (Wallace 1958; Hart 1979; Eliade 1972). *Breaking process*, or using the various *confusion techniques*, applied during sleight of hand, tent shaking, or shock statements or shock behaviors (saying or doing the unexpected), is also widely practiced (Atkinson 1992a; Kalweit 1992; Howard 1990; Eliade 1972; Murphy 1964; Balikci 1963). Having the client go on a quest to find some unusual thing or event, and other "rites of passage, is very common (Jilek 1982) and can be seen as more specifically related to adolescents and the preventing or lessening of the emotional turmoil encountered at puberty through public initiation into adulthood (Turner 1969, 1970a; see references in Bettelheim 1962; Mahdi et al. 1987).

Storytelling, or the use of metaphors for creating a cognitive shift without going on an actual quest, is used in many cultures (Bettelheim 1977; Mahdi et al. 1987; Campbell 1972, 1990). Using *third persons* (e.g., spirit entities) to deliver messages or obtain healing information (Atkinson 1992a; Laderman 1987; Powers 1986) or assigning *profound intellectual insight* to individuals (analogous to spirit guides--see Kearney 1979; Fuchs 1964) is popular, as is the assumption (*the raising of expectations*) that something will occur (*future pacing* or *self-fulfilling prophecies*), that the person will be healed if certain acts--for example, confessing (La Barre 1964), carrying amulets or charms (Hart 1979; Halpern and Foley 1979; Rush 1974)--are performed. This is closely connected to the well-known placebo effect. Along with this, subtle accusations are made with implications of cause, thus allowing the client to fill in the blank and come to therapeutic conclusions (Rush 1974, 1994).

Roleshifting, and the assuming of appropriate roles to enhance therapeutic effect, is common (Atkinson 1992a:192-193). The use of *hypnosis* or *trance states* is commonplace in many curing ceremonies even in disguised forms (Kalweit 1992; Jilek 1982; Powers 1986; Balikci 1963). Closely related to this is the use of mind-altering drugs, often taken by the shaman (therapist) and/or the client in order to commune with spirits for answers to cause and effect and information on proper procedures (Kalweit 1992; Lewis 1992; Wolf 1991; Dobkin De Rios 1990; Eliade 1972). The use of *double binds* and other *paradoxical implications or procedures* is likewise evident in the literature (Kalweit 1992; Bateson 1972:201-227; Turner 1969). What is of interest is that many Western psychologists and psychiatrists believe *they* invented many of these approaches.[4]

Along with all the above reframing techniques, the clinical anthropologist must inform and move toward a termination ritual (end of cure or cure is complete) and social reintegration of the individual or family. Therapy cannot be indefinite (or no cure can be accomplished), and, as illness is usually a metaphor of social functioning, social reintegration (often more symbolic than tangible because of the impersonal nature of our culture) is absolutely necessary.

Cross-Cultural Counseling

Moreover, when reviewing the bibliographical entries of current and popular works on cross-cultural counseling and therapy (Comas-Diaz and Griffith 1988; Sue and Sue 1990; Lee and Richardson 1991; Furuto et al. 1992; van der Veer 1992; Vargas and Koss-Chioino 1992; Carter 1995) and then checking the entries of specific authors, one finds many, many references to the works of anthropologists. This is not an accusation of plagiarism, but, instead, a statement designed to place anthropological data in proper perspective in terms of their obvious relevance to the clinical setting.

With respect to cross-cultural counseling/therapy, from an anthropological perspective, the anthropologist, when in other cultures, can use the concept of HRMs to diagnose both the social and the physical manifestations of illness, which then can be correlated to indigenous belief systems regarding cause and effect. Counseling and therapy within the context of another culture would involve assuming the role and understanding the procedures for curing, as understood and practiced by specialists. Attempting to use Western concepts and practices--for example, getting the client to talk about personal issues, admit to emotional problems--is usually non-productive. In Southeast Asia, for example, among the Hmong of Laos, discussing intimate family matters with an outsider is inappropriate at best, and to admit a psychological problem would be quite unusual. Individual psychology, which demands a concept of individualism in the first place, is not part of their illness philosophy, as mentioned in Chapter 4. The indigenous curer, the shaman, the herbalist, and so on, are in the best position to offer assistance in these matters. For the Hmong in Sacramento, California (and other areas of the United States), the shaman is still the preferred specialist, as only about ten percent of Hmong refugees have abandoned their indigenous beliefs (Vang and Lewis 1990:3, although Capps 1994 has found that shamanism and ancestor worship are no longer in evidence in Kansas City). Within this ten percent, and this figure is bound to rise as more and more children are exposed to Western beliefs and practices, there are still problems of applying Western psychological techniques. In fact, if the Hmong do not see the counselor as an educator, someone with knowledge they can use, and someone who is in a position of authority, the process is doomed to failure. Moreover, referring to the process of dealing with families in a psychological/psychiatric fashion is stigmatizing and is bound to be so for many years.

Collecting information from most Southeast Asians, especially those who have come in contact with the criminal justice system, is a difficult task, and the safest way to begin is by commencing a discussion of kinship terminology and relations. This can be a long-term project, and those in the criminal justice system (e.g., probation officers) often do not have the time to engage such a process, which is unfortunate.[5] When a situation needs to be resolved, rapport with the family is not entirely necessary. Instead, if the counselor is seen as someone in legitimate authority,[6] and someone who understands the culture's HRMs and avoids tapping into them, the family members can simply be given directives that will usually be carried through. If the directives are unrealistic (i.e., if the family members cannot put the directives in place), then counseling and such directives are a waste of time. For example, a teenage boy apprehended for robbery has caught on to the ideas of individualism and equality (as opposed to collectivism and inequality as being the natural order of the world), but not responsibility for actions. A directive that *excludes* helping the family to bring a community power base into the problem solving, to help keep an eye on the teenager, on a 24-hour-a-day basis will have little effect. Moreover, if the probation officer or counselor makes a promise to a Hmong, Lao, Vietnamese, or Cambodian, and then does not follow through, trust is lost not only for this particular individual, but for others in authority (e.g., police) as well.

With respect to Russian families, one likewise has the problem of collecting information regarding family conflict and other intimate information. With Russian families, as opposed to Southeast Asian families, an authoritarian position is the worst posture to assume. Further, Russian families are not very warm to the roles of psychologist and/or psychiatrist, as these represent, in large measure, repressive instruments of the state.[7] Rapport building is absolutely necessary with the Russian family, with participation- observation being the ideal. Current concepts in Western psychology are not open to this, as participation in the family is considered to bias the psychological process (transference and countertransference) in a possibly nonproductive manner. Moreover, high levels of alcohol abuse among Russian males present a different challenge and almost force an orientation of alcohol abuse away from the genetic model to social causes; psychology, for the most part, may not be prepared to confront these longstanding social issues.

Once again, all approaches are designed to reshape or reframe information in order to balance or rebalance the individual's health within a social context (Powers 1986:177-179). The use of language, verbal and non-verbal, and the use of symbols, cultural and otherworldly, comprise the therapeutic tool kit for healing. Healing is defined not as the use of psychology, but, instead, as the use of language, wrapped around social issues, in order to educate.[8]

ANTHROPOLOGISTS AS EXPERT
WITNESSES IN COURT EVALUATIONS

Physical anthropologists have, for many years, been called as expert witnesses in terms of identification of human remains (Krogman and Iscan 1986; Rathbun and Buikstra 1984; Maples 1994). Anthropologists from other subfields have also been called to offer expert testimony regarding numerous social issues in both criminal cases (cross-cultural issues of dangerousness, drug use, etc.) and civil cases (racial issues, child custody, individual/family social functioning after accidents, etc.--see Rosen 1977 and his discussion of some of the problems involved). As a clinical anthropologist, it is almost 100 percent certain that at some time you will be called to testify or your records will be subpoenaed. There are anthropologists who object to anthropology and anthropologists being "used" in adversarial proceedings. I am of a different opinion with two qualifications. First, and referring to child custody cases, the clinical anthropogist should do everything in his or her power to move the couple toward mediation and resolving the problem that is leading them toward litigation, that is, their inability to communicate in a manner that leads toward conflict resolution. Litigation is simply a method of using the legal system to continue to solve that problem. Once in the litigation arena, the respondent and petitioner will lose control of their lives.

Second, the "expert" better have a good understanding of how the system works, or he or she will (a) be used as a "hired gun" and/or (b) be subject to public humiliation on the witness stand for "pretending" to be expert, but shown otherwise.

Licensing

Our legal system is adversarial; it is one side against the other, and he or she who has the best information, and knows how to present it, usually wins.

Now, I used the word "best." This does not mean truth or fact; "best" is always opinion. Do not look for truth in the legal system, but, instead, look for interpretations of information presented to the courts. If you are called by the courts to offer expert testimony, your adversary, the lawyer who represents the opposition to your opinion, will attempt, in any way possible, to discredit you and what you have to say. There are no current licensing requirements for clinical anthropologists. One reason for this is that anthropologists have traditionally been educators and, unlike the medical and psychological communities, have spent little time in promoting themselves as experts in the area of human behavior. Also, there is no clear legal expression as to what it means to be "doing anthropology."[9] Attorneys, however, may attempt to discredit testimony on the basis of this non-licensed status. Licensing, however, does not mean or confer competence or credibility; how you present yourself, who you are, what you do, how long you have done it, your publications, your formal education, your teaching experience, all these *can* add up to credibility. Moreover, it is up to the judge to determine whether or not your testimony will be accepted, not licensing, although some judges need to be gently reminded of this. Additionally, if licensing were the criterion for competence and credibility, then why would the attorney still attempt to discredit the expert, even *when* licensed? The answer to this is simple: Licensing, obviously, is not that critical to the attorney; discrediting testimony in defense of the client is the objective.

As Yozwick (1994:32-33) states:

The state never goes after a profession demanding that it be regulated. It is the profession that goes to the state proposing legislation to regulate that particular profession.

It is your right to choose not to be licensed. In most states, no license is required in order to counsel, guide or instruct others. . . . Regardless of which state you live in, these licensing laws do not affect you if you work as a consultant.

In fact, trade restraint is another definition for licensing, enforced by the state and, moreover, is usually administered by professional peers. . . .

Most people are under the impression that a licensed profession protects the public. Does it? How many people have been flim-flammed by realtors and insurance agents in this country? . . .

Licensing protects only the profession licensed. People should have the right to choose and evaluate the kind of service they get in return for their money. If you give people an honest service, they will return, and it will be by your reputation that you will either stand or fall. We are already over-regulated in the U.S. What we really need is deregulation.

In short, an organization, for example, the American Psychological Association or the California Psychological Association, approaches the State for licensing for several reasons. The first and foremost is trade restriction, to cut down competition in the market place. The second reason involves quality control, or some standard by which to judge performance, which is related to the third issue, that is, protection of its members from the public (i.e., malpractice).

So what does licensing mean? It means that the person is recognized by an organization as belonging to that organization. Beyond that, nothing. Competence and credibility are earned as the individual applies his or her knowledge. Keep in mind that the knowledge and tools at the individual's disposal may not lead to assessments or evaluations that represent an agreed upon reality by other members of that profession or other professionals, from other disciplines, who likewise study and evaluate human behavior, that is, anthropologists, sociologists, and so on.

Defining the Expert

Who, then, can be an expert in a court of law?   As Melton et al. (1987:17-18) state:

Assuming that mental health professionals' opinions should be admissible in at least some instances, the question arises as to which mental health professionals should be considered experts by the courts. Traditionally, this question has been answered by examining educational credentials, particularly with respect to discipline . . . .

Our own preference is for establishment of qualifications that are both broader and narrower than those commonly used; these should focus not only on educational attainments, but also on *experience in the relevant area and on the evaluation procedures used.* This preference is based on an assumption that the law should use a functional approach to evaluation of qualifications, as in fact is suggested in Rule 702 (which uses a criterion of probable assistance to the trier of fact). The prevailing standard as to qualifications should be broader, in that *the available research gives no basis for the historic preference for medically trained experts. The level of knowledge about forensic practice is not predictable by discipline, either among general clinicians or among clinicians with special forensic training. . . . [t]here is no basis for excluding social workers from competency evaluations; indeed, trained laypersons reach conclusions similar to those of mental health professionals. On the other hand, the standard as to qualifications should be narrower, in that training as a mental health professional by itself is insufficient to guarantee a specialized knowledge of forensic mental health.* [emphasis mine]

There is nothing in Melton et al. to suggest, imply, or demand that licensing stand as the or even a qualification to expert status in human behavior. My own preference is not to license, but instead to maintain a voluntary registry of *practicing* clinical anthropologists. I emphasize "practicing" because there is a great difference between being an intellectual in the field and actually applying techniques in a clinical setting. The former requires an extensive research of the literature in many fields, fieldwork, and a good memory for authors, dates, and cultural content, while the latter requires all of these plus the knowledge of what happens when you interact with others, along with specific tools of intervention (tools gleaned from the anthropological literature), so that the knowledge can be applied. If the individual is not practicing clinical anthropology, he or she cannot claim to be an expert in this area.

Psychological Testing

Another method employed by attorneys to discredit experts giving anthropological evaluations is that of psychological testing. I have already discussed the issue of testing in Chapter 4 and will only offer a review at this point. First, psychological testing is not cross-culturally applicable, so, therefore, it must be ethno-biased. If it is ethno-biased, then the meanings assigned to such testing will be continuously changing as culture, and thus psychology (perceptions, emotional reactions, attitudes, beliefs, etc.), changes. Psychological testing does not measure psychological processes so much as it does the questions answered about life situations experienced at the moment the test is taken. They cannot measure the past, as that is under a continual process of evaluation and renegotiation by the individual, and they cannot predict the future.

Second, I respectfully challenge any expert, even the designers of such tests, to definitely--without question, without hedging, without qualifications--state explicitly what these tests mean. I am not interested in what they are *supposed* to test for; my interest is, What do they *really* mean?

Third, as mentioned in Chapter 4, these tests are attempts to be analogues of medical testing. For example, if you go to the doctor and she orders a urine test to check for diabetes, the results of what is or is not in the urine give direction to the doctor's next procedure. If the ketone level is within normal limits, then diabetes is not an issue. The procedures for gathering the urine sample (i.e., when urine is collected, how it is stored, etc.) have to be taken into consideration. Urinalysis is, therefore, a main consideration for the diagnosis of diabetes. In other words, if the tests are negative, a diagnosis of diabetes will be withheld.

When it comes to psychological testing, on the other hand, another, very interesting procedure occurs. For example, suppose a male is accused of child molestation, and he denies the charges. The district attorney in the case asks the court for a psychological evaluation, and the individual is ordered to the office of a court-appointed clinical psychologist. The clinical psychologist, in his/her process of interviewing, administers psychological tests--in this case, for example, the MMPI and Rorschach. If the results come back, "Not clinically significant," these tests are then not referred to again. Instead, the clinical psychologist will rely on interviews with the accused, reports presented to the court, police records, interviews with significant others, and so on. On the other hand, if the MMPI or Rorschach results come back "clinically significant," then the significance of this will be elaborated upon in great detail and with flowing artistic license, using information collected during other interviews, police reports, and so on. In other words, when the test results are "significant," they are used in conjunction with the other information available in the case. When the test results are "not significant," they are not treated in the same way. My question is, What, then, is the significance of testing? My opinion is that tests are divination procedures subject to the personal reality of the psychologist, a reality conditioned by the tradition of his or her profession plus his or her artistic license. And, as with ordeal-type divination procedures, the purpose is to uncover information to bolster the accusations rather than to balance or negate.

Fourth, such psychological testing has no predictive value. The MMPI, for example, cannot tell you if a person will rape, kill, commit suicide, become a hermit, run for the presidency, or take up an animal rights cause for the SPCA.

Taking all these objections into consideration, there is no substitution for numerous, personal interviews with the client, interviews with others who have had extensive interaction with the client, and access to police and probation records. Human behavior is social behavior; what people will do is dependent upon what they have done with others in the past and with whom they will interact in the future. Using these parameters, I have great difficulty with a psychological evaluation that places emphasis on testing and on unproven and culture-bound psychological concepts rather than on detailed examinations of actual social functioning. The cry from the psychological community is that the testing is an expedient, an indicator because of time limitations. I seriously question this thinking, especially when a report could have rather overwhelming consequences for the lives of many individuals. The only way social functioning can be tested is through observing social interaction. Rape, murder, child molestation, theft, drug abuse, emotional abuse, all of these are social issues and cannot and do not occur outside of a social setting. Such behaviors cannot and do not occur outside of the context of interaction (historically, currently, and in the future) with other people. Psychological testing does not test social interaction, the most important criterion in predicting behavior in the future.[10]

Personality, which many of the psychological tests claim to measure (e.g., MMPI--Minnesota Multiphasic *Personality* Inventory), is, as I stated in Chapter 3, a product of a person's rule-setting tool kit, his or her style of delivery, and, of course, any genetic predispositions that are, in all likelihood, wrapped around this. I know of no psychological testing that uncovers such tools and style of delivery or attempts to correlate these into personality. Any such test, if developed, would have to be administered in a contextual frame representing each role the person plays during the course of a day, week, or longer. This would show that the individual has many personalities, which is normal, and that psychological testing has little to do with actual behavior.

NUTRITIONAL COUNSELING

Nutrition plays a very large part in physical and emotional health. Combining this with the communication principles mentioned above, one comes to the conclusion that the information we put in our bodies (and how our bodies and souls interpret this information)--that is, the pathogens, toxins, nutrients (food, etc.), and symbols (language, verbal and non-verbal)--defines much of what each culture calls illness and disease. In a word, much of this information intrusion can be included under the term *life style*. The clinical anthropologist needs to understand information intrusion on many levels, and how this translates into individual or group life style, and, within this, she or he must have a specialized knowledge of nutritional issues, just as she or he does the interpersonal and group communication issues.

For example, a family comes to you with a child diagnosed with hyperactivity, attention deficit disorder, (ADD), or both (ADHD). Keep in mind that these are Western biomedical terms and may have little to do with the actual causes of behavior that led to this diagnosis. Such a diagnosis does not mean that the behavior is genetic in a strict sense, that is, that there is a locus on some chromosome that translates as ADD. Hyperactivity and ADD can mean many things. They can mean that the child lacks positive attention from others, that this is the expected manner of interaction/communication in the home environment (implied rules), or that our concept of emotional maturity is not in line with behavioral expectations. They could also mean that the child has metabolic problems brought about by poor nutrition, mineral toxins (copper, lead, etc.) from drinking tap water, allergic reactions to milk, and so on, and this does not exploit all the possibilities. According to Coles (1987: 44-46), ADD is not clearly defined in the first place and is not, therefore, diagnosable. Moreover, "[t]he medical use of the diagnosis, whether it is called Attention Deficit Disorder or one of the earlier terms, has been the official basis for treating this 'disorder' with drugs, mostly Ritalin. Consequently, if the diagnosis is faulty, prescribing the drugs becomes questionable" (1987:44).

Numerous parents have come to me over the years very much concerned that the school psychologist has suggested that their child be on Ritalin, or that the child was on Ritalin and their justifiable fears regarding long-term use. It is a physiological fact that the long term use of anti-psychotic and tranquilizing drugs can lead to organic problems such as Parkinson's disease and tardive dyskinesia. "Long term" is not clearly defined--it could be a year. In a vast majority of the cases, a change in nutrition, combined with a different communication style at home and more parental contact with the school (parent-teacher-child meetings), significantly diminished the problem behavior. The use of Ritalin, or other such prescription drugs, is, again, an instant fix, a treating of symptoms and not causes, and is prescribed mainly so that teachers and parents do not have to make changes in their information input with the child (see Armstrong 1995). Ritalin, and a vast number of the prescriptions drugs are not fit for human consumption, deal mainly with symptoms, and create more medical conditions, often untreatable, over time.

Moreover, if a condition is undiagnosable, then the prescription of anything other than nutrition, rest, continued information gathering, and perhaps a different style of communication is the irresponsible practice of medicine. The prescription of Ritalin in these cases is only one example of Western bio-medicine at its worst. As Foss and Rothenberg (1987:85) state:

Holistic practitioners view biomedicine as after-the-fact treatment. As such, bio-medical practice begins once disease has been found. Holistic practice, on the other hand, sees its role as emphasizing the maintenance of health prior to the appearance of disease. This shift in orientation places the holistic effort in the arena of disease prevention and health maintenance as opposed to the "crisis care of pathology."

I see ADD, in most cases, as a diagnosis of social illness (see Shiloh 1977:443). In other words, attention deficits and other categories of learning disabilities, for the most part, are social issues. The disease model attached to the symptoms surrounding these issues is an illusion created and maintained by Western biomedicine and psychology. Problems of attention and learning are preventable if we care enough to teach parenting skills (how to intimately and respectfully communicate with one another) within our grammar school and high school curriculums and to introduce and reinforce the basics of sound nutrition instead of fastfoods. One only has to look toward the format of television programing--the rapid switching from one frame of reference to another (a form of electronic psychosis), the commercial breaks that interrupt continuity, the violence, and the impulsive nature of thoughts and behaviors--to understand a major cause of the short attention span and learning disabilities. We also need to come to the conclusion that people simply have different styles of learning, that some children emotionally mature later than others, and that the factory approach to education pushes more of our children out of the system rather than fostering the idea that education is useful as well as potentially fun.

Holistic Medicine

Holistic medicine has not had the impact on health planning that one might expect. Certainly, the congressional debate over a comprehensive medical care package indicates that prevention is not a high priority. For one thing, it is difficult to measure prevention; if medical problems do not occur, then they do not qualify as problems for consideration. Second, in order to practice prevention, the public needs to be informed about specific aspects of health, not about the generalities like "stay away from fat," "don't smoke," "don't abuse alcohol," and so on. The shift away from consulting your medical doctor to seeing other health practitioners (e.g., naturopathic doctors and chiropractors) or even consulting a book has been discouraged by Western biomedicine. We have become too complacent, believing in the myth of a perfected medical system, and we are willing to engage in a destructive life style and then hope and pray that medical miracles, "magic bullets," will be available to deal with any contingency. This has not happened. Although catastrophic illness does cost a great deal of money, the vast majority of visits to the doctors are for self-limiting conditions, physical-emotional problems that wax and wane *until* some devastating physical breakdown occurs. These visits are symptoms of interpersonal communication problems, a destructive life style, and a polluted environment. With proper information-- and this information is neither magical nor complicated--a person can manage, in large measure, his or her own health. Moreover, many of the supplements (vitamins, minerals, and herbs) useful in treating everyday health concerns can be purchased at a local health food store or grown in your home or backyard. Again, informed choice is the key.

Prevention vs. Reaction to Disease

Most of the catastrophic illnesses (i.e., cardiovascular problems leading to ischemic heart disease, stroke, diabetes, liver problems, etc.) are directly related to a destructive life style, poor nutritional habits, and lack of precaution when dealing with toxic substances that are commonplace in every home (Quillin 1994). Specific information on prevention and even information that allows a promise of longevity (we have not developed any acceptable short-term methods of measuring longevity except with mice and rats) are available. However, and according to a number of medical doctors (Kent 1994a; Whitaker 1994), such specific preventative information will *not* be forthcoming in the near future. For one thing, thinking prevention and informing the public are not part of the current medical model. It would take a paradigm shift (Kuhn 1967) of great proportions to move in that direction. Second, the effect on our economy could be "devastating" if the focus shifted to prevention overnight; the government and insurance companies would *save* a great deal of money.

Along with this, taking nutrition seriously opens up many alternative systems, and competition will not be welcomed by the established medical community. In fact, the current situation, with the FDA attempting to purge libraries of any information in scientific journals that even remotely suggests that there are health benefits from or curing aspects to the use of vitamins, minerals, and herbs, reminds me of Galileo being forced by the Catholic church to withdraw his contention that the Earth revolves around the Sun, rather than the Earth being the center of the universe, under the threat of torture. Such a recanting can be seen on the copyright page of Murray (1994), and I quote:

IMPORTANT: PLEASE READ

The information in this book is intended to increase your knowledge about natural remedies and by no means is intended to diagnose or treat an individual's health problems or ailments. The information given is not medical advice nor is it presented as a course of personalized treatment. There may be risks involved in connection with some of the natural remedies suggested in this book, just as there may be risks involved in connection with prescription drugs. Therefore, before starting any type of natural remedy or medical treatment, or before discontinuing any course of medical treatment you may now be undergoing, you should consult your own health-care practitioner.

There are no disclaimers to any of the editions of any of the texts, in my possession, on Western biomedical diagnoses and procedures written by MDs. The reason for this is that the medical profession has cornered the market on truth in diagnosis and curing. Through legislation, medical practitioners have created a trade restriction that cuts down on the individual's choice of health systems. This position needs to be challenged in the courts because it is literally killing people. Yes, "snake oil" is still being sold to many people, and this is precisely why more research into herbal products, vitamins, and minerals is crucial in order to accurately inform the public. Moreover, there are many prescription drugs and surgical procedures that do not do what they claim to do and they are on the market with the FDA's blessings (see Grossinger 1995:42-43). Coronary bypass surgery is an example; it does not do what it claims, and yet chelation therapy, known for years and used as a preventative strategy, would eliminate many cardiovascular problems. Consider the thousands of women (yes, mainly due to vanity and cultural directives) who have been permanently injured (another example of medical intervention creating metabolic chaos) by breast implants, and who were told that the procedures were safe. Such cosmetic surgery is not, in my opinion, the practice of medicine and is engaged in, in the vast majority of cases, for purely financial gain without really considering long-term effects. But, again, my main emphasis is prevention, and that will take a shift in the individual's thinking about responsibility for health.

One final observation--Finkler (1994a:192) states, with respect to Spiritualist movements in Mexico:

Paradoxically, as a folk healing movement, Spiritualist beliefs exert little hegemonic force in Mexico on a national scale, but by transforming patients' existence through incorporation into a community of persons healed spiritually, they have created a religious movement comprising thousands of people. In so doing, Spiritualist ministrations have promoted, on an aggregate level, religious pluralism in Mexico.

Spiritualism thereby contributes to advancing social change by mobilizing a sizable population and fomenting a growing movement that furnishes Mexicans with new options for religious participation. While Spiritualist healing may change a couple's day-to-day interaction, on an aggregate level the movement fails to restructure Mexican society in ways that could benefit its participants economically or politically. . . . *On the other hand, biomedicine, by treating individual bodies without transforming people's lives, fails to contribute to new social forms for the collectivity. It succeeds only in maintaining its hegemony as the major authorized provider of health care legitimated by the state.* [emphasis mine]

Health is important, especially when you are unhealthy. In a society with a health system that is oriented toward disease and is economically predisposed to be so, there is little incentive to promote preventative medicine. However, preventive medicine that encourages health-directed life styles, including good nutrition, use of supplements, antioxidants, and longevity, offers a means to actually transform society. As illness is a metaphor, a concentration on disease may represent a significant signal about the direction of Western culture in general. That is to say, if illness represents a metaphor of physical and social well-being, then maintaining a disease model may, in fact, maintain a diseased society. A preventative model of medicine would certainly "contribute to new social forms for the collectivity" in our own culture.

CLINICAL ANTHROPOLOGISTS AND LIFE-STYLE COUNSELING

Concept of Balance

As I stated earlier, and in my opinion, clinical anthropology should represent a holistic endeavor. Many emotional and/or emotional and consequent behavioral problems can be directly connected to a person's day-to-day life style, nutritional habits (Pfeiffer 1975, 1978, 1987a, 1987b; Mowrey 1990; Werbach 1991; Murray 1994), and communication patterns. The analogy used and shared by many cultural groups is that of balance. Your body/brain/mind needs internal information input of a specific quality and quantity every day. This input need is in the form of food, water, sleep, and exercise, as well as social information. The input of more information than the body needs (information intrusion resulting in information overload), such as protein and fat, can accumulate or be stored as fat tissue and represent macro-toxins. Also, there is a need for a certain balance of minerals in the body, as these are necessary for healthy bones (calcium), blood (iron), nerves (potassium, calcium, iron, zinc, etc.), and so on. Lack of calcium can lead to conditions such as rickets, lack of iron can lead to blood-oxygen problems often termed *anemia*, and lack of sufficient zinc can elevate copper in the brain, which can then lead to emotional as well as devastating physical problems, that is, enlarged prostate and prostate cancer. An overload of this information, however, can result in micro-toxicity.

Then there are the vitamins, which are, for the most part, catalysts that allow reactions to occur or act as transporters so that minerals can get to specific parts of the body. For example, calcium works synergistically with vitamin D in order to produce bone tissue. Thus, too little or too much of either of these can lead to an unbalancing of the system. Moreover, everyone's needs are different, and these needs change over time. Life style--that is, what one eats, exercise, and the use of alcohol, tobacco, and other drugs (prescribed or otherwise)--and social skills for dealing with stressors all combine to define, in large measure, health. One's chosen life-style evolves out of training early in life, the behaviors of one's peers, and images and words emanating from the mass media, either as sales pitches or as behaviors/attitudes depicted in movies, television sitcoms, or music. Choice, then, is, for the most part, limited to the choices presented by one's culture. Any individual, marriage, or family communication counseling/therapy that neglects these data is only considering part of the picture. Expanding choices, be this in the area of interpretation of life events, different behavioral possibilities, or possible life style changes (i.e., educating the person), is the nature of all counseling and therapy; the content and specific processes involved in delivery of this information, however, differ from culture to culture.

Many choices (i.e., smoking, abuse of alcohol, ingesting large amounts of hydrogenated vegetable oil or animal fat, using too much salt, falling asleep at night in front of the television, use of electric blankets, working night shifts, etc.) are unbalancing to the human body and, taken in combination, will result, over time, in illnesses and disease. These choices are a social, not a psychological issue, as people will engage in the choices presented to them. Further, people do not always make healthy choices often because the models around them are not engaging in healthy choices either. We know a great deal about the consequences of certain behaviors on our emotional and physical health, and I believe it is irresponsible *not* to inform people. A person can only have a choice if such choices are known.

For example, when I was growing up in the 1940s and 1950s, it seemed that almost everyone smoked. Of course, there were a few odd balls who did not; it was a life style pattern, much the same as reading the Sunday paper or listening to "The Shadow" or "Inner Sanctum." Television in the 1950s and early 1960s would not have been television without the ads depicting smokers as the picture of health, with love, sex, and manhood billowing out from every puff of smoke.

Smoking is very, very bad for your health and, in conjunction with other life style practices, unbalances the body, through the intrusion of many different types of toxins (free radicals), to the point of catastrophic illness, that is, heart problems, emphysema, and lung cancer.

The addictiveness of tobacco is usually attributed to nicotine, but research conducted at the Philip Morris Research Center over ten years ago found that a by-product of cigarette smoke, acetaldehyde, is perhaps just as addictive as nicotine (Raloff 1994a). Moreover, smokers who use alcohol encounter the same substance, acetaldehyde, as the first breakdown product of alcohol metabolism, which the researchers think "may be responsible for the addictive properties leading to alcoholism" (1994a:294).

Tobacco can be found in a natural state in North America, South America, Australia, specific islands in the South Pacific, and Africa (Wilbert 1987:1) and was introduced to Europe from the Americas during the first New World contacts. Tobacco became a desired product (people got addicted to it), and was/is grown commercially in many areas of the world. Europeans did not have any experience with tobacco, and it immediately became an everyday (casual, social, etc.) addition (and addiction) to ongoing life styles. Tobacco, however, as used in the Americas, was not consumed in the same casual manner as it was in Europe (Wilbert 1987), and although there was casual use, the importance of tobacco in shamanism overshadowed the casual aspects, in many cases. In short, because Europeans did not have experience with tobacco, and because they did not have any mystical ritual set associated with the plant and its use, its addictive nature has led to its abuse. Smokers literally *abuse* tobacco, in the same way people abuse alcohol and mind-altering prescription drugs. In this case, tobacco can be seen as *information intrusion*, analogous to pathogens in terms of cause and effect.

The use of tobacco has come under heavy attack in recent years and manufacturers have come up with clever symbols to sell the product. Benson & Hedges, for example, has come up with, "a welcome sign for people who smoke," which is a takeoff on the yin and yang symbol, complete with a cigarette and smoke. The yin and yang symbol represents balance and health, and, obviously, Benson & Hedges, through the juxtaposition of symbols, is attempting to associate smoking *with* balance and even health.

The use of alcohol, like cigarettes in earlier years, is directly related to life style as presented through the mass media. People are depicted as being healthy, having fun, and enjoying adventure, along with sexual overtones. In fact, drinking beer is one of the defining factors of youth and "maleness" in our North American culture (some others are owning a pickup truck, chasing women, and never asking for directions).

The abuse of alcohol leads to all kinds of health problems, both physical and social. Alcohol is a factor in interpersonal and intergroup violence, marriage and family conflict, work absenteeism, automobile accidents, and suicides (Goodwin 1992:146). The social issues connected with, for example, drunk driving/auto accidents are complicated indeed, and one has to wonder if the legal system, at least in California, really wants the drunk driver off the road. Consider, for the moment, your average drunk driver and where he or she gets drunk. Many people get drunk not at home, but, instead, at a bar. Most drunk drivers are apprehended after leaving a bar, especially late at night. All a police officer has to do is park within sight of a favorite watering hole, around midnight or 1 A.M., and pull over anyone driving away from the establishment. If, on the other hand, bars had to close at 9 A.M. there would be far fewer drunk drivers on the road and far fewer arrests. Of course, one has to consider the economic and political ramifications. Money would be lost by the bars, by the lawyers, and by the courts, and any politician who attempted to put through such legislation would encounter serious obstacles from special interest groups.

Is drunk driving a manifestation of alcoholism and personality problems? Is it a product of economics and the social spacing of bars with respect to where a person lives? Is it a product of advertising the "in" places to socialize? Is it a product of the rapid transit system? Is it a product of images presented by the mass media a la "Cheers," commercials, and the like? Or is it a combination of these things? Keep in mind that no amount of psychological testing or evaluation in such a case would ever uncover the social and economic factors mentioned above (see Helman 1994:194-223).

Returning specifically to the physical health risks of drinking alcohol, outside of suicide, injuries from falls, auto accidents, and fights, there are numerous health problems that result from its long-term use. These include gastrointestinal problems, liver disorders, heart problems, and destruction of brain tissue (Goodwin 1992:146-147). Not only are these conditions directly related to the abuse of alcohol itself, but also they are related to complicated nutritional and digestive issues that accompany alcohol abuse (Mitchell and Herlong 1986; Kruesi and Rapoport 1986; Munro et al. 1987; Seitz and Simanowski 1988; Shils 1988; Keen and Gershwin 1990; Heath 1991; Heaney 1993). In actuality, the hazards of alcohol abuse are only minimally considered in the mass media; commercial advertising of a life style that includes alcohol far outweighs any mention of the adverse effects of alcohol abuse. As Western biomedicine is reactive, rather than preventive, this is not surprising.

Other drugs enter into life style. These include marijuana, amphetamines, cocaine, heroin, and certainly the prescription drugs, like Prozac and Valium, and they have become just as much connected to life style as alcohol and tobacco. Looked at from another perspective, prescription drugs (i.e., tranquilizers and neuroliptic drugs) are designed to be abused in the sense that they are used on a daily basis, often over long periods of time. If a person uses a tranquilizer to deal with what are essentially social issues (e.g., stress evolving from relationship issues and work stress) then the tranquilizer, in and of itself, does not address these issues, nor do those (psychiatrists) who prescribe them.

Sleep Patterns and Life Style

Sleep patterns, also associated with life style, are likewise related to health and behavior. As Jarrett (1989:131) states:

[I]t is becoming clear that some, if not all, patients with a major depressive illness have a reversible disruption in the physiological regulation of the sleep-wake cycle and reductions in the amplitudes of the body temperature rhythm and circadian neuroendocrine secretory profile. It can therefore be postulated that a depressive illness is frequently associated with a pathophysiological disturbance in the regulation of circadian biological rhythm. [also see Kupfer et al. 1988b]

Disregulated sleep (information alteration and/or insufficient information) habits can evolve out of work patterns (working night shifts, for example), anxiety over unfinished work (you know, *The Protestant Ethic and the Spirit of Capitalism*), looping on information regarding relationship issues, and the consequent insomnia, drug use/abuse, noise pollution, allergies, eating habits, and so on, most of which are social, not psychological issues.

Who Chooses What You Eat?

As mentioned earlier, information on nutrition proper is extremely important. Fat and oil intake is of definite consequence with respect to cardiovascular disease, in that some types of fat are more likely to clog up the arteries than others (information intrusion). For example, vegetable oils, with the exception of olive, are proving to be a health risks especially when hydrogenated to resemble butter. Margarine, often considered marginal in the average North American diet, appears to be one of our highest sources of fat intake (Raloff 1994b).[11]

Further, food chemists and manufacturers have developed a fat substitute that is low in calories (Adler 1994). Fat, because of the size of the molecules (between .01 and 5 micrometers) is experienced by the human nervous system as "fat." Particles below .01 micron are perceived as "watery," and those above 5 microns are interpreted as "powdery or chalky" (1994:296). Procter & Gamble has spent "25 years and $250 million" developing a fat substitute called Olestra, which, according to the experts involved in its development, is not metabolized by the body. However, this product can cause numerous digestive problems (i.e., diarrhea, cramping, etc.), removes essential vitamins from the body, and, therefore it is not neutral information to the system. Instead, it is information intrusion, and, in my opinion, it will push the body toward chaos if ingested frequently and over time. Moreover, its use is mainly in the manufacture of junk food ("Experts Urge FDA," November 18:A24). This type of food substitute will simply add to digestive problems that are already epidemic in our culture.

The FDA, as of this writing, has approved Olestra, and I advise the reader to avoid it like the plague. What I find most interesting is that, through chemistry, food manufacturers are attempting to *maintain* a life style that includes fat or fat-like substances. We can learn to live without the "yummy taste" of fat; humans are actually pretty adaptable, given half a chance and appropriate choices. Further, it is difficult to predict what effect such "living better through chemistry" will have on the human body over time (remember the chaos issue mentioned earlier). One might come to the conclusion that Western biomedicine, the pharmaceutical companies, the FDA, and food manufacturers, view us as simply one big experiment. The knowledge gained might be very useful in space travel, but, in day-to-day living, we end up with, for the most part, very unhealthy citizens (physically and socially).

Proper nutrition is a misnomer unless it is balanced with appropriate vitamins and minerals, and what is appropriate cannot be left to the judgment of the Food and Drug Administration (Dean et al. 1993:126-129). Many vitamins and minerals are lost during food processing, and soils have been depleted of certain minerals, for example, zinc. Males often have a deficiency in this area that needs to be replaced by supplements.

Women are often deficient in calcium and vitamin B_6, which can lead to mood swings and painful periods. Further, we are so into fast foods, literally, that we "chow down" often without sufficient chewing. Moreover, we eat what is considered a balanced diet by blending meat, vegetables, tubers, greens, and oils in the same meal, which leads to digestive problems and malabsorption of essential macro- and micronutrients (vitamins and minerals). Our digestive systems were designed to eat food in sequence, beginning perhaps with fruit in the morning and tubers and vegetables later in the day. Protein from meat was occasional and, more than likely, eaten on its own, as were insects. Our protoancestors did not combine all these food items at once, and to do so invites digestion problems. Moreover, the cooking of food is a fairly recent development, and certainly came after our digestive systems were fully formed and in their present functioning state.[12] Cooking destroys essential enzymes in meats and vegetables; cooking fractionates food. Household pets, dogs and cats, likewise consume foods that are similar to those found in our current human diet, that is, foods that have been cooked, combinations of meats and vegetables, and so on. It is interesting that dogs and cats come down with illnesses similar to those of their human caretakers, that is, obesity, both malignant and benign tumors, leukemia, and so on. Is there a message here? I believe so.

OVERVIEW OF CHAPTERS 4 AND 5

Within Western culture, and keeping in mind the special considerations due the diverse cultural groups with respect to diagnosis and application,[13] the concept of HRMs can be applied to both physical and social issues, as the one is analogous to the other. Our current knowledge of human physiology allows us, in a general sense, to understand the types of HRMs (information intrusion) underlying (causing) many of the symptoms treated by Western biomedicine.

Identifying such HRMs should be the focal point of intervention rather then merely treating symptoms. Most catastrophic medical situations are not trauma injuries, but long-term effects of life style (nutrition, drug abuse, etc.). In conjunction with this, we must consider the way we communicate with one another, with the personalized interpretation of negative bits (rejection) leading to and/or exacerbating existing physiological problems. All psychological problems are culture bound, and attempting to force Western theories into the emotional and behavioral manifestations encountered in other cultures is non-productive in terms of understanding and intervention. In fact, it is rudely ethnocentric.

In short, the model presented by Western biomedicine, and especially the terminology and diagnostic categories encountered in Western psychiatry, is not the model to apply cross-culturally. The Western psychiatric and psychological models are, for the most part, second level and apply only to limited situations. The use of a first-level model (i.e., the uncovering of HRMs) is helpful in all systems and cultures as a means of initially diagnosing system stress factors. At the same time, the cultural content itself offers insights in terms of stress reduction by understanding in-the-culture attitudes and behaviors that could be utilized to reduce this stress rather than importing foreign ideas and technology. Moreover, the language used in this model is not emotionally charged, nor does it reduce the individual to a label or symptom.

NOTES

1. Forensic anthropology has traditionally and primarily been associated with the physical aspects of human identification, although anthropological involvement in forensics has expanded over the last few years.

2. I consider therapeutic any information/education that allows individuals in a social unit (i.e., family, marriage, or larger system) to function in a more harmonious and cooperative fashion. Thus, marriage and family therapy involves an education and communication skills approach to dealing with problems in social living.

3. The specifics of cross-cultural counseling will be outlined in a companion volume in preparation, *The Holistic Health Practitioner: Anthropology in Clinical Context*.

4. For example, see Bandler and Grinder (1975), Grinder et al. (1977), and Erickson and Rossi (1979) for an overview and discussion of Ericksonian hypnotherapeutic techniques. Erickson was familiar with the anthropological literature and interacted frequently with anthropologists like Bateson, but just how much of his therapeutic technique was borrowed from anthropologists and how much was independent invention is difficult to determine.

5. Probation officers are as important in their function of managing as the police are in apprehending offenders. The government is willing to put more police officers on the street in order to *react* to crime, but there does not seem to be a similar willingness to hire more probation officers to *prevent* crime.

6. If you are a female counselor, and please do not take offense at this, you may not be seen as a person with a legitimate, decision-making status.

7. According to some Western psychiatrists, we do not have to go to other cultures to observe the repressive nature of psychiatry (Szasz 1972, 1977, 1994).

8. Some years ago Ruesch (1973) used the words "therapeutic communication" to describe *the* process used in psychotherapy. See Powers (1986) for an informative discussion of therapeutic communication in context. Also see Wierzbicka (1992) for a more general consideration of language and its relationship to cognition, emotions, and everyday interaction patterns.

9. There is no clear statement as to what "doing psychology" really means either, except by virtue of the fact that an individual can call himself or herself a psychologist after obtaining a degree in psychology at a college or university and a license to practice. There are as many different concepts of psychology and brands of therapy as there are people in the field.

10. See Rush (1992a, 1995a) for the Rush Dangerous Behavior Quotient (Rush-DBQ), a behavioral check list that requires the evaluator to collect substantial data about the individual's social interaction patterns in order to make a prediction. Although there is no way of predicting behavior, this check list has been very useful for developing a index of probability. There is no reference to psychological testing in the Rush-DBQ.

11. As Schauss (1985:8) states: "In essence, as a modern society *many of us increasingly abdicate our responsibility for our diet, letting it go by default to non-family members.*" In fact, we have turned our diets, and health, over to the fast-food restaurants and convenience food manufacturers, who, in turn, saturate us with salt, fat, and sugar.

12. See Aiello and Wheeler (1995) for an opposite and, in my opinion, unsupportable position.

13. A detailed description of the diagnosis and application of concepts will be found in a companion volume, *The Holistic Health Practitioner: Anthropology in Clinical Context.*

CHAPTER 6

Culture and Conflict

This chapter moves toward a consideration of larger social issues, although they stem from the same model as applied to family systems. Included in the chapter is a look at the nature of conflict and violence, and how the mass media, as well as the government, shapes the legitimacy of violence as a choice of action for solving conflict.

Much of the psychological and psychiatric literature, because it focuses on the individual, tends to neglect the larger picture effecting individual behavior; this chapter, although briefly, questions the belief in fee will, fee choice, and individual responsibility. A consideration of how specific systems reward deception in social interaction is also included, as well as a discussion of social defection resulting from individuals not seeing themselves as coupled to the larger system. International conflict, and the connection to HRMs, is likewise considered.

THE NATURE OF CONFLICT

Conflict is a normal part of culture, both within and without. Social relationships are beset with misunderstanding, competing goals, and different perspectives of how things ought to be. Much of the day-to-day conflict is diminished greatly through the establishment of implied rules and rituals, as mentioned earlier. Implied rules establish routines and expectations. Along with implied rules there are the kinship terms that establish ideal interaction patterns and expectations and act as a barometer for understanding problems and problem resolution.

Explicit rules, often enacted by decree or through vote or negotiation, likewise serve to limit conflict. And, in state-type societies, where people can be anonymous, impersonal policing and decision-making agencies (courts) evolve to maintain order when competing goals collide. But, even with rules, roles, and policing agencies, there will always be conflict between individuals and groups, which leads to withdrawal, verbal altercations, physical violence between individuals and groups, and more creative stress-reducing mechanisms. As mentioned, conflict seems to be the normal order of things, as it opens the door to new possibilities and new social arrangements.

One point to keep in mind: Conflict, of whatever intensity, does not occur in a vacuum. Conflict does not occur outside of a social context. Yes, there is a psychology to conflict. However, if the contextual social issues out of which the conflict emerges are not considered *and* dealt with, conflict usually continues. Dealing with conflict and violence as if it were an individual psychological issue is as pointless as saving a drowning man who cannot swim and then throwing him back into the water.

THE BIOLOGICAL MODELS OF CONFLICT

Genetic and Metabolic Issues

Biological and genetic theories (information alteration, inherited information) of conflict and/or violent behavior are a supreme example of attributing the causes strictly to the individual and the malfunctioning of biology. In a limited number of cases, biological functioning can be directly tied to conflict between individuals or groups and aggression toward one's self. Even before there was any understanding of genetics, neurochemistry, and associated behavioral outcomes, we had the "bad seed" model. That is to say, some people were considered to be just "born bad." Period. From the moment of birth, in a very limited number of cases, you have the psychopath, an individual who is without a social conscience, an individual who behaves according to his or her own inner directives without the least care and concern for the consequences to others. In early human groups (i.e., bands and tribes), such individuals would have been weeded out before too much damage was done to the group, much the same as a wolf will destroy pups with antisocial behavior patterns.

In current Western society, however, such individuals survive and usually live to prey on others time and time again. And, although statistically they make up a small proportion of what I will call "social conflict generators," they can inflict a tremendous amount of emotional and physical violence on society.

Expanding on this for a moment, individuals who are "born bad" are never, ever born independent of a social context. In other words, we are not at a point of epidemiological sophistication where we understand the total cause and effect of maternal stress, environmental toxins (including electromagnetic fields), and food additives and the relationship to fetal development. We do know some of the effects of alcohol ingestion and other drugs on fetal development (see Lewis 1989:1402; Finnegan and Kandall 1992), but the effects of chronic emotional stress are not well understood, nor are they measurable at this time. Keep in mind that the "more or less" genetic issue in neurochemistry, as mentioned in Chapter 3, combined with maternal stress, could tip the balance in brain biochemical development through either periodic or sustained hormonal dumping.

Staying with genetics for a moment, the 47-XYY chromosome theory, popular some years ago, suggested that certain chromosomal attributes pushed the individual into antisocial, criminal acts. More research indicated, however, that this particular chromosome issue does not seem to be statistically relevant to delinquent or antisocial behavior (see McGuire and Troisi 1989). Also, attention deficit disorders (ADD) and learning disabilities, considered to have a genetic base and to be tied to behavioral problems at school and at home, need to be seriously reconsidered, as I stated in Chapter 5 (see Coles 1987; Peele 1989; Armstrong 1995).

Also within the biological model are the metabolic, hormonal, and nutritional issues that can lead to or exacerbate social conflict. These include inborn metabolic errors (e.g., PKU [phenylketonuria] and Tay-Sachs disease), single-gene abnormalities (e.g., microcephaly), chromosomal aberrations (e.g., Down's syndrome), and polygenic familial syndromes, which can be a combination of the above (see Szymanski and Crocker 1989). It is quite clear that hormonal abnormalities, as well as hormonal changes that occur during maturation and in monthly and yearly cycles, can have profound effects on behavior. Cushing's syndrome, for example, caused by a continual release of cortisol from the adrenal glands, can lead to chronic depression accompanied by agitation or manic phases. In Western culture, suicidal ideation is common with this condition, along with delusions and hallucinations.

Addison's disease, caused by adrenocortical insufficiency, can manifest itself in weakness, anorexia, nausea, salt craving, and a decrease in smell and taste. Hyperthyroidism (thyrotoxicosis), an elevation of thyroid hormones, can bring about insomnia, anxiety, irritability, and episodes of violence in Western culture (see Droba and Whybrow 1989).

All of the above (i.e., genetic and biological problems) can all fit into one or the other categories of *information loss, information alteration,* or *inherited information,* as discussed in Chapter 3. However, from a statistical perspective, these genetic/metabolic issues do not add significantly to cultural conflict. I have seen several cases of *genuinely* identifiable genetic and metabolic issues directly connected to social conflict. However, the small samples I worked with some years ago at two psychiatric hospitals (one in Colorado and the other in Ontario, Canada) indicated that only a fraction of a percent of social conflict could be directly correlated to these conditions. Some of these conditions so limit an individual's mental abilities to interact with society that the constant supervision necessary, in itself, cuts down on social conflict. Conflict between family members, certainly, can arise out of having to care for these individuals.

Central Nervous System Injury and Brain Tumors

War has been the ghastly laboratory for experimental work on brain injury. Projectiles (intrusive information) penetrating specific areas of the brain have allowed researchers to understand a great deal about what happens when brain injury occurs. Damage to the orbital region of the frontal lobe can lead to impaired social judgment, while damage to other areas of the frontal lobe (i.e., behind the forehead) can lead to a lack of creativity and inflexibility (see Andreasen 1984:118-120). The frontal area of the skull is often a point of impact during fights or automobile accidents, and, certainly, a portion of antisocial behavior is the result of such injuries.

On the other hand, injuries to the rear portion of the left frontal lobe and adjacent areas of the temporal lobe can result in specific language difficulties (aphasias). Not being able to put thoughts into words, for example, can be an extremely frustrating process, but just how much of this type of brain damage results in social conflict is difficult to say. I suspect, however, that it is minimal.

Tumors in certain portions of the brain have been directly linked to violent behavior. In June of 1966, "an ex-GI named Charles Whitman climbed to the top of a tower on the campus of the University of Texas at Austin and started firing a rifle at random at people walking below. He killed fourteen people before he himself was killed by police. The autopsy showed that the reason for his bizarre behavior lay in a tumor in the brain near a tissue known as the amygdala" (Brown 1976:4).

The above example illustrates the potential for social conflict to evolve out of alteration of internal information (tumors). Research done with cats years ago showed that stimulation of the amygdala produced a sham rage. However, there is, in all likelihood, a social component connected to the Whitman case mentioned above. The question becomes, What will a person do with rage? Will a person, in every case, pick up a gun, climb a tower, and randomly kill people? The answer to this question is unequivocally "No." When people go into rages, their choices of behavior are socially conditioned. Some people lash out at others verbally; others lash out physically with knives, baseball bats, or guns; still others withdraw. Rage can just as well be turned inward, as in the case of suicide or high-risk behaviors (e.g., drug abuse).

From whom and under what circumstances do people acquire and then act on specific choices? Well, it is reasonable to assume that in the Charles Whitman case, his choice was conditioned, in part, by his military experience.

Others acquire their choices from observing parents or peers. Still others can acquire their choices by watching television or movies. We have all been exposed to the choice of physically injuring others, and yet only a small portion of the public engages in that choice under *any* circumstances. The news media and the politicians who benefit from certain types of legislation promote an illusion of unrestrained violence. Keep in mind, however, that people will act on the choices they have learned in the social milieu from which they draw information. Behavioral choice is not simply a product of individual psychology but, instead, a dynamic process of total social living.

Nutrition and Behavior

The human body is able to create, using primary substances from the environment, specific life-sustaining amino acids. These inner-manufactured products are called non-essential because they do not have to be continuously taken into the system (information input) except when, for one reason or another, there are metabolic deficiencies resulting is a deficiency. The non-essential amino acids are asparagine, aspartate (aspartic acid), alanine, cysteine, glutamine, glutamate (glutamic acid), glycine, proline, serine, and tyrosine. On the other hand, there are many essential amino acids that our bodies cannot synthesize (although bacteria existing in our intestines may secrete small amounts of certain of these during their metabolic processes). The essential amino acids are arginine (necessary for infants and small children) histidine, isoleucine, leucine, lysine, methionine, phenylalanine, threonine, tryptophan, and valine. Amino acids are the building blocks for proteins. Along with amino acids, there are carbohydrates, lipids, acids, enzymes, and so on, all functioning to maintain a certain balance in the body. When there is too much or too little of an essential or non-essential amino acid in the body, this will have an effect, either immediate or over time, on total metabolic functioning. The concept of balance, as mentioned in earlier chapters, is part of the philosophy of many medical systems around the world wherein health is a maintenance of balance, which includes social relationships and/or relationships with superordinate agencies. Although I will approach nutrition in greater detail in another volume, it is important to understand how behavior is affected by what we put in our bodies.

First, we need to illustrate what happens when certain foods or substances create imbalance in the body and, more specifically, in neural functioning. Ethanol (CH_2OH), for example, can be considered a perfect food in that it does not have to be broken down before entering the bloodstream. It is removed from the body by enzymes in the liver, but, before alcohol is metabolized and removed from the body, it has an effect on total body functioning. In short, it unbalances the body's metabolic processes.

One of the most obvious effects of drinking ethyl alcohol is that one's consciousness is altered and external information is processed differently. Why? What kind of a neurochemical and/or electrical increase or decrease does alcohol consumption promote? In a word, how does alcohol *unbalance* the system? The biochemical effects of alcohol are complicated, but seem to involve Gama-aminobutyric acid and calcium ion channel complexes (see Tabakoff and Hoffman 1992).

The alteration of either can have profound effects, depending upon the amount of alcohol consumed, on neural functioning. Some effects include feelings of all-powerfulness, a lessening of inhibitions, and, at higher levels of consumption, depression, lack of motor control, slurred speech, blackout, and death. Alcohol offers us an instant look at what certain "foods" can do to neural functioning. This may seem like an extreme example, but what are the effects of other foods or lack of specific nutrients on neural functioning?

Over the past 100 years, we have become increasingly aware of the effects of certain deficiencies in vitamins and minerals (see Carpenter 1993; Masdeu and Solomon 1989:200-201). Research in this area is incomplete at best, and I refer the reader to the research of Pfeiffer (1987a, 1987b), Chafetz (1990), Schoenthaler (1991), and Werbach (1991). According to these researchers, nutrition has a profound effect on mood and behavior. One of the problems with such research is that each person has different nutritional needs that can change over the course of a day. Moreover, as the body ages, nutritional needs are likewise altered and, because Western biomedicine works, for the most part, from a disease model, a clearer understanding of nutritional needs, health, and behavior is not right around the corner.

When considering less than optimum nutrition (e.g., when a child goes to school on an empty stomach or with inadequate protein intake), does this have anything to do with the fight he or she gets into shortly before lunch? And if it does, why does the child go to school hungry in the first place? Poverty? Choices learned at home from parents who eat the same way? Media conditioning to eat fast, fractionated foods laden with fat, salt, and iodine? Staying up late at night, getting up late, and not having enough time to eat in the morning? A concern about how one looks, so breakfast is skipped in order to lose a few more ounces? The child, of course, is referred to the school psychologist, who looks for attention deficit disorder (ADD), dysfunctional family dynamics, or drug abuse, often without considering the other social factors mentioned above. If diet is brought up, however, it is never considered as important as the psychological issues. Why? Because we live in a society that promotes the illusion of individualism and freedom of choice, which fits in well with psychodynamic theories; the model blinds us to the reality that people are influenced by the behaviors of others. To simply tell the child to "eat better" does nothing to alter the choices at home. If the person is living at the poverty level, how does one intercede in that system without violating civil rights and the freedom to choose what one eats for breakfast? The usual diagnosis offered by psychiatrists and psychologists in many of these cases (i.e., conduct disorder) essentially leaves the problem up to the individual--it is not seen as encased in a composite of information emanating from the society within which he or she lives. So what do we do? We punish the child.

Why do people consume alcohol? Why do people maintain certain less-than-optimum nutritional standards? The answer is not simple, but it lies in the choices presented to the individual by other family members, the mass media, and governmental agencies. If a person abuses alcohol, he or she is labeled an alcoholic. If a person eats too much and is obese, is anorexic, or practices bulimia as a dieting mechanism, as you can see, we have terms for them as well. If a person is within normal weight limits and is not anorexic or bulimic, but maintains a very poor quality diet, this person is considered normal, but, in fact, all of these individuals are responding to social messages, and to initially consider any of the above to be suffering from some sort of neurosis is ludicrous. Why do people abuse alcohol? Is it because of a weakness or sickness or genetic problem? No. People abuse alcohol because it is one among many social choices for dealing with social issues, and I respectfully challenge any psychiatrist or psychologist to show me that alcohol and/or other drug abuse is without primary social cause and effect. One of the basic reasons that drug rehabilitation programs fail for a vast majority of the participants is that the social conditions that led to the abuse are not altered. In fact, altering some of these social issues would require vast changes in our culture.

Nutrition, what we eat and do not eat, has a profound, yet not thoroughly appreciated effect on behavior. But, as important as it is, when it comes to conflict in social living, the way we learn to communicate interpersonally and between groups in our family of origin is head and shoulders above all the other considerations mentioned thus far, for this is where we learn our first choices for behaving.

Conflict and Communication

In the preceding chapters, I have discussed at length how people set rules and, at the same time, tell the person who he or she is in the group. Out of this, the individual develops a group worth, or positive and negative reference points that he or she uses to compare all other incoming data. High Risk Messages (HRMs), both cultural and social, represent the negative reference points out of which most social conflict is generated. Yes, social conflict evolves out of disputes over territory, money, and competing political ideologies. However, at the center of all this is the HRM. Understanding HRMs, and the universal processes engaged in to reduce stress, helps us to understand the fact that conflict is a natural feature of social living; life is trouble. The goal, then, is to reduce conflict by understanding its common denominator. Before reexamining HRMs, let us take a look at some of the social elements that allow us to predict points of social conflict.[1]

Choices

When you observe people over a period of time, it becomes clear that there is a high level of general predictability in human behavior. This is because people act on the choices they have for dealing with specific situations. It is a matter, then, of cataloging choices. Yes, people can expand choices, and this can happen out of a conscious desire as well as situational expedience. The desire to expand choices is itself a choice. Most people run on autopilot, and, although you can teach an old dog new tricks, most people are creatures of habit. Moreover, under stress, people have a tendency to revert to one or a combination of the basic stress reducing strategies, that is, physical and verbal fighting, withdrawal, freezing up, emotional conversion, and sexual behavior.

Further, people will develop a cluster of strategies for use in different environments. In other words, an individual may have the choice of listening to an employer when being critiqued without getting sarcastic or violent. On the other hand, this same individual may become extremely agitated or violent while being critiqued by his or her spouse. If the strategy of listening during periods of conflict was not initially an element of the relationship rules in the marriage (either implied or explicit), then it is not a choice. Thus, the first choices one learns for dealing with others within specific environments, combined with relative stress, become prime factors for predicting behavior and understanding social conflict in general.

The Mass Media

The owners and operators of the mass media (i.e., movies, television, etc.,) maintain that their influence on viewer choices of behavior is minimal at best. Although this is not explicitly stated as such, it is certainly implied in the messages that flow into our homes. Yes, it is our choice to watch certain programs, but people will watch and be influenced by what is available. There is research that indicates that the news media may serve to increase criminal activity, as well as suicide, (see Phillips 1974, 1983; Strasburger 1995; Macbeth 1996), through suggestion and, in my opinion, through an implication that what they are reporting is the norm. The average viewer of the 6 o'clock news is likely to reach the conclusion, after daily reports of murder and mayhem, that there is a burglar for every home, a rapist and murderer on every corner, and a convicted felon in every parking lot looking for a victim. This is not the truth; it is an illusion created by the media in order to attract viewers or readers through sensationalism. This can create a great deal of anxiety on the part of the viewers, but, more important, it gives an impression to a certain percentage of the viewers that "everyone is into rape, murder, and so on and, therefore, it is okay to do these things." Youth, especially males who are searching for an identity, are in a status of limited power and anomie, and much of the conflict-oriented criminal behavior can seem very attractive, especially when it is presented in such a graphic, heroic manner without consequences or conscience.[2]

Now, when I am talking about identity, I am referring not to the psychological component of identity, whatever that is, but to the social aspects. Identity is, in large measure, a product of how the individual interprets the social world around him or her, and how one interprets involves learned choices. Keep in mind that those early choices learned in one's family of origin are very important, and thus the choices we have as parents for communicating with our children become of prime importance when considering how the individual will handle conflict in social relations.

As Milgram (1963, 1974) pointed out very dramatically years ago, people will go along with perceived authority to the point of committing violent acts. Is this a flaw in human morality? Is this evidence of psychopathology deep within the human soul? "No," to both questions. We are a group animal, our basic model of authority comes from our parents or caretakers, and it becomes a choice to go along with their authority. Keep in mind that teens who rebel against parental authority may not necessarily rebel against others seen as being in authority.

The larger question here is, Do we in fact have freedom of choice? I would say, "Definitely not," unless all possible choices are known to the individual along with the potential outcome of each choice. People are free to choose from the choices seen as viable to them, and, as people are creatures of habit, choices equal habits. Social interaction becomes a series of behavioral sequences, both positive and negative from a social value standpoint, and, in this sense human, behavior is very predictable once you understand both choices/habits and behavioral sequences.

People alter their choices when dealing with others only under certain circumstances: (1) they acquire new information, a new choice, and feel motivated to act upon it; (2) they are forced to engage in a new behavior, but this does not mean that the behavior will continue once the power is withdrawn; (3) under stress, and sometimes connected to number 2, the individual might arbitrarily or accidentally try something else, and, if it produces positive results, it may continue; (4) possibly connected to numbers 2 and 3, the individual and/or group members decide consciously to break up negative behavioral sequences, and, if results are positive, the behavior may continue; (5) through analogous thinking, the individual and/or group recognizes a behavior that was useful in one situation could be useful in another; and (6) if a person knows that he or she is being observed in order to document negative behavior, that individual may alter behavioral responses to avoid detection (this does not necessarily mean that certain behaviors are no longer a part of the individual's choice repertoire and will never be engaged in again). This may not exploit all the possibilities, but, after a life of mechanically behaving, new choices do not just automatically fall out of the air. If they did, society would amount to a bunch of arbitrary behavior not directed to group cooperation (which, for the genetic reductionists, *is* self-interest). You need habits, you need behavioral sequences, and you need limited choices, so that there is a sense of conformity and expectation. Keep in mind that the choices one has for relating to others and to one's environment can be used to define a specific culture. All individuals within a specific culture may not have the same choices or even be aware of specific choices, that is , choices not within his or her status, communication tool kit, and so on. Freedom of choice, once again, is an illusion.

Stress and Choices

As Monahan (1981:153) states:

One concept that may provide an organizing principle for many of the issues in violent prediction is that of stress. Stress can be understood as a state of imbalance between the demands of the social and physical environment and the capabilities of the individual to cope with these demands. . . . The higher the ratio of demands to resources, the more stress is experienced. Stress is thus to be thought of in terms of transactions between persons and their environments over time.

If you change the word "capabilities" to "choices," you then begin to understand the advantages of choices when dealing with others in terms of lowering social conflict. Choices, for the most part, and in this present context of interpersonal and group conflict, relate specifically to how you communicate with others, how you send and interpret information. Keep in mind the five general strategies that people will engage in when under stress (see Chapter 3).   A person's choices expand dramatically when he or she understands what is happening when talking and listening, when desired goals are more clearly defined, and when these are combined with specific interpersonal and group communication tools. And, again, where do our choices come from? From what those around us are doing, and this includes parents, teachers, peers, police, those depicting the patterns of social interaction in the mass media (movies, sitcoms, news broadcasts), and government officials. If people see conflict being settled with more conflict, then this is the model they will use. The model of solving conflict with more conflict is likewise employed by our government; we do not see the behind-the-scenes negotiation in an attempt to avoid the conflict. Why? Is it not sensational enough? Would people not be interested in understanding how diplomacy works? What would be the outcome, in terms of public opinion for both sides, if diplomatic endeavors were made more public? What effect would this have on reducing conflict simply through public opinion? The problem is that the needs, opinions, and agendas of citizens are often at odds with government needs and agendas.

Impulsivity

According to Segal et al. (1988:756, 762):

Danger to others was related most strongly to impulsivity and irritability and was also significantly associated with disorders of thought form, thought content, and judgment, expansive mood, and inappropriate affect.

One surprisingly clear finding in our study is that the degree of impulse control as perceived by clinicians is the most important aspect of the person's clinical state in determining disposition.

Let us take a close look at this statement. First, "thought form" and "thought" are socially conditioned, even when under the influence of drugs. Second, "judgment" brings us back to the choices one learns. Third, "expansive mood," meaning the expression of emotions, is likewise, and in most cases, culturally conditioned as well.[3] Fourth, "inappropriate affect" is also culturally determined. This leaves us with "impulse control," which, according to Segal et al., is the "most important" factor when considering dangerousness.

Impulsivity, however, is also a learned social issue. We currently live in a society that *demands* instantness. We have instant credit, instant communications via telephone and FAX, nearly instant delivery of catalog items (next-day air), instant relationships/sex, buy now and pay later; everything has to happen *now*. We are a culture that hates to wait for anything. We do not like waiting in lines, we demand fast foods, we expect instant service, and traffic jams are unbearable. Impulsiveness evolves from a technology that allows instant communication; impulsiveness also evolves from an economic system that is geared to *not* delaying gratification. So, when people are impulsive, is this purely an individual psychological issue? I think not. Impulsivity is not the key to violence and conflict, but it certainly sheds more and more light on socially learned factors that can lead to conflict and violence.

Interpersonal Conflict

Conflict in social living primarily involves tapping into a person's HRMs, keeping in mind that this is a two-way street. People send information, and the receiver places a meaning on the perceived messages. All information is compressed and is, therefore, subject to interpretation.

HRMs, as you will recall from earlier chapters, are learned as the individual learns the rules, at first in the family of origin, and then while interacting in other groups. These rules, along with the learned tools, are designed to create conformity and expectations within these primary systems, but they are also designed to aid interaction in the larger arena of life outside of the family. The rules and tools learned in one's family of origin act as templates or stepping-off points for adding to, or subtracting from, processes and strategies for dealing with "strangers." Herein lies the big secret behind most of the conflict we experience in day-to-day living. There is nothing mystical about this; there is nothing Oedipal about this; there is nothing pathological about this except in a small number of cases stemming from genetic or metabolic issues, physical brain damage or tumors, and nutritional issues. *Conflict is generated as we send and receive information and activate HRMs.* When this happens, stress goes up, and our culturally taught and personally learned reactions to stress (i.e., models from parents, friends, television, school) come into play, that is, verbal and physical fighting, withdrawing, freezing up, emotional conversion, and sexual behavior. Variables that lead to conflict include who the person sending the message is (i.e., you will interpret the messages from close friends differently than those from strangers or enemies), your mood at the time (i.e., if you are having a "bad day," interpretations will be different than if you are having a "good day"), drugs (i.e., conflict is more likely to occur when drinking alcohol than when smoking marijuana), and implied rules regarding how you and the other person dealt with conflict in the past.

Marital Conflict

In our culture, *all* couples entering matrimony are incompatible. This is because, as you will recall from Chapters 3 and 5, each person enters the relationship with different rules for operating a marriage, different tools for communicating within the relationship, different styles of tool use, different histories from which to draw experiences, and different sets of HRMs. This surely equals *incompatibility,* which leads to misunderstanding, which leads to high-risk communication patterns and activated HRMs. This, in turn, leads to stress and distrust, which leads to a 50/50 chance of divorce, as negative information builds up in the system, making interaction problematical and problem solving impossible. Incompatibility, in reality, is not the problem. The problem is, How does one live intimately with another human being without creating a "war"? Incompatibility, for the most part, is a difference in cultural *content.* The processes of intimate living, once understood and practiced, cut across and through such differences. Although I will go into this in great detail in a companion volume (*The Holistic Health Practitioner: Anthropology in Clinical Context*), let me point out just a few factors that help to clarify processes in social conflict and the elements necessary for intimate living.

First of all, we spend very little formal time educating children about interpersonal communication. They are not instructed in *listening processes* and why one should listen in the first place. Second, we do not explicitly instruct children in sending *positives,* along with a recognition that each person is different in his or her needs for positives. Third, by the time the child is ready to leave the family of origin, there is little or no conception of *processes for shutting off unwanted behavior that are low risk*. And, fourth, the child learns to be an individual with free choice and usually negotiates in terms of what he or she wants, which leads to "no win" situations. *Negotiation,* then, is the fourth process that is absolutely necessary in intimate living. And fifth, at times negative bits need to be sent, and *message escalation* becomes a necessary adjunct to dealing with unwanted behavior.

The tools or strategies currently learned by our children, and then replayed in their families of procreation, are neither good nor bad, neither right nor wrong, but many strategies are highly likely to activate HRMs in others--they are high risk. Just as children learn the types of foods the family prepares, they likewise learn to ingest and utilize the communication strategies presented in that environment. Such learning is not a matter of individual pathology, but, instead, a matter of enculturation. Again, there is no such thing as common sense in communication. People act on the choices at their disposal regardless of their effectiveness or abrasiveness.

Child and Spousal Abuse

Conflict between males and females resulting in spousal abuse is likewise, in most instances, not an issue of individual pathology. In fact, most spousal abuse actually originates during the dating phase of the relationship, when the couple interacts within an illusion that they are getting to know one another by discussing the car they want to buy, the house on the hill, the trips to the Caribbean, the number of children they will have, sexual behavior, and by bitching and moaning about parental control or parental abuse. Very rarely does the couple ever discuss, in detail, how they will communicate with one another--how they will listen, how they will send positive messages, how they will deal with the negative behavior of one another, and how they will negotiate. Of course, these four preceding factors are not as romantic as discussing a trip to the Caribbean, but, without a set of agreed-upon communication tools (the processes for intimate living mentioned above), the couple only enters the marriage as incompatible as ever--*even more so.* Why? Because, once they become husband and wife they have to act out these roles, and, if they have not discussed the roles and the tools they will use within them (as well as within the roles of parents), their models of behavior are usually those of their parents or their exact opposite (polarity). And, even if the respective parents did a "good job," the rules of relating may not fit in the next generation. For example, in my generation, spanking children was considered appropriate disciplinary behavior. It was a tool for setting rules. Currently, spanking a child could be considered child abuse.

Spousal abuse does not happen in a vacuum. It takes at least two for abuse to happen, one to abuse and the other to perceive it as abuse. But there is a third actor, and that is society itself. The definition of abuse changes as cultural ideals change. What is considered abusive today would not necessarily have been considered abusive fifty years ago. Moving in another direction, what is considered child abuse today (e.g., spanking) was the norm when I was growing up in the 1940s and 1950s. Today, as mentioned above, spanking is considered abusive and is grounds for legal action and possible loss of custody of your child.

This brings me back to stress, the choices of action a person has and will use under stress, and the tools for living intimately with others. Stress is generated in relationships as the individual interprets information and activates HRMs. As communication tools and behavioral choices for dealing with stress in intimate living are learned, approaching domestic violence from a psychological perspective seems to miss the point. Recently (January 26, 1993) the state of California amended Domestic Violence Diversion, AB 226, for example, to exclude couples counseling. The Orange County Probation Department's, "Guidelines for Batterers' Treatment Programs," developed in response to the new amendment, states (page 1):

I. Principles/Philosophy of Treatment Providers
  1. Domestic violence is a crime and can never be condoned.
  2. The primary focus must be on stopping the violence, not saving the relationship.
  3. Violence is the responsibility of the batterer.
  4. Treatment providers should work cooperatively and communicate with interrelated agencies such as law enforcement, the courts, battered women's shelters, probation, district attorney's office, victim advocates, etc.
  5. Treatment providers must be culturally sensitive and should strive to reflect the community's cultural diversity. . . .

Violence is a time-honored tool for dealing with human relationships. The state of California and the federal government, for example, use violence on a daily basis for dealing with specific social issues. As Parkin (1987:205) states:

Sometimes the use of violence is justified by those in authority as a necessary response to opposition, but it is rarely referred to as such, and is more normally couched in acceptable idioms (e.g. "state of emergency", "measures taken in the interests of national security", "detention centers", etc.). This sense of violence clearly presupposes questions of institutionalized legitimacy, so that the rule-goverened physical force exerted by, say, prison wardens in the performance of their duty is not in the eyes of the law called violence, but becomes so if in some way the wardens are found to have gone beyond certain standards of conduct.

I do not condone violence per se, and there is a time and a place for it, just as the state determines when violence is in its best interest. If, for example, you yell and scream at a police officer while he or she is giving you a speeding ticket, violence is likely, if not considered necessary, depending upon the words used and emotional content.

In amending AB 226, the state of California is attempting to install another approach to family violence; Orange County is going along with the amendment. The amendment, however, is put together from a psychological perspective that includes beliefs in the existence of individual free will, freedom of choice, and individual responsibility. Violence is not just the responsibility of the batterer. The state is willing to assign blame without first asking what it has done to prepare its citizens for intimate family living. The state quickly acknowledges that the individual needs to be tested in order to obtain a driver's license, but no such instruction or testing is necessary to get a marriage license, a license that initiates a set of behaviors and responsibilities that are a thousand times more complex than driving a car. The statuses of husband, wife, and parent have somehow ended up on the bottom of the heap.

Further, number 5 above (i.e., being "culturally sensitive") is really a curious addition if violence is the responsibility of the batterer. If we assume that behavior occurs in a vacuum, that choices are consciously thought out along with consequences of actions, then we can blame and theoretically tame the violent behavior of the spouse beater. Unfortunately, that is not how behavioral choices develop, nor is it how thoughts become actions or how behaviors come into play.

In fact, we do very little thinking about what we do, and it is certainly not very clear why people do things except that these are their choices under certain social conditions and emotional sets. People act and react according to what others are doing, regardless of the culture to which we are referring. Therefore, if we are to be culturally sensitive, then behavior can not be seen as a simple manifestation of a single, misdirected soul. To be culturally sensitive would involve the significant others in a person's life. To be culturally sensitive, one has to look at the elements in society that direct choices of behavior, and these include the relative importance we place on husband, wife, and parent roles and skills as well as the types of models presented in the mass media.

Family Violence, a Template of Social Violence

We are obviously a society, along with many others, that condones physical violence as a strategy for resolving conflict. The mass media tend to focus on social violence as a method to boost ratings. In the action films, murder is viewed as fun and necessary; little remorse is shown, and the pain and suffering of survivors is not revealed. But the real question is, Why is there so little violence when compared to the amount of social interaction? The answer lies in the fact that we do not interact with the vast majority of people in our social environment. We ignore most people, although we do have ritual behaviors that at least allow us to initiate interactions with almost anyone. In the urban world we exist within nets of relationships. In fact, the vast majority of violence occurs not between strangers but between those known to us.

Statistically, males tend to be more physically violent than females, although I suspect that there is equality in verbal violence. According to Betz and Fitzgerald (1993:361):

Discussions of male socialization and its conflicts and stresses emphasize variables such as emotional restrictiveness and difficulties with intimacy, and generally examine interventions to assist men to live fuller psychological lives. Conspicuous by its absence is any sustained attempt to analyze and intervene in what can only be considered one of the most serious social problems of our age--male violence against women. Although such investigations are beginning to appear in the specialized literature on aggression and victimization--e.g. *Violence and Victims* and *Victimology*-- these studies are generally not being conducted by counseling psychologists nor are they written about in the core counseling psychology literature.

It is assumed in the above statement, extracted from a review of the literature,[4] that males learn when and where to be violent. However, "emotional restrictiveness" and "difficulties with intimacy" do not necessarily lead to violence. Moreover, I am not sure what *emotional restrictiveness* means, as people have different methods of emotional expression, and, thus, it becomes an issue of interpretation. Because a female cries and openly expresses her feelings using verbs and adverbs, this does not mean that such expression is better than, superior to, or more preferred than not saying anything and withdrawing. Both expressions are laden with emotion. The real issue is what is on the person's mind, that person's choices for revealing thoughts and under what conditions, and the tools the receiver (the wife, in this case) has for getting the person to express ideas without feeling threatened. Getting the husband (or wife) to talk without ordering, warning, name-calling, using sarcasm, or withdrawing love is one of the keys to successful intimate living.

Moreover, to assume that, because a person uses a lot of emotion words, shows a wide range of emotional expression, and freely talks about things, this person is living a "fuller psychological life" is an illusion. North American males do not have as much trouble with intimacy as many North American females (or psychologists) think. What both males *and* females have trouble with is *trust*. It is very common in counseling sessions for the wife to state that the husband avoids intimacy and emotional expression on specific issues. A common male reply to this is "Well, when I do reveal how I'm feeling, it is used against me during a future discussion." In short, the husband does not trust what the wife will do with the openness. Or, "If I really tell her how I'm feeling, we get into more of an argument because it isn't what she wants to hear. My reality is denied."

In many, many cases, it is not that males want to avoid intimacy and discussions with emotional content. It is that the wife *both* wants it and does not want it at the same time. Males often find themselves in the double bind of "Tell me what's on your mind, but it better not be negative because you will pay!" Once again, male violence is not created in a vacuum and stems, in large measure, from the way we communicate, and this takes at least two people.

With respect to male-female violence Levinson's (1989) research is instructive and has some far-reaching implications that fit with the themes in this work. He states (1989:103-104):

In general, it seems that in societies without family violence, husbands and wives share in domestic decision making, wives have some control over the fruits of family labor, wives can divorce their husbands as easily as their husbands can divorce them, marriage is monogamous, there is no premarital sex double standard, divorce is relatively infrequent, husbands and wives sleep together, men resolve disputes with other men peacefully, and intervention in wife beating incidents tends to be immediate. . . . One should not be surprised, for example, to find that shared decision making in the household predicts the absence of wife beating . . . . male dominance in decision making predicts wife beating . . . . equality and closeness in the marital relationship lead to low rates of family violence. The central conclusion I reach from these findings is that *family violence does not occur in societies in which family life is characterized by cooperation, commitment, sharing and equality.* [emphasis mine]

Family interaction patterns can also be seen as the template with which to measure social functioning in general. Violence between family members initiates a rule that says violence is *a* or *the* method of resolving conflict. Social violence involves a mosaic of factors; it is not simply the product of individual pathology and can only be conceived of in that way when society needs someone or something (i.e., handguns, assault weapons) to blame. Social violence affects everyone, and singular causes only cloud the issue. However, prevention does involve a simple solution, and that is encouraging, educating, and rewarding individuals to participate in families in a non-hurtful, healthy, and cooperative manner. This means educating in terms of HRMs, explicit and negotiable rules of division of labor, explicit relationship rules, and a clearer definition of the roles involved in marital/family relationships.

Divorce and Social Violence

In North American cultures, divorce begins with dating, for it is during that time that many of the rules of the relationship (implied rules) are set. Such rules, in many cases, are only renegotiated with great difficulty and usually with outside help. As the system matures and life situations change, the inability to renegotiate the rules leads to stress, and stress, as mentioned in Chapter 3, can lead to verbal and physical violence. Although Levinson's research suggests that an equal ability for both husband and wife to divorce is a factor in low levels of husband-wife violence, frequency of divorce is also a predicting factor (1989:103). When a complex, urban society makes it easy to defect from one's primary family units (family of origin and family of procreation), that society then loses its most valuable mechanism of social recognition and social control and motivator for positive social action.

But there is a larger issue, and that is the message that easy divorce sends to its citizens: family life is not important; the roles of husband, wife, and parent are not important. The intrusive message has gone from "Choose your spouse wisely and know how to manage the system--get the rules and roles straight" to, "Divorce is a method of correcting bad choices." When you undermine the most important roles a citizen can play--that is, husband, wife, and parent (not doctor, lawyer, and politician)--you undermine society, and, in such a situation, violence increases at all levels of society.

Just as simply as effective family systems can be developed, one can likewise mold violent, dangerous behavior within that same unit.

Military Training and a Model for Creating the Violent Criminal

Taking this a step further, the creation of male violence (or female violence) is best observed in the procedures used for training loving, gentle, caring males to kill. I am referring to military training. The steps are as follows: First, the person is disoriented by being inducted into the service. He is put through an impersonal medical exam and then shipped to boot camp. At boot camp, the individual is told that he no longer is a human being, but, instead, belongs to the government to do with as it deems fit. This disorientation, in most cases, regresses the individual to a dependent, almost infantile position.

Second, verbal abuse from one's drill instructor (D.I.) is frequent, usually uncalled for, and sometime capricious. Personal space is violated; if orders are not followed immediately, verbal abuse, along with some type of humiliating punishment, quickly follows. This amounts to emotional and physical abuse, abuse that is sustained. Anger and resentment build out of this, but the expression of these emotions cannot be directed at the D.I. or any of the officers. If they are expressed in these directions, severe penalties result. The direction of these emotions has to be selective. And who does the selecting? The government.

Third, the new recruit sees the same verbal abuse directed at others; D.I.s are not noted for their tact when disciplining. In fact, disciplining in front of others is the rule as it seems to create a connection between the person being disciplined and the observers; that is, "This could be you if you step out of line."

Fourth, the D.I. and other specialists teach the recruit how to abuse others, this time using, for the most part, armed and unarmed combat.[5]

A recent publication by Athens (1992) outlines essentially three steps for creating a dangerous and violent criminal.[6] First, the child is brutalized (verbally and physically) over a period of time by someone seen as in authority, for example father, mother, or older brother. Second, this individual observes this person in authority brutalizing others. And, third, this authority figure coaches him (or her) to brutalize others. Now, what is the difference between Athens's discussion and the process experienced in the military? Nothing. But what the comparison does do is inform us that, given the right conditions, people can learn to be violent and that this violence can be pointed in specific directions. Further, violent people can be created at any age, and violence is a behavior to be developed and utilized by the government--it is not a choice to be engaged in by the individual citizen on his or her own. There is unsettling incongruence here.

Male violence is, for the most part, not a product of individual psychopathology, but, instead, a product of society's priorities. If you teach people how to communicate in intimate relationships, if you bolster the roles of husband, wife, and parent, male-female physical and emotional violence will drop significantly. There is no mystery to this. As Segall (1991:176) states:

Landau (1984) examined statistics on criminal acts of violence in a dozen industrialized nation states for more than a decade spanning the mid-1960's through the late 1970's. During that period, all but one reported either stable or increasing homicide rates and robbery rates (Japan was the exception). *Landau's primary use of these data was to provide a preliminary test of a model which predicts that the probability of violence and aggression as reactions to stress will increase when social support systems fail or malfunction.* Using inflation rates as his major measure of social stress and ratio between marriage and divorce rates as his main social support measure, Landau found parallels in changes of these indices in every country but Japan.

There, an *increase* in social stress (as indexed by inflation) and a *decrease* in the strength of the family was accompanied by a considerable increase in suicide. As possible reasons for this departure from the overall picture found in this 12-nation sample, Landau suggested that strong social control mechanisms beyond the family exist in Japan, notably in schools, local communities and work places. He also cited the fact of much citizen participation in crime prevention in collaboration with professional law enforcement agents in Japan, as well as three important social control mechanisms embedded in Japanese cultural phenomena, namely a strong sense of shame, a sense of duty and loyalty, and respect for human relationships. Switzerland was another partial exception in this sample, in that while measures of aggression and violence increased, there was a greater increase in suicide rates. [emphasis mine]

Humans as Small-Group Animals, Involvement in Larger Groupings, and Social Collapse

Miller's number and Carneiro's mathematics of conflict (see Chapter 1) hold a very important truth: Humans are a small group animal. Groups fracture from irreparable conflict and, theoretically at least, can only come together into larger groups (over 125), initially at least, by consent, probably in the face of some crisis, real or supernaturally inspired. As numbers increase, available statuses decrease, and the power base alters accordingly. Handling interpersonal conflict moves slowly away from family/kinship responsibility to more impersonal methods as the social groupings within a geographical area gradually increase. Sanctions or police actions are necessary because of our tendency to see ourselves as "us" and others as "them." Such polarity promotes a communication style that is high risk and behaviors that are not conducive to cooperation. Although this is a bit simplistic, it will serve as a bridge from band/egalitarian living to urban non-egalitarian social groupings.

Once in the urban milieu, the manner in which the government responds to its citizens--its style of communication and actual behaviors for the "good" of its citizens--is likewise a key to stability or collapse. Also, if the citizens do not have other models with which to compare their lives (relative deprivation-- a form of information intrusion), and/or if there are supernatural sanctions that justify and validate ruler(s)/ruled communication patterns, stability over long periods of time is possible. In urban settings, however, when there is the possibility of comparing life styles in other systems, when there is little or no positive "stroking" of its citizens (as is the case in most urban societies), when the individual and group are afforded little input (their "story" is not listened to), and when the individual is dictated to and more and more laws are passed because the government is fearful of losing its power, the result is a great deal of instability. During periods of social instability, the worst possible thing for a government to do is to become repressive. The message (a negative bit) to its citizens is, "We don't trust you." What is of interest is that the more laws that are enacted to deal with conflict, the more conflict that is generated. The powers that be spend more and more time enforcing laws and building a larger and larger police force; collapse is inevitable. Any society that rules with power without consent and then loses that power loses its ability to positively influence its citizens. As Tainter states (1990:193):

Collapse is fundamentally a sudden, pronounced loss of an established level of sociopolitical complexity.

A complex society that has collapsed is suddenly small, simpler, less stratified, and less socially differentiated. Specialization decreases and there is less centralized control. The flow of information drops, people trade and interact less, and there is overall lower coordination among individuals and groups. Economic activity drops to a commensurate level, while the arts and literature experience such a quantitative decline that a dark age often ensues. Population levels tend to drop, and for those who are left the known world shrinks.

Information overload, especially if it is information of a repressive nature, is a key factor in collapse. People stop looking toward a common good and, instead, defect, that is, are demotivated and often engage in social sabotage. Early warning signs are manifest in art forms that express violence and decadence, crime rates that increase, and general relationships between citizens that deteriorate. Certainly, we can look to environmental factors-- overproduction of land, crop failure, population increases, and so on. (see Tainter 1990:194 for his list of key factors)--but the interplay between individuals and between individuals and their government is of prime importance. People go to their death in defense of systems within which they feel acceptance; in reverse, people destroy systems within which they are anonymous.

What would be a personal and small-group motivation for participating in an urban complex? Stress reduction. If, instead, there is continual stress enhancement--that is, lack of food, lack of resources, lack of acceptance (all representing information loss or deprivation); more and more information intrusion (laws) of a nature suggesting a troubled society; and more and more energy output with fewer and fewer rewards--society will inevitably revert to a lower information input-output level or a level where losses can be minimized. This is called social defection.

Deception in Interpersonal and Intercultural Interaction

Conflict can evolve out of deception or accusations of deception. In order to fully understand deception and how this relates to conflict, we must first comprehend information distortion, how it evolved, the purpose it serves, and not only how to recognize deception in day-to-day encounters, but also how to deal with it in a low risk manner.

Deception is very common in other species (see Dawkins and Krebs 1978; Mitchell and Thompson 1986; Krebs and Dawkins 1984; Guilford and Dawkins 1991; Griffin 1992), and, therefore it must serve some purpose other than as an aberrant communication strategy. Thus, we have to determine, within the general rule-setting nature of communication, more specific purposes for verbal and non-verbal messages. When animals are commun- icating, between species and within species, we have at least three possibilities:

1. To communicate about self or inform--to give directives or instructions regard- ing the status of one's self, for example, anger, in heat, direction of food, hunger, affection, and so on;
2. To manipulate or control others--to give misleading information or even lack of information in order to misdirect. Purpose: to acquire food, to avoid being the meal of others (being discovered or detected), to protect offspring, and so on;
3. To support an ongoing process of adaptation--this might likewise be considered manipulation, but it benefits both the sender and the receiver over time as the re- ceiver adapts to the misinformation, thus increasing its survivability. On the other hand, the sender is adapting as well, becoming more and more clever in its behav- ior to deceive.

No evidence has survived (at least paleontologists and archaeologists have not as yet found evidence) of deception in our protoancestors. In contemporary monkeys and apes, researchers have noticed the use of alarm calls to distract aggressive intentions or to draw attention away from food sources (see de Waal 1989), but this does not necessarily mean that contemporary and prehistoric behaviors coincide. However, one of our protoancestors' assumed survival mechanisms was the ability to observe other animals and, through analogous thinking, imitate their behaviors in some way. Interspecies deception, therefore, would have had great survival value. Using analogous thinking, *intra*species deception would have always been a possibility if *inter*species deception existed, for once you utilize a strategy in one environment, it is reasonable to assume that it will be utilized in others. Stated another way, once interspecies deception becomes a standard process in avoiding predators, acquiring food, and so on, deception as a communication process would have been accepted under certain circumstances; it becomes an implied rule and, at the same time, a definite possibility in *all* interpersonal interaction. And, because we develop a distinction between "us" and "them" (see Chapter 1) when dealing with other cultural groups, it is more of a given than a possibility.

According to Griffin (1992:196), "[I]n the long run, 'cheating' by transmitting inaccurate information works only if most signaling is reasonably accurate." Most people, most of the time, do not consciously engage in deception. Deception, except that evolving out of certain categories mentioned below, involves a definite measure of conscious calculation. But let us back up a moment in order to better appreciate when people are most likely to deceive.

Social Deception and Defection

In terms of basic survival, deceptive signals have been used in all manner of food acquisition and in conflict between groups and between groups members, for example, shamanic illusions to effect cures. First and foremost, then, people will deceive if it is perceived as in their best interest or in the best interest of others (this may be more of an illusion or a statement after the fact to explain behavior--more deception). As the nature of human systems changes, the nature and specific purpose of deception changes. For example, in small, face-to-face groups, such as a small band with limited numbers who have to rely upon each other for survival, information distortion for individual gain at the expense of others would have had low individual and group survival potential.

At the other end of the spectrum, where there is no personal relationship defined by kinship (blood, fictive, marriage) or other binding relationship with a duration (time) factor, the individual is likely to maximize gain for self at the expense of others. This is termed *social defection*. Such defection is most common where there is anonymity, geographical mobility, and few (if any) solid ties to others, ties represented by recognized, agreed-upon, and somehow enforced rights and obligations. Such is the case in current urban society, where deception, rather than being simply individual pathology, is, in fact, a very normal and expected part of social living. In our culture, we expect people to tell "the truth, the whole truth, and nothing but the truth," and we expect people to keep their word, and be "up-front" with us, but these are ideals that do not represent what actually goes on, not out of individual pathology, but simply because of the nature of large urban settings.

Lies, deception, distortion, malingering, and the withholding of information, then, appear to be universal factors and not the private domain of the human animal. These communicative behaviors, therefore, can be seen as strategies or tools for personal or group survival. At the small-group level (i.e., among our ancestors of 30,000 years ago and still among the surviving bands existing in the world today) information sending between members is of a different nature in terms of survival. Individual survival is dependent upon group survival. Moreover, there is an equality of access to information except that which is considered by the group as the domain of men, women, or other limited specialists. Social cooperation, and thus group survival, is enhanced by relatively accurate sending and receiving of information. Moreover, because of close social living, deception is more difficult to engage.

This is altered in the state-type, urban complex, wherein there are many diverse groups within a larger system. In such systems, there is often competition between groups, or, at the very least, one group does not see mutually agreed-upon cooperation with other groups as necessary for survival. Control mechanisms to prevent excessive predation between individuals and groups evolve in order to maintain order. Such mechanisms are police, courts, and so on. What this tells us is that humans are a small-group animal, and when they are placed in large groups and faced with anonymity, survival becomes an individual and a small-group matter. Lying, distortion, malingering, and the withholding of information increase in proportion to the "us" vs. "them" distinction because it is seen as necessary--honesty is not necessarily the best policy. In many, many cases, deception is in the individual's or the group's best interest, especially when "belonging to" a larger system (i.e., the urban complex, or society) is so abstract as to be outside of individual and group comprehension. Fortunately or unfortunately, this is the case in the nation-state, and it then becomes crucial that the government pay special attention to the needs of its people or the people will defect. The government, however, has its own agenda, which is often in conflict with its citizens' needs unless the citizenry is supposed to support that agenda. In cultures where the government is supposed to serve the needs of its citizens, but does not, this amounts to the government defecting from its people.

Groups within can develop very different goals from those of the dominant society, with some goals being considered antisocial. In the urban setting, one does not have to look very far to do cross-cultural research. Within this "us" vs. "them" setting, honesty and confessing can lead to conviction. For example, a Hell's Angels gang, apprehended for cooking amphetamines in the desert, will lie, cheat, distort, and withhold information in order to avoid prosecution by the criminal justice "gang."

Family court services will stand as another example. Many a parent has lost custody of his/her children by being honest and confessing to alcohol abuse or verbal/physical abuse of children. Moreover, many a parent has lost custody of, or visitation rights to, his or her children because of distortions presented by the other spouse and believed by the family court counselor. In the former, honesty is punished; in the latter, distortion is rewarded. Logic and social circumstances defend the lie, the distortion, the withholding of information. From a sociological perspective, apprehension and punishment for wrongdoing are essential for bringing order or balance to the state, an abstract entity. Most of the time, however, this order or balance is not returned to the families or neighborhoods within which the crime occurred. As the crime is seen as impersonal, so is the punishment. When dealing with the state, a person's best policy *is* to deceive. This has less to do with psychology than it does with the social realities that exist within the urban complex (see Barnes 1994; Lewis and Saarni 1993; Miller and Stiff 1993; Hyman 1989; and Rogers 1988 for further discussions of sociological and psychological aspects of deception).

Finally, in a society where big businesses, such as insurance companies, are known to lie, cheat, and steal; where sales people are rewarded for distorting in order to sell a product; where television ads misrepresent the nature of a product in order to influence the consumer; where politicians cover up the truth, twist motives, and outright lie, the message to the average person is, "It is all right to lie, cheat, and steal." Where, day after day, rape, murder, gang activity, theft, deception, and the like, as presented by the mass media, are offered as the norm and not isolated incidences, such behavior can be justified and engaged in by many "borderline people" because they think everyone does it. There is a direct correlation between the media news reporting of rape and murder, drive-by shootings, arson, theft, and so on, and the increases in similar behaviors in the days that follow (see Phillips 1974, 1983; Lagerspetz 1991).

Deception and the Potential for Conflict

Deception, when detected, leads to conflict. The secret is to discourage deception, but, at the same time, to understand deception as a strategy in certain situations. These situations include those when interactions are defined by one or both parties as "us" vs. "them," those when the individual or group can defect from social obligations because of mobility or the anonymity factor of urban living, and those when it is "in one's best interest to deceive," as it maximizes gain, at least in the short term.

Because of the nature of human information processing, information is always distorted or biased. This comes about as a byproduct of normal information processing, that is, the generalizing, deleting, and distorting process, combined with time lag, and the input of new information that alters old information. Certain emotional conditions give rise to mass distortion of information, as well as the alteration of brain chemistry and consequent interpretation of information through the ingestion of psychotropic drugs. For the most part, in these cases, we are not talking about purposeful distortion (the taking of psychotropic drugs is purposeful, but the behaviors engaged in after the fact usually are not--they are, in a sense, unpredictable in that the person may engage in behaviors never considered when off drugs).

Purposeful distortion, on the other hand, is the conscious effort to restructure information for personal or group gain, with a lie equaling signal falsification and distortion equaling information alteration. Keep in mind, however, that such distortion cannot be simply boiled down to individual psychology or psychopathology, but, instead, reflects social attitudes and survival realities. Deception by government, when detected, breeds conflict, as it is a message of distrust, and distrust is a message of individual and group nonacceptance. In other words, if the government is practicing deception, it is telling its citizens that they are unworthy and are subjects rather than citizens of the state. Especially with democratic governments, each time the government or its representatives deceive the public and it is detected, this will breed great stress and distrust of government that is difficult to forget or forgive. Individual citizens are less tolerant of government deception than that of friends, neighbors, or even strangers. Government deception is a sign of defection from the public good. If wrongdoings by government agencies (i.e., FBI, CIA, BATF, FDA, IRS, etc.) are not *quickly* and *severely* dealt with to the satisfaction of the citizens, social stress will increase geometrically. This will lead to a defection of the citizenry and can also lead to the creation of millenarian-type movements that can be quite militant, that is, militias with charismatic leaders, religious cults, etc. These types of groups can be seen as warning signs of growing social dissatisfaction--symptoms, if you will--which, if suppressed or ignored, can lead to armed confrontation, extremes in "us" vs. "them" confrontations (e.g., racism), and so on. Governments can react to such groups in several ways. The first, which is most popular in the United States, is to suppress information (through control of the mass media) about government wrongdoing and then use the mass media to discredit such groups. The second is to really start listening to the public not through special interest groups, but through senators and representatives, thus obtaining more realistic (not statistical by testing a selected number of people in a selected area of the country) input through a vote on government policy, including all those issues that have so polarized this country over the past thirty years, that is, the public's preference for medical care (preventive vs. reactive), educational direction in our schools, gun legislation, and, probably most important, a dialogue about family dynamics and what to do, at the local level, to improve family life. This would act as a process of social reintegration so badly needed in the country. It is not that I am naive enough to believe that there is any one answer to the problems inherent in urban living, but the ability for the average person to talk--and be heard, acknowledged, and counted as important--*is* the process of social reintegration. The government does not, however, like what it hears (negative information intrusion--HRM activation at that level), and this is the fear to ever engage in such a policy other than at the local level. When you tap into the HRMs of people in power, you risk unbridled retaliation.

CULTURAL CONFLICT

Cultures collide for a number of reasons, resulting, at the very least, in harsh words and, at the very most, warfare. A good review of many of the factors that lead to warfare can be found in Harrison (1973) and Groebel and Hinde (1991). Konner's discussion (1982:186-194) regarding specifically interpersonal conflict attempts to correlate social and psychological aspects with neurobiological factors. Harris (1989, 1979, 1978), however, enters ecological factors into the explanation arena. All of the issues posed by the above authors are likewise discussed in more recent terms in Haas (1990). Obviously, all the factors mentioned by these authors have a part to play in terms of conflict and its expression, be these attempts at negotiation or warfare.

As Ross (1993:21) states:

Conflict and cooperation occur in specific cultural settings. Culture is the particular practices and values common to a population living in a given setting. It is a shared, collective product that provides a repertoire of actions and a standard against which to evaluate the actions of others. . . . Culture is often manifest in the shared symbols and rituals which invoke common responses and easily link the interests and actions of individuals to those of the larger collectivity. . . . Viewing conflict as cultural behavior helps explain why disputes over seemingly similar substantive issues can be handled so dissimilarly in different cultures.

The culture of conflict refers to a society's specific norms, practices, and institutions associated with conflict. Culture defines what people value and what they are likely to enter into disputes over, suggests appropriate ways to behave in particular kinds of disputes, and shapes institutions in which disputes are processed. In short, *a culture of conflict is what people in a society fight about, whom they fight with, and how they go about it.* [emphasis mine]

Although culture does define what people value, and thus the cultural HRMs, cultures in the macro sense only collide out of the efforts of the representatives (usually the efforts of from five to seven people--remember Miller's number) of specific cultures. For it is through communication strategies and resulting mutual understanding, or lack of it, that cooperation or conflict emerges.

The importance of genetics and neurological problems, except in limited individual cases, takes a definite back seat to the communication set and setting within which people find themselves. And, as mentioned earlier, each person brings to that setting rules, tools, style, history, and HRMs (the set). These, in my mind, are the prime variables for conflict, be this between friends, husband and wife, neighbors, or cultures. Boiling these variables down further, and as a starting point, how people send (symbolic output) and how they receive (symbolic input--interpretation) are the primary factors for initially understanding the dynamics of conflict or cooperation. At a very basic level (the *process* level) the individual needs to understand what happens when people talk and listen, that is, the concept of HRMs, the rules that people play by (the fact, we all operate under a different set of rules and values), the perceived roles we play and the statuses we display, the possible stress reactions when HRMs are tapped into, and how implied rules are built.

At the next level of analysis, the individual needs to apply these processes, using specific content, when communicating with others. This is easier when individuals are speaking the same language and from a similar cultural orientation, keeping in mind that without understanding what happens on the basic level, speaking the same language and having the same cultural orientation do not necessarily cut down on conflict. In fact, when dealing with people that you perceive as similar to you, you might assume there is more understanding than really occurs. At this basic level of analysis, the individual *must* assume he or she *does not* understand. Because all communication equals compressed data, and because each individual has his or her own program for decompressing the data, the reader can then appreciate why understanding is difficult. The fact that communication is redundant, as discussed by Colby (1958) some years ago, allows for much of the understanding that does occur.

At the third level of analysis, which involves cross-cultural issues, the individual must understand certain basic concepts about that specific culture, and these, again, are that culture's specific HRMs. A way to this understanding is through learning the language, but, certainly, an understanding of cultural HRMs can be developed from others who do speak the language and understand interaction patterns and attitudes toward perceived outsiders.

Moreover, there are universal HRMs that apply to all cultures, and these include voice tone and facial gestures, ordering, warning, threatening, name-calling, interrupting, violation of body space, and hitting, to name some of the more obvious (see Rush 1995c). It is not enough just to show respect, because how one does that differs from culture to culture.

The Purpose of Conflict

Conflict does serve many purposes, one of which is to open a door to redefining social behavior between individuals and groups and to redefining goals (see Sluka 1992). What is of interest is that the same categories of information used in diagnosis, as presented in Chapter 4, can be used in diagnosing intra- as well as intercultural conflict. Whether we are dealing with conflict over scarce resources (insufficient information, loss of information) or leaders attempting to improve their general power base (information imbalance, insufficient information), we are considering differing types of information input and output.

INTERNATIONAL CONFLICT

International conflict, including economic sanctions, the breaking off of diplomatic relations, and warfare, can stem from a multitude of issues, all evolving out of how each of the parties involved is perceiving the information presented by the other(s).[7] More specifically, and once again, cultural and personal HRMs come into play. And there are certain rules to the initiation of such conflict. Whenever the representatives of one country threaten, name-call, invade territory or in some way insult the honor of the other, stress will increase, and that country's strategies, as utilized in the past and under similar circumstances, will come into play. There is nothing too complicated about this. The question as to why wars start has been debated over the centuries, and the answers include competition for scarce resources, biological issues involving aggression and population control, assassinations stemming from fanatical causes, to even accidental shots fired. But, once again, war, as well as all other forms of conflict, evolves from how the parties involved interpret the motives of the other, the strengths and weaknesses of the other, and, probably most important of all, misinterpretation and the tapping into HRMs. Not all conflict can or should be avoided. Because conflict, in one form or another, is universal and observable across species, it must serve a purpose. That purpose appears to center around change.

Factors that are involved in limiting international conflict are not too different from those limiting conflict between husband and wife or in any relationship wherein the participants will be interacting over a period of time. The dynamics of this are discussed in detail in *Process in Cultural Sensitivity* (see Rush 1995c). However, it must be kept in mind that humans are a small-group animal, and, beyond a certain level of abstraction (perhaps the tribe), social control methods need to be in place at the small-groups level, that is, the family, neighborhood, and community. Without such social control mechanisms (that are family based and basically agreed upon), oppression, through the use of impersonal police forces, military personnel, and, in this day and age, the mass media, becomes a natural consequence of urban living (see Carneiro 1970; Haas 1982; Wenke 1984). Any culture that cannot resolve conflict at the community level without oppressive measures only hypo-critically enters the international arena as a problem solver. Obviously, if the tools and skills are not available at one level, how will they magically appear at another, larger, and more complicated level?

Conflict with Nature

One aspect usually left out of the nature of conflict is conflict *with* nature. As urban people often see themselves as disconnected from nature, the indiscriminate rape of nature, stemming from greed, special interest groups, and eventually government policy, will bring us to the ultimate conflict--our removal, *by nature*, as a viable species from the face of this planet. As Gall (1978:47) stated some years back, "The system always kicks back." The planet as a system, certainly within a larger system, has its own HRMs.

OVERVIEW

Interpersonal and group conflict emerges from the way individuals and groups send and interpret information. Because we all have a separate reality, the probability of conflict is almost guaranteed in any interaction. It is decreased, however, as the interactants understand what is happening as they are talking and listening and have sufficient tools to engage feedback for clarification.

Conflict, however, is an inevitable consequence of social and international living; it is a given. Because conflict is ever present, it is intertwined with the change factor, which appears to be connected to all organic and inorganic systems. Those professionals who see conflict as merely individual pathology, or an issue of individual psychology, are naive at best.

As a generalization, large amounts of conflict can produce large amounts of change, and certain types of rapid changes (i.e., separation and divorce, violent political takeover, the overtaxing of environmental resources, etc.) lead to system breakdown. In the large picture, system breakdown can lead to a more adaptive system--the "better mousetrap," so to speak. At the individual level, however, rapid change evolving out of conflict, especially within the family, can be traumatic, to say the least.[8]

Even when individuals do understand, at least in a general sense, what is happening as they talk and listen, competing goals and wants often stand in the way of successful negotiation. However, all humans share the same basic needs. Negotiating on this level would seem to be the starting point for reducing much of human conflict at the interpersonal as well as at the intercultural level.   In order to do this, however, each individual needs to understand that it is in his or her best interests to belong to the larger system (i.e., the nation or global Community), to be intimately connected to this larger system and personally recognized and needed. Humans, though, are a small-group animal, and identification with these. large and abstract entities is difficult at best. National or global "good" has to be synonymous with individual "good" and recognized as such by the individual and the small groups to which he or she belongs; such a congruence signals a high level of individual and social health. This is one of the reasons that nation-states are unstable, with instability directly correlated to numbers of police and laws. More police and laws translates into more instability. When individuals and groups do not see belonging to the larger social matrix as in their best interest, they defect and devolve to small groupings, which are seen as having higher survival potential.

Government defection is directly correlated to how these administrators or "rulers" see the public, that is, as subjects or citizens. The more the government sees the public as subjects, the higher the defection rate, which is accompanied by more policy that benefits the government and those in power. When government determines what is in the best interest of the public, the members of the public become subjects. Democratic nation-states are most stable when the members of the public are seen as citizens with an equal say in the development of policy, policy that benefits the citizens and not solely the figureheads of the state. Social reintegration, and the health of the nation, begins when the citizen becomes an active participant in the designing of public policy at the local *and* national levels. Such decisions, when left up to the pressure from special interest groups or the private opinions and agendas of senators and representatives, communicate to the average citizen that he or she does not count--rejection at a symbolic and highly significant level. Rejection is the cornerstone of HRM development, rejection breeds stress, and stress moves people to action.

NOTES

1. This material is taken from *Evaluation of Dangerous Behavior* (1992a) and *Evaluation and Communication with the Violent Juvenile (1995a),* both by John A. Rush and available from the author.

2. Through the mass media, some of our most vulnerable youth learn that the gun, a symbol of power similar to the Acheulean Hand Axe, as mentioned in Chapters 1 and 2, is a means of obtaining this identity. The gun, a symbol of power, is then prosecuted by the state. This is certainly not a logical response, but it does correspond, again, to the suppression of symptoms rather than dealing with cause.

3. For example, Arabs and Mexicans use emotions as an expression of sincerity. Anglo-Americans often misinterpret this as a sign of aggression (see Kochman 1983;

Ortony et al. 1990; Rush 1995c).

4. It is the belief of many in the therapeutic community that male violence is, in part, a result of lack of intimacy and restricted emotional expression, with the conclusion that violence is both a way to halt intimacy and a release of all that pent-up emotion. I seriously question this cause and effect position (a reduction to individual pathology) because the wider social dimension is not considered. Once violence becomes selective (i.e., toward one's spouse) the communication patterns of *both* husband and wife need to be examined, as the whole interaction pattern can be seen as a negative interaction sequence, a sequence conditioned by implied rules.

5. I am not sure that the brain/mind really makes a distinction between verbal and physical abuse. I suspect that, for the most part, they are one and the same.

6. I am taking some liberties with Athens's discussion, but I believe the central premise to be correct.

7. Keep in mind that the conflict evolves out of individual and small-group endeavors; in this day and age, cultures in the large sense are never in conflict. It is the representatives who, out of purpose or ignorance, initiate conflict and convince citizens to join in by appealing to cultural HRMs.

8. Stabilizing the family, however, would have consequences of its own, consequences regarding the manifestation of illness behavior, economic priorities, the need for policing agencies, how we treat our planet, and general government policy. I would predict that, by diminishing conflict at the family level, and as family members set a priority of holistic health, energies that currently are channeled away from the family in pursuit of money and status would remain in and with the family. Diminished conflict at that level would decrease conflict (and social change in general) throughout the entire social fabric, but it would have some interesting and unpredictable effects on the work habits and economics of this country. Keep in mind that it is an illusion to believe that we will solve all social ills by stabilizing the family and returning it to the position of main socializing unit (instead of the television set, schools, and the local mall); by enhancing the status of husband, wife, and parent; and by teaching useful communication processes and tools. Urban complexes, in and of themselves, foster illness and disease for many reasons including the concentration of toxins (metaphorically similar to the body concentrating toxins), information overload (noise, electromagnetic fields, etc.) anomie, and so on.

CHAPTER 7

Conclusion

The final chapter is a summary of concepts assembled to build the model of human behavior that is then used as a stepping-off point in the diagnostic procedures and thera- peutic processes. The necessity of having a nutritional base is likewise mentioned--health is a holistic phenomenon.

This chapter, once again, underscores the educational nature of clinical anthropology, with a goal of increasing individual and system choice of action for stress reduction.

BASIC PROCESSES

Clinical anthropology is a dynamic and holistic approach to individual, family, and system health. It is founded on understanding basic processes in human biological and social development. Some of these basic processes include analogous thinking, language and communication potential, and the com- pression and chunking of data. Along with analogous thinking is the concept of polarity, which means that, if a person has one model in his or her mind, the exact opposite is likewise available. Analogous thinking was and is an important feature in the development of consciousness, creativity, and group and individual realities.

The compression and chunking of information lead to generalizations, which, again, are useful in storing information, but can also lead to overgeneralization and mind sets that many times inhibit seeing or approaching things from other directions.

There are limits on information processing and storage in the human brain. In prehistoric times, with the death of a group member, specialized information often died as well. Information, over time, was increasingly stored outside of the individual or group, and this has proved to be of paramount importance in terms of individual, group, and cultural survival.

As humans are a small-group animal, numerous grouping mechanisms, designed to keep the individual oriented toward the group, evolved. These include the fear of rejection, the accumulation of High Risk Messages (HRMs) during rule setting, food sharing, sexual restrictions, home base, implied rules (overlearning and negative/positive behavioral sequences), and roles. Further, HRMs, leading to physio-emotional stress reactions and action, can emanate from environmental factors (i.e., predators, weather, accidents, pathogens, etc.) as well as from significant others within one's groups of orientation.

All of the above factors or concepts are used to explain individual and group behavior within a social milieu. Moreover, these concepts are necessary for explaining environmental stressors, and individual and group stress reactions, including disturbed communication patterns, conflict, and violence. Further, the HRMs concept is then useful in designing strategies for altering communication patterns, for lowing stress, and for enhancing cooperative potential. Going a step further, and maintaining a holistic approach, the concept of HRMs and the informational categories are a useful starting point for uncovering causal factors in illness in general (physical and emotional).

BASIC INFORMATION CATEGORIES FOR
DIAGNOSING ILLNESS AND DISEASE

Information classes (i.e., information intrusion, information loss, etc.) are used as categories for diagnosing or evaluating illness/disease. Combined with this is the use of HRMs for diagnosing the physical and/or emotional reaction(s) to the informational class(es).

The curing of a physio-emotional illness is accomplished through a process of reframing or altering the body or mind's interpretation of the particular information category. For example, in regard to Western biomedicine, a person with a staphylococcus infection (information intrusion--a HRM with respect to biological functioning) would be given a broad-spectrum antibiotic designed to alter (destroy) the intrusive information. On the other hand, the patient, knowing that he or she is receiving the antibiotic, reframes the illness/disease (social expression of HRM) around the concept of hope. Stress goes down, and physiological functioning returns to normal as the infection subsides. Keep in mind that this represents the disease model in Western biomedicine. Clinical anthropologists would also be interested in preventing illness by understanding its underlying causes, much of which are related to nutrition and overall lifestyle, and by engaging a life style that boosts rather than degrades immune functioning.

The same procedure occurs when the individual is looping on rejection (social HRM). A part of the procedure for curing or alleviating stress is the framing and reframing of the HRM. By placing a different, stress-reducing meaning on the message, the individual exits the loop. Specific techniques used for the reframing of socially constructed HRMs include analysis, storytelling or metaphors, paradoxes, future pacing, self-fulfilling prophecies, and so on.

Balance is then restored through ritual termination and social reintegration. Social reintegration can occur on three levels: (1) a recognition ritual as performed by significant others (i.e., other family members); (2) a symbolic ritual when a recognition ritual is impossible because significant others are not available or cannot or will not understand the part they play in the development of illness symptoms; and (3) recognition by the individual, at the second level (i.e., neighborhood, community, church) and third level (i.e., town or city, state, nation) that social involvement or participation is a worthwhile and necessary part of the whole.

Again, the information within which HRMs are being activated (i.e., the family, work, etc.) likewise needs to be altered, and/or the individual needs to apply alternative interpretations to such information in order to prevent HRM activation or lessen the impact. Placing the blame on others, however, needs to be avoided through appropriate reframing. Blame is only useful if further individual and social stress is, for some reason, necessary, as most HRMs are activated out of ignorance of the patterns of human information processing.

The concepts of information categories, HRMs, implied rules, and the framing and reframing of information represent a model or methodology for diagnosing or evaluating medical/curing systems throughout the world. These terms are relatively neutral, and do not contain the biases embodied within other Western terms, that is, Oedipus complex, schizophrenia, depression, psychosis, and so on. For this reason, and in my opinion, this approach represents a more useful form of analysis, very different from that found in Western psychology or psychiatry.

NUTRITION AND LIFESTYLE

Nutritional information is also important to any approach to holistic health. Nutrition and life style play a major part in our overall health, mental functioning, and ability to deal with daily stressors. Moreover, in an environment impacted with chemicals and electromagnetic fields with carcinogenic potential, it is crucial that individuals be informed about research regarding the antioxidant and anti-cancer potential of specific foods and supplements. *Reacting* to disease and/or social and individual illnesses, rather than *educating* with the goal of *preventing*, represents, in my opinion, an obsolete paradigm.

CLINICAL ANTHROPOLOGY AS AN EDUCATIONAL PROCESS

The overall process used in delivering information for restoring biological and social system functioning is educational. Such an educational process represents a balancing, rebalancing, or preventative approach to physical, emotional, and social health. Because this is an educational approach, the clinical anthropologist has to take a more dynamic role in information delivery. Although I have used the terms diagnosis and cure, which are "copyrights" in terms of the practice of Western biomedicine, I am using these concepts in a larger sense. As an educator, the clinical anthropologist evaluates individual and systems information input and output and counsels regarding more healthy alternatives, be this in the way of interpersonal communication style or life style habits in general. The clinical anthropologist cures no one because he or she is not responsible for anyone's health. The clinical anthropologist's responsibility is to approach clients with concern and kindness and to be a model of the tools and life style presented during health system evaluation and intervention.

Bibliography

Abraham, R., and Shaw, C. 1983. *Dynamics: The Geometry of Behavior,* Part Two, *Chaotic Behavior.* Santa Cruz, Calif.: Visual Mathematics Library, Aerial Press.

"Acupuncture Give Knees a Lift." 1994. *Science News* 145(20):319.

Adler, T. 1994. "Designer Fats." *Science News* 124(19):296-297.

Aiello, L., and Wheeler, P. 1995. "The Brain and the Digestive System in Human and Primate Evolution." *Current Anthropology* 36(2):199-221.

Alcena, V. 1994. *The African American Health Book.* New York: Birch Lane Press.

Alexander, L. 1979. "Clinical Anthropology: Morals and Methods." *Medical Anthropology* 3(1):61-108.

Allegro, J. 1970. *The Sacred Mushroom and the Cross.* London: Hodder & Stoughton.

Althen, G. 1988. *American Ways: A Guide for Foreigners in the United States.* Yarmouth, New Hampshire: Intercultural Press, Inc.

Amazing Medicines the Drug Companies Don't Want You to Discover. 1993. Tempe, Ariz.: University Medical Research.

Anderson, R. 1991. "The Efficacy of Ethnomedicine: Research Methods in Trouble." *Medical Anthropology* 13:1-17.

Andreasen, N. 1984. *The Broken Brain: The Biological Revolution in Psychiatry.* New York: Harper & Row.

Armstrong, T. 1995. *The Myth of the A.D.D. Child: 50 Ways to Improve Your Child's Behavior and Attention Span Without Drugs, Labels, or Coercion.* New York: Viking Press.

Athens, L. 1992. *The Creation of Dangerous Violent Criminals.* Urbana: University of Illinois Press.

Atkinson, J. 1987. "The Effectiveness of Shamans in an Indonesian Ritual." *American Anthropologist* 89:342-355.

Atkinson, J. 1992a. *The Art and Politics of Wana Shamanship.* Berkeley: University of California Press.

Atkinson, J. 1992b. "Shamanism Today." *Annual Review of Anthropology* 21:307-330.

Axelrod, R. 1980a. "Effective Choice in the Prisoner's Dilemma." *Journal of Conflict Resolution* 24:3-25.

Axelrod, R. 1980b. "More Effective Choices in the Prisoner's Dilemma." *Journal of Conflict Resolution,* 24:379-403.

Axelrod, R. 1984. *The Evolution of Cooperation.* New York: Basic Books.

Bahn, P., and Vertut, J. 1988. *Images of the Ice Age.* London: Bellew Publishing Company.

Balikci, A. 1963. "Shamanistic Behaviors Among the Netsilik Eskimos." *Southwestern Journal of Anthropology* 19(4):380-396.

Balzer, M. 1987. "Behind Shamanism: Changing Voices of Siberian Khanty Cosmology and Politics." *Social Science and Medicine* 24(12):1085-1093.

Bandler, R., and Grinder, J. 1975. *Patterns of the Hypnotic Techniques of Milton H. Erickson, M.D., Vol. 1.* Cupertino, Calif.: Meta Publications.

Banton, M. (ed.) 1965. *Political Systems and the Distribution of Power.* A.S.A. Monograph, No. 2, London: Tavistock.

Barnes, B. 1988. *The Nature of Power.* Chicago: University of Illinois Press.

Barnes, J. A. 1994. *A Pack of Lies: Towards a Sociology of Lying.* New York: Cambridge University Press.

Barzini, L. 1965. *The Italians.* New York: Bantam Books.

Basso, K. 1989. "Southwest: Apache." In *Witchcraft and Sorcery of the American Native Peoples,* ed. D. Walker, 167-190. Moscow: University of Idaho Press.

Bastien, J. 1987. "Cross-Cultural Communication Between Doctors and Peasants in Bolivia." *Social Science and Medicine* 24(12):1109-1118.

Bateson, G. 1972. *Steps to an Ecology of Mind.* New York: Ballantine Books.

Bean, L. 1976. "California Indian Shamanism and Folk Curing." In *American Folk Medicine,* ed. W. Hand, Berkeley: University of California Press, 109-123.

Beidelman, T. 1963. "Witchcraft in Ukaguru." In *Witchcraft and Sorcery in East Africa,* eds. J. Middleton, and E. Winter, London: Routledge & Kegan Paul, 57-98.

Beinfield, H., and Korngold, E. 1991. *Between Heaven and Earth: A Guide to Chinese Medicine.* New York: Ballantine Books.

Beiser, M. 1985. "A Study of Depression Among Traditional Africans, Urban North Americans, and Southeast Asian Refugees." In *Culture and Depression: Studies in the Anthropology and Cross-Cultural Psychiatry of Affect and Disorder,* eds. A. Kleinman and B. Good, Berkeley: University of California Press, 272-298.

Berne, E. 1973. *T/A: Transactional Analysis in Psychotherapy.* New York: Ballantine Books.

Berry, J., Poortinga, Y., Segall, M., and Dasen, P. 1992. *Cross-Cultural Psychology: Research and Applications.* New York: Cambridge University Press.

Bettelheim, B. 1962. *Symbolic Wounds: Puberty Rites and the Envious Male.* Collier Books, New York.

Bettelheim, B. 1977. *The Uses of Enchantment: The Meaning and Importance of Fairy Tales.* Vintage Press, New York.

Betz, N., and Fitzgerald, L. 1993. "Individuality and Diversity: Theory and Research in Counseling Psychology." *Annual Review of Psychology,* 44:343-381.

Bickerton, D. 1990. *Language and Species.* Chicago: University of Chicago Press.

Binford, L. 1987. "Were There Elephant Hunters at Torralba?" In *The Evolution of Human Hunting,* eds. M. Nitecki and D. Nitecki, New York: Plenum Press, 47-105.

Bloom, F. 1989. "Basic Molecular Genetic Neuroscience." In *Comprehensive Textbook of Psychiatry*, 5th ed., ed. H. Kaplan and B. Sadock, vol. 1, Baltimore: Williams & Wilkins, 137-143.

Boissevain, J., and Mitchell, J. (eds.). 1973. *Network Analysis: Studies in Human Interaction*. The Hague: Mouton.

Bonner, J. 1980. *The Evolution of Culture in Animals*. Princeton: Princeton University Press.

Bornoff, N. 1991. *Pink Samurai: Love, Marriage and Sex in Contemporary Japan*. New York: Pocket Books.

Bott, E. 1971. (1st ed. 1957). *Family and Social Network*. London: Tavistock Publications.

Bower, B. 1990. "Modern Humans May Need Redefining." *Science News* 137(15):228.

Bower, B. 1992a. "Neandertals to Investigators: Can We Talk?" *Science News* 141 (15):230.

Bower, B. 1992b. "Erectus Unhinged." *Science News* 141(25):408-411.

Bower, B. 1993. "Marital Tiffs Spark Immune Swoon. . . ." *Science News* 144(10):153.

Bower, B. 1994. "Child Sexual Abuse: Sensory Recall. . . . and Treating Survivors." *Science News* 145(23):365.

Briggs, J., and Peat, F. 1989. *Turbulent Mirror: An Illustrated Guide to Chaos Theory and the Science of Wholeness*. New York: Harper & Row.

Brodwin, P. 1992. "Guardian Angels and Dirty Spirits: The Moral Basis of Healing Power in Rural Haiti." In *Anthropological Approaches to the Study of Ethnomedicine*, ed. M. Nichter, Philadelphia: Gordon and Breach Science Publishers, 57-74.

Brown, D. 1991. *Human Universals*. Philadelphia: Temple University Press.

Brown, H. 1976. *Brain and Behavior*. Toronto: Oxford University Press.

Brown, M. H. 1990. *The Search for Eve*. New York: Harper & Row.

Brown, P., and Inhorn, M. 1990. "Health Issues in Human Populations." In *Medical Anthropology: Contemporary Theory and Method*, ed. T. Johnson and C. Sargent, New York: Praeger, 187-214.

Buckley, T., and Gottlieb, A. (eds.). 1988. *Blood Magic: The Anthropology of Menstruation*. Berkeley: University of California Press.

Buettner-Janusch, J. 1966. *Origins of Man*. New York: John Wiley & Sons.

Calvin, W. 1983. *The Throwing Madonna*. New York: McGraw-Hill.

Calvin, W. 1990. *The Ascent of Mind*. New York: Bantam Books.

Campbell, Jeremy. 1982. *Grammatical Man: Information, Entropy, Language, and Life*. New York: Simon & Schuster.

Campbell, Joseph. 1969. *The Mask of the Gods*. Vol. 1, *Primitive Mythology*. New York: Penguin Books.

Campbell, Joseph. 1972. *The Hero with a Thousand Faces*. Princeton: Princeton University Press.

Campbell, Joseph. 1988a. *The Power of Myth*. New York: Doubleday.

Campbell, Joseph. 1988b. *Historical Atlas of World Mythology: The Way of the Animal Powers*. Vols. 1 and 2. New York: Harper & Row.

Campbell, Joseph. 1989a. *The World of Joseph Campbell: Transformation of Myth through Time*. Vol. 1, Program No. 5. St. Paul: HighBridge Productions (Audio tape).

Campbell, Joseph. 1989b. *The World of Joseph Campbell: Transformation of Myth through Time*. Vol. 3. St. Paul: HighBridge Productions (Audio tapes).

Campbell, Joseph. 1990a. *The Transformation of Myth Through Time*. New York: Harper & Row.

Campbell, Joseph. 1990b. *The Transformation of Myth Through Time*, with Bill Moyer. Programs 1-5. St. Paul: HighBridge Productions (Video tapes).

Cannon, W. 1942. "'Voodoo' Death." *American Anthropologist* 44(2):169-178.

Cannon, W. 1989 (orig. 1915). *Bodily Changes in Pain, Hunger, Fear and Rage*. Birmingham, Ala.: Behavioral Sciences Library.

Capps, L. 1994. "Change and Continuity in the Medical Culture of the Hmong in Kansas City." *Medical Anthropology Quarterly* 8(2):161-177.

Carneiro, R. 1970. "A Theory of the Origin of the State." *Science* 169:733-738.

Carpenter, K. 1993. "Nutritional Chemistry." In *The Cambridge World History of Human Disease*, ed. K. Kiple, New York: Cambridge University Press, 140-146.

Carper, J. 1993. *Food--Your Miracle Medicine: How Food Can Prevent and Cure Over 100 Symptoms and Problems*. New York: HarperCollins.

Carter, R. 1995. *The Influence of Race and Racial Identity in Psychotherapy: Toward a Racially Inclusive Model*. New York: John Wiley & Sons.

Casti, J. 1989a. *Alternate Realities: Mathematical Models of Nature and Man*. New York: John Wiley & Sons.

Casti, J. 1989b. *Paradigms Lost: Images of Man in the Mirror of Science*. New York: William Morrow.

Caudill, W. 1958. *The Psychiatric Hospital as a Small Society*. Cambridge: Harvard University Press.

Chafetz, M. 1990. *Nutrition and Neurotransmitters: The Nutrient Bases of Behavior*. Englewood Cliffs, N.J.: Prentice-Hall.

Chalmers, N. 1980. *Social Behavior in Primates*. Baltimore: University Park Press.

Chomsky, N. 1957. *Syntactic Structures*. The Hague: Mouton.

Chomsky, N. 1968. *Language and Mind*. New York: Harcourt, Brace & World.

Chomsky, N. 1975. *Reflections on Language*. New York: Pantheon Books.

Chomsky, N. 1980. *Rules and Representations*. New York: Columbia University Press.

Chomsky, N. 1985. *Knowledge of Language: Its Nature, Origin and Use*. New York: Praeger.

Chrisman, N. and Johnson, T. 1990. "Clinically Applied Anthropology." In *Medical Anthropology: Contemporary Theory and Method*, ed. T. Johnson and C. Sargent, New York: Praeger, 93-113.

Clark, L., Watson, D., and Reynolds, S. 1995. "Diagnosis and Classification of Psychopathology: Challenges to the Current System and Future Directions." *Annual Reviews in Psychology* 46:121-153.

Cohen, D. 1991. "The Augustan Law on Adultery: The Social and Cultural Context." In *The Family in Italy from Antiquity to the Present*, ed. D. Kertzer and R. Saller, New Haven, Conn.: Yale University Press, 109-126.

Cohen, M. 1989. *Health and the Rise of Civilization*. New Haven, Conn.: Yale University Press.

Colby, B. 1958. "Behavioral Redundancy." *Behavioral Science* 3:317-322.

Coles, G. 1987. *The Learning Mystique: A Critical Look at "Learning Disabilities."* New York: Pantheon Books.

Comas-Diaz, L., and Griffith, E. 1988. *Clinical Guidelines in Cross-Cultural Mental Health*. New York: John Wiley & Sons.

Crocker, J. 1985. *Vital Souls: Bororo Cosmology, Natural Symbolism, and Shaman-*

ism. Tucson: The University of Arizona Press.

Darwin, C. 1859. *The Origin of Species by Means of Natural Selection*. London: John Murry.

Darwin, C. 1871. *The Descent of Man, and Selection in Relation to Sex*. London: John Murry.

David, A., and Tapp, E. 1993. *The Mummy's Tale: The Scientific and Medical Investigation of Natsef-Amun, Priest in the Temple of Karnak*. New York: St. Martin's Press.

Davies, P., and Gribbin, J. 1992. *The Matter Myth*. New York: Simon & Schuster.

Dawkins, R. 1976. *The Selfish Gene*. New York: Oxford University Press.

Dawkins, R., and Krebs, J. 1978. "Animal Signals: Information or Manipulation?" In *Behavioral Ecology: An Evolutionary Approach*, ed. J. Krebs and N. Davies, Oxford: Blackwell, 282-315.

Dean, W., Morgenthaler, J., and Fowkes, S. 1993. *Smart Drugs II: The Next Generation*. Menlo Park, Calif.: Health Freedom Publications.

Dennett, D. 1978. *Brainstorms*. Cambridge: MIT Press.

Dennett, D. 1991. *Consciousness Explained*. Boston: Little, Brown.

Dentan, R. 1988. "Ambiguity, Synecdoche and Affect in Semai Medicine." *Social Science and Medicine* 27(8):857-877.

Devor, E. 1993. "Genetic Disease." *The Cambridge World History of Human Disease*, ed. K. Kiple, New York: Cambridge UniversityPress, 113-125.

De Waal, F. 1989. *Peacemaking Among Primates*. Cambridge: Harvard University Press.

Di Chiara, G., and Imperato, A. 1988. "Drugs Abused by Humans Preferentially Increase Synaptic Dopamine Concentrations in the Mesolimbic System of Freely Moving Rats." *Proceedings National Academy of Science* 85(14):5274-5278.

Dobkin De Rios, M. 1990. *Hallucinogens: Cross-Cultural Perspectives*. Bridport, Dorset, UK: Prism Press.

Donald. M. 1991. *Origins of the Modern Mind: Three Stages in the Evolution of Culture and Cognition*. Cambridge: Harvard University Press.

Douglas, M. (ed.) 1991a. *Constructive Drinking: Perspectives on Drink from Anthropology*. New York: Cambridge University Press.

Douglas, M. 1991b. "A Distinctive Anthropological Perspective." In *Constructive Drinking: Perspectives on Drink from Anthropology,* ed. M. Douglas, New York: Cambridge University Press, 3-15.

Droba, M. and Whybrow, P. 1989. "Endocrine and Metabolic Disorders." In *Comprehensive Textbook of Psychiatry*, 5th ed., ed. H. Kaplan and B. Sadock, vol. 2, Baltimore: Williams & Wilkins, 1209-1220.

Dugdale, D., and Eisenberg, M. 1992. *Medical Diagnostics*. Philadelphia: W. B. Saunders.

Durkheim, E. 1933. *The Division of Labor in Society*. New York: The Free Press.

Durkheim, E. 1951. *Suicide: A Study in Sociology*. London: The Free Press.

Durkheim, E. 1964. *The Rules of Sociological Method*. London: The Free Press.

Edelman, G. 1987. *Neural Darwinism: The Theory of Neuronal Group Selection*. New York: Basic Books.

Edelman, G. 1988. *Topobiology : An Introduction to Molecular Embryology*. New York: Basic Books.

Edelman, G. 1989. *The Remembered Present*. New York: Basic Books.

Edelstein, L. 1987. *Ancient Medicine*. Baltimore: Johns Hopkins University Press.

Eden, D. 1990. "Acute and Chronic Job Stress, Strain, and Vacation Relief." *Organizational Behavior and Human Decision Making Processes* 45:175-193.

Eisner, R. 1987. *The Road to Daulis: Psychoanalysis, Psychology, and Classical Mythology*. Syracuse, N.Y.: Syracuse University Press.

Eldredge, N. 1985. *Time Frames: The Rethinking of Darwinian Evolution and the Theory of Punctuated Equilibria*. New York: Simon & Schuster.

Eldredge, N. 1991. *The Miner's Canary*. New York: Prentice-Hall Press.

Eliade, M. 1972. *Shamanism: Archaic Techniques of Ecstasy*. Princeton: University of Princeton Press.

Engel, G. 1977. "The Need for a New Medical Model: A Challenge for Biomedicine." *Science* 196:126-136.

Erickson, K. 1966. *Wayward Puritans: A Study in the Sociology of Deviance*. New York: John Wiley & Sons.

Erickson, M. and Rossi, E. 1979. *Hypnotherapy: An Exploratory Casebook*. New York: Irvington Publishers.

Estes, C. 1992. *Women Who Run With the Wolves: Myths and Stories of the Wild Woman Archetype*. New York: Ballantine Books.

Etkin, N. (ed.). 1986. *Plants in Indigenous Medicine and Diet: Biobehavioral Approaches*. Bedford Hills, N.Y.: Redgrave Publishing Company.

Evans-Pritchard, E. 1937. *Witchcraft, Oracles, and Magic among the Azande*. Oxford: Oxford University Press.

"Experts Urge FDA to Approve Artifical Fat Despite Side Effects." 1995. *Sacramento Bee*, November 18, sec. A, p.24.

Falk, D. 1987. "Hominid Paleoneurology." *Annual Review of Anthropology* 16:13-30.

Fardon, R. (ed.). 1987. *Power and Knowledge: Anthropological and Sociological Approaches*. Edinburgh: Scottish Academic Press.

"FDA Raid Report: The Insider's Guide to Illegal and Unconstitutional Acts by the FDA." *Life Extension* (May):1-5.

Fedigan, L. 1986. "The Changing Role of Women in Models of Human Evolution." *Annual Review of Anthropology* 15:25-66.

Field, M. 1960. *Search for Security*. Chicago: Northwestern University Press.

Finkler, K. 1994a. "Sacred Healing and Biomedicine Compared." *Medical Anthropology Quarterly* 8(2):178-197.

Finkler, K. 1994b. *Women in Pain: Gender and Morbidity in Mexico*. Philadelphia: University of Pennsylvania Press.

Finnegan, L., and Kandall, S. 1992. "Maternal and Neonatal Effects of Alcohol and Drugs." In *Substance Abuse: A Comprehensive Textbook*, ed. J. Lowinson, P. Ruiz, R. Millman, Baltimore: Williams & Wilkinns, 628-656.

First, M. (ed.). 1994. *Diagnostic and Statistical Manual of Mental Disorders (DSM-V)*. Washington, D.C.: American Psychiatric Association.

Firth, R., Hubert, J., and Forge, A. 1970. *Families and Their Relatives*. New York: Humanities Press.

Fortes, M. 1969. *Kinship and the Social Order: The Legacy of Lewis Henry Morgan*. Chicago: Aldine.

Fortes, M. 1976. "Foreward." In *Social Anthropology and Medicine*, ed. J. Loudon. A.S.A. Monograph No. 13, London: Academic Press.

Foss, L., and Rothenberg, K. 1987. *The Second Medical Revolution: From Biomedi-*

cine to Infomedicine. Boston: New Science Library.

Foulks, E. 1972. *The Arctic Hysterias of the North American Eskimo*. Anthropological Studies, No. 10. Washington, D.C.: American Anthropological Association.

Fowles, D. 1992. "Schizophrenia: Diathesis-Stress Revisited." *Annual Review of Psychology* 43:303-326.

Frayer D., Wolpoff, M., Thorne, A., Smith, F., and Pope, G. 1993. "Theories of Modern Human Origins: The Paleontological Test." *American Anthropologist* 95(1):14-50.

Frazer, J. 1890. *The Golden Bough: A Study of Comparative Religion*. London: Macmillan.

Freud, S. 1946 (orig. 1918). *Totem and Taboo*. New York: Vintage Press.

Fried, M. 1967. *The Evolution of Political Society*. New York: Random House.

Fuchs, S. 1964. "Magic Healing Techniques Among the Balahis in Central India." In *Magic, Faith, and Healing*, ed. A. Kiev, New York: Free Press, 121-138.

Furuto, S., Biswas, R., Chung, D., Murase, K., and Ross-Sheriff, F. 1992. *Social Work Practice with Asian Americans*. Newbury Park, Calif.: Sage Publications.

Gadon, E. 1989. *The Once and Future Goddess*. New York: Harper & Row.

Gaines, A. (ed.). 1992a. *Ethnopsychiatry: The Cultural Construction of Professional and Folk Psychiatries*. Albany: State University of New York Press.

Gaines, A. 1992b. "Ethnopsychiatries: The Cultural Construction of Psychiatries." In *Ethnopsychiatry: The Cultural Construction of Professional and Folk Psychiatries*, ed. A. Gaines, Albany: State University of New York Press, 5-50.

Gall, J. 1978. *Systemantics*. New York: Simon & Schuster.

Gardner, H. 1983. *Frames of Mind*. New York: Basic Books.

Gershon, E., and Rieder, R. 1992. "Major Disorders of Mind and Brain." *Scientific American* 267(3):126-133.

Gerszten, G., and Allison, M. 1991. "Human Soft Tissue Tumors in Paleopathology." In *Human Paleopathology: Current Syntheses and Future Options*, ed. D. Ortner and A. Aufderheide, Washington, D.C.: Smithsonian Institution Press, 257-260.

Gimbutas, M. 1989. *The Language of the Goddess*. San Francisco: Harper and Row.

Glass, L., and Mackey, M. 1988. *From Clocks to Chaos: The Rhythms of Life*. Princeton: Princeton University Press.

Glass-Coffin, B. 1992. "Discourse, Dano, and Healing in North Coastal Peru." In *Anthropological Approaches to the Study of Ethnomedicine*, ed. M. Nichter, Philadelphia: Gordon & Breach, 33-56.

Gleick, J. 1987. *Chaos: Making a New Science*. New York: Viking.

Gluckman, M. 1944. "The Logic of African Science and Witchcraft: An Appreciation of Evans-Pritchard's *Witchcraft, Oracles and Magic Among the Azande* of the Sudan." *Human Problems in British Central Africa* 1:61-71.

Goffman, E. 1963. *Stigma: Notes on the Management of Spoiled Identity*. Englewood Cliffs, N.J.: Prentice-Hall.

Goodall, J. 1986. *The Chimpanzees of Gombe*. Cambridge: Harvard University Press.

Goodwin, D. 1992. "Alcohol: Clinical Aspects." In *Substance Abuse: A Comprehensive Textbook*, ed. Lowinson, P. Ruiz, and R. Millman, Baltimore: Williams & Wilkins, 144-150.

Gordon, T. 1970. *Parent Effectiveness Training*. New York: Peter W. Wyden.

Gottlieb, A. 1988. "Menstrual Cosmology among the Beng of Ivory Coast." In *Blood Magic: The Anthropology of Menstruation*, ed. T. Buckley and A. Gottlieb, Berkeley: University of California Press,55-74.

Graham, J. 1987. *The MMPI: A Practical Guide.* New York: Oxford University Press.

Greenberg, J., Turner, C., and Zegura, S. 1986. "The Settlement of the Americas: A Comparison of the Linguistic, Dental, and Genetic Evidence." *Current Anthropology* 27:477-497.

Greenfield, S. 1987. "The Return of Dr. Fritz: Spiritist Healing and Patronage Networks in Urban, Industrial Brazil." *Social Science and Medicine* 24(2):1095-1108.

Greenwood, M., and Nunn, P. 1992. *Paradox and Healing: Medicine, Mythology, and Transformation.* Victoria, B.C.: Paradox.

Griffin, D. 1992. *Animal Minds.* Chicago: University of Chicago Press.

Grinder, J., DeLozier, J., and Bandler, R. 1977. *Patterns of the Hypnotic Techniques of Milton H. Erickson, M.D.* Vol. 2. Cupertino, Calif.: Meta.

Grmek, M. 1989. *Diseases in the Ancient Greek World.* Baltimore: Johns Hopkins University Press.

Groebel, J., and Hinde, R. (eds.). 1991. *Aggression and War: Their Biological and Social Bases.* New York: Cambridge University Press.

Grossinger, R. 1995. *Planet Medicine: Origins.* Berkeley: North Atlantic Books.

Guilford, T., and Dawkins, M. 1991. "Receiver Psychology and the Evolution of Animal Signals." *Animal Behavior* 42:1-14.

Haas, J. (ed.). 1982. *The Evolution of the Prehistoric State.* New York: Columbia University Press.

Haas, J. 1990. *The Anthropology of War.* New York: Cambridge University Press.

Halpern, B., and Foley, J. 1979. "Bajanje: Healing Magic in Rural Serbia." In *Culture and Curing: Anthropological Perspectives on Traditional Medical Beliefs and Practices,* ed. P. Morley and R. Walis, Pittsburgh, Pa.: University of Pittsburgh Press, 40-56.

Hamilton, W., Axelrod, R., and Tanese, R. 1990. "Sexual Reproduction as an Adaptation to Resist Parasites: A Review." *Proceedings of the National Academy of Sciences* 87: 3566-3573.

Hammell, J. 1995. "FDA Investigated at Congressional Hearing." *Life Extension* 1(11):10-16.

Hand, W. (ed.). 1976. *American Folk Medicine.* Berkeley: University of California Press.

Harner, M. 1984. *The Jivaro: People of the Sacred Waterfalls.* Berkeley: University of California Press.

Harris, M. 1968. *The Rise of Anthropological Theory.* New York: Thomas Y. Crowell.

Harris, M. 1978. *Cows, Pigs, Wars and Witches.* New York: Vintage Press.

Harris, M. 1979. *Cultural Materialism.* New York: Random House.

Harris, M. 1989. *Our Kind.* New York: Harper Perennial.

Harris, M., and Ross, E. (eds.) 1987. *Food and Evolution: Toward a Theory of Human Food Habits.* Philadelphia: Temple University Press.

Harrison, R. 1973. *Warfare.* Minneapolis: Burgess.

Hart, D. 1979. "Disease Etiologies of Samaran Filipino Peasants." In *Culture and Curing: Anthropological Perspectives on Traditional Medical Beliefs and Practices,* ed. P. Morley and R. Walis, Pittsburgh: University of Pittsburgh Press, 57-98.

Harvey, P. and Gow, P. (eds.). 1994. *Sex and Violence: Issues in Representation and Experience.* Routledge, New York.

Headley, L. (ed.). 1983. *Suicide in Asia and the Near East.* Berkeley: University of

California Press.

Heaney, R. 1993. "Nutritional Factors in Osteoporosis." *Annual Review of Nutrition* 13: 287-316.

Heath, D. 1991. "A Decade of Development in the Anthropological Study of Alcohol Use: 1970-1980." In *Constructive Drinking: Perspectives on Drink from Anthropology*, ed. M. Douglas, New York: Cambridge University Press, 16-69.

Helman, C. 1994. *Culture, Health and Illness*. Oxford, England: Butterworth-Heinemann.

Herdt, G. 1987. *Guardians of the Flutes: Idioms of Masculinity*. New York: Columbia University Press.

Hinde, R., and Groebel, J. (eds.). 1991. *Cooperation and Prosocial Behavior*. New York: Cambridge University Press.

Hinsie, L., and Campbell, R. 1976. *Psychiatric Dictionary*. New York: Oxford University Press.

Ho, D. 1993. "Relational Orientation in Asian Social Psychology." In *Indigenous Psychologies: Research and Experience in Cultural Context*, ed. U. Kim and J. Berry, Newbury Park, Calif.: Sage Publications, 240-259.

Hockett, C. 1960. "The Origins of Speech." *Scientific American* 203(3):89-96.

Hoffman, W. 1896. *The Menomini Indians*. Bureau of American Ethnology, Annual Report 1892-93, Pt. 1. Washington, D.C.: Smithsonian Institution.

Hofstadter, D., and Dennett, D. 1981. *The Mind's I*. New York: Basic Books.

Howard, J. 1990. *Oklahoma Seminoles: Medicines, Magic, and Religion*. Norman: University of Oklahoma Press.

Hsu, F. 1955. *Americans and Chinese*. London: Cresset Press.

Hurtado, A. 1990. "Introduction to the Bison Book Edition." In *California Indian Nights*, ed. E. Gifford and G. Block, Lincoln: University of Nebraska Press.

Hyman, R. 1989. "The Psychology of Deception." *Annual Review of Psychology* 40: 133-154.

Jackson, F. 1991. "Secondary Compounds in Plants (Allelochemicals) as Promoters of Human Biological Variability." *Annual Review of Anthropology* 20:505-546.

Jarrett, D. 1989. "Chronobiology." In *Comprehensive Textbook of Psychiatry*. 5 ed., ed. H. Kaplan and B. Sadock, vol. 1, Baltimore: Williams & Wilkins, 125-131.

Jaynes, J. 1990. *The Origin of Consciousness and the Breakdown of the Bicameral Mind*. New York: Houghton Mifflin.

Jelinek, A. 1977. "The Lower Paleolithic: Current Evidence and Interpretations." *Annual Review of Anthropology* 6:11-32.

Jilek, W. 1982. *Indian Healing: Shamanic Ceremonialism in the Pacific Northwest Today*. Blaine, Wa.: Handcock House.

Johanson , D., and Shreeve, J. 1989. *Lucy's Child: The Discovery of a Human Ancestor*. New York: William Morrow.

Johanson, D., and White, T. 1980. "On the Status of *Australopithecus afarensis*." *Science* 207:1104-1105.

John, E. R. 1976. "A Model of Consciousness." In *Consciousness and Self-Regulation*, Vol. 1, ed. G. Schwartz and D. Shapiro, New York: Plenum Press, 1-50.

Johns, T. 1990. *With Bitter Herbs They Shall Eat It: Chemical Ecology and the Origins of Human Diet and Medicine*. Tucson: University of Arizona Press.

Johnson, T., and Sargent, C. (eds.). 1990. *Medical Anthropology: Contemporary Theory and Method*. New York: Praeger.

Kalweit, H. 1988. *Dreamtime and Inner Space: The World of the Shaman*. Boston: Shambhala.

Kalweit, H. 1992. *Shamans, Healers, and Medicine Men*. Boston: Shambhala.

Kaplan, H. 1989. "History of Psychosomatic Medicine." In *Comprehensive Textbook of Psychiatry*. 5 ed., ed. H. Kaplan and B. Sadock, vol. 2, Baltimore: Williams & Wilkins, 1155-1160.

Kaplan, H., and Sadock, B. 1991. *Synopsis of Psychiatry*. 6 ed. Baltimore: Williams & Wilkins.

Katz, S. 1987. "Fava Bean Consumption: A Case for the Co-Evolution of Genes and Culture." In *Food and Evolution: Toward a Theory of Human Food Habits*, ed. M. Harris and E. Ross, Philadelphia: Temple University Press, 133-159.

Kearney, M. 1980. "Spiritualist Healing in Mexico." In *Culture and Curing: Anthropological Perspectives on Traditional Medical Beliefs and Practices*, ed. P. Morley and R. Wallis, Pittsburgh: University of Pittsburgh Press, 19-39.

Keen, C., and Gershwin, M. 1990. "Zinc Deficiency and Immune Function." *Annual Review of Nutrition* 10:415-431.

Keesing, F. 1939. *The Menomini Indians of Wisconsin*. Vol. 10. Philadelphia: American Philosophical Society.

Kent, S. (ed.). 1994a. "FDA Tyranny in Action." *Life Extension Report* 14(4):25-32.

Kent, S. 1994b. "The Life-Extension Lifestyle." *Life Extension Report* 14(9):65-69.

Kertzer, D., and Saller, R. (eds.). 1991. *The Family in Italy from Antiquity to the Present*. New Haven Conn.: Yale University Press.

Kety, S., and Matthysse, S. 1988. "Genetic and Biochemical Aspects of Schizophrenia." In *The New Harvard Guide to Psychiatry*, ed. A. Nicholi, Cambridge: Harvard University Press, 139-151.

Kiev, A. (ed.). 1964. *Magic, Faith, and Healing*. New York: Free Press.

Kinghorn, A., and Balandrin, M. (eds.). 1993. *Human Medicinal Agents from Plants*. Washington, D.C.: ACS.

Kiple, K. (ed.). 1993. *The Cambridge World History of Human Disease*. New York: Cambridge University Press.

Klein, R. 1989. *The Human career: Human Biology and Cultural Origins*. Chicago University of Chicago Press.

Kleinman, A., and Good, B. (eds.). 1985. *Culture and Depression: Studies in the Anthropology and Cross-Cultural Psychiatry of Affect and Disorder*. Berkeley: University of California Press.

Kline, P. 1981. *Fact and Fantasy in Freudian Theory*. New York: Methuen.

Knight, C. 1991. *Blood Relations: Menstruation and the Origins of Culture*. New Haven, Conn.: Yale University Press.

Knowler, W., Pettiti, D., Bennett, P., and Williams, R. 1983. "Diabetes Mellitus in the Pima Indians: Genetic and Evolutionary Considerations." *American Journal of Physical Anthropology* 62:107-114.

Knowler, W., Pettiti, D., Saad, K. and Bennett, P. 1990. "Diabetes Mellitus in the Pima Indians: Incidence, Risk Factors and Pathogenesis." *Diabetes and Metabolism Review* 6:1-27.

Kochman, T. 1983. *Black and White Styles in Conflict*. Chicago: University of Chicago Press.

Konner, M. 1982. *The Tangled Wing: Biological Constraints on the Human Spirit*. New York: Holt, Rinehart and Winston.

Kosek, M. 1990. "Medical Genetics." In *Current Medical Diagnosis and Treatment*, ed. S. Schroeder, M. Krupp, L. Tierney, Jr., and S. McPhee, Norwalk, Calif.: Appleton & Lange, 1118-1139.

Kosslyn, S., and Koenig, O. 1992. *Wet Mind: The New Cognitive Neuroscience*. New York: Free Press.

Krebs, J., and Dawkins, R. 1984. "Animal Signals: Mind Reading and Manipulation." In *Behavioral Ecology: An Evolutionary Approach*. 2nd ed., ed. J. Krebs and N. Davies, Sunderland, Mass.: Sinauer, 380-402.

Krogman, W., and Iscan, M. 1986. *The Human Skeleton in Forensic Medicine*. Springfield, Ill.: Charles C. Thomas.

Kruesi, M., and Rapoport, J. 1986. "Diet and Human Behavior: How Much Do They Affect Each Other?" *Annual Review of Nutrition* 6:113-130.

Kuhn, T. 1967. *The Structure of Scientific Revolutions*. Chicago: University of Chicago Press.

Kunitz, S. 1989. *Disease Change and the Role of Medicine: The Navajo Experience*. Berkeley: University of California Press.

Kuper, A. 1988. *The Invention of Primitive Society*. London: Routledge.

Kupfer, D., Monk, T., and Barchas, J. (eds.). 1988a. *Biological Rhythms and Mental Disorder*. New York: Guilford Press.

Kupfer, D., Frank, E., Jarrett, D., Reynolds III, C., and Thase, M. 1988b. "Interrelationship of Electroencephalographic Sleep Chronobiology and Depression." In *Biological Rhythms and Mental Disorder*, ed. D. Kupfer, T. Monk, J. Barachas, New York: Guilford Press, 1-26.

La Barre, W. 1964. "Confession as Cathartic Therapy in American Indian Tribes." In *Magic, Faith, and Healing*, ed. Kiev, A. New York: Free Press, 36-49.

LaBruzza, A., and Mendez-Villarrubia J. 1994. *Using DSM-IV: A Clinician's Guide to Psychiatric Diagnosis*. Northvale, N.J.: Jason Aronson.

Laderman, C. 1987. "The Ambiguity of Symbols in the Structure of Healing." *Social Science and Medicine* 24(4):293-301.

Lagerspetz, K. 1991. "Media and the Social Environment." In *Aggression and War: Their Biological and Social Bases*, ed. J. Groebel and R. Hinde, New York: Cambridge University Press, 164-172.

Lakoff, G., and Johnson, M. 1980. *Metaphors We Live By*. Chicago: University of Chicago Press.

Landau, S. 1984. "Trends in Violence and Aggression: A Cross-Cultural Analysis." *International Journal of Comparative Sociology* 24:133-158.

Landy, D. (ed.). 1977. *Culture, Disease, and Healing: Studies in Medical Anthropology*. New York: Macmillan.

Lappe, F. 1991. *Diet for a Small Planet*. New York: Ballantine Books.

Lappe, M. 1994. *Evolutionary Medicine: Rethinking the Origins of Disease*. San Francisco: Sierra Club Books.

Larsen, C. 1995. "Biological Changes in Human Populations with Agriculture." *Annual Review of Anthropology* 24:185-213.

Last, M. 1976. "The Presentation of Sickness in a Community of Non-Muslim Hausa." In *Social Anthropology and Medicine*, ed. L. Loudon, A.S.A. Monograph 13. London: Academic Press, 104-149.

Leak, G., and Christoper, S. 1982. "Freudian Psychoanalysis and Sociobiology." *American Psychologist* 37(3):387-395.

Leakey, R., and Lewin, R. 1992. *Origins Reconsidered: In Search of What Makes Us Human*. New York: Doubleday.

Leakey, R., and Walker, A. 1980. "On the Status of *Australopithecus afarensis*." *Science* 207:1103.

LeDoux, J. 1994. "Emotion, Memory and the Brain." *Scientific American* 270(6): 50-57.

Lee, C., and Richardson, B. (eds.). 1991. *Multicultural Issues in Counseling: New Approaches to Diversity*. Alexandria, Va.: American Counseling Association.

Leutwyler, K. 1994. "Sick, Sick, Sick. Neurotic? Probably, says DSM-IV." *Scientific American* 271(3):17-18.

Leutwyler, K. 1995. "The Price of Prevention." *Scientific American* 272(4):124-129.

Levinson, D. 1989. *Family Violence in Cross-Cultural Perspective*. Newbury Park, Calif.: Sage Publications.

Levi-Strauss, C. 1967. *Structural Anthropology*. New York: Doubleday-Anchor Books.

Levi-Strauss, C. 1969 (orig. 1949). *The Elementary Structures of Kinship*. Boston: Beacon Press.

Levi-Strauss, C. 1970. *The Raw and the Cooked: Introduction to a Science of Mythology*. New York: Harper Torchbooks.

Levy, R. 1978a. "Eastern Miwok." In. *Handbook of North American Indians*. Vol. 8, ed. R. Heizer, Washington, D.C.: Smithsonian Institution, 398-413.

Levy, R. 1978b. "Costanoan." In *Handbook of North American Indians*, Vol. 8, ed. R. Heizer, Washington, D.C.: Smithsonian Institution, 485-495.

Lewin, R. 1987. *Bones of Contention*. New York: Simon and Schuster.

Lewis, D. 1989. "Adult Antisocial Behavior and Criminality." *Comprehensive Textbook of Psychiatry*. 5th ed., ed., H. Kaplan and B. Sadock, vol. 2, Baltimore: Williams & Wilkins, 1400-1405.

Lewis, G. 1976. "A View of Sickness in New Guinea." In *Social Anthropology and Medicine*, ed. J. Loudon, A.S.A. Monograph No. 13, London: Academic Press, 49-103.

Lewis, M., and Saarni, C. (eds.). 1993. *Lying and Decption in Everyday Life*. New York: Guilford Press.

Lewis, T. 1992. *The Medicine Men: Oglala Sioux Ceremony and Healing*. Lincoln University of Nebraska Press, Lincoln.

Lieberman, L. 1987. "Biocultural Consequences of Animals Versus Plants as Sources of Fats, Proteins, and Other Nutrients." In *Food and Evolution: Toward a Theory of Human Food Habits*, ed. M. Harris and E. Ross, Philadelphia: Temple University Press, 225-258.

Lieberman, P. 1991. *Uniquely Human: The Evolution of Speech, Thought, and Selfless Behavior*. Cambridge: Harvard University Press.

Loudon, J. (ed.). 1976. *Social Anthropology and Medicine*. A.S.A. Monograph No. 13. London: Academic Press.

Lupton, D. 1994. *Medicine as Culture: Illness, Disease and the Body in Western Societies*. Thousand Oaks, Calif.: Sage Publications.

Lutz, C. 1985. "Depression and the Translation of Emotional Worlds." In *Culture and Depression: Studies in the Anthropology and Cross-Cultural Psychiatry of Affect and Disorder*, ed. A. Kleinman and B. Good, Berkeley: University of California Press, 63-101.

Macbeth, T. (ed.). 1996. *Tuning in to Young Viewers*. Thousand Oaks, Calif.: Sage

Publications.

Macfarlane, A. 1970. *Witchcraft in Tudor and Stuart England.* New York: Harper & Row.

Macrone, M. 1992. *By Jove!* New York: Cader Books.

Magner, L. 1992. *A History of Medicine.* New York: Marcel Dekker.

Mahdi, L., Foster, S., and Little, M. (eds.). 1987. *Betwixt and Between: Patterns of Masculine and Feminine Initiation.* La Salle, Ill.: Open Court.

Mair, L. 1969. *Witchcraft.* Toronto: McGraw Hill.

Malinowski, B. 1927. *Sex and Repression in Savage Society.* London: Routledge & Kegan Paul, Trench, Trubner.

Malinowski, B. 1929. "Kinship." *Encyclopaedia Britannica.* 14th ed., Vol. 13:403-409.

Mann, M. 1986. *The Sources of Social Power.* Vol. 1, *A History of Power from the Beginning to A.D. 1760.* New York: Cambridge University Press.

Maples, W. 1994. *Dead Men Do Tell Tales: The Strange and Fascinating Cases of a Forensic Anthropologist.* New York: Doubleday.

Marr, D. 1982. *Vision.* San Francisco: W. H. Feeman.

Marshack, A. 1991. *The Roots of Civilization.* New York: Moyer Bell.

Marwick, M. 1964. "Witchcraft as a Social Strain-Gauge." *Australian Journal of Science* 26:263-268.

Mascie-Taylor, C. 1995. *The Biological Anthropology of Disease.* In *The Anthropology of Disease,* ed. C. Mascie-Taylor, New York: Oxford University Press, 1-72.

Masdeu, J., and Solomon, S. 1989. "Clinical Neurology and Neuropathology." In *Comprehensive Text Book of Psychiatry,* 5th ed., H. Kaplan and B. Sadock, vol. 1, Baltimore: Williams and Wilkins, 176-218.

Matossian, M. 1989. *Poisons of the Past.* New Haven, Conn.: Yale University Press.

May, R. 1991. *The Cry for Myth.* New York: W. W. Norton.

Mayer, P. 1970 (orig. 1954). "Witches." In *Witchcraft and Sorcery,* ed. M. Marwick, Baltimore: Penguin Books, 45-64.

McGrew, W. 1979. "Evolutionary Implications of Sex Differences in Chimpanzee Predation and Tool Use." In *The Great Apes,* ed. D. Hamburg and R. McCown, Menlo Park, Calif.: Penjamin & Cummings, 441-464.

McGue, M., Pickens, R., and Svikis, D. 1992. "Sex and Age Effects on the Inheritance of Alcohol Problems: A Twin Study." *Journal of Abnormal Psychology* 101(1): 3-17.

McGuire, M., and Troisi, A. 1989. "Aggression." In *Comprehensive Textbook of Psychiatry,* 5th ed., ed. H. Kaplan and B. Sadock, vol. 1, Baltimore: Williams & Wilkins, 271-282.

McKenna, T. 1992. *Food of the Gods.* New York: Bantam Books.

McLuhan, M. 1962. *The Gutenberg Galaxy.* New York: Signet Books.

McNeill, W. 1989. *Plagues and People.* New York: Anchor Books.

Melton, G., Petrila, J. Poythress, N., and Slobogin, C. 1987. *Psychological Evaluations for the Courts.* New York: The Guilford Press.

Middleton, J., and Winter, E. 1963. *Witchcraft and Sorcery in East Africa.* London: Routledge & Kegan Paul.

Milgram, S. 1963. "Behavioral Study of Obedience." *Journal of Abnormal and Social Psychology* 67:371-378.

1974. *Obedience to Authority.* New York: Harper & Row.

Miller, G. 1956. "The Magical Number Seven, Plus or Minus Two: Some Limits on

Our Capacity for Processing Information." *Psychological Review* 63:81-97.

Miller, G., and Stiff, J. 1993. *Deceptive Communication*. Thousand Oaks, Calif.: Sage Publications.

Mills, S. 1991. *The Essential Book of Herbal Medicine*. New York: Penguin Books.

Milton, K. 1987. "Primate Diets and Gut Morphlogy: Implications for Hominid Evolution." In *Food and Evolution: Toward a Theory of Human Food Habits*, ed. M. Harris and E. Ross, Philadelphia: Temple University Press, 93-116.

Milton, K. 1993. "Diet and Primate Evolution." *Scientific American* 269(2):86-93.

Mitchell, J. (ed.). 1969. *Social Networks in Urban Situations*. Manchester, England: Manchester University Press.

Mitchell, M., and Herlong, H. 1986. "Alcohol and Nutrition: Caloric Value, Bioenergetics, and Relationship to Liver Damage." *Annual Review of Nutrition* 6:457-474.

Mitchell, R., and Thompson, N. (eds.). 1986. *Deception: Perspectives on Human and Nonhuman Deceit*. Albany: State University of New York Press.

Mollica, R., and Lavelle, J. 1988. "Southeast Asian Refugees." In *Clinical Guidelines in Cross-Cultural Mental Health*, ed. L. Comas-Diaz and E. Griffith, New York: John Wiley & Sons.

Monahan, J. 1981. *Predicting Violent Behavior: An Assessment of Clinical Techniques*. Beverly Hills, Calif.: Sage Publications.

Moore, J. 1984. "Parasites That Change the Behavior of Their Host." *Scientific American* 250(5): 108-115.

Moore-Howard, P. 1982. *The Hmong--Yesterday and Today*. Lansing, Mich.: PAJ NTAUB, PLIA YANG.

Moore-Howard, P. 1989. *The Iu Mien: Tradition and Change*. Sacramento, Calif.: Sacramento City Unified School District.

Morgan, E. 1990. *The Scars of Evolution: What Our Bodies Tell Us About Human Origins*. New York: Oxford University Press.

Morgan, L. 1870. *Systems of Consanguinity and Affinity of the Human Family*. Smithsonian Contributions to Knowledge No.17; 4-602. Washington, D.C.: Smithsonian Institution.

Morgan, L. 1877. *Ancient Society: Researches in the Lines of Human Progress from Savagery through Barbarism to Civilization*. New York: Holt.

Morley, P., and Walis, R. (eds.). 1979. *Culture and Curing: Anthropological Perspectives on Traditional Medical Beliefs and Practices*. Pittsburgh: University of Pittsburgh Press.

Morsy, S. 1990. "Political Economy in Medical Anthropology." In *Medical Anthropology: Contemporary Theory and Method*, ed. T. Johnson and C. Sargent, New York: Praeger, 26-46.

Morton, J. 1977. *Major Medicinal Plants: Botany, Culture and Uses*. Springfield, Ill.: Charles C. Thomas.

Mowrey, D. 1986. *The Scientific Validation of Herbal Medicine*. New Canaan, Conn.: Keats.

Mowrey, D. 1990. *Next Generation Herbal Medicine*. New Canaan, Conn.: Keats.

Munro, H., Suter, P., and Russell, R. 1987. "Nutritional Requirements of the Elderly." *Annual Review of Nutrition* 7:23-49.

Murdock, G., Wilson, S., and Frederick, V. 1978. "World Distribution of Theories of Illness." *Ethnology* 17(4):449-470.

Murphy, J. 1964. "Psychotherapeutic Aspects of Shamanism on St. Lawrence Island,

Alaska." In *Magic, Faith, and Healing*, ed. A. Kiev, New York: Free Press, 53-83.

Murray, M. 1994. *Natural Alternatives to Over-the-Counter and Prescription Drugs*. New York: William Morrow.

Myerhoff, B. 1976. "Shamanic Equilibrium: Balance and Mediation in Known and Unknown Worlds." In *American Folk Medicine*, ed. W. Hand, Berkeley: University of California Press, 99-108.

Nadel, S. 1957. *The Theory of Social Structure*. London: Cohen & West.

Naeser, M. 1992. *Outline Guide to Chinese Herbal Patent Medicines in Pill Form*. Boston: Boston Chinese Medicine.

Nesse, R., and Williams, G. 1994. *Why We Get Sick: The New Science of Darwinian Medicine*. New York: Times Books.

Neumann, E. 1972. *The Great Mother: an Analysis of the Archetype*. Princeton: Princeton University Press.

Nichter, M. (ed.). 1992. *Anthropological Approaches to the Study of Ethnomedicine*, Philadelphia: Gordon and Breach.

Nuckolls, C. 1992. "Deciding How to Decide: Possession-Mediumship in Jalari Divination." In *Anthropological Approaches to the Study of Ethnomedicine*, ed. M. Nichter, Philadelphia: Gordon and Breach Science Publishers, 75-101.

Nunes, E., and Rosecan, J. 1987. "Human Neurobiology of Cocaine." In *Cocaine Abuse*, ed. H. Spitz and J. Rosecan, New York: Brunner/Mazel, 48-94.

Oakley, D. 1985. "Cognition and Imagery in Animals." In *Brain and Mind*, ed. D. Oakley, London: Methuen, 1-42.

Obeyesekere, G. 1985. "Depression, Buddhism, and the Work of Culture in Sri Lanka." In *Culture and Depression: Studies in the Cross-Cultural Psychiatry of Affect and Disorder*, ed. A Kleinman and B. Good, Berkeley: University of California Press, 134-152.

O'Brien, J. 1992. "It's That Time of the Year." *Omni* 14(11):28.

Ody, P. 1993. *The Complete Medicinal Herbal*. London: Dorling Kindersley.

Ohnuki-Tierney, E. 1984. *Illness and Culture in Contemporary Japan: An Anthropological View*. New York: Cambridge University Press.

Oken, D. 1989. "Current Theoretical Concepts in Psychosomatic Medicine." In *Comprehensive Textbook of Psychiatry*, 5th ed., ed. H. Kaplan and B. Sadock, vol.2, Baltimore: Williams & Wilkins, 1160-1169.

Ornstein, R. 1991. *The Evolution of Consciousness*. New York: Prentice-Hall Press.

Ortony, A., Clore, G., and Collins, A. 1990. *The Cognitive Structure of Emotions*. New York: Cambridge University Press.

Oyama, S. 1989. "Ontogeny and the Central Dogma: Do We Need the Concept of Genetic Programming in Order to Have an Evolutionary Perspective?" In *Systems and Development*, ed. M. Gunnar and E. Thelen, Hillsdale, N.J.: Lawrence Erlbaum, 1-34.

Palacio, J. 1991. "Kin Ties, Food, and Remittances in a Garifuan Village in Southern Belize." In *Diet and Domestic Life in Society*, ed. A. Sharman, J. Theophano, K. Curtis, and E. Messer, Philadelphia: Temple University Press, 119-146.

Park, G. 1967. "Divination and Its Social Context." In *Magic, Witchcraft, and Curing*, ed. J. Middleton, Garden City, N.Y.: Natural History Press, 233-254.

Parkin, D. 1987. "Controlling the U-Turn of Knowledge." In *Power and Knowledge: Anthropological and Sociological Approaches*, ed. R. Fardon, Edinburgh: Scottish Academic Press, 49-60.

Parsons, A. 1969. *Belief, Magic, and Anomie: Essays in Psychosocial Anthropology.* New York: Free Press.

Parsons, T. and Shils, E. (eds.). 1962. *Toward a General Theory of Action.* New York: Harper & Row.

Pasnau, R., and Fawzy, F. 1989. "Stress and Psychiatry." *Comprehensive Textbook of Psychiatry,* 5th ed., ed. H. Kaplan and B. Sadock, vol. 2, Baltimore: Williams & Wilkins, 1231-1240.

Paul, R. 1976. "Did the Primal Crime Take Place?" *Ethos* 4:311-352.

Pavlov, I. 1941. *Conditioned Reflexes and Psychiatry.* New York: International Publishers.

Peele, S. 1989. *Diseasing of America: Addiction Treatment Out of Control.* Lexington Books, Lexington.

Pellett, P. 1987. "Problems and Pitfalls in the Assessment of Human Nutritional Status." In *Food and Evolution: Toward a Theory of Human Food Habits,* ed. M. Harris and E. Ross, Philadelphia: Temple University Press, 163-180.

Pennisi, E. 1993. "Chemical Revelations." *Science News* 143(1):8-10.

Penrose, R. 1994. *Shadows of the Mind: A Search for the Missing Science of Consciousness.* New York: Oxford University Press.

Peristiany, J. (ed.). 1970. *Honour and Shame: The Values of Mediterranean Society.* Chicago: University of Chicago Press.

Perls, F., Hefferline, R., and Goodman, P. 1951. *Gestalt Therapy: Excitement and Growth in the Human Personality.* New York: Dell Publishing Company.

Pfeiffer, C. 1975. *Mental and Elemental Nutrients.* New Canaan, Conn.: Keats.

Pfeiffer, C. 1978. *Zinc and Other Micro-Nutrients.* New Canaan, Conn.: Keats.

Pfeiffer, C. 1987a. *The Healing Nutrients Within: Facts, Findings and New Research on Amino Acids.* New Canaan, Conn.: Keats.

Pfeiffer, C. 1987b. *Nutrition and Mental Illness.* Rochester, N.Y.: Healing Arts Press.

Pfeiffer, J. 1982. *The Creative Explosion: An Inquiry into the Origins of Art and Religion.* New York: Harper & Row.

Phillips, D. 1974. "The Influence of Suggestion on Suicide: Substantive and Theoretical Implications of the Werther Effect." *American Sociological Review* 39:340-354.

Phillips, D. 1983. "The Impact of Mass Media Violence on U.S. Homicides." *American Sociological Review* 48:560-568.

Polster, E., and Polster, M. 1973. *Gestalt Therapy Integrated.* New York: Random House.

Poundstone, W. 1992. *Prisoner's Dilemma.* New York: Doubleday.

Powers, W. 1986. *Sacred Language: The Nature of Supernatural Discourse in Lakota.* Norman: University of Oklahoma Press.

Pribram, C. 1976. "Self-consciousness and Intentionality: A Model Based on an Experimental Analysis of the Brain Mechanisms Involved in the Jamesian Theory of Motivation and Emotion." In *Consciousness and Self-Regulation,* ed. G. Schwartz and D. Shapiro, vol. 1, New York: Plenum Press, 51-100.

Prieditis, A. (ed.). 1988. *Analogica.* Los Altos, Calif.: Morgan Kaufmann.

Prigogine, I., and Stengers, I. 1984. *Order out of Chaos.* New York: Bantam Books.

Prochiantz, A. 1989. *How the Brain Evolved.* New York: McGraw-Hill.

Quillin, P. 1994. *Beating Cancer With Nutrition.* Tulsa, Okla.: Nutrition Times Press.

Radcliffe-Brown, A. 1952. *Structure and Function in Primitive Society.* London: Cohen & West.

Radcliffe-Brown, A. 1964 (Orig. 1922). *The Andaman Islanders*. New York: Free Press.

Raloff, J. 1993. "EcoCancers: Do Environmental Factors Underlie a Breast Cancer Epidemic?" *Science News* 144(1):10-13.

Raloff, J. 1994a. "Cigarettes: Are They Doubly Addictive?" *Science News* 145(19): 294.

Raloff, J. 1994b. "Margarine is Anything but a Marginal Fat." *Science News* 145(21): 325.

Rathbun, T., and Buikstra, J. (eds.). 1984. *Human Identification: Case Studies in Forensic Anthropology*. Springfield, Ill.: Charles C. Thomas.

Reid, W. 1989. *The Treatment of Psychiatric Disorders: Revised for the DSM-III-R*. New York: Brunner/Mazel.

Renfrew, C., and Zubrow, E. (eds.). 1994. *The Ancient Mind: Elements of Cognitive Archaeology*. New York: Cambridge University Press.

Reynolds, V., and Reynolds, F. 1965 . "Chimpanzees of the Budongo Forest." In *Primate Behavior*, ed. I. DeVore, New York: Holt, Rinehart & Winston, 368-425.

Rheingold, H. 1991. *Virtual Reality*. New York: Summit Books.

Riches, D. (ed.). 1986. *The Anthropology of Violence*. New York: Basil Blackwell.

Riches, D. 1987. "Power as a Representational Model." In *Power and Knowledge: Anthropological and Sociological Approaches*, ed. R. Fardon, Edinburgh: Scottish Academic Press, 83-104.

Ricoeur, P. 1971. "The Model of the Text: Meaningful Action Considered as Text." *Social Research* 38(3):423-447.

Ridley, M. 1993. *The Red Queen: Sex and the Evolution of Human Nature*. New York: Macmillan.

Rightmire, G. 1992. "*Homo erectus*: Ancestor or Evolutionary Side Branch?" *Evolutionary Anthropology* 1(2):43-49.

Rivlin, R., and Gravelle, K. 1984. *Deciphering the Senses: The Expanding World of Human Perception*. New York: Simon & Schuster.

Robbins, J. 1987. *Diet for a New America*. Walpole, N.H.: Stillpoint.

Rogers, C. 1965. *Client Centered Therapy*. Boston: Houghton Mifflin.

Rogers, R. (ed.). 1988. *Clinical Assessment of Malingering and Deception*. New York: Guilford Press.

Roonwal, M., and Mohnot, S. 1977. *Primates of South Asia*. Cambridge: Harvard University Press.

Rosen, L. 1977. "The Anthropologist as Expert Witness." *American Anthropologist* 79(3):555-578.

Ross, C., and Pam, A. 1995. *Psuedoscience in Biological Psychiatry: Blaming the Body*. New York: John Wiley & Sons.

Ross, E. 1987. "An Overview of Trends in Dietary Variation from Hunter-Gatherer to Modern Capitalist Societies." In *Food and Evolution: Toward a Theory of Human Food Habits,* ed. M. Harris and E. Ross, Philadelphia: Temple University Press, 7-56.

Ross, M. 1993. *The Culture of Conflict*. New Haven, Conn.: Yale University Press.

Rozin, P. 1987. "Psychobiological Perspectives on Food Preferences and Avoidances." In *Food and Evolution: Toward a Theory of Human Food Habits*, ed. M. Harris and E. Ross, Philadelphia: Temple University Press, 181-206.

Rubel, A., O'Nell, and Collado-Ardon, R. 1991. *Susto: A Folk Illness*. Berkeley: University of California Press.

Ruesch, J. 1973. *Therapeutic Communication: A Descriptive Guide to the Communication Process as the Central Agent in Mental Healing.* New York: W. W. Norton.

Ruesch, J., and Bateson, G. 1968. *Communication: The Social Matrix of Psychiatry.* New York: W. W. Norton.

Rush, J. 1974. *Witchcraft and Sorcery: An Anthropological Perspective of the Occult.* Springfield: Charles C. Thomas.

Rush, J. 1976. *The Way We Communicate,* 2nd ed. Shelburne Falls, Mass.: Humanity Publications.

Rush, J. 1978. *Communication Skills Training Manual.* Shelburne Falls, Mass.: Humanity Publications.

Rush, J. 1990. (1st ed. 1988). *Managing Aggressive/Violent Behavior.* Workbook prepared for the California State Board of Corrections, STC Program.

Rush, J. 1992a. (1st ed. 1987). *Evaluation of Dangerous Behavior.* Workbook prepared for the California State Board of Corrections, STC Program.

Rush, J. 1992b. *Listening: Purpose and Process.* Workbook prepared for the California State Board of Corrections, STC Program.

Rush, J. 1993a. (1st ed. 1987). *Approaches to Stress Management.* Workbook prepared for the California State Board of Corrections, STC Program.

Rush, J. 1993b. *Techniques in Crisis Counseling.* Workbook prepared for the California State Board of Corrections, STC Program.

Rush, J. 1994. *Curing and Crisis in an Italian Kindred: The Adaptive Role of the Fattucchiera.* Unpublished Ph.D. Dissertation, Columbia Pacific University, Ann Arbor: Mich.: U.M.I. Dissertation Services.

Rush, J. 1995a. (1st ed. 1990). *Evaluating and Communicating with the Violent Juvenile.* Workbook prepared for the California State Board of Corrections, STC Program.

Rush, J. 1995b. (1st ed. 1992). *Dealing with Lies and Denial.* Workbook prepared for the California State Board of Corrections, STC Program.

Rush, J. 1995c. (1st ed. 1993). *Process in Cultural Sensitivity: An Anthropological Perspective of Cross-Cultural Conflict.* Workbook prepared for the California State Board of Corrections, STC Program.

Rusting, R. 1992. "Why Do We Age?" *Scientific American* 267(6):130-141.

Sahlins, M. 1976. *Culture and Practical Reason.* Chicago: University of Chicago Press.

Saler, B. 1964. "Nagual, Witch, and Sorcerer in a Quiche Village." *Ethnology* 3(3): 305-328.

Savage, W. 1990. *Comic Books and America, 1945-1954.* Norman: University of Oklahoma Press.

Schank, R. 1990. *Tell Me A Story.* New York: Charles Scribner's Sons.

Schauss, A. 1985. *Nutrition and Behavior.* New Canaan, Conn.: Keats Publishing.

Schoenthaler, S. 1991. "Applied Nutrition and Behavior." *Journal of Applied Nutrition* 43(1):131-150.

Schultes, R., and Hofmann, A. 1980. *The Botany and Chemistry of Hallucinogens.* Springfield, Ill.: Charles C. Thomas.

Scott, A. 1995. *Stairway to the Mind: The Controversial New Science of Consciousness.* New York: Springer-Verlag.

Scudder, J. 1994 (orig. 1984). *Specific Diagnosis.* Sandy, Og.: Eclectic Medical.

Segal, S., Watson, M., Goldfinger, S., and Averbuck, D. 1988. "Civil Committment in the Psychiatric Emerrgency Room." *Archives of General Psychiatry* 45:748-763.

Segall, M. 1991. "Cultural Factors, Biology and Human Aggresion." In *Aggression and War: Their Biological and Social Bases*, ed. J. Groebel and R. Hinde, New York: Cambridge University Press, 173-188.

Seitz, H., and Simanowski, U. 1988. "Alcohol and Carcinogenesis." *Annual Review of Nutrition* 8:99-119.

Selye, H. 1956. *The Stress of Life*. New York: McGraw-Hill.

Sept, J. 1992. "Was There No Place Like Home." *Current Anthropology* 33(2):187-207.

Sharp. L 1966. "Steel Axes for Stone Age Australians." In *Readings in Anthropology*, ed. J. Jennings and E. Hoebel, New York: McGraw-Hill.

Sheikh, A., and Sheikh, K. (eds.). 1989. *Eastern and Western Approaches to Healing: Ancient Wisdom and Modern Knowledge*. New York: John Wiley & Sons.

Shiloh, A. 1977. "Therapeutic Anthropology: The Anthropologist as Private Practitioner." *American Anthropologist*, Vol. 79, No. 2:443.

Shils, M. 1988. "Magnesium in Health and Disease." *Annual Review of Nutrition* 8:429-460.

Shimony, A. 1989. "Eastern Woodlands: Iroquois of Six Nations." In *Witchcraft and Sorcery of the American Native Peoples*, ed. D. Walker, Moscow: University of Idaho Press, 167-190.

Siegel, R. 1989. *Intoxication: Life in Pursuit of Artificial Paradise*. New York: E. P. Dutton.

Sigerist, H. 1951/1961. *A History of Medicine*, 2 vols. New York: Oxford University Press.

Simoons, F. 1994. *Eat Not This Flesh: Food Avoidances from Prehistory to the Present*. Madison: University of Wisconsin Press.

Singleton, P., and Sainsbury, D. 1993. *Dictionary of Microbiology and Molecular Biology*. New York: John Wiley and Sons.

Skinner, A. 1915. "Associations and Ceremonies of the Menomini Indians." *Anthropological Papers of the American Museum of Natural History* 13(2), New York: American Museum of Natural History.

Skinner, B. F. 1972. *Beyond Freedom and Dignity*. London: Jonathan Cape.
1974 *About Behaviorism*. New York: A. Knopf & Son.

Skultans, V. 1988. "Menstrual Symbolism in South Wales." In *Blood Magic: The Anthropology of Menstruation*, ed. T. Buckley and A. Gottlieb, Berkeley: University of California Press, 137-160.

Sluka, J. 1992. "The Anthropology of Conflict." In *The Paths to Domination, Resistance, and Terror*, Nordstrom, C. and Martin, J. (eds.), Berkeley: University of California Press, 18-36.

Smith, C. 1978. "Tubatulabal." In *Handbook of North American Indians*. Vol. 8, ed. R. Heizer, Washington, D. C.: Smithsonian Institution, 437-445.

Spindler, G. 1955. *Sociocultural and Psychological Processes in Menomini Acculturation*. Publications in Culture and Society, No. 5. Berkeley: University of California Press.

Spindler, L. 1952. "Witchcraft in Menomini Acculturation." *American Anthropologist*, 54:593-602.

Spindler, L. 1989. "Great Lakes: Menomini." In *Witchcraft and Sorcery of the Amer-*

ican Native Peoples, ed. D. Walker, Moscow: University of Idaho Press, 39-74.

Spiro, M. 1982. *Oedipus in the Trobriands*. Chicago: University of Chicago Press.

Stein, H. 1987. *Developmental Time, Cultural Space*. Norman: University of Oklahoma Press.

Steiner, R. (ed.). 1985. *Folk Medicine: The Art and the Science*. Washington, D.C.: ASC Publications.

Stewart, I. 1989. *Does God Play Dice? The Mathematics of Chaos*. New York: Basil Blackwell.

Stinson, S. 1992. "Nutritional Adaptation." *Annual Review of Anthropology* 21:143-170.

Strasburger, V. 1995. *Adolescents and the Media: Medical and Psychological Impact*. Thousand Oaks, Calif.: Sage Publications.

Stringer, C., and Gamble, C. 1993. *In Search of the Neanderthals: Solving the Puzzle of Human Origins*. New York: Thames and Hudson.

Sue, D., and D. Sue. 1990. *Counseling the Culturally Different: Theory and Practice*. New York: John Wiley & Sons.

Sullivan, L. 1988. *Icanchu's Drum: An Orientation to Meaning in South American Religions*. New York: Macmillan.

Sulloway, F. 1979. *Freud: Biologist of the Mind*. New York: Basic Books.

Szasz, T. 1972. *The Myth of Mental Illness*. Frogmore, St. Albens, Hertz: Paladin Press.

Szasz, T. 1977. *The Manufacture of Madness: A Comparative Study of the Inquisition and the Mental Health Movement*. New York: Harper & Row.

Szasz, T. 1994. *Cruel Compassion: Psychiatric Control of Society's Unwanted*. New York: John Wiley & Sons.

Szymanski, L., and Crocker, A. 1989. "Mental Retardation." In *Comprehensive Textbook of Psychiatry*, 5th ed., H. Kaplan and B. Sadock, vol. 2., Baltimore: Williams & Wilkins, 1728-1771.

Tabakoff, B., and Hoffman, P. 1992. "Alcohol: Neurobiology." In *Substance Abuse: A Comprehensive Textbook*, ed. J. Lowinson, P. Ruiz, and R. Millman, Baltimore: Williams & Wilkins, 152-185.

Tainter, J. 1990. *The Collapse of Complex Societies*. New York: Cambridge University Press.

Tatai, K. 1983. "Japan." In *Suicide in Asia and the Near East*, ed. L. Headley, Berkeley: University of California Press, 6-58.

Templeton, A. 1993. "The 'Eve' Hypothesis: A Genetic Critique and Reanalysis." *American Anthropologist* 95(1):51-72.

Thorwald, J. 1963. *Science and Secrets of Early Medicine*. New York: Harcourt, Brace & World.

Thwaites, R. (ed.). 1896-1901. *The Jesuit Relations and Allied Documents: Travels and Explorations of the Jesuit Missionaries in New France, 1610-1791*, Vol. 1. Cleveland: Burrows Brothers.

Tobin, J, and Friedman, M. 1983. "Spirits, Shamans, and Nightmare Death: Survivor Stress in a Hmong Refugee." *American Journal of Orthopsychiatry* 3(3):439-448).

Torrey, E. F. 1980. *Schizophrenia and Civilization*. New York: Jason Aronson.

Torrey, E. F. 1986 (orig. 1972). *Witchdoctors and Psychiatrists*. New York: Jason Aronson.

Triandas, H. 1987. "Cross-Cultural Psychology as the Scientific Foundation of Cross-Cultural Training." In *Intercultural Skills for Multicultural Societies*, ed. C. Dodd and F. Montalvo, Washington, D.C.: Sietar International, 23-44.

Trinkaus, E. 1986. "The Neandertals and Modern Human Origins." *Annual Review of Anthropology* 15:193-218.

Trinkaus, E., and Shipman, P. 1993. *The Neandertals: Changing the Image of Mankind*. New York: Alfred A. Knopf.

"Tuned into High-Tech Psychedelics." 1992. *Sacramento Bee*, August 10, sec. C, pp. 1,3.

Turner, V. 1968. *The Drums of Affliction*. Oxford, Eng.: Clarendon Press.

Turner, V. 1969. *The Ritual Process: Structure and Anti-Structure*. Chicago: Aldine.

Turner, V. 1970a. "Betwixt and Between: The Liminal Period in *Rites de Passage*." In *The Forest of Symbols*, V. Turner, London: Cornell University Press, 93-111.

Turner, V. 1970b. "Lunda Medicine and the Treatment of Disease." In *The Forest of Symbols*, V. Turner, London: Cornell University Press, 299-358.

Tuttle, R. 1988. "What's New in African Paleoanthropology?" *Annual Review of Anthropology* 17:391-426.

Tyler, E. 1871. *Primitive Culture*. London: John Murry.

Tyrer, P., and Steinberg, D. 1993. *Models for Mental Disorders: Conceptual Models in Psychiatry*. New York: John Wiley & Sons.

van der Veer, G. 1992. *Counseling and Therapy with Refugees: Psychological Problems of Victims of War, Torture and Repression*. New York: John Wiley & Sons.

Vang, L., and Lewis, J. 1990. *Grandmother's Path, Grandfather's Way*. Rancho Cordova, Calif.: Vang & Lewis.

van Praag, H. 1993. *"Make-Believes" in Psychiatry or The Perils of Progress*. New York: Brunner/Mazel.

Vargas, L., and Koss-Chioino, J. (eds.). 1992. *Working with Culture: Psychotherapeutic Interventions with Ethnic Minority Children and Adolescents*. San Francisco: Jossey-Bass.

Veldee, M. 1994. "Nutrition." In *Tietz Textbook of Clinical Chemistry*, ed. C. Burtis and E. Ashwood, E., Philadelphia: W. B. Saunders Company, 1236-1274.

Vernant, J. 1988. *Myth and Society in Ancient Greece*. New York: Zone Books.

Vernant, J., and Vidal-Naquet, P. 1988. *Myth and Tragedy in Ancient Greece*. New York: Zone Books.

Vigilant, L., Pennington, R., Harpending, H., Koche, T., and Wilson, A. 1989. "Mitochondrial DNA Sequences in Single Hairs from a Southern African Population." *Proceedings, National Academy of Science* 86:9350-9354.

Vigilant, L., Stoneking, L., Harpending, H. Hawkes, K., and Wilson, A. 1991. "African Populations and the Evolution of Human Mitochondrial DNA." *Science* 253:1503-1507.

Walker, D. (ed.). 1989. *Witchcraft and Sorcery of the American Native Peoples*. Moscow: University of Idaho Press.

Wallace, A. 1958. "Dreams and the Wishes of the Soul: A Type of Psychoanalytic Theory Among the Seventeenth Century Iroquois." *American Anthropologist* 60 (2): 234:248.

Wallace, A. 1960. "An Interdisciplinary Approach to Mental Disorder Among the Polar Eskimos of Northwest Greenland." *Anthropolgica* 11(2):1-12.

Wallace, A. 1961. "Mental Illness, Biology, and Culture." In *Psychological Anthro-*

pology, ed. F. Hsu, Homewood: Dorsey Press, 254-295.

Wasson, R. 1967. *Soma, Divine Mushroom of Immortality*. New York: Harcourt & Brace.

Watson, C., and Ellen, R. (eds.) 1993. *Understanding Witchcraft and Sorcery in Southeast Asia*. Honolulu: University of Hawaii Press.

Watson, R. 1977. "An Introduction to Humanistic Psychotherapy." In *Psychotherapies: A Comparative Casebook*, ed. S. Morse and R. Watson, New York: Holt, Rinehart & Winston, 1-31.

Weigert, A., Teitge, J., and Teige, D. 1986. *Society and Identity*. Cambridge: Cambridge University Press.

Weiss, B. 1980. "Nutritional Adaptation and Cultural Maladaptation: An Evolutionary View." In *Nutritional Anthropology: Contemporary Approaches to Diet and Culture*, ed. N. Jerome, R. Kandel, and G. Pelto, New York: Redgrave, 147-180.

Weiss, R. 1988. "Women's Skills Linked to Estrogen Levels." *Science News* 134(22): 341.

Wenke, R. 1984. *Patterns in Prehistory: Humankind's First Three Million Years*. New York: Oxford University Press.

Werbach, M. 1991. *Nutritional Influences on Mental Illness*. Portland, Oreg.: Bergner Communications.

Westermeyer, J. 1982. *Poppies, Pipes, and People: Opium and Its Use in Laos*. Berkeley: University of California Press.

Westermeyer, J. 1983. "A Comparison of Refugees Using and Not Using a Psychiatric Service: An Analysis of DSM-III Criteria and Self-Rating Scales in Cross-Cultural Context." *Journal of Operational Psychiatry* 14(1):36-41.

Whitaker, J. 1994. "It's Time to Give Henry Waxman His Walking Papers." *Health and Healing* 4(5):8.

White, L. 1949. *The Science of Culture*. New York: Grove Press.

White, R. 1989. "Visual Thinking in the Ice Age." *Scientific American* 261(1) :92-99.

Wierzbicka, A. 1992. *Semantics, Culture, and Cognition: Universal Human Concepts in Culture-Specific Configurations*. New York: Oxford University Press.

Wilbert, J. 1987. *Tobacco and Shamanism in South America*. New Haven, Conn.: Yale University Press.

Williams, W. 1992. *The Spirit and the Flesh: Sexual Diversity in American Indian Culture*. Boston: Beacon Press.

Winokur, G., and Clayton, P. (eds.). 1994. *The Medical Basis of Psychiatry*. Orlando, Fla.: W. B. Saunders Company.

Wobst, M. 1974. "Boundary Conditions for Paleolithic Social Systems: A Simulation Approach." *American Antiquity*, April:147.

Wolf, F. 1991. *The Eagle's Quest: A Physicist finds Scientific Truth at the Heart of the Shamanic World*. New York: Simon & Schuster.

Wynn, T. 1989. *The Evolution of Spacial Consciousness*. Urbana: University of Illinois Press.

Yap, P. M. 1977. "The Culture-Bound Reactive Syndromes." In *Culture, Disease, and Healing: Studies in Medical Anthropology*, D. Landy, New York: Macmillan, 340-349.

Yeatman, G., and Dang, V. 1980. "Cao Gio (Coin Rubbing)." *Journal of the American Medical Association* 244(24):2748-2749.
Yozwick, C. 1994. *Legal and Administrative Aspects of a Holistic Health Practice.* Birmingham, Ala.: Clayton School of Natural Healing.

Index

About the Author

JOHN A. RUSH is a Naturopathic Physician and Certified Medical Hypnotherapist. Dr. Rush is also an ethnobotanist and maintains an extensive garden of medicinal herbs from all over the world. He also instructs for the California State Board of Corrections in their STC Program, conducts research in communication patterns, nutrition, and stress reactions for CommunEfect, a nonprofit corporation, and is a part-time instructor in cultural and physical anthropology at Cosumnes River College, Folsom, California, and at Sacramento City College, Sacramento, California. Dr. Rush earned his Ph.D. in Anthropology from Columbia Pacific University, and is the author of numerous books and texts including *Witchcraft and Sorcery: an Anthropological Perspective of the Occult* (1974).

ISBN 0-275-95571-0

HARDCOVER BAR CODE